ROBERTO SAVIANO

ZeroZeroZero

*Translated from the Italian
by Virginia Jewiss*

ALLEN LANE
*an imprint of*
PENGUIN BOOKS

ALLEN LANE

UK | USA | Canada | Ireland | Australia
India | New Zealand | South Africa

Allen Lane is part of the Penguin Random House group of companies
whose addresses can be found at global.penguinrandomhouse.com.

Originally published in Italian by Feltrinelli Editore, Milan 2013
First published in the United States of America by The Penguin Press 2015
First published in Great Britain by Allen Lane 2015
001

Copyright © Roberto Saviano, 2013
Translation copyright © Penguin Random House LLC

The moral right of the author has been asserted

Printed in Great Britain by Clays Ltd, St Ives plc

A CIP catalogue record for this book is available from the British Library

HARD BACK ISBN: 978–1–846–14769–2
TRADE PAPERBACK ISBN: 978–1–846–14771–5

This book is dedicated to all my Carabinieri bodyguards
to the fifty-one thousand hours we've spent together
and to those still ahead. Wherever they may be.

I'm not afraid they'll trample me.

Trampled grass soon becomes a path.

—BLAGA DIMITROVA

# CONTENTS

# ZERO
# ZERO
# ZERO

# COKE #1

The guy sitting next to you on the train uses cocaine, he took it to get himself going this morning; or the driver of the bus you're taking home, he wants to put in some overtime without feeling the cramps in his neck. The people closest to you use coke. If it's not your mother or father, if it's not your brother, then it's your son. And if your son doesn't use it, your boss does. Or your boss's secretary, but only on Saturdays, just for fun. And if your boss doesn't, his wife does, to let herself go. And if not his wife, then his lover—he gives her cocaine instead of earrings, in place of diamonds. And if they don't, the truck driver delivering tons of coffee to cafés around town does; he wouldn't be able to hack those long hours on the road without it. And if he doesn't, the nurse who's changing your grandfather's catheter does. Coke makes everything seem so much easier, even the night shift. And if she doesn't, the painter redoing your girlfriend's room does; he was just curious at first but wound up deep in debt. The people who use cocaine are right here, right next to you. The police officer who's about to pull you over has been snorting for years, and everyone knows it, and they write anonymous letters to his chief hoping he'll be suspended before he screws up big time. Or the surgeon who's just waking up and will soon operate on your aunt. Cocaine helps him cut open six people a day. Or your divorce lawyer. Or the judge presiding over your lawsuit; he doesn't consider it a vice, though, just a little boost, a way to get more out of life. The cashier who hands you the lottery ticket you hope is going to change your life. The carpenter who's installing the cabinets that cost you a month's salary. Or the workman who came to put together the IKEA closet you couldn't figure out how to assemble on your own. If not him, then the manager of your condo building who is just about to buzz you. Or your electrician, the one who's in your bedroom right now, moving the outlets. The singer you are listening to to unwind, the parish priest you're going to talk to about finally getting confirmed because your grandson's getting baptized, and he's amazed you've put it off for so long. The waiters who will work the wedding you're going to next Saturday; they wouldn't be able to last on their feet all that time if they didn't. If not them, then the town councillor who just approved the new pedestrian zones, and who gets his coke free in exchange for favors. The parking lot attendant who's happy now only when he's high. The architect who renovated your vacation home, the mailman who just delivered your new ATM card. If not them, then the woman at the call center who asks "How may I help you?" in that shrill, happy voice, the same for every caller, thanks to the white powder. If not her, your professor's research assistant—coke makes him nervous. Or the physiotherapist who's trying to get your knee working right. Coke makes him more sociable. The forward who just scored, spoiling the bet you were winning right up until the final minutes of the game. The prostitute you go to on your way home, when you just can't take it anymore and need to vent. She does it so she won't have to see whoever is on top or under or behind her anymore. The gigolo you treated yourself to for your fiftieth birthday. You did it together. Coke makes him feel really macho. The sparring partner you train with in the ring, to lose weight. And if he doesn't, your daughter's riding instructor does, and so does your wife's psychologist. Your husband's best friend uses it, the one who's been hitting on you for years but whom you've never liked. And if he doesn't, then your school principal does. Along with the janitor. And the real estate agent, who's late, just when you finally managed to find time to see the apartment. The security guard uses it, the one who still combs his hair over his bald spot, even though guys all shave their heads these days. And if he doesn't, the notary you hope you never have to go back to, he does it to avoid thinking about the alimony he has to pay his ex-wives. And if he doesn't, the taxi driver does; he curses the traffic but then goes all happy again. If not him, the engineer you have to invite over for dinner because he might help you get a leg up in your career. The policeman who's giving you a ticket, sweating profusely even though it's winter. The squeegee man with hollow eyes, who borrows money to buy it, or that kid stuffing flyers under windshield wipers, five at a time. The politician who promised you a commercial license, the one you and your family voted into office, and who is always nervous. The professor who failed you on your exam. Or the oncologist you're going to see; everybody says he's the best, so you're hoping he can save you. He feels omnipotent when he sniffs cocaine. Or the gynecologist who nearly forgets to throw away his cigarette before going in to examine your wife, who has just gone into labor. Your brother-in-law, who's never in a good mood, or your daughter's boyfriend, who always is. If not them, then the fishmonger, who proudly displays a swordfish, or the gas station attendant who spills gas on your car. He sniffs to feel young again but can't even put the pump away correctly anymore. Or the family doctor you've known for years and who lets you cut the line because you always know just the right thing to give him at Christmas. The doorman of your building uses it, and if he doesn't, then your kids' tutor does, your nephew's piano teacher, the costume designer for the play you're going to see tonight, the vet who takes care of your cat. The mayor who invited you over for dinner recently. The contractor who built your house, the author whose book you've been reading before falling asleep, the anchorwoman on the evening news. But if, after you think about it, you're still convinced none of these people could possibly snort cocaine, you're either blind or you're lying. Or the one who uses it is you.

# GOD SAVE THE COKE

"Two facts I've read in the papers say it all. A small amount of stuff costs less than a glass of wine and 11 percent of bank notes in circulation test positive for cocaine."

"Mark, you seem well informed on the subject. Why's that?"

"It's part of my job. I've always been good with numbers and reeling out a few statistics makes a good impression on your audience. We call it entertainment. We take the more interesting clients to dinner and try to give them a good night out. Most of the time it's a real pain because you're going to get bored, no matter what they say. They've spent the weekend sailing and seen an unforgettable starry sky? Interesting. Or they've just bought a new hat for their wife who can't wait to show it off at Ascot? Just as interesting. Then there's the client who wants a really good time that evening and you get him what he asks for. If you know some stories about the stuff and you throw in a few facts to impress him, well, you're home and dry. You just have to be their best friend for a few hours."

"And you, Steven, would you like to introduce yourself?"

"Yes. I'm Steven, as you said, and I'm a broker like the others.

Actually, an ex-broker. I say that so that I'm honest from the start. I didn't have to come here, but I thought it was important. I started doing coke when I was really young. I did it to keep awake. In front of the monitors from seven in the morning till late at night. Non-stop, with the boss breathing down your neck, threatening you'll miss out on the Christmas bonus that year. How could I cope?"

"We're not here to judge. This is the place to solve a problem. A place that no one knows exists, since it's the problem itself that gets ignored. It's the problem that doesn't exist. It's not group therapy, it's not a confessional. And the methods are not conventional ones; some might say they're unorthodox. Almost a professional breach. Sharing news that has passed unobserved, halting the flow of information. Breaking the ice on the surface and plunging into freezing water. Are we heightening awareness? Perhaps. Even if often, for those who work with numbers, the numbers lose their meaning, substance, value."

"Yes, sure. Have you ever heard of fat-finger syndrome? It's happened to me a couple of times. Always in the evening, when the histograms in front of you are just a blur of colours. Your client has asked you to sell and by mistake, because you're tired, or stressed or whatever, you press the wrong button and you buy. In a fraction of a second you've fucked up a whole day's work. You've lost your bonus money, you've lost your client's money, and you've made your company lose money. And all that because of one button."

"I see. And when did you decide to quit?"

"When a friend of mine, to tease me because I kept standing him up with the excuse that I was at work, had the clever idea of sending me an old article from the *Telegraph*. It was about this guy, Darren Liddle, a young broker who wasn't even 30 and one morning he leapt from the 19th floor of the Hilton in London. He was really bright, always gave 100 percent at the office. He was an analyst and a trader, just like me, and had worked his arse off for that job at Credit Suisse. Years of study and sacrifice, and then to keep up with the pace he'd looked for some help and had found it. Like we did. Only he couldn't handle it and started getting hallucinations and becoming paranoid. He used to see enemies everywhere. One day he couldn't cope anymore. He said he was being chased by 'gangs of vigilantes' and maybe he thought that by leaping out of the window they would stop following him. They tried talking him down, but it was too late and just after his girlfriend got to the room, Darren threw himself off the building. When I finished reading the article I began shaking and sweating. I was dripping onto the keyboard and the more I tried to control myself the worse it got. My boss noticed and he sent me home. It had never happened before. I must have looked scary."

"Who'd like to speak?"

"My name is Tom. I'm 52 and I'm a survivor. In my time you didn't need a master's degree in economics and a PhD in maths to do business. All you needed was a telephone and some contacts. Sociability was the best weapon. The trick was to anticipate what the other person was going to do next. You were a good broker if you could drill into the human soul better than everyone else. It's a talent you're born with, but it has to be cultivated and nurtured like a rare plant. You water it too much or too little and the plant dies. Moving wealth around is hard work. You know when my profession first started? In 1623. Have you ever heard of the Wind Trade? There was a time in Holland when everyone went crazy for tulips. You had to have at least one; otherwise you were a nobody. Prices soared and demand went up and up. And the traders started selling bulbs that didn't yet exist.

"They were selling the future, you see? In the end the bubble burst: the market price for tulips dropped and those who were anxiously waiting for a bulb that didn't yet exist, and had paid its weight in gold, ended up ruined. Then technology arrived, the Net, computers with ten screens. The economy changed. You buy and sell what you don't have. It's the economy of the intangible: clients and operators have multiplied by ten, a hundred, a thousand! The job has stayed more or less the same: you're a middleman who gets an order from the trader who gets an order from the agent who gets an order from a pensions fund or something. You have to plunge into the market to make a deal with buyer and seller and bring home your tidy commission. It's shockingly simple, but try thinking of this procedure multiplied ten, a hundred, a thousand times! Simultaneously. And by then you find that a country's government no longer has the majority and everyone's in a state of agitation, political instability fuels profiteering and from one second to the next you have to start all over again. How do you keep up? I've seen kids who boast that they've been out until four in the morning and they get to the office before you. I'm not stupid. I know how they do it. I know what they take. And so, here I am. A middle-aged man who snorts just like the youngsters, to keep up with them."

"My name is Luke and I work in offices in Lombard Street. I knew the City was rotten with cocaine. Everyone knows it, but they're careful not to say it. There are more policemen in the City than in any other part of London, but the traders who sniff all hours of the day go unnoticed. I reckon they think a trader behind bars is no big deal; it's better to concentrate on real crime. What's the problem if someone takes drugs and does his job well? If coke helps you perform better and makes you and your society richer, then where's the crime? That's how I've always seen it. Even when people suggested that an extra push would help, I always said no. I'm a proud man, and I wanted to do it on my own. Then the crisis blew up. The number of clients doubled, everyone was anxious to ride that storm, and in order to keep up I had to put my pride to one side. Now the risks were even greater, but we had to pretend we knew what we're doing. I don't regret it because I was at a crossroads, and I had to choose what I thought was the best path at that moment."

"Thank you all, gentlemen, for having shared a part of your stories. You all know why we're here today. The companies you work for are worried and they felt that group therapy was necessary to try to restore performance levels. There's no doubt that your profession is stressful, but the solutions you have come up with to deal with the pressure are no longer effective. You have reached peak performance and now the

side effects outweigh the results – absenteeism, mistakes, obsessive be-
haviour – all harmful to those around you.

"I've done some research on each of you. I've seen your records and
have some idea of who you are: you are pioneers at a frontier that others
are unable to see. You have the power to look into the future. But this
power has a price, an entrance charge that many of you don't even know
you are paying. I'm not here to persuade you that this system is right or
wrong. This isn't a psychoanalysis session, or a self-help group. I won't
be asking you to hug each other or make amends. I want to understand
and want *you* to understand. You have some envelopes in front of you.
Inside there's some writing, and I'd like each of you in turn to read it
out loud. These articles are the result of various studies into the world
of cocaine here in Britain. You see, over the years I've come to realize
that in our country coke enjoys a unique characteristic: invisibility. It's
not spoken about, apart from when it reaches the headlines. It's never
discussed, except to limit it to events that cause a stir. It's taboo, and
has to remain like that because it's convenient for everyone. For you, for
work. For your companies, for their profit. For your clients, who gain
from it. But what do you know about the stuff you sniff? You are the
bridgehead between a declining economy and a future beyond all imagination, and yet you are only part of the story of cocaine. What happens in the City stays in the City. Isn't that what you say? I believe that
the first step in overcoming a problem is awareness. And so I'm asking
you: what do you know about the petrol that fuels you and this country?
What do you know about an asset that's so much like those commodi-
ties you trade each day? There's not much difference between speculat-
ing on the prices of petroleum, on corn or on government bonds. Your
work has much more in common with the drug market than you could
possibly imagine. Mark, could you start please?"

"Yes, sure.

Great Britain is a country of consumers. £6 billion is spent on
drugs each year, of which £1 billion alone is spent on the 25 to

30 tons of imported cocaine. We live in what has been described as the European cocaine capital. There are one million consumers of white powder and one person in ten has admitted to having tried it at least once. It's an epidemic that affects above all young people from 16 to 24, who make up half of consumers. The wholesale price of cocaine is the highest in Europe, but the retail price is among the lowest due to the widespread use of cutting agents. The coke that arrives in Britain has a 65 percent level of purity because it has already been cut with other substances, including a drug called Levamisole, used for treating intestinal worms in livestock. And this level is destined to decrease further when it reaches the hands of those controlling the sale, going as low as 5 percent on the streets of Scotland. The result is a market divided into two. On the one hand, there's the majority of consumers who cannot afford to pay the £120 asked by the Peruvian or Bolivian retailers and sniff white powder cut with benzocaine, widely used because it has an anaesthetizing effect similar to that of coke; and on the other hand there's an elite that spends in order to have the best quality and knows where to obtain it: in the City. One last statistic: in the 16 to 59 age group, those who consume alcohol three or more times a week are three times more likely to have consumed a drug in the last year and six times more likely to have consumed a Class A drug, including cocaine, compared to those who don't drink."

"They're just numbers, doctor. We're living on an island buried under a blanket of coke. So what? I don't know how to buy stuff in the East End, but I know that at Canary Wharf, all you have to do is put a number into your mobile, and wait for some guy who's dressed just like you – grey suit and freshly polished shoes – to answer at the other end. At that point you arrange a meeting and if you don't have cash then you can pay him by bank transfer. Nothing simpler. Maybe one day they'll even give you a receipt, so you can deduct it on your tax return. Doesn't it work like that everywhere?"

"Luke, you're perfectly right. It's a perversion of the capitalist system. The more it expands, the more energy it requires. Do the names Stephen Perkins and Richard Crawford mean anything to you? Please, Luke, open your envelope."

"Stephen had always worked in the black gold market. The fluctuations in petroleum sent shockwaves to the base of his spine. Then he realized that to steer a straight course his iron will was not enough, and he began to drink. On the day that he came to the notice of the Financial Services Authority, Stephen was buying 7 million barrels of petroleum too casually, causing a huge rise in the price per barrel. Those transactions, made well into the middle of the night under the effect of alcohol, cost his company nearly $10 million.

Richard Crawford is the one who chases after the baddies. He's the head of the anti-fraud department of First Direct, a division of HSBC. He has everything: money, family, career. Then the family falls apart, desperation turns to vice, and coke and alcohol dry up his bank account. Though he's earning £65,000 a year, Crawford has difficulty keeping up with his 'recreational' expenses. But finding the money is no problem. He is sitting on a mountain of money every single day. The account holders he's supposed to be protecting from fraud certainly aren't going to notice small withdrawals. To cover himself, he selects bank customers whose current accounts are at high risk of fraud. He knows who they are; that's his job. Over eight months of withdrawal after withdrawal, the head of the anti-fraud department removes £173,000 from the accounts of his customers which end up in the accounts of aliases invented by him, until he is arrested and jailed for three years and eight months."

"Ours is an underground economy. Until not long ago if you wanted a beer you had to get on the tube and go to another area. Today you can spend the whole night in the City. You go from one nightclub to another, through to the morning. If you're not too tired and off your face you can even go straight to the office."

"These are stories people tell us when they first arrive. It's a kind of initiation. Do you remember Christen Schnor?"

"I knew him well. I knew all his family. I wasn't surprised when they found him hanged in that suite at the Carlton Tower Hotel."

"He was a big shot, one of those who used to get six-figure bonuses. Rumour has it that before he put an end to it, he organized a fake robbery at his maxi-villa in Cannes. His wife had worked it all out. She knew that Christen would try sooner or later to settle his debts in one way or another."

"Excuse me if I interrupt, gentlemen, but there's something I don't understand. How can anyone build up debts when they have salaries and bonuses that ordinary people can only dream of?"

"It's not hard, doctor. There are go-getting 25-year-olds who, in order to hook a client, will take them around for a whole week. You see them again the following Monday and they're as fresh as a rose. If you ask them what they've done and you know them well enough to get an honest answer, they'll tell you the last thing they remember is closing the office door behind them – and then waking up somewhere with a bill of more than £5,000 to pay. Entertainment expenses which then interfere with your private life, and if you're no good at managing it, your career ends at 30."

"Management is everything. You know the rules, you know all the secret codes for ordering coke along with your favourite cocktail. You know that at Leadenhall you're sure of finding something. You know which clubs to join where members are guaranteed special treatment. Do you remember Anthony Alexander?"

"Before they caught him he was a real institution. He used to bring you coke along with the drinks."

"That's why it's important to learn how to manage it. What slays you is how easy it is to get the cocaine. If money's no problem, and for us it's not, then buying a wrap of stuff is as hard as ordering a gin and tonic."

"Knowing how to manage it is everything. Not like that customer portfolio manager at Barclays in Basingstoke a few years ago. What was his name?"

"David Frith."

"That's him. He was young, the girls liked him and he was good at numbers. The drugs squad had been keeping an eye on him for a year, and by listening to his telephone calls – which were recorded as part of bank protocol – they discovered that David was delivering the drug to his 'clients' during the lunch break. You understand, doctor? David was selling coke to people like him. He was a colleague who was supplementing his salary by tapping money from other colleagues. If he's doing the whole seven and a half years they gave him, he'll still be in prison."

"And then, if you want to make that leap, you have to think big. It's like in finance. You look around and see they're all richer than you. But you've studied, you've worked your arse off, you've slaved away like a packhorse, but the bloke sitting next to you on the tube has an original Armani suit. In reality, but you only discover this only later, he's no richer than you and when he looks at you he's thinking exactly the same thing. Those who are really stuffed full of money are a tiny percentage, but you carry on asking yourself: 'Why them and not me?' Luck and intelligence. Not necessarily in that order. In any case, they've managed to break the bank, and while you enjoy your winnings at the slot machine, they've robbed the casino. You have to know how to wait for the chance and take it. Anyway, returning to us, David Frith was a kid who loved fast cars. Trevor Collenette? Well, he knew how to think big."

"In the end they discovered that Trevor had nothing to do with it. They'd framed him."

"Excuse me, gentlemen, who's Trevor Collenette?"

"Trevor worked for Lloyds TSB until 2006, the year he retired. I remember it well, because I arrived a month later. He couldn't sit around doing nothing, so he began to cultivate his passion: sailing. All hell broke loose shortly after, when we heard that he'd been arrested in Gibraltar for smuggling cocaine. He'd crossed the Atlantic on *Gin*, a yacht that was to carry him – and three other crew – from the Caribbean to Europe. Customs officials climb on board and find coke worth £8 million. When the news arrived here in London there were all kinds of reactions, but most people were gripped by excitement. They couldn't believe that such a mild man who loved the sea and had always shown a tireless dedication to work could possibly have thought up such a daring job. For us it was a dream. We want to get rich gambling on the future, and Trevor would have succeeded if it hadn't been for the customs officers who had discovered that false glass fibre bottom where the stash of coke slabs had been hidden. In the end, what's the difference? That 50-year-old had us all fooled. For almost two months Trevor became our hero. He stubbornly denied all involvement, he repeated tirelessly that he hadn't put the drugs there, that he didn't even know there was a secret compartment, that someone had taken advantage of his good faith. And in the end they released him, all accusations were dropped.  He really was innocent."

"Gentlemen, what emerges once again from your words is a partial view of the phenomenon. Awareness means a clear view. It means living in the present and not always projecting into the future, as your profession requires. You've mentioned various names. Brokers of greater or lesser talent who have been involved with cocaine along the way. Now I'll give you a name: Curtis Warren. Does that mean anything to you? Please, Tom, open your envelope."

"Toxteth is one of the poorest suburbs of Liverpool. Houses here cost less than half in comparison with the rest of the country. It's a district abandoned to itself which in 1981 saw rioting and the streets laid to waste. There were dozens of injuries and arrests in the clashes between people living there and police. Curtis Warren grows up on those streets and a few months after the riots of 1981, at barely 19, he ends up in prison for blackmailing a prostitute and her client. His release marks a turning point in his life. While working as a bouncer in the Liverpool clubs he comes into contact with dealers and smugglers, including Brian Charrington, owner of a car dealership and a coke operator. And here begins the legend of "Cocky" Curtis Warren, regarded as the richest and most powerful criminal in British history. Cocky is an ideal blend of ambition and strategic planning. With his partner, he heads straight to the source. He sails with him to Venezuela and reaches an agreement with the Cali cartel in Columbia to smuggle enormous quantities of cocaine. But for this business to work there has to be a well-thought-out plan. Charrington's yacht is perfect for the crossing: it can transport as much as 1,000 kilos of goods, which Cocky intends to hide in steel containers concealed in lead ingots. The x-rays at customs are useless and as an extra precaution Cocky finds out the exact length of the drill bits used by the customs officers in order to calculate at what depth to put the cocaine under the lead ingots: in that way they would be safe even if they encountered the most scrupulous police controls. The business can start, but after only two voyages a tip-off puts Cocky and his partners in trouble. He's back in prison, and this time for over a year, until almost miraculously all charges are dropped and Cocky is free again with a wealth of £87 million, the profit from the first voyage from Venezuela to England. With that fortune he builds an empire. He moves to Sassenheim, in Holland, a quiet village that becomes a stronghold from which he runs an organization that manages 500 kilos of

drugs each month and from which he forms alliances with the
Columbian cartels, with the Turkish mafia and with the Mo-
roccan underground in Spain, who deal respectively in cocaine,
heroin and cannabis. Cocky alone is in command. Intelligent,
shrewd, cautious, scrupulous in his personal life, with a prodi-
gious memory, Curtis decides and moves the pawns in the way
he considers most effective. It is the perfect application of the
principles of efficiency – in other words, the relationship between aims and concrete results. Behind his furious gaze is a
thoroughly modern *homo oeconomicus*, who in 1997 enters Britain's *Sunday Times* Rich List. Cocky buys cocaine on credit
from the South American cartels, then transports it to Bulgaria,
the safest destination in Europe. He has devised a most im-
aginative plan: the cocaine has to reach the winery he has purchased in Bulgaria and is then put into bottles of wine that will
be transported to the Netherlands and from there, by air, they
arrive in the United Kingdom. Once in Liverpool, awaiting the
shipment will be a team of chemists, hired for the purpose, who
will extract the drug ready for sale. But the Dutch authorities
are tapping his mobile phone and wreck the whole plan, seizing
400 kilos of cocaine.

Cocky likes to go it alone, but he knows that his empire
cannot risk ending up in pieces if anything were to happen to
him. Anything whatsoever. The drug traffic he runs between
South America and Europe is now a well-established business.
All of the protagonists are bound together by indissoluble links,
and he has devised a perfect plan for laundering the trafficking
profits, where speed of execution plays a fundamental role. The
key point is this: the money from drug sales has to remain on
the street for as little time as possible. It has to be moved to
London to be changed into high denomination German and
Dutch bank notes. At this point it is directed towards tax ha-
vens or lawful financial activities. It's a mechanism that is hard

to obstruct. This is why, when Cocky is arrested on October 24, 1996, his business affairs aren't affected by the boss's departure. On the contrary, he carries on earning money to the point that, in 2005, the Dutch authorities accuse him of running a drug-trafficking group from his prison cell. But the accusations are dismissed on appeal for lack of evidence. And yet it's not only his finances that increase, but also the years of imprisonment he still has to serve, because in 1999 Cocky leaves a fellow Turkish inmate in a pool of blood. The prisoner dies and Cocky cries self-defence, but he isn't believed and gets another four years.

In June 2007, having served two-thirds of the total sentence of sixteen years, he is released and returns to his home country, only to end up back in jail in 2009, sentenced to thirteen years in prison for trying to get a million-pound consignment of cannabis to Jersey. In all these years, the police haven't managed to discover the whereabouts of his proverbial fortune. The treasury of the English drugs baron – transformed maybe into elusive hotels, resorts and vineyards spread throughout Europe – remains hidden. Meanwhile, the Crown Prosecution Service has obtained a High Court order that on his release he is prevented from using public telephones, from carrying more than £1,000 in cash and from having multiple bank accounts, restrictions never before made in English history, which ought to prevent Warren from going back to making money from drug trafficking. If then, by March 2014, he had repaid the £198 million, the fruit of his criminal activity according to the Jersey police, Warren would have been released from prison. But not having done so, he will have to stay in jail for another ten years.

"Awareness, gentlemen. What effect does it have, finding out about the journey cocaine makes? What it's like outside the City? How does it feel, thinking about how the powder you've sniffed has passed through hundreds of invisible hands that have packaged, dispatched, received, supplied, stockpiled, and then worked and distributed it in every corner of the country? Nothing? It has no effect?"

"It's written there in the file, doctor. *Homo oeconomicus*. The principle of efficiency. If you're trying to get us to confess that we're not much different from Curtis Warren because we're applying rationality to obtain a result, then I'll satisfy you straightaway. We're money traffickers. We're the ones making money when everyone's losing it. We are the children of Gordon Gekko. We've really embraced his words: 'Greed is good'. You said it yourself at the start. We're an elite who live in an ivory tower, who've never heard of the area where Cocky was born. And you know why? Because our world works. Without us, not even you would exist."

"We're not the champions of morality. We and our country. We behave like the top of the class and we look away when our front doormat gets dirtied. It's a kind of self-defence. But should we feel guilty about this?"

"Gentlemen, this isn't about the ethics of a country that doesn't realize it's one Europe's most lucrative drug markets. Today we are trying to establish whether and to what extent the information we are exchanging might be of use to you. When you leave here you will probably go back to your desks, switch on your iPads, your iPhones and your two mobile phones, and you'll start talking to six people at the same time. You'll be shouting out orders and developing strategies and models to fit data into. Maybe one day you'll go back to performing as you were before your managers started wondering whether your bloodshot eyes are the result of too many hours in front of the monitors or substance abuse. Your bosses, just like you, gentlemen, are not stupid. They know the world they live in and accept its strengths and weaknesses. They know your needs and they're not scandalized, because they've been there themselves. And they also know it's not to be spoken about, except with shrinks like us when things aren't going right. In other words, when the money isn't moving around as much as before. Go back to your lives and think no more about these hours wasted in group reading of doubtful taste. Or perhaps – and this is what I hope – something might have clicked. The veil is lifted, and things you used to take for granted are no longer so. That's the power of words. It's your choice. Steven, please, continue the reading."

> "The Irish coastline is famous for its seas, which are often stormy, and for its violent winds. The 7,500 rugged miles that extend from the waters of the Atlantic as far as Dublin are known as the Irish Box. For forty years criminal organizations have been exploiting this long stretch – which is difficult to control because of the bad weather conditions – for landing their cargoes more or less undisturbed: it is reckoned that for every consignment intercepted by the Irish authorities, another nine reach their destination."

"Just a few steps away, gentlemen, is the Wild West, didn't you know? And we live in a hunting reserve that's being attacked daily. You are educated people. You've been to smart schools, you think you know the world, and yet a simple piece of information like this catches you by surprise. You've reached the top of the social pyramid and you're convinced you live at the centre of the universe. And you know what I say? You're right. The centre is right here. Carry on, Steven. Thank you."

> "It is calculated that between 1996 and 2007, the Royal Navy and British customs seized 18.36 tons of cocaine along the sea routes, with a retail value of £1.5 billion."

"You handle money without touching it, gentlemen. Can you imagine £1.5 billion? How much space would so much money take up? How could it pass under our eyes without our noticing it? And where does it end up?"

"June 24, 2007. HMS *Ocean*, the largest ship in the Royal Navy, stops a boat in the Caribbean that's probably on its way to Europe with its cargo: 485 kilos of cocaine with a street value in Britain of £29 million.

In July 2007, Irish naval frogmen dive into the sea off Cork where a ship has capsized in bad weather. They bring up packs containing approximately 1.5 tons of cocaine worth hundreds of millions of pounds.

November 2008. The sailing boat *Dances with Waves* is rescued during a storm off the Irish coast: found on board is a fortune of cocaine worth £134 million.'

"Are you keeping count, gentlemen?"

"The Irish coast is generally a point of transit, as Brian Wright well knows. Nicknamed 'The Milkman', he hit the news headlines in 1996 when *Sea Mist*, one of the trawlers he used for smuggling, was forced to take shelter in Cork harbour after a storm at sea on its way to England. Nearly 600 kilos of cocaine were found on board."

"What's the weight of the money you send with one click to the other side of the ocean? What's the weight of £1 million? And £80 million – the value of the cocaine seized on *Sea Mist* – how much does that weigh? Can you imagine how much space 600 kilos take up?"

"The Milkman earned his nickname from the fact that he 'always delivers', just like the milkman who arrives promptly each morning with the milk. Risk runs in his blood. He loves gambling, betting and horse racing. He keeps company with British showbiz personalities and attends VIP events. Before the *Sea Mist* case, he was seen as a young businessman who turned everything he touched into gold. But horses are not the secret of his success and it isn't through bribing a few jockeys that he manages to accumulate £100 million, rent a luxury apartment in Chelsea, buy a £2-million villa in the south of Spain and a house in Frimley, Sussex."

"Another £100 million, gentlemen, and properties spread across Europe."

"After the *Sea Mist* 'incident' it took another eleven years of investigations to piece together the information on Brian Wright and build up a full picture. It's not easy identifying the leads. The Milkman likes to be in the limelight, but is highly skilled in covering every movement, physical and financial. He has interests in Australia, France, Switzerland, Spain, Venezuela, the Caribbean, Mexico, the United States, South Africa and Northern Cyprus without his name appearing in any clearly definable manner. He pays no tax and appears to have no bank accounts: even his car was registered not in his but his son's name. He's an elusive spectre. For this reason, the investigators begin to dig around him, starting from his closest collaborators, until they understand how his organization operates. The Caribbean is the point where the traffic starts. It is there that The Milkman's vessels arrive. They are then boarded by sailors who have the task of collecting the drugs thrown into the sea from other ships or from planes. Then they set sail for Great Britain, passing the Irish Box. But a trawler or a ship is too conspicuous and so the cocaine is divided and transferred onto smaller local boats, perhaps hired sailing yachts that have access to unsuspecting tourist ports.

"All under our nose, gentlemen."

"The authorities discover that between 1996 and 1998 the organization managed to get 7 boats to Great Britain in this way, carrying 3 tons of coke valued at somewhere around £300 million.

February 1999. 472 kilos of cocaine are seized in a ware-house run by a member of the group at Leigh-on-Sea, Essex. It is worth £61 million."

"Three hundred plus sixty-one, gentlemen."

"Nine members of the organization end up in handcuffs. For The Milkman, this is a serious blow. He flees to Northern Cyprus, which has no extradition treaty with Great Britain, enabling him to continue running his organization. Things work out for a while, but his presence on the island doesn't go unnoticed, to the point that The Milkman fears the government will send him to Turkey where the rules of extradition are applied. After six years, he decides to move to Spain, where he feels safer and can intensify his business interests. But he is arrested in 2005 and sentenced in 2007 to thirty years' imprisonment for drug trafficking."

"Gentlemen . . ."

"If you're going to ask us if we've added up all the millions of pounds that you're shooting at us, I can tell you straight-away: no, I haven't even tried. You've forced us to face up to the reality, I admit that. This island of ours is like a colander where everyone involved in drug trafficking finds their way in. But we're not blind, or deaf. We read the newspapers too."

"So, gentlemen, if I ask you who Colin 'Smigger' Smith is, you'll certainly know who I'm talking about?"

"The bloke they bumped off a few years ago outside a gym in Liverpool?"

"Him. And do you know the motive?"

"A settling of scores?"

"In a certain sense, yes. Luke, would you please read your sheet of paper?"

"The Snow King, Colin 'Smigger' Smith, has built up his success on his word. Like his fellow citizen 'Cocky' Curtis Warren, Colin doesn't need to show his power by showing off or with acts of violence. It's far more effective to have important relations with those who really count. And those who really count are the Colombian narcos, particularly those of the Cali Cartel. He buys coke from them with a handshake, as if it were a gentleman's agreement. The Colombians trust the Snow King because they have always done good business with the Liverpool mafia. And the Colombians give credit to Stephen Lawlor, the Snow King's man and bodyguard, when he organizes a shipment of 500 kilos. They give him credit because those 500 kilos will be cut, becoming almost a ton of white powder to be sold on the streets and at that moment they'll have earned enough in Liverpool to pay the Colombians and to live the high life in nightclubs in the capital. Before the cocaine reaches the United Kingdom, there's a stopover in Amsterdam. Lawlor knows every detail of the operation, but in May 2001 he is killed. And that is what the Snow King assures the Colombians: the man who knows it all is dead. The Cartel is patient for a while. After all, the Snow King has never let them down. But time passes and word reaches the ears of the Colombians: Smith has tricked them; he knows perfectly well where the 500 kilos are. Before condemning him to death, the Cartel asks Smith for evidence that the goods really were taken from him with Lawlor's death, even just a newspaper report.But there's nothing of the kind, and in 2007 the Snow King is assassinated: two shots at point blank range from a pump-action shotgun."

"Does the Liverpool mafia really exist?"

"Gentlemen, I think it's time to hand over to Tom."

"'The Colombian cartels have always had a weakness for the city of Liverpool and for its port, which can handle around

seven hundred thousand containers a year. A terminal that's so
busy and with an industrial zone among the largest in Europe
is ideal for those looking for a safe landing place on the Old
Continent. But a profitable and lasting commercial initiative
needs reliable partners, like the Liverpool mafia, which includes various criminal gangs who have cut their teeth in Smack
City, the city of heroin. Colombia and Mexico, thanks first to
the Cali Cartel and then to the Sinaloa and Los Zetas cartels,
have never before been so close to the United Kingdom."

"Follow the money, gentlemen. Isn't that what they say? Thank you,
Tom. Read the rest."

"January 2009: Anthony Spencer, aged 61, probably the head of
a drug smuggling group, is arrested after the police discover 100
kilos of amphetamines and 50 kilos of cannabis at a Dutch
farm. During investigations the group was filmed by the police
as they were burying purpose-built safes in a rural area which
could store up to 140 kilos of various drugs. August 12, 2009.
A gang of four people is arrested for having imported 8.5 kilos
of cocaine from Colombia. Street value after being cut: £2 million.

May 30, 2010. Five men are arrested on a trawler at the Isle
of Wight before they can retrieve 11 watertight sacks that have
been tied with ropes to a signal buoy in the English Channel –
as though they were lobster pots – and dropped into the sea by
a container ship. In them were a total of 225 kilos of pure cocaine. Value: £53 million.'

July 2010. Five men are arrested in Manchester and charged
with international drug trafficking. The cocaine is stockpiled in
a warehouse and hidden inside metal pipes. Value: £25 million.

September 2009. Seven members of an organization are accused of having bribed several baggage handlers at Heathrow

Airport to bring in 12 kilos of cocaine from Brazil. Street value after being cut: £4.5 million.

February 11, 2011. Dritan Bullari and Olger Bullari are sentenced to six years for handling drugs. They concealed and transported the goods, 4 or 5 kilos each time, in vehicles from which they had removed the passenger airbag.

June 2011. Found in the bathroom of the *Louise*, a luxury yacht moored at Southampton, are 1.2 tons of purest cocaine. Street value: £300 million.'

June 26, 2011. Corby, Northamptonshire. Six men are arrested and accused of importing cocaine from the Netherlands and from France. Five kilos of white powder are found in the plane used for the transport. Value: £1,700,000.'

July 2011. Two Poles attempt to bring 17 kilos of cocaine into the United Kingdom by plane from Colombia in sacks containing live tropical fish. Wholesale value: £1.6 million.

October 27, 2011. Twenty-four members of a criminal organization are arrested for having planned the importation of 40 tons of drugs from Central and South America to the United Kingdom hidden in tinned fish or in pellets. Value: £1.4 billion.

June 11, 2012. A cargo ship from Brazil, moored at Silvertown, has 30 kilos of cocaine hidden among its cargo of cane sugar. Retail value: £3 million.

September 2012. Gary Pattison, a 52-year-old florist from Hull, is sentenced to eighteen years' imprisonment for having imported 84 kilos of cocaine hidden in boxes of chrysanthemums. Value: £23.5 million.

October 10, 2012. Emma McCue-Smith of Radcliff is jailed for six years for having imported from Holland, through the Channel Tunnel, 10 kilos of pure cocaine hidden inside a blanket specially designed and draped over the back of her horse. Retail value: £5 million.

"This, gentlemen, is the country where we live, where we work, where we bring up our children. And where we pretend that nothing of what we have read about is happening. It's the first time I find myself in front of a group like yours and when your bosses asked me in what way I intended to help you, well, I didn't know what to say. And after these two hours spent with you, I still have mixed ideas. I'm convinced that you don't want to be helped. I look into your eyes and see your boredom when faced with the facts I have given you. You are asking how all of this will be of use to you. I'm really wondering, looking at your expressions, if the word really does have the power I have given it up to now. I'm wondering whether I'm deluding myself, whether this power really can change things. Now it's up to you. It's your choice."

Silence.

# 2

# THE LESSON

"They were all sitting around a table, right here in New York, not far from here."

"Where?" I asked instinctively.

He gave me a look that said he couldn't believe I was stupid enough to ask a question like that. What I was about to hear was an exchange of favors. The police had arrested a young man in Europe a few years back. A Mexican with an American passport. He was sent to New York, where they let him stew in the swamp of the underworld instead of in jail. Every now and then he'd spill some news to keep from being arrested. Not an informer exactly, but pretty close, something that didn't make him feel like a rat, but not one of those silent as stone types either. The police would ask him generic questions, nothing specific enough to expose him in front of his gang. They needed him to say which way the wind was blowing, what the mood was, rumors of meetings or wars. No proof or evidence, just rumors. They'd collect the evidence later on. But now that wasn't enough. The young man had recorded a speech on his iPhone at a meeting he'd gone to. A speech that made the police uneasy. Some of them, whom I'd known for years,

wanted me to write about it somewhere, to make noise, to see what
sorts of reactions it got in order to find out if the story I was about to
hear really went the way the young man said it had, or if it had been
staged, a little theater piece. They wanted me to shake things up in the
world where those words had been uttered, where they'd been heard.

The police officer waited for me in Battery Park, on a little jetty. No
hat or dark glasses, no ridiculous disguise. He showed up in a brightly
colored T-shirt and flip-flops, with a smile that said he couldn't wait to
spill his secret. His Italian was full of dialect, but I could understand
him. He wasn't looking for complicity of any sort; he had orders to tell
me about the speech and didn't waste time. I remember the story perfectly; it has stayed inside me. The things we remember aren't stored
merely in our heads; I'm convinced that other parts of our bodies remember too. The liver, testicles, fingernails, ribs. When you hear such
words, they get lodged there. Each body part sends what it remembers
to the brain. More and more I realize that I remember with my stomach, which stores up the beautiful as well as the horrendous. I know
that certain memories are there, because my stomach moves. My diaphragm, that membrane rooted at the very core of my body, creates
waves. The diaphragm makes us pant and shudder, but it also makes us
piss, defecate, and vomit. That's where the pushing during childbirth
starts. Where everything starts. And I'm sure there are places that collect much worse, that store up the waste. I don't know exactly where
that place is inside of me, but I know it's full. My place of memories, of
waste, is saturated. That might seem like a good thing, but it isn't. Because if the waste doesn't have anywhere to go it starts worming its way
into places it shouldn't. It thrusts itself into places that collect different
sorts of memories. That policeman's story filled up forever the part of
me that remembers the worst things. Those things that resurface just
when you start thinking everything's going better, when you start
imagining you'll finally be able to go home, when you tell yourself it
really was worth it after all. It's in moments like that when the dark
memories resurface from somewhere, like an exhalation, like trash in a

dump, buried and covered over by plastic, that somehow finds its way to the surface and poisons everything.

The police officer told me that the young man, his informer, had heard the only lesson worth learning—that's what he called it—and had recorded it on the sly. Not to betray anyone, but to be able to listen to it again. A lesson on how to be in the world. And he let the officer hear the whole thing; they listened together, sharing the young man's earbuds.

"Now you have to write about it. Let's see if somebody gets pissed off . . . which would mean that the young man's telling the truth. If you write about it and nobody does anything, then either it's just a load of crap from some B-grade actor, and our Chicano friend is making fools of us . . . or nobody believes the bullshit you write." He laughed.

I nodded without promising anything; I was just trying to understand the situation. Supposedly it was an old Italian boss talking to a group of Latinos, Italians, Italian Americans, Albanians, and former Kaibiles, the notorious Guatemalan elite soldiers. At least, that's what the young man said. No facts, statistics, or details. Not something you learn against your will; you just enter the room one way and you come out changed. You're still wearing the same clothes, have the same haircut, your beard is still the same length. No signs of being initiated, no cuts over your eyebrows, no broken nose, and you haven't been brainwashed with sermons either. You go in, and when you come out, at first glance you look exactly the same as when you were pushed through the door. But only on the outside. Inside you're completely different. They didn't reveal the ultimate truth to you, they merely put a few things in their proper place. Things you hadn't known how to use before, that you'd never had the courage to take in.

The police officer read me the transcription he'd made. They'd met in a room not far from where we were, seated in no particular order, randomly, not in a horseshoe like they do at ritual initiations. Seated like they do in a club in some small town in southern Italy, or on Arthur Avenue in New York City, to watch the soccer game on TV. But there

was no soccer game on TV in that room, and this was no gathering of
friends. They were all members of criminal organizations, of all different ranks. The old Italian gets up. They knew he was a man of honor,
that he'd come to the United States after living in Canada for a long
time. He begins talking without even introducing himself; he doesn't
need to. He speaks a bastard Italian, some dialect thrown in, mixed
with English and Spanish. I wanted to know his name, so I asked the
police officer, trying to sound casual, as if it were a passing curiosity.
He didn't bother answering me. There were only the boss's words.

> Them folks who think they can get by with justice, with laws
> that are equal for everybody, with hard work, dignity, clean
> streets, with women same as men, it's only a world of fags who
> think it's okay to make fools of themselves. And everyone
> around them. All that crap about a better world, leave it to them
> idiots. To the rich idiots who can afford such luxuries. The lux-
> ury of believing in a happy world, a just world. Rich people with
> guilty consciences, or with something to hide. Whoever rules
> just does it, and that's that. Sure, he can say he rules for the
> good, for justice and liberty and all. But that's just sissy stuff;
> leave all that to the rich fools. Who rules, rules. Period.

I tried asking how he was dressed, how old he was. Cop questions,
things a reporter or a nosy obsessive would ask, believing that the
typology of a boss who'd give this sort of speech can be had in the
details. The police officer ignored me and kept on talking. I listened,
sifting his words like sand in hopes of finding the nugget, the name. I
listened to his words but was searching for something else. I was searching for clues.

"He wanted to explain the rules to them, capish?" the police officer
said. "He wanted them to really get into it. I'm sure he's not lying. This
isn't some lazy Mexican wank, I'm telling you. I swear on my life, even
if no one believes me."

The police officer buried his nose in his notebook and started reading again.

> The rules of the organization are the rules of life. Government laws are the rules of one side that wants to fuck the other side. And we ain't gonna let ourselves get fucked by nobody. There's people who make money without taking any risks, and they're always gonna be afraid of those who make money by risking everything. If you risk it all, you have it all, capish? But if you think you gotta save yourself, or that you can do it without jail time, without fleeing, without going into hiding, then let me make it clear right from the start: you are not a man. And if you're not a man, you can leave this room right now, and don't even hope to ever become one, 'cause you will never ever be a man of honor.

The police officer looked at me. His eyes were two narrow slits, as if he were trying to see words he remembered all too well. He had read and listened to that testimony dozens of times.

> *Crees en el amor?* Love ends. *Crees en tu corazón?* Your heart stops. No? No love and no heart? So, do you believe in *coño*, in pussy? Well, even pussies dry up after a while. You believe in your wife? Soon as your money runs out, she'll tell you you're neglecting her. You believe in your children? As soon as you stop giving them money they'll say you don't love them. You believe in your mama? If you don't nurse her, she'll say you're an ungrateful child. Listen to what I'm tellin' you. You need to live, *vivir*. You got to live for yourselves. It's for yourselves that you need to know how to be respected, and how to show respect. *La famiglia*. Respect the people who are useful to you and despise the ones who aren't. The people who can give you something get your respect, and the ones who are useless lose it. Somebody

who wants something from you, doesn't he respect you? Somebody who's afraid of you? So what happens when you got nothing to give? When you got nothing left? When you're no longer useful? Then you're *basura*, rubbish. If you have nothing to give, then you're nothing, *nada, nulla.*

"So," the police officer said, "I understood right then and there that the boss, this Italiano, was somebody who counts, who knows what life's about. Really knows. That Mexican kid couldn't have come up with that speech on his own. The spic dropped out of school at sixteen; they fished him out of a gambling den in Barcelona. And the way this guy talks, his Calabrian dialect, how could some actor or braggart ever invent that? If it weren't for my wife's grandmother I never would have understood a word of it."

I'd heard dozens of speeches on Mafia moral philosophy—in penitents' confessions and wiretappings. But this was different; it was like training for the soul.

I'm talkin' to you; I even like some of you. Some of you, I'd like to smash your face. But even if I like you the best, if you got more pussy or more money than me, I want you dead. If one of you becomes my brother, and I make him my equal in the organization, then one thing is clear: He's gonna try to fuck me over. Don't think a friend will be forever a friend. I'll be killed by somebody I shared my food with, my sleep, everything. I'll be killed by somebody I ate with, somebody who gave me shelter. I don't know who it'll be or I'd already have eliminated him. But it'll happen. And if he doesn't kill me, he'll betray me. Rules are rules. And rules are not laws. Laws are for cowards. Rules are for men. That's why we have rules of honor. Rules of honor don't tell you you have to be good, just, upright. Rules of honor tell you how to rule. What you have to do to handle people, money, power. Rules of honor tell you how to behave if you want to rule, if you want to fuck the guy above you, if you don't want to be fucked by the guy below you. There's no sense explaining them. Rules of honor exist, period. They evolved on their own, on and through the blood of every man of honor. How do you choose?

Was that question for me? I searched for the right answer.

How can you choose, in a few seconds, a few minutes, hours, what you should do? If you choose wrong, you'll pay for it for years, for that quick decision. The rules are always there, but you got to know how to recognize them, you got to understand when they really count. And then there's God's laws. God's laws are contained in the rules. God's laws—the real ones, though, not the ones they use to make poor fools tremble with fear. But remember this: You can have all the rules of honor you want, but still, only one thing's for certain. You're a man only if you know deep down what your destiny is. Poor fools grovel, because it's easier. Men of honor know that everything dies, everything passes away, nothing lasts forever. Journalists start out wanting to change the world and end up wanting to be editor in chief. It's easier to condition them than to corrupt them. Each one matters only for himself and for the Honored Society. And the Honored Society says you matter only if you rule. You can choose how, later. You can rule with an iron fist or you can buy consensus. By spilling blood or giving it. The Honored Society knows that every man is weak, depraved, vain. It knows that people don't change; that's why rules are everything. Bonds of friendship are nothing without rules. Every problem has a solution, from your wife who leaves you to your group that splits up. The solution merely depends on how much you offer. If

things go poorly, you merely offered too little. Don't go looking
for other explanations.

It seemed like a university seminar for aspiring bosses. What was this?

You have to know who you want to be. If you rob, shoot, rape,
deal drugs, you'll make money for a while, but then they'll take
you and crush you. You can do it. Sure, you can do it. But not
for long, 'cause you don't know what might happen to you; people will fear you only if you stick a pistol in their mouth. But as
soon as you turn your back, what happens? As soon as a job
goes wrong? If you belong to the organization, you know there's
a rule for everything. If you want to make money, there's ways
to do it; if you want to kill, there are motives and methods; if
you want to get ahead, you can, but you have to earn respect,
trust, you have to make yourself indispensable. There's even
rules for if you want to change the rules. Whatever you do outside the rules, you never know how it might end. But whatever
you do that follows the rules of honor, you always know exactly
what it's going to get you. And you know exactly how the people around you will react. So if you want to be an ordinary
man, just keep doing what you're doing. But if you want to
become a man of honor, you got to have rules. And the difference between an ordinary man and a man of honor is that the
man of honor always knows what's happening, while the ordinary man gets screwed by chance, bad luck, or stupidity. Things
happen to him. But the man of honor knows what's gonna happen, and he knows when. You know exactly what belongs to
you and what doesn't; you know exactly how far you can push
yourself, even if you want to push past every rule. Everybody
wants three things: power, pussy, and money. Even the judge
when he condemns bad people, even the politicians, they want
*dinero* and pussy and power, but they want to get it by showing

they're indispensable, defenders of the law or the poor or who knows what. Everybody wants money, even though they go around saying they want something else, or doing things for other people. The rules of the Honored Society are rules for controlling everybody. The Honored Society knows you can have money, pussy, and power, but it also knows that the man who's capable of giving up everything is the one who decides everybody else's fate. Cocaine. That's what cocaine is. All you can see, you can have it. Without cocaine, you're nothing. With cocaine, you can be whoever you want. If you sniff cocaine, you screw yourself all on your own. The organization gives you rules for moving up in the world. It gives you rules for killing and for how you're gonna be killed. You want to lead a normal life? You want to be worth nothing? Fine. All you need to do is not see, not hear. But remember this: In Mexico, where you can do whatever you want, get high, fuck little girls, drive as fast as you like, the only ones who really rule are the ones who have rules. If you do stupid stuff, you got no honor, and if you got no honor, you got no power. You're just like everybody else.

The police officer pointed his finger at a particularly worn page of his notebook. "Look, look at this . . . he wanted to explain absolutely everything. How to live, not just how to be a mafioso. How to live."

You work, a lot. You have some money, *algo dinero*. Maybe some beautiful women. But then they leave you, for somebody more handsome, with more *dinero* than you. You might have a decent life—pretty unlikely—or a shitty life, like everybody else. But when you end up in jail, the ones on the outside, who think they're clean, will insult you, but you will have ruled. They'll hate you, but you'll have bought yourself everything good in life, everything you wanted. You'll have the organization behind you. It might happen that you suffer some, and maybe they'll even kill you. The organization backs whoever's strongest, obviously. You can climb mountains with rules of flesh, blood, and money. But if you become weak, if you make a mistake, you're fucked. If you do good, you'll be rewarded. If you make a bad alliance, you're fucked; if you make a mistake in war, you're fucked; if you don't know how to hold on to power, you're fucked. But these wars are permitted, they're allowed. They're our wars. You might win and you might lose. But on only one condition will you always lose, and in the most painful way possible: if you betray the organization. Whoever tries to go against the Honored Society has no hope of surviving. You can run from the law but not from the organization. You can even run from God, 'cause God can wait forever for the fugitive. But you can't escape the organization. If you betray it and run, if they screw you and you run, if you don't respect the rules and you run, somebody's gonna pay. They'll come looking for you. They'll go to your family, to your allies. Your name will be on the list forever. And nothing can ever erase it. Not time, not money. You're fucked for all eternity, you and your descendants.

The police officer closed his notebook. "The kid, it was like he came out of a trance."

And then the officer told me what the young man had asked him: "So am I betraying the organization now, letting you listen to this?"

"Write about it," the police officer said to me. "We got our eye on him. I'll put three guys on his ass, twenty-four hours a day. If someone tries to close in on him, we'll know he wasn't bullshitting, that it isn't some joke, this is a real boss talking."

That story really stunned me. Where I come from, it's what they've always done. But it was strange to hear those same words in New York. Where I come from, you don't join merely for the money; you do it above all in order to belong, to have a structure, to move as if on a chessboard. To know exactly which piece to move and when.

"It's risky, I think," I said to him.

"Do it," he insisted.

"I don't think so," I replied.

I couldn't sleep. I tossed and turned. It wasn't the story itself that struck me so much. It was the whole chain that left me perplexed. I'd been contacted to write the story of a story of a story. The source—the old Italian—I trusted instinctively. A bit because, when you're far from home, whoever speaks your language, I mean your very same language—same codes, same locutions, same vocabulary, same omissions—you recognize immediately as one of your own, as someone to pay attention to. And also because his speech was delivered at the right time, to exactly the people who needed to hear it. If those words were true, they signaled a most dreadful turning point. The Italian bosses, the last remaining Calvinists of the West, were training new generations of Mexicans and Latin Americans, the criminal bourgeoisie born of drug trafficking, the most ferocious and hungry recruits in the world.

I couldn't stay still. My bed felt like a wooden plank, my room like a cell. I wanted to pick up the phone and call that police officer, but it was two in the morning and I didn't want him to think I was crazy. I went to my desk and started an e-mail. I would write about it, but first I had to understand more. I wanted to listen to the actual recording. That training lesson about how to be in the world wasn't only for mafia affiliates but for anyone who decides they want to rule on this Earth. Words no one would utter with such clarity unless he were training people. When you talk publicly about a soldier, you say he wants peace and hates war, but when you're alone with him, you train him to shoot. That speech was an effort to bring Italian organized crime traditions into South American organizations. That kid wasn't boasting at all.

I got a text. The young man, the informer, had wrapped himself around a tree while driving. It wasn't revenge. Just a fancy Italian car he didn't know how to drive, and he slammed it into a tree. End of story.

## 3.

# BIG BANG

Don Arturo is an elderly gentleman who remembers it all. And he'll talk about it to anyone who's willing to listen. His grandchildren are too big, he's already a great-grandfather, and he prefers to tell the little ones other stories. Arturo tells of how one day a general arrived, dismounted his horse, which seemed incredibly tall but was merely a healthy animal in a land of skinny, arthritic beasts, and ordered that all the *gomeros*—the peasants who raised opium poppies—be rounded up. Burn all the fields: It was an order. That's the way the government works. Do it or end up in jail. For ten years. Jail, the *gomeros* all thought, the sooner the better. Growing grain again was worse than going to jail. But during those ten years their children wouldn't be able to grow poppies, and the land would be seized or, in the best of circumstances, devastated by drought. The *gomeros* merely lowered their eyes: Their lands and their poppies would all be burned. Soldiers arrived and dumped diesel fuel on the soil, the flowers, the mule tracks, the paths leading from one estate to another. Arturo told how fields once red with poppies were now stained black with buckets of dark, dense diesel fuel, how a foul smell saturated the air. Back then, the work was all done by hand; those big poison pumps didn't exist yet. Bucketfuls of stench. But that's not the reason old Arturo remembers it all. He remembers because it was there that he learned how to recognize courage, and that cowardice tastes of human flesh. The fields caught fire, but slowly. Not a sudden burst of flame, but row by row, fire contaminating fire. Thousands of flowers, stems, and roots catching fire. The peasants all watched, and so did the police and the mayor, the women and the children. A painful spectacle. Then all of a sudden they saw screaming balls of fire come shooting out of the nearby bushes. Living flames, it seemed, leaping and gasping for breath. But the fire hadn't suddenly come to life—these were animals. Asleep among the poppies, they hadn't heard the noise or smelled the diesel fuel, which they'd never smelled before. Flaming rabbits, stray dogs, even a small mule. All on fire. There was nothing to be done. No amount of water can put out diesel flames on flesh, and besides, the land all around was on fire. The howling beasts were consumed right before the people's eyes. And that wasn't the only tragedy. The *gomeros* who had gotten drunk while dumping the fuel, they too caught fire. They drank cerveza as they worked, and then fell asleep in the brush. The fire took them, too. They howled a lot less than the animals, staggering around as if the alcohol in their veins were feeding the fire from within. No one went to help them; no one ran over with a blanket. The flames were too fierce.

That's when Don Arturo saw a dog, all skin and bones, run toward the fire. The dog dove into that inferno and came out with two, three, finally six puppies, rolling each one on the ground to put out the flames. Singed, spitting smoke and ashes, covered in sores, but alive. They stumbled after their mother, who walked past the people gazing at the fire. She seemed to look right at each one of them, her eyes piercing the *gomeros*, the soldiers, and all the other miserable human beings who were just standing there. An animal senses cowardice. And respects fear. Fear is the more vital instinct, and deserves more respect. Cowardice is a choice, fear is a state of mind. That dog was afraid, but she dove into those flames to save her young. Not one man had saved another man. They'd let them all burn to death. That's how the old man told it. There is no right age for understanding. To him it came early, when he was only eight. And he remembered this truth till he was ninety: Beasts have courage and know what it means to defend life. Men boast about courage, but all they know how to do is obey, crawl, get by.

For twenty years there were only ashes where poppies had once grown. Then one day, Arturo recalled, a general came. Another one. On estates in every corner of the Earth, there's always someone who appears in the name of a powerful figure, someone with a uniform, boots, and a horse—or an SUV, depending on when we're talking about. He ordered the peasants to become *gomeros* again, Arturo remembered. Enough with grain, time for poppies again. Drugs again. The United States was preparing for war, and before the guns, before the bullets, tanks, planes, and aircraft carriers, before the uniforms and boots, before everything else, the United States needed morphine. You don't go to war without morphine. If any of you have been in pain, excruciating pain, you know what morphine is: peace from suffering. You don't go to war without morphine, because war is suffering, broken bones, and lacerated flesh. There are treatises and demonstrations, candles and pickets for people's outrage. But for burning flesh there's only one thing: morphine. Maybe you live in the part of the world that is still fairly tranquil. You know the cries of hospital wards, of women in labor, of the sick, of children who scream and joints that dislocate. But you've probably never heard the screams of a man hit by a bullet, his bones shattered by a submachine gun or shrapnel, his arm or half his face ripped off. Those are real cries, the only ones memory cannot forget. Our memory of sounds is fleeting; memories are linked to actions, contexts. But the cries of war never go away. Veterans and reporters, doctors and career soldiers all wake up to those cries. If you've heard the screams of a dying man, or one lying wounded in the middle of a battlefield, there's no point spending money on psychoanalysts or seeking comfort. You'll never forget those screams. Only chemistry can stop them, soothe them, only chemistry can lessen the pain. At the sound of those cries, the other soldiers all turn to stone. Nothing is less militaristic than the screams of someone wounded in battle. Only morphine can silence those cries and let the others go on thinking they'll get off scot-free, come out unscathed, be victorious. And so the United States, which needed morphine for war, asked Mexico to increase its opium production, and even helped build a railroad to facilitate transportation. How much opium was needed? Lots. As much as possible. Arturo had grown up by then. He was almost thirty, already had four kids. He wasn't about to set fire to his fields, as his father had done. He knew what would happen—first they'd ask, then they'd order him to do it. So when the general left, Arturo took the back roads and caught up with him. He intercepted the general's caravan and negotiated. He would sell a portion of his opium on the black market. The bulk would go to the government, which would sell it to the United States military; the rest he'd smuggle out, for those Yankees who wanted to enjoy a little opium or morphine. The general accepted the proposal in exchange for a hefty cut. And on one condition: "You get your opium across the border yourself."

Old Arturo is like a sphinx. None of his children are narcos. None of his grandchildren are narcos. None of their wives are narcos. But the narcos respect him because he was the first opium smuggler in the entire area. Arturo went from *gomero* to broker. He didn't simply grow poppies; he mediated between producers and traffickers. He kept it up until the 1980s, and that was only the beginning, because back then most of the heroin that made its way to America was handled by Mexicans. Arturo had become a powerful, well-to-do man. But something ended his activity as opium broker. That something was Kiki. After the Kiki ordeal Arturo decided to go back to growing grain. He abandoned opium and the men who dealt in heroin and morphine. It's an old story, the one about Kiki. From many years ago. But it's a story that Arturo never forgot. So when his children said they wanted to traffic in coke, just as he had in opium, Arturo realized the time had come to tell them the story of Kiki. If you don't know it, it's well worth hearing. Arturo took his children outside the city and showed them a hole, now full of flowers, most of them dried. A deep hole. And he told them the story. I'd read it but hadn't understood how decisive it was until I got to know the strip of land called Sinaloa, a paradise where people endure punishments worthy of the worst inferno.


The story of Kiki is linked to that of Miguel Ángel Félix Gallardo, whom everyone knows as El Padrino, the Godfather. Félix Gallardo worked for the Federal Judicial Police of Mexico, and then worked as a bodyguard for the family of Governor Leopoldo Sánchez Celis, from which perch he began amassing his understanding and his power. As a police officer he tracked smugglers, studied their methods, uncovered their routes, arrested them. He knew everything. He hunted them down. Eventually he would go to their bosses and propose that they organize, but under one condition—that they choose him as their boss. Whoever accepted became part of the organization, whoever preferred to remain independent was free to do so. And later killed. Arturo agreed to join. The era of transporting marijuana and opium on a large scale had begun for Félix Gallardo. He got to know personally every inch of every access route into the United States: where you could climb over, where trucks or horses could slip through. There weren't any cartels in Mexico back then; Félix Gallardo created them. Cartels. Everyone calls them that now, even kids who don't really know what the word means. Most of the time, it's exactly the right word. Groups that manage coke, coke capital, coke prices, coke distribution. That's what cartels are. After all, "cartel" is the economic term for a group of producers who agree on prices, production levels, and how, when, and where to distribute. This holds for the legal as well as the illegal economy. The prices in Mexico were decided by only a few drug cartels. El Padrino was considered the Mexican czar of cocaine. Under him were Rafael Caro Quintero and Ernesto Fonseca Carrillo, known as Don Neto. In Colombia, the rival

Cali and Medellín cartels were in the midst of a full-blown war to control cocaine trafficking and routes. Massacres. But Pablo Escobar, lord of Medellín, also had problems outside Colombia: The U.S. police, whom he couldn't manage to bribe, were sequestering too many of his shipments off the coast of Florida and in the Caribbean, and he was losing tons of coke. Airport bribes were getting so high that he was losing lots of money. So Escobar decided to ask Félix Gallardo for help. Escobar, El Magico, and Félix Gallardo, El Padrino, understood each other right away. And they reached an agreement. The Mexicans would get the coke into the United States. Félix Gallardo knew the U.S.-Mexico border, and for him all corridors were open. He knew the routes marijuana took—the same ones that opium took—and now cocaine would take them as well. El Padrino trusted Escobar; he knew he wouldn't become a rival because the Colombian boss wasn't strong enough to set up his own man in Mexico. Félix Gallardo didn't guarantee Escobar exclusivity. He'd give Medellín priority, but if Cali or other smaller cartels asked him to handle their shipments, of course he'd take them on as well. To profit from everyone without becoming anyone's enemy is a difficult praxis in life, but at that moment at least, when lots of cartels needed to cross the border, it was possible to squeeze money out of all of them. More and more money.

The Colombians usually paid cash for each shipment. Medellín would pay—first in pesos, then in dollars—and the Mexicans would get their load into the United States. But after a while, El Padrino realized that currency could depreciate and that cocaine was more profitable: It would be a real coup to distribute it directly in the North American market. So when the Colombian cartel started commissioning more shipments, El Padrino demanded to be paid in goods. Escobar accepted; it even seemed like a better deal. And in any case, he couldn't not accept. If a shipment was easy to transport, if it could be hidden in trucks or trains, 35 percent of the coke went to the Mexicans. If it was tricky and had to pass through underground tunnels, the Mexicans got 50 percent. Those impassible routes, that border, those nearly two thousand miles of Mexico sutured to the United States, became El Padrino's greatest resource. The Mexicans went from being transporters to actual distributors. Now it was they who would place the coke with the American organizations, with the bosses, area managers, and pushers. It wasn't just the Colombians anymore. Now the Mexicans could aspire to have a seat at the business table too. That and more. Much more. That's how it works in big companies too; the distributor often becomes the producer's main competitor, and its earnings surpass the head company's.

But El Padrino was clever and understood that it was essential to maintain a low profile. Especially with the whole world watching Escobar, El Magico, and Colombia. So he tried to be prudent. To lead a normal life, to be a leader rather than an emperor. And he paid attention to the details, knew that every move had to be oiled, that every checkpoint, every officer in the area, every mayor of every village they went through had to be paid off. El Padrino knew he had to pay. To make sure your good fortune was understood to be everyone's good fortune. And—most important—to pay before anyone had time to talk, betray, blab, or offer more. Before he could sell himself to a rival clan or to the police. The police were key. He'd been an officer himself once. Which is why they found someone who could guarantee their shipments would move smoothly: Kiki. Kiki was a cop who could guarantee impunity from the state of Guerrero to the state of Baja California. From then on, entry into the United States was smooth. Caro Quintero practically worshipped Kiki, and often invited him to his home. He'd tell him how a boss should live, what his lifestyle should be, how he should appear to his men: rich, well-off, but not too ostentatious. You have to make them believe that if you thrive, they'll thrive too. That the people who work for you will thrive too. They have to want your business to grow. If instead you show them that you have it all, they'll want to take something from you. It's a fine line, and success lies in never overstepping it, never giving in to the allure of a life of luxury.

Kiki got drugs through everywhere with remarkable ease, and El

Padrino's clan paid willingly. It seemed that Kiki could bribe everyone, could get everything across the border smoothly. It was because of this extraordinary trust, which Kiki had earned over time, that they began talking to him about something they never had mentioned to anyone: El Búfalo. After the umpteenth tractor trailer loaded with Colombian coke and Mexican grass made it over the American border, Kiki was taken to Chihuahua. He'd heard people mention El Búfalo a thousand times, but he'd never understood what it was exactly, a code name, a special operation, a nickname? El Búfalo was not the boss of bosses, or some sacred, venerable beast, even though it was usually spoken of with reverence. El Búfalo was one of the biggest marijuana plantations in the world. Over 1,300 acres of land and something like 10,000 peasants working it. Every protest movement in the world, from New York to Athens, from Rome to Los Angeles, was characterized by marijuana use. Parties without joints? Political demonstrations without joints? Impossible. Weed, the symbol of a light buzz, of togetherness and feeling good, of sweet relaxation and friendship. For a long time almost all the marijuana that Americans smoked, the grass consumed in universities in Paris and Rome, the weed toked at Swedish demonstrations and on German picket lines, was grown in El Búfalo; that's where it came from, before mafias delivered it around the world. They needed Kiki to get more trucks through, more trains full of El Búfalo gold. And Kiki agreed.

On the morning of November 6, 1984, 450 Mexican soldiers invaded El Búfalo. Helicopters rained down soldiers, who ripped up marijuana plants and seized what had already been harvested, entire bales ready for drying and chopping. Between what was sequestered and what was burned, $8 billion worth of weed went up in smoke. El Búfalo and all its plantings were under the control of Rafael Caro Quintero's clan, and it operated with the full protection of the police and army: The ranch was vast and was the main economic resource of the area. Everybody profited from El Búfalo. Caro Quintero couldn't believe that with all the money he'd invested to oil the machine, to bribe the police and the army, a military operation of this scale could have escaped his notice. Even the military planes in the area would notify him before taking off, ask his authorization. No one could understand what happened. The Mexicans must have been pressured by the Americans. The DEA, the U.S. Drug Enforcement Administration, must have stuck its nose in El Búfalo business.

Caro Quintero and El Padrino were alarmed. The two shared a deep trust; they cofounded the organization that held the monopoly on drug trafficking in Mexico. They asked everyone who worked for them, at every level, to investigate everyone in their pay. Because they should have known about the raid in advance. Normally they were warned if the authorities were going to strike, and they themselves would make sure some drugs were found. A good amount, if the police officer responsible had news cameras with him, or needed to climb the ranks. A little less if he wasn't one of their men. Kiki talked with everyone, with Don Neto, with El Padrino's political cronies. He wanted to sound them out, figure out what the cartel aristocracy's next move would be.

One day he was on his way to see his wife, Mika; they didn't meet for lunch very often, only when Kiki was serene and not too swamped with work. They would meet somewhere far from his office, in one of the nicer neighborhoods of Guadalajara.

Kiki put his badge and pistol in a drawer, left his room, and stepped outside. He went over to his pickup, and five men, three near the engine and two near the bed, pointed pistols at him. Kiki raised his hands, tried to recognize the faces of the men threatening him. He was loaded into a beige Volkswagen Atlantic. His wife was waiting for him, and when he didn't show, she called his office. Kiki was taken to Lope de Vega Street. He knew the house well, two stories, with a veranda and a tennis court. It belonged to one of El Padrino's men. He'd been found out. Because Kiki wasn't the umpteenth Mexican police officer in the pay of the drug lords, he wasn't an extremely talented but corrupt cop who had become El Padrino's alchemist. Kiki was with the DEA.

His real name was Enrique Camarena Salazar. An American of

Mexican origins, he'd joined the DEA in 1974. He started working in California and then was sent to the Guadalajara branch. For four years Kiki Camarena mapped the country's major cocaine and marijuana trafficking networks. He got to thinking about infiltrating, because police operations were merely arresting campesinos, dealers, drivers, killers, little guys, when the real problem was elsewhere. He wanted to get beyond the mechanism of big arrests, spectacular in terms of numbers but insignificant in terms of importance. Between 1974 and 1976, when a joint task force of the DEA and Mexico set out to eradicate opium production from the mountains of Sinaloa, there were four thousand arrests, all growers and transporters. But if you didn't arrest the bosses, if you didn't arrest the people pulling the strings of the whole operation, the organization was destined to live forever, to regenerate continuously. Kiki was trying to penetrate deeper and deeper into the Golden Triangle—the states of Sinaloa, Durango, and Chihuahua—a vast marijuana and opium production area. Kiki's mother was against the idea. She wasn't happy about his work, didn't want her son taking on the world's drug kingpins all by himself. But Kiki simply said, "Even though I'm just one person, I can make a difference." That was his philosophy. And it was true. But they betrayed him. Very few people knew about the operation, and one of those very few had talked. His kidnappers took him into a room and began torturing him. They had to do an exemplary job. No one was ever to forget how Kiki Camarena was punished for his betrayal. So they recorded it all on tape, because they needed to prove to El Padrino that they had done everything possible to make Kiki spill what he knew. They wanted every word he uttered as he was beaten and tortured to be recorded, so they could catch every clue, even the most insignificant shred of information. At that point anything could turn out to be useful. They wanted to know how much Kiki had already talked and who the other members of his team were. They started with slaps in the face and punches to his Adam's apple, to take his breath away. They blindfolded him, tied his hands, and then broke his nose and the bone above his eyes. When he lost consciousness his torturers called a doctor. They washed the blood off and splashed ice water on him, until he came to. Kiki wept from the pain. But he didn't talk. They asked how the DEA got its information, who gave it to them. They wanted names. But there were no names. They didn't believe him. They tied electric wires to his testicles and started giving him shocks. The tape records screams and thuds, as his body was hurled in the air by the electric current. Then, Kiki's hands and feet tied to a chair, one of his torturers placed a screw on his head and began turning. The screw entered his skull, piercing flesh and bone, the pain was excruciating. Kiki merely repeated, "Leave my family alone." "Please, don't hurt my family." At every slap, every extracted tooth, every electric shock, the pain was made worse by the thought that it would be multiplied on Mika, Enrique, Daniel, and Erik, his wife and three children. It's the thing he repeats most often on the tape. No matter what sort of relationship you have with your family, when you know they might pay for something you've done, the pain becomes unbearable, as does the thought that someone else will suffer because of you, for a choice you made.

When pain takes hold of your body it generates reactions that are unexpected, unthinkable. You don't produce some huge lie in the hope that it will end, because you fear you'll be found out and the pain will come back, even more agonizing this time, if such a thing is even possible. Pain makes you say exactly what your torturers want to know. But the most unbearable thing that happens when the pain becomes intolerable is the complete loss of psychological orientation. You're on the floor, in a pool of your own blood and piss and drool, your bones broken, and despite all this—you don't have any choice—you continue to place your trust in them. To trust their logic, their nonexistent pity. The pain makes you lose all judgment, makes you blurt out your deepest fears. It makes you beg for mercy, above all for your family. How could you possibly think that someone capable of burning your testicles or screwing a piece of metal into your head would heed your prayers to spare your family? But Kiki begged anyway, unable to gauge the rest.

How could he imagine that his prayers were feeding their hunger for revenge, their savagery?

They broke his ribs. At a certain point on the tape you hear him ask, "Could you bandage them for me, please?" His ribs had pierced his lungs, and it felt like crystal shards were slicing his flesh. One of his torturers lit some charcoal, like they were going to grill a steak. They heated a rod until it was red hot, and then stuck it up his rectum. They raped him with a boiling hot rod. His screams are impossible to listen to; no one can keep from turning off the recorder, from walking out of the room where the tape is played. Whenever Kiki's story is told there's always someone who recalls that the judges who listened to those tapes couldn't sleep for weeks. They tell about the policemen who vomited when they had to draft the report on those nine hours of tapes. Others would weep as they wrote, or plug their ears and shout, "Enough!!!!" They tortured Kiki, all the while asking how he arranged it all. Asking for names, addresses, bank accounts. But Kiki was the only one. He had organized the infiltration all by himself, with the consent of a few of his supervisors and the help of a small support unit in Mexico. That was the strength of his undercover operation—he operated alone. But those few—very few—Mexican police officers who knew about it, who'd been tried and tested with years of experience, they sold themselves. They sold out to Caro Quintero.

It seemed clear from the start that the Mexican police were involved. Testimonies reveal that the kidnapping was carried out with the help of corrupt police officers in the pay of the Guadalajara cartel. But Los Pinos—the president's residence—did nothing; no investigations were launched, no answers given. The Mexican government blocked every initiative, played down the whole affair, saying, "Someone's simply gone missing—he could be sunbathing in Guadalajara. It's not a priority." They would not admit to the kidnapping. Washington also advised the DEA to let it drop and accept what had happened, since political relations between Mexico and the United States were too important to be compromised over some disappeared agent. But the DEA couldn't accept such a defeat. They sent twenty-five of their men to Guadalajara to investigate. What ensued was a huge manhunt for Kiki Camarena. El Padrino began to feel suffocated. Touching Kiki had probably been a bad move. But when you have an entire contingent of political allies, and above all when you think you've taken care of everything, down to the last detail, you have the arrogance of power. And the power of money. They had to make an example out of Kiki. The trust they'd had in him was absolute, so the punishment had to be unforgettable. It had to go down in history, to stay lodged in people's memories.

Kiki's body was found a month after the kidnapping, near La Angostura, a small village in the state of Michoacán, sixty miles south of Guadalajara. Dumped along the side of a country road. His tortured body was still bound, gagged, and blindfolded. The Mexican government lied, declaring that the body, wrapped in plastic, had been found there by a peasant. But FBI investigations on the soil traces on his skin confirmed that the body had been placed there only later; it had been buried somewhere else first. Buried in that hole where Don Arturo, the elderly opium smuggler, placed flowers, that hole where he took his children. And when his grandchildren and his grandchildren's children asked his permission to join the cartels, to work for the drug lords, to give them land, Arturo didn't say a word. Once a respected opium boss, he had renounced everything, but his descendants regretted his decision; they couldn't understand it. Until the old man brought them all to that hole and told them about Kiki, and about that dog he'd seen when he was a little boy. It was his way of explaining what his refusal meant. It was his way of entering the fire and carrying out his puppies. Don Arturo knew he had to have the courage of that dog.

Kiki Camarena's story shouldn't hurt anymore, maybe it doesn't even need to be told anymore, because by now it's well known. A story one might think is marginal, which took place on an unknown, insignificant strip of land. But Kiki's story is central. It's the origin of the world, I'm tempted to say. It's essential to understanding where our modern world begins, its birth pains, its principal path. What we experience today, the economy that regulates our lives, is determined more by what Félix Gallardo, El Padrino, and Pablo Escobar, El Magico, decided and did in the eighties than by anything Ronald Reagan and Mikhail Gorbachev decided or did. Or at least that's how I see it.

Various testimonies relate that in 1989 El Padrino convened all the most powerful Mexican drug lords in a resort in Acapulco. While the world was preparing for the fall of the Berlin Wall, while the past of the cold war, iron curtains, and insuperable borders was being buried, the future of the planet was silently being planned in this city in southwestern Mexico. El Padrino decided to subdivide his activity and assign various segments to traffickers the DEA hadn't fixed their eyes on yet. He divided his territory into zones, or *plazas*, each entrusted to men with exclusive rights to manage his assigned *plaza*. Whoever traveled through territory beyond their control had to pay the ruling cartel. In this way, traffickers would no longer enter into conflict over control of strategic areas. Félix Gallardo created a model of cohabitation for the cartels.

But subdividing his territory also presented other advantages. Four years had passed since the Kiki story, and for El Padrino, it was still an open wound. He hadn't thought it possible to be duped like that. Which is why it was so important to strengthen the chain, to prevent a weak link from bringing the entire organization to its knees. If it was no longer a single unit, the authorities could no longer bring it down in a single blow; the politicians could no longer compromise it if they withdrew their protection or the winds shifted. What's more, autonomous management allowed for increased business potential for each group, and each boss would keep close watch on his *plaza*. Investments, market research, competition—all these things provided more work and more opportunities. To put it succinctly, El Padrino was staging a revolution, the significance of which the entire world would soon come to realize: He was privatizing the drug market in Mexico and opening it up to competition.

They say that the meeting at the Acapulco resort wasn't rowdy or loud. There was no fighting, no melodrama, no comedy. They arrived, parked, and took their places at the table. There were few bodyguards and a menu fit for an important occasion, such as a baptism—the baptism of the new narco power. El Padrino arrived after the others had already started eating. He took his place and proposed a toast. A toast with several glasses, one for each territory to be assigned. Glass in hand, he stood and asked Miguel Caro Quintero to do the same: The Sonora corridor had been assigned to him. After the applause died down, they drank. The second glass was for the Carrillo Fuentes family: "For you, Ciudad Juárez." A new glass, and this time he turned to Juan García Ábrego, to whom he assigned the Matamoros corridor. Then it was the Arellano-Félix brothers' turn: "For you, Tijuana." The last glass was for the Pacific coast. Joaquín Guzmán Loera, El Chapo, and Ismael Zambada García, El Mayo, got to their feet even before being called. They were expecting to get that zone; they'd been viceroys there, and now, finally, they were kings. The division was done; the new world created. It might be just a legend, but I've always believed that only a legend of this sort has the necessary symbolic force to give birth to an actual foundation myth. Like an ancient Roman emperor who summons his heirs and assigns each of his children a portion of his possessions. El Padrino needed to inaugurate the new era with a sovereign gesture, or needed at least for a story like this to get around.

So the drug cartels were born that day, and today, more than twenty years later, they still exist. A new breed of criminal organization, with the means and the power to decide prices and influences, either with some new rule or law decided around a table, or with TNT and thousands of deaths. There's no one way to decide the price and distribution of cocaine.

El Padrino would still supervise the operations: He was the ex-cop, the one with the contacts, so he would still be the point man. But he didn't get to see his plan put into effect. When Kiki's body was found almost four years earlier it was immediately clear that his colleagues at the DEA would not rest until justice was done for the horror endured by one of their own. Relations between the Mexican and American governments grew increasingly tense. The nearly two thousand miles that join Mexico and the United States, that long tongue of land that licks America's ass—as the carriers like to say—and as a result of licking, manages to slip in whatever it wants, was guarded day and night with a rigor and intensity never before seen. One of Rafael Caro Quintero's associates confessed that Kiki's body had originally been buried in a wooded park west of Guadalajara, not where it was found. Soil samples from the park matched those found on the victim's skin. Kiki's clothes had been destroyed, on the excuse that they were putrid, but it was clearly an attempt to erase the evidence. At that point the DEA launched the biggest homicide investigation ever undertaken by the United States up till then. It was called Operación Leyenda—Operation Legend. The search for the murderers turned into a manhunt. The American agents followed every possible scent. Five policemen who admitted taking part in the plot to unmask Camarena were arrested. They all named as instigators Rafael Caro Quintero and Ernesto "Don Neto" Fonseca Carrillo.

Caro Quintero tried to flee. He couldn't believe that Mexico, his realm, would hand him over to the DEA. He, who had always bought everyone, paid a commander of the Federal Judicial Police of Mexico 60 million pesos for safe passage. He managed to get to Costa Rica. But don't think you can bring your old life with you when you flee. You flee, that's it. In other words, you die in some way. But Caro Quintero took someone with him—his girlfriend, Sara Cristina Cosío Vidaurri Martínez. Sara wasn't a boss. She didn't know how to live in hiding. It may seem easy to live somewhere far away, to forge a new identity. You don't think it will really take that much, other than money. Yet to live in hiding is a form of torture that inflicts a psychological pressure few can endure. After months living so far away, Sara couldn't take it anymore, and she called her mother in Mexico. The police knew she'd call sooner or later and had been monitoring the phone. This was the mistake that allowed the DEA to locate the boss, his house, his new life. They went and got him. Caro Quintero and Don Neto refused to collaborate with the authorities and laid the blame for Kiki's murder on their boss, El Padrino. All they did was kidnap him, they said. It was probably some sort of agreement they'd made with El Padrino, who had the protection of Mexican politicians and high-ranking officials. But in the four years following Kiki's death, the American police had been chipping away at all of Félix Gallardo's protections. To get to El Padrino they had to isolate the entire network that defended him: politicians, judges, police, and journalists. Many of those who had been paid by the Guadalajara clan to protect El Padrino and his associates were arrested or fired. Among the accused was a certain Miguel Aldana Ibarra, the director of INTERPOL in Mexico, a repository of all sorts of information on investigations and cocaine trafficking. He too was in El Padrino's pay: He would pass information first to the narcos and then to his superiors. El Padrino was arrested on April 8, 1989. A few years later he was transferred to the El Altiplano high security prison, where he is still serving his forty-year sentence.

El Padrino and Ernesto Fonseca Carrillo are behind bars, but Caro Quintero is another matter: On August 9, 2013, he was allowed to breathe the fresh air of freedom again. A federal court in Guadalajara found a "formal" irregularity in Caro Quintero's trial for the kidnapping, torture, and murder of Kiki Camarena: The federal court that tried him was not authorized to do so because Kiki was a DEA agent, not a diplomatic or consular agent, so Caro Quintero should have been tried in a regular court. Such quibbles were enough to set one of the biggest Mexican bosses free. But he is still wanted for various federal crimes in the United States, and the U.S. Department of State has allocated a $5 million reward for anyone able to provide information leading to his arrest. The Americans want to see him behind bars again, American bars this time.

. . .

The murder of Kiki Camarena and all that ensued represents a turn-ing point in the fight against Mexican drug trafficking. The level of impunity that the cartels enjoyed was revealed: To kidnap a DEA agent in plain daylight, right outside the U.S. consulate, and then torture and kill him far exceeded anything they had done in the past, all they had dared to do up till that moment. Kiki had been remarkably in-sightful: He had understood before anyone else that the structure had changed, that it had become much more than a band of gangsters and smugglers. He'd understood that they were now battling drug manag-ers. He'd understood that the first step was to break the ties between institutions and traffickers. He'd understood that mass arrests of the small-time henchmen who do the dirty work were pointless if they didn't behead the bosses, if they didn't radically alter the dynamics that allowed the bosses to flood the markets with money and grow stronger. Kiki witnessed the birth of this unstoppable criminal bour-geoisie. He was more interested in the flow of money than in stopping the killers or dealers. Kiki had understood what the United States has trouble grasping even today: You have to strike at the head. You have to hit the bosses, the big bosses—the limbs merely carry out orders. He had also understood that the producers were weakening compared with the distributors. It's a law of economics, and thus also of drug trafficking. The Colombian producers were in crisis, as were the Me-dellín and Cali cartels, as were the FARC fighter groups, the Revolu-tionary Armed Forces of Colombia.

Kiki's death ignited American public opinion about the drug prob-lem in a completely new way. After his body was found, many Ameri-cans, starting in Calexico, California, Kiki's hometown, began wearing red ribbons, a symbol of pain and profanation of flesh. And they asked people to stop doing drugs in the name of the sacrifice Kiki had made in the war against drugs. In California they organized Red Ribbon

Week, a campaign that later spread throughout the country. It's still celebrated every October as part of a drug prevention campaign. And Kiki's story ended up on TV and film.

Before he was arrested, El Padrino had managed to convince the bosses to give up opium in order to concentrate on cocaine coming from South America on its way to the United States. Not that marijuana and opium poppy cultivation have disappeared from Mexico. They're still there, and the export business carries on. They've become less important, though, supplanted by cocaine and later by ice or methamphetamines. The decisions made during that meeting in Acapulco a few months before El Padrino was arrested helped the organizations grow, but without the guidance and recognized authority of the boss a fierce territorial dispute broke out among those who were still free. By the early 1990s the cartels had started warring among themselves, a war waged far from any media hype, since very few people believed in the existence of drug cartels. But as the conflict gradually became more bloody the protagonists' names became better known, acquired popularity. They are sharks who, in order to dominate the drug market, which today is worth between $25 billion and $50 billion a year in Mexico alone, are eroding Latin America at its very foundations.

The economic crisis may be destroying democracies, destroying work, destroying hopes, destroying credit, destroying lives. But what the crisis is not destroying, and instead is strengthening, are criminal economies. If you look through the wound of criminal capital, all the vectors and movements appear different. If you ignore the criminal power of the cartels, all the interpretations of the crisis seem based on a misunderstanding. In order to understand it you have to look at this power, stare it in the face, look it right in the eye. It has built the modern world, generated a new cosmos. This was the Big Bang.

COKE #2

It's not heroin, which turns you into a zombie. And it's not pot, which mellows you and makes your eyes bloodshot. Coke is a performance-enhancing drug. On coke you can do anything. Before it explodes your heart and turns your brain to mush, before your dick goes soft forever and your stomach starts oozing pus—before all this happens, you'll work more, fuck more, play more. Coke is the comprehensive answer to the most pressing concern of our day: the absence of limits. On coke, you'll live more. You'll network more—the first commandment of modern life. And the more you network, the happier you'll be, the more fun you'll have, the more emotions you'll experience, the more you'll sell. Whatever it is you sell, you'll sell more of it. More. Always more. But our bodies don't run on "more." At a certain point the excitement has to die down, our bodies have to return to a state of calm. Which is precisely where coke intervenes. It's very exacting, because it has to make its way to the synaptic juncture—to the exact point where individual cells divide—and inhibit a fundamental mechanism. It's like when you're playing tennis and you've just hit a winner straight down the line: Time stands still and everything is perfect, peace and strength are perfectly balanced inside you. That sensation of well-being is triggered by a microscopic drop of a neurotransmitter, which lands right in the synaptic juncture of a cell and stimulates it. That cell then infects the one next to it, and so on and so on, until millions of cells are stimulated, an almost instantaneous swarm. Life lights up. You move back to the baseline, and so does your opponent; you're ready to play the next point, and that feeling of a second ago is now just a distant echo. The neurotransmitter has been reabsorbed, the impulses between one cell and the next have been blocked. This is where coke comes in. It inhibits the reabsorption of neurotransmitters, so your cells are always turned on; it's like Christmas all year long, lights twinkling 365 days a year. The neurotransmitters coke is most crazy about, the ones it never wants to do without, are dopamine and norepinephrine. The first allows you to be the center of the party, because everything is so much easier now. Easier to talk, to flirt, to be nice, to feel you're liked. The second, norepinephrine, is sneakier. It amplifies everything around you. A glass breaks? You hear it before everyone else. A window slams? You're the first to realize it. Someone calls you? You turn even before they've finished saying your name. That's how norepinephrine works. It raises your state of alertness; the world around you fills with threats and dangers, turns hostile; you're always expecting to be harmed or attacked. Your fear-alarm responses speed up, your reactions become immediate, no filters. This is paranoia; the door is wide open. Cocaine is the body's fuel. It is life cubed. That is, before it consumes you, destroys you. The extra life that coke seems to have given you, you'll pay for later, at loan-shark interest rates. But later doesn't count. It's all here and now.

# 4

# THE WAR OVER WHITE PETROL

Mexico is the origin of everything. If you disregard Mexico, you'll never understand the destiny of democracies transformed by drug traffic. If you disregard Mexico, you'll never find the route that follows the smell of money, you won't realize how the odor of criminal money becomes a winning smell that has very little to do with the stench of death, poverty, barbarity, and corruption.

In order to understand cocaine, you have to understand Mexico. Those nostalgic revolutionaries who have taken refuge elsewhere in Latin America or grown old in Europe look upon this land like it's a former lover who has found herself a rich man yet still seems unhappy, whereas you remember how, when she was young and poor, she would offer herself with a passion that the rich man who has bought her with marriage will never know. On the surface Mexico can seem a place of unending and incomprehensible violence, a land that never stops bleeding. But it also retells a familiar story, a story of rampant civil war, because the warlords are powerful and the forces that should check them are corrupt or weak. As in feudal times, as in the Japan of the samurai and shogun or the tragedies of William Shakespeare. But Mexico is not some distant land that has caved in on itself. It is not some new Middle Ages. Mexico is now, here, and the warlords in question are masters of the most sought after goods in the world, the white powder that brings in more money than the oil wells.

The white petrol wells are in the state of Sinaloa, on the coast. Sinaloa, with rivers flowing down from the Sierra Madre to the Pacific, is so spectacular you can't believe there's anything else here but blinding sunlight and bare feet on the sand. That's how a student would like to answer his geography teacher when asked about the area's natural resources. But he should say, "Opium and marijuana, ma'am." If his school has walls, it's because Sinaloa's grandfathers cultivated marijuana and opium. Today, thanks to cocaine, Sinaloa's sons have universities and jobs. But if the student were to answer that way he would get a slap in the face and a black star next to his name. Better to repeat what it says in the textbooks: The region's riches are fish, meat, and organic produce. Yet Chinese merchants brought opium to Sinaloa back in the 1800s. Black poison, they called it. And since then, Sinaloa has been full of opium. You can grow opium poppies just about anywhere; they grow wherever grain grows. All they need is the right climate: not too dry, not too humid, no frost, no hail. The climate's good in Sinaloa; it almost never hails, and it's close to the sea.

The Sinaloa cartel is hegemonic. In Sinaloa, drugs provide jobs for everyone. Entire generations have fed themselves thanks to drugs. From peasants to politicians, police officers to slackers, the young and the old. Drugs need to be grown, stocked, transported, protected. In Sinaloa, all who are able are enlisted. The cartel operates in the Golden Triangle, and with over 160 million acres under its control, it's the biggest cartel in all of Mexico. It manages a significant slice of U.S. cocaine traffic and distribution. Sinaloa narcos are present in more than eighty American cities, with cells primarily in Arizona, California, Texas, Chicago, and New York. They distribute Colombian cocaine on the American market. According to the Office of the United States Attorney General, between 1990 and 2008 the Sinaloa cartel was responsible for the importation and distribution of at least two hundred tons of cocaine, as well as vast quantities of heroin, into the United States.

Until El Chapo's arrest in 2014, Sinaloa was his realm and he was viewed in the United States as having a significance akin to a head of state. Coke, marijuana, amphetamines: Most of the substances that Americans smoke, snort, or swallow have passed through his men's hands. From 1995 to 2014 he was the big boss of the faction that emerged from the ashes of the Guadalajara clan after the Big Bang in 1989. El Chapo, aka Shorty, five feet five inches of sheer determination. El Chapo didn't lord it over his men, didn't dominate them physically; he earned their trust. His real name is Joaquín Archivaldo Guzmán Loera, born on April 4, 1957, in La Tuna de Badiraguato, a small village with a few hundred inhabitants in the Sierra Madre mountains in Sinaloa. Like every other man in La Tuna, Joaquín's father was a rancher and farmer, who raised his son on beatings and farmwork. These were the years of opium. El Chapo's entire family was involved: a small army devoted to the cultivation of opium poppies, from dawn to dusk. El Chapo started at the bottom: Before he was allowed to follow the men along impassable roads to the poppy fields he had to stay at his mother's side and bring his older brothers their lunch. One kilo of opium gum brought in eight thousand pesos for the family, the equivalent of seven hundred dollars today. The head of the family had to get the gum into the next step of the chain. And that step meant a city, maybe even Culiacán, the capital of Sinaloa. No easy feat if you're merely a farmer, but easier if the farmer in question, El Chapo's father, is related to Pedro Avilés Pérez—a big-shot drug lord. The young El Chapo, having reached the age of twenty, began to see a way out of the poverty that had marked the lives of his ancestors. At that time it was El Padrino, Miguel Ángel Félix Gallardo, who ruled in Sinaloa: Together with his partners, Ernesto "Don Neto" Fonseca Carrillo and Rafael Caro Quintero, he controlled the coming and going of every drug shipment in Mexico. Joining the organization was a natural step for the young El Chapo, as was accepting his first real challenge: handling the drugs from the fields to the border. If you want to get to the top, you can't take pity if someone makes a mistake, you can't back down when underlings make excuses for not keeping to the schedule. If there was a problem, El Chapo eliminated it. If a peasant was enticed by someone with a fatter wallet, El Chapo eliminated him. If a driver with a truckload of drugs got drunk and didn't deliver his shipment the next morning, El Chapo eliminated him. Simple and effective.

El Chapo soon proved himself trustworthy, and in a few years' time he was one of the men closest to El Padrino. He learned many things from El Padrino, including the most important one: how to stay alive as a drug trafficker. Just like Félix Gallardo, in fact, El Chapo lived a quiet life, not too ostentatious, not too many frills. El Chapo married four times and fathered nine children, but he never surrounded himself with hordes of women.

When El Padrino was arrested and the race to find an heir began, El Chapo decided to remain loyal to his mentor. He was methodical, and didn't flaunt his power. He wanted to keep his family beside him, wanted his blood bonds to be his armor. He moved from Sinaloa to Guadalajara, the last place El Padrino lived before his arrest, while he based his organization in Agua Prieta, a town in the state of Sonora, convenient because it borders the United States. El Chapo remained in the shadows, and from there he governed his rapidly growing empire. Whenever he traveled, he did so incognito. People would say they'd spotted him, but it was true only one time out of a hundred. El Chapo and his men used every form of transport available to get drugs into the United States. Planes, trucks, railcars, tankers, cars. In 1993 an underground tunnel was discovered, nearly fifteen hundred feet long, sixty-five feet belowground. Still incomplete, it was going to connect Tijuana to San Diego.

These were years of settling scores against rivals, of escapes and murders. On May 24, 1993, Sinaloa's rival cartel, Tijuana, recruited some trustworthy killers to strike at the heart of the Sinaloa cartel. Two important travelers were expected at the Guadalajara airport that day:

El Chapo Guzmán and Cardinal Juan Jesús Posadas Ocampo, who, as archbishop of the city, had railed constantly against the drug lords' power. The killers knew that El Chapo was traveling in a white Mercury Grand Marquis, a must for drug barons. The cardinal was in a white Mercury Grand Marquis as well. The Tijuana hit men started shooting at what they believed to be the boss of Sinaloa's car, and others—El Chapo's bodyguards, maybe—returned fire. The airport parking lot suddenly became hell. The shoot-out left seven men dead, among them Cardinal Posadas Ocampo, while El Chapo managed to escape, unscathed. For years people wondered if the killers really wanted to eliminate the inconvenient cardinal, or if chance had merely played a bad joke on Posadas Ocampo that morning. It was only recently that the FBI declared the killing a tragic case of mistaken identity.

El Chapo was arrested on June 9, 1993. He continued to manage his affairs from prison with scarcely a hitch. The maximum security prison Puente Grande, where he was transferred in 1995, became his new base of operations. After eight years, however, El Chapo could no longer afford to remain behind bars: The Supreme Court had approved a law making it much easier to extradite narcos to the United States. American incarceration would mean the end of everything. So El Chapo chose the evening of January 19, 2001. The guards were bribed handsomely. One of them—Francisco Camberos Rivera, known as El Chito, or the Silent One—opened the door to El Chapo's cell and helped him climb into a cart of dirty laundry. They headed down unguarded hallways and through wide-open electronic doors to the inner parking lot, where only one guard was on duty. El Chapo jumped out of the cart and leaped into the trunk of a Chevrolet Monte Carlo. El Chito started it up and drove him to freedom.

El Chapo became everybody's hero, a legend. He kept on running his cartel with the help of his closest collaborators: Ismael Zambada García, known as El Mayo; Ignacio Coronel Villarreal, known as Nacho, who was killed on July 29, 2010, during a raid by the Mexican military; and his adviser, Juan José Esparragoza Moreno, who was known as El Azul, or Blue, because of his dark complexion. These men were the undisputed princes of Mexican drug trafficking for about a decade after the Sinaloa cartel was founded in 1989.

For years El Chapo also allied himself with the Beltrán Leyva family—a criminal gang led by four brothers skilled at intimidation and kickbacks, and especially good at infiltrating the political and judicial systems and the Mexican police force. They even had connections in INTERPOL offices in the U.S. embassy and at the Mexico City airport. The Beltrán Leyvas were a small, family-run army, and El Chapo trusted them. They'd always stuck with him, even when his authority was threatened. In 2003, for example, two years after his escape from prison, when there was a power vacuum in the state of Tamaulipas, in particular around Nuevo Laredo, a strategically essential corridor that leads to Texas, right to the famous Interstate 35, the road on which 40 percent of drugs coming from Mexico travel. But power vacuums don't exist for drug lords. And if they do, they're very short-lived. The first rule is to occupy a territory, so the pretenders rush in when a boss falls. The area became a ferocious battleground. El Chapo entrusted the job of taking possession of northeastern Mexico before anyone else could to one of the four Beltrán Leyva brothers: Arturo, who founded the armed wing Los Negros and identified the right man to run it.

Edgar Valdez Villarreal is called "La Barbie"—the nickname this big kid with blond hair and blue eyes was saddled with when he joined his high school football team in Laredo, Texas. "You look like Ken," the coach declared, "but I'm going to call you Barbie." Barbie's American dream wasn't a college degree or a nicer house than the one his immigrant father had. His dream was a sea of money, which could be had across the border in Nuevo Laredo. His American passport added to his appeal. Barbie liked women, and women liked him. He loved Versace clothes and fancy cars. He couldn't have been more different from El Chapo, but El Chapo knew how to get past a first impression. He smelled the blood that was soaking the Nuevo Laredo *plaza*, and the newcomer's longing for affirmation. Los Negros was going to have to fight Los Zetas, the bloodthirsty armed wing of the Gulf cartel with a bent for macabre spectacle that was surging into the power vacuum in northeastern Mexico as well. Barbie accepted enthusiastically and decided to use the same weapons as his adversaries: a film clip on YouTube of men kneeling, some bare chested, all of them clearly beaten. Zetas condemned to death. If Los Zetas were going to use the Internet to broadcast its ferocity, Los Negros would too. The horror escalated, feeding on itself, an endless loop from the streets to the web and back.

Fear and respect go hand in hand, they're two sides of the same coin: power. The coin of power has a shiny, bright side and a worn, opaque one. Bloodthirstiness strikes fear in one's rivals, but not respect, that luminescent patina that allows you to open every door without having to break it down. It's all a question of attitude: To be number one you have to know how to act like you're number one. El Chapo was never satisfied, never rested on his laurels. After throwing himself into the capture of Nuevo Laredo he decided he wanted the *plaza* of Ciudad Juárez too, that other outpost on the U.S. border, traditionally controlled by the Carrillo Fuentes family.

Los Negros made the first move. On September 11, 2004, Rodolfo Carrillo Fuentes—he and his brother Vicente ruled the Juárez cartel—was killed in the parking lot outside a multiplex cinema in Culiacán, in the heart of Sinaloa territory. He was with his wife. Their bodyguard was helpless against El Chapo's hit men, who fired from all directions, riddling the couple's bodies with bullets. The message was clear: Sinaloa once respected the boss of the Juárez cartel, Amado Carrillo Fuentes—the eldest of the Carrillo Fuentes brothers—but it no longer respected his family. The road to open war was short, and the Juárez cartel's revenge didn't take long. Vicente ordered one of El Chapo's brothers killed: Arturo, El Pollo, or Chicken, was murdered in the maximum security prison of Almoloya de Juárez on December 31. It was a tough blow for El Chapo, but it didn't make him back down. For years the border city of Juárez was transformed into a war zone—no holds barred—between El Chapo and the Carrillo Fuentes men. But in the end El Chapo got the upper hand, undermining the foundations of his enemies in Juárez.

Years earlier Amado Carrillo Fuentes had transformed the Juárez cartel from a group of bandits into a clan of well-groomed businessmen who favored Brioni and Versace suits. Appearance above all, even when you're wearing handcuffs: Let the media crowding outside your villa immortalize you in a white Abercrombie tracksuit with "NY" on your chest, as Amado's son Vicente Carrillo Leyva did in 2009. Amado had grown up in close contact with the cartels. His uncle was Ernesto "Don Neto" Fonseca Carrillo, boss of the Guadalajara organization and El Padrino's partner. Violence was Amado's daily bread, but money can sometimes prove more effective than violence, and the respect that Amado had managed to earn for himself over time was in part the fruit of the big tips he lavished on his men, the sports cars he gave to powerful people, his generous donations to build churches, like the one it is said he had built in his native village of Guamuchilito.

Amado had inherited the cartel that Rafael Aguilar Guajardo had founded in the 1970s. A rival of the Tijuana and Gulf cartels from the outset, this cartel had taken advantage of its strategic position across the U.S. border from El Paso, Texas, to build a powerful base, which needed to be defended. Amado was just the man. Prudent, patient, clever, he moved his pawns without getting his own hands dirty. He made shrewd investments, including an entire fleet of Boeing 727s, which he used to transport cocaine from Colombia to Mexico. But Boeings weren't suitable to cover the last leg—from Mexico to the United States. He needed smaller, more agile means, such as Cessnas; the air taxi company Taxceno (Taxi Aéreo del Centro Norte) used them and Amado became a major shareholder of it. People started calling him El Señor de los Cielos, the Lord of the Skies.

The coke war was fought with money. The most sizable expenditure—$5 million a month—was for kickbacks to officials, police, and the military all over Mexico, for stipends and gifts. Another sizable budget item was for entertainment, such as the so-called Palace of the Thousand and One Nights, which Amado bought in Hermosillo, in the state of Sonora. Situated provocatively a few hundred yards from the governor's residence, the Palace of the Thousand and One Nights is a garish place whose onion domes recall Russian Orthodox churches and the Kremlin, and whose white walls, now hidden under thick graffiti, recall the palaces of the maharaja.

No one knew Amado's whereabouts. He moved around constantly among the many residences he had scattered throughout the country. Eccentricity and ostentation, compensated for with shrewd financial decisions and an obsession with security, made him the iconic drug lord. Handsome and fierce, intelligent and cocky, courageous and tenderhearted. A hero for his time. He established ties with some Guadalajara bosses, got control of airports and clandestine runways, and bribed José de Jesús Gutiérrez Rebollo, head of the National Institute to Combat Drugs, who with his men became Amado's armed wing, using the institute's rich network of information to wipe out Amado's enemies and competitors, in exchange for enormous kickbacks. He even planned on striking an agreement with the federal government: Mexico would get 50 percent of his property; his collaboration in reducing violence among cartels; and his guarantee that drugs would not infest Mexico but only the United States and Europe. In exchange Amado would get peace and tranquillity to do his business.

But it wasn't to be. On November 2, 1997, along the Autopista del Sol—the Sun Highway—that runs from Mexico City to Acapulco, the police made a gruesome discovery: three cadavers in barrels filled with cement, bodies of three renowned plastic surgeons who had disappeared a few weeks earlier. Freed from the cement, their bodies bore witness to the tortures they endured before being killed: gouged-out eyes and broken bones. They'd been beaten so badly that one of the bodies had to be tied together to keep it from falling to pieces. Two of them had died of asphyxia, strangled with cables, the third of a bullet to the back of his neck. Their crime? Having the courage to operate on Amado Carrillo Fuentes, who, like many drug lords, wanted a total makeover. Four months earlier, on July 4, 1997, the Lord of the Skies had died in room 407 of the Santa Monica Hospital in Mexico City, after undergoing plastic surgery and liposuction under a false name. An overdose of Dormicum, a powerful sedative used during postop, had proved fatal. His heart, already weakened by cocaine, had given out. It's still unclear whether anyone was at fault, whether his death was accidental or intentional. Such a bizarre end for a sovereign generates legends of immortality as well as endless, malicious gossip. Some say his own vanity killed him, but it's more likely that he wanted to alter his appearance in order to escape the police and his enemies.

Amado's death created a huge power vacuum. His brother Vicente took over the cartel, but relations between Carrillo Fuentes and rival groups became increasingly precarious. In 2001, after El Chapo Guzmán escaped from prison, many Juárez cartel members decided to follow him and to join the Sinaloa cartel. On April 9, 2010, the Associated Press announced that the Sinaloa cartel had finally won the battle against the Juárez men. But the media epitaph did not prevent the Juárez cartel from continuing to wage war. A war that made Ciudad Juárez the most dangerous and violent city in the world, with nearly two thousand homicides a year.

In July 2010, on a street in the center of the city, a car bomb set off by a cell phone killed a federal police agent, a doctor, and a musician who lived in the area. These last two had heard gunshots and gone out into the street in order to help a man in a police uniform lying wounded on the ground. But as the narcos revealed after their arrest, he was merely the bait to attract the attention of the feds. A message spray-painted in black was found on a wall near the attack: "What happened on Calle 16 septiembre will happen to all the authorities who continue to back El Chapo. Cordially, the Juárez cartel. And anyway, we have other car bombs."

"*Carne asada!* Grilled meat!" It's a cry you hear every day as you wander the crowded streets of Ciudad Juárez. If it weren't for the agitated tone and the adrenaline in their voices it would sound like two Mexicans organizing a Sunday cookout. Instead, it's the code narcos use to say that someone's been killed. The killings continue undisturbed. Mutilated, decapitated bodies. Bodies exposed in public for the sole purpose of guaranteeing the status quo of fear. Bodies like that of the lawyer Fernando Reyes, suffocated with a plastic bag, wacked several times in the head with a shovel, thrown in a ditch, and covered first with quicklime and then with dirt.

In order to try to stop the Juárez cartel, the Mexican authorities offered a reward of 30 million pesos, and the U.S. government up to $5 million, for information leading to the arrest of Vicente Carrillo Fuentes, known as the Viceroy but actually the real king of the organization since his brother Amado's death. On October 9, 2014, Vicente was captured in Torreón, Coahuila, during a federal police operation that concluded without any shots fired. When stopped at a checkpoint he showed a fake driver's license registered to a Jorge Sánchez Mejía, but the federal forces, who had been after him for several months, were not fooled: He was the chief of one of the most violent drug cartels Mexico had ever known. Along with the Viceroy, they arrested his ever-present bodyguard, a figure without whom the narcos never leave their hideouts.

Vicente's arrest could lead to a loss of power of the Juárez cartel, as the Mexican authorities hope, but just as happened in the past, it could also create a power vacuum to be filled with violence and terror.

"*Carne asada! Carne asada!*"


El Chapo didn't believe in showing his rage. He saw no point. He punished those who deserved it with death, but even when applying this definitive sentence, he didn't allow any emotion to shine through. El Chapo was rational in his bloodthirstiness. Alfredo Beltrán Leyva, the

Beltrán Leyva brother known as El Mochomo—as the red desert ants that eat anything and survive everything are called in Sinaloa—was the complete opposite: instinctive, hot-tempered, aggressive. He loved the good life and wanted a steady stream of people coming to see him, especially women. El Mochomo was the Beltrán Leyva brother entrusted with the most public role. But El Chapo realized that Alfredo was dangerous. Being showy doesn't fit well with being a fugitive; you're too easy a target. The state of alert increased significantly when El Chapo found out that the Beltrán Leyvas were negotiating with Los Zetas. A scission was inevitable. Which meant blood.

Alfredo Beltrán Leyva was arrested in Culiacán in January 2008, together with three members of his security corps. He was found in possession of almost a million dollars, luxury watches, and a small arsenal, including frag grenades. A tough blow for Sinaloa, because Alfredo supervised drug trafficking on a large scale, handled the organization's money laundering, and bribed the police. He was the cartel's foreign minister. But as the Beltrán Leyva brothers saw it, El Chapo was behind Alfredo's arrest. They had to respond in kind, and it was easy to decide where to strike.

Édgar Guzmán López was only twenty-two , but he had a brilliant career ahead of him because he was El Chapo's son. In May 2008, he went for a stroll with some friends in a shopping center in Culiacán. To check out the shop windows and the *chicas*. A peaceful day. On their way back to their car, which they left in the parking lot, they saw fifteen men approaching, in uniforms and blue bulletproof vests. The men moved in unison, like soldiers, and the boys were petrified, immobile. Before the men opened fire, the boys managed to read what was on their bulletproof vests: FEDA, which stood for Fuerzas Especiales de Arturo, or Arturo's Special Forces. These were the men of Arturo Beltrán Leyva, the brother known as El Barbas. To prepare for the break with the Sinaloa cartel he'd created a unit with the same structure and discipline as the army and special police corps. They used heavy weapons, including the lethal P90 personal defense weapon, and were charged with protecting the bosses and eliminating hit men of rival cartels. Now, in 2008, baptized in the blood of El Chapo's son, the Beltrán Leyva cartel was born. The brothers handled cocaine, marijuana, and heroin, thanks in part to their complete control of the principal airports in the states of México, Guerrero, Quintana Roo, and Nuevo León. Other activities included human trafficking; prostitution; money laundering, through hotels, restaurants, and resorts; extortion; abduction; and arms trafficking. From South to North America, they managed corridors that moved tons of drugs. It was a new, small cartel, but one determined to carve out a sizable slice of power. But the Mexican authorities were eager to put the family out of business right away, so when Arturo threw a party in the winter of 2009, they didn't let the opportunity pass.

For El Barbas, a Christmas party is not a Christmas party if there's no entertainment. Money was no object, so he invited artists such as Los Cadetes de Linares and Ramón Ayala, winner of two Grammy Awards and two Latin Grammys with over a hundred albums, to play at his house in one of the most exclusive neighborhoods of Cuernavaca. Plus twenty or so call girls. The Mexican navy's special forces surrounded the building. The shoot-out left several bodies on the ground, but not Arturo's; he managed to escape. The Mexican navy was on his trail, though, and they found him less than a week later, in another residential neighborhood. Determined not to let Arturo escape again, the navy decided to do things big: two hundred marines, two helicopters, and two small army tanks. The battle lasted nearly two hours, and when it was finished, Arturo and four of his men were dead. The photo of his corpse made the rounds on the Internet: His pants lowered to show his underwear and his T-shirt rolled up to show his naked chest covered in lucky charms and bills, dollars as well as pesos. One last humiliation for the enemy. The army denied it had touched his body, but there was a strong suspicion that the humiliation techniques so dear to new cartels such as Los Zetas and Beltrán Leyvas themselves were contaminating the very men paid to eliminate them. The army and the narcos were becoming more and more alike.

Vengeance came immediately after Arturo Beltrán Leyva's death: Four relatives of one of the soldiers who lost his life in the operation were killed. Meanwhile, a decapitated head was left in front of Arturo's tomb, in the Jardines del Humaya cemetery in Culiacán. Arturo's brother Carlos Beltrán Leyva was arrested about ten days later by the Mexican federal police in Culiacán: He had shown a fake driver's license when the police stopped him. Some people held that it was El Chapo again who provided the police with information that led to Carlos's arrest.

After Arturo's death, a civil war over leadership broke out within the cartel: On one side were lieutenants Edgar "La Barbie" Valdez Villarreal and Gerardo "El Indio" Álvarez Vázquez; on the other, Héctor Beltrán Leyva, El H, and his right-hand man, Sergio Villarreal Barragán, a former Mexican federal police agent, known as El Grande or King Kong, because he was over six feet five. All but Héctor were arrested in 2010; El H took the reins of what remained of the cartel. The United States had put a price on his head of $5 million, and the Mexican government was offering 30 million pesos. Héctor was a sort of financial genius; after years of anonymity he succeeded in controlling the group, thanks to his business talent and his ability to maintain good relations with his new allies, Los Zetas.

But the race was soon over for him too. On October 1, 2014, Héctor was arrested in San Miguel de Allende, Guanajuato. He was enjoying dinner at a seafood restaurant together with the financial operator of his cartel when the special forces of the Mexican army swooped in. Though he initially passed himself off as a refined businessman and artwork trader, he and his tablemate were carrying pistols exclusively issued to the military. But confirming his proverbial elegance, he let them handcuff him without resisting.

Héctor was the last of the Beltrán Leyva brothers still at large. After his arrest the Mexican authorities believe the cartel will lose most of its influence on the country. But thrones do not remain empty for long in the narco-trafficking world. The real question is: Who will be the new leader?

The war between the Beltrán Leyvas and their old Sinaloa partners not only devastated Culiacán and Sinaloa, it has made its way to the United States, to Chicago, where the twins Margarito and Pedro Flores, two Americans with Mexican roots, operated. Their fleet of trucks connected Los Angeles to cities in the Midwest twenty-four hours a day, seven days a week. They were serious, efficient distributors. They guaranteed their customers two tons of coke and heroin a month, from the border all the way to the shores of Lake Michigan. But they were greedy: They worked with the Sinaloa cartel, but they didn't disdain working with the Beltrán Leyvas either. When El Chapo found out, he sent some men to Chicago to keep his distribution monopoly from being put at risk by rival cartels. At the same time that the Flores twins were receiving threats from Sinaloa, the DEA set its sights on them. They were arrested in 2009. In part thanks to the testimonies of Margarito and Pedro, who turned informers, the Americans were able to add a few more pieces to the complex puzzle of El Chapo's and the Beltrán Leyvas' movements.

A few months earlier the U.S. government had delivered another blow to the king of Sinaloa by arresting 750 members of his cartel in the United States. An army. American presidents don't talk much about it, but there are entire legions of narcos within their borders. During the twenty-one months of the operation, more than $59 million in cash, more than 12,000 kilos of cocaine, more than 7,000 kilos of marijuana, more than 500 kilos of methamphetamine, about 1.3 million ecstasy pills, more than 8 kilos of heroin, 169 weapons, 149 vehicles, 3 airplanes, and 3 boats were seized in various states, from the East to the West coasts. An enormous success but a worrisome one, for its very scale was alarming. The American authorities looked the Sinaloa cartel in the eye, and what they saw was a multinational corporation with connections and branches all over the world, on whose boards sat supermanagers handling relations in every corner of the planet. Narco executives on Sinaloa salaries acted as contact points in numerous South American countries. And El Chapo was well along in conquering western Africa and making inroads in Spain.

For El Chapo, total domination over the 370 or so miles of border between Mexico and Arizona was the flywheel of his personal economy. He followed the market: When the demand for *hielo*—crystal meth— surged, he was there. A terrible drug—it costs less than coke and eats you up sooner. When you overdo it you start feeling the parasite effect: worms crawling under your skin. So you scratch yourself raw trying to cut open your flesh to get rid of them. It's the side effect of a drug that otherwise has the same effect as coke, only bigger and worse. Request for it was on the rise, but there was no boss, no one who knew how to transform an opportunity into a river of money. El Chapo saw the opportunity; the Sinaloa cartel was ready. And he had the right man to manage the new business: Ignacio Coronel Villarreal, who became the King of Crystal. All you need to produce methamphetamine are clandestine labs and the right chemical substances. If you have good contacts on the Pacific coast, it's not hard to get precursor shipments from China, Thailand, and Vietnam. And it's very profitable: For every dollar you invest in raw materials, you'll earn ten on the street.

That is Sinaloa's great gift: the speed with which it sniffs out every new business opportunity. Sinaloa colonizes. Sinaloa wants to rule. Only Sinaloa.

El Chapo has a clear vision of today's world: The West is in trouble; its ideals are in conflict with the market's iron logic, so it needs lands without laws, lands without rights. Mexico has cocaine and the United States has cocaine users. Mexico has the cheap labor the United States needs. Mexico has soldiers and the United States has weapons. The world's drowning in unhappiness? Mexico has the solution: cocaine. El

Chapo grasped all this. He became the king of the narcos, the Steve Jobs of cocaine, with the mystical authority of the pope. Which is why February 22, 2014, will go down in history, for Mexico and the entire world. On that day, Joaquín Guzmán Loera, El Chapo, the most wanted narco on the planet, was arrested. At 6:40 A.M. in a hotel in the center of Mazatlán, in Sinaloa state. A maxi operation by Mexican marines and in collaboration with the DEA: two helicopters and six land artillery units. But not a single shot was fired. The most dangerous fugitive in Mexico, with a price of $5 million on his head, was hiding out in Sinaloa. Maybe that's where he'd been for the past thirteen years, hiding in the region that made him what he was, that offered him protection.

The military operation had been launched about ten days before: Law enforcement officers had managed to identify several residences in Culiacán, El Chapo's stronghold, where he usually stayed. The man who had been a master at digging tunnels to get drugs into the United States relied on them for his own getaways too: Several of his residences were connected by underground passageways. The military nearly caught him more than once, but he always managed to escape. Several members of the Sinaloa cartel had been arrested, though; El Chapo's inner circle was shrinking. Earlier that week a raid of his ex-wife Griselda López's house turned up some weapons and a tunnel that fed to the sewers. Mexico's drug lord would clamber through the sewers to get from one hiding place to another.

What's most extraordinary is that El Chapo was caught by surprise in Mazatlán, a tourist town. He wasn't hiding up in the Sierra mountains, as most people thought. And his hotel in Mazatlán was nothing fancy: an ordinary building, with a nondescript lobby and a simple room. The way he'd always lived.

In Mexico his arrest was followed with the same anxiety as the World Cup finals, with more interest than a presidential election. Rumors of his arrest or murder had circulated for years. Which is why, on February 22, no one could believe it had actually happened. Thousands of tweets: "Is it really him? Where's the proof?" "I won't believe it till I see the photo of El Chapo in handcuffs." "El Chapo is still El Chapo, they don't have him!" Many tweeters did not hide their disappointment; many expressed their solidarity with the boss; many wrote in English. A hashtag was even created: #FreeChapo. These tweets say more about the world today than most articles and political powwows.

Verifying El Chapo's capture proved to be as agonizing as the arrest itself. At first there were just unconfirmed reports: The Associated Press gave out the news at 9:54 A.M., after receiving a tip-off from an anonymous American official. The Mexican authorities did not confirm it, however. Meanwhile, word of his arrest started spreading all over the Internet. The Mexican authorities called a press conference for 11:30, but the secretary of state canceled it, leading people to think it wasn't him. But the photo of a bare-chested man with a mustache, arrested by a soldier in camouflage, started to circulate. It sure looked like him, but thirteen years had passed since the last official photos; it could just be a close resemblance. Everyone waited with bated breath. At 12:08 the secretary of the interior, Miguel Ángel Osorio Chong, called a new press conference, this time for 1:00 P.M. Would the rumors be denied or confirmed? Doubts were quelled at 12:33; the Mexican authorities confirmed the arrest on CNN. But still no official announcement. El Chapo's fans were hoping it was all a terrible mistake. At 1:20 El Chapo's photo disappeared from the DEA's most wanted list. That's how the Americans confirmed the news. They beat out the Mexican confirmation, which came a few minutes later, in the form of a tweet by President Enrique Peña Nieto, expressing his gratitude for the work of the security forces. In truth, he was patting himself on the back for the most important arrest since he'd taken office. At 2:04 a federal police helicopter landed in front of the group of reporters gathered in a navy hangar. During the press conference they confirmed what everyone already knew: El Chapo had been arrested. They filled in some details, about where and when. The attorney general of Mexico read the list of people arrested and goods seized: thirteen men, ninety-seven large guns, thirty-six handguns, two grenade launchers, forty-three vehicles, sixteen houses, and four farms. Only one thing was missing: the man himself. El Chapo made his entrance at 2:11, captured by photographers as he was escorted across the square to the police helicopter: black jeans and white shirt, neat hair and mustache. Looking a little tired and not in the least cocky as Mexican marines in camouflage hold him by the arms and make him lower his head. No presentation to the media, just these few photos to confirm his arrest. At 3:00 P.M., word was given that El Chapo was behind bars at the Penal del Altiplano, the prison in Almoloya de Juárez, in México state.

A few years earlier El Chapo had formed a new tie with the United States. In August 2011, his young wife Emma, an American citizen, tranquilly gave birth to twin girls in a clinic in Lancaster, near Los Angeles. The DEA knew but couldn't do anything, because Emma, twenty-two at the time, had a clean record. El Chapo's men had accompanied her to Lancaster, but she did take one precaution: Emma left the father's name blank on the twins' birth certificates. But everyone knows who the father is. The Mexican and American authorities exulted after El Chapo's arrest, but alongside their messages on social networks were others, posted by regular people who considered El Chapo a hero, a benefactor, a Mexican god. The most widespread reaction was disbelief: "El Chapo is too clever to let himself be caught"; "El Chapo is too smart to let himself be framed"; "impossible that they nabbed him two feet from his stronghold." As if El Chapo had orchestrated it all, as if he had decided that the moment for his arrest had come. There are all sorts of theories: Maybe he sensed that he was becoming too big a story politically, and the only way his cartel could keep doing business would be if he was arrested. Or maybe he knew a big feud was about to erupt, so he took himself out of the equation to avoid being killed by a new generation of Sinaloa narcos eager to take his place. Some have even quietly insinuated that his *fedelissimo*, El Mayo, also in hiding and fearing his own arrest or murder, sold his boss's head. In fact, the press had been expecting El Mayo's arrest for days, but to their surprise, El Chapo was arrested instead. The only certainty is ambiguity. At any rate, it's hard to believe that it was purely a police action, because, as everyone knows, nothing in Sinaloa happens without El Chapo's blessing. The king is dead, long live the king.

# 5

# FRIEND KILLER

Matamoros, in the state of Tamaulipas in northeastern Mexico, rises on the southern bank of the Rio Bravo and is connected to the Texas city of Brownsville by four bridges. Those four bridges are like four pipelines through which white petrol is pumped into the United States. Here it's the Gulf cartel that rules. In 1999 it was bringing up to fifty tons of cocaine into the United States every month, and its power had spread from the Gulf of Mexico to parts of the Pacific, areas conquered with violence, corruption, and agreements with other narco groups. The Gulf cartel was number one. And its number one was Osiel Cárdenas Guillén.

Osiel had heard the story a million times. El Padrino arrived last, took a seat, and toasted the new territory bosses. Sure, the details changed from one teller to the next, as unsteady as April showers, but the gist was always the same: The new world had been created at that meeting.

"If you can have the whole world, why be satisfied with just a piece?" This was said to be his retort to an impudent interlocutor who'd annoyed him for the umpteenth time with the story of El Padrino and the division of the kingdom. Osiel was born angry. Quarrelsome as a boy, tough as a teenager, violent as a young man. A blind, senseless rage that he nourished and nursed constantly, and that his lively intelligence made sadistic and demonic. He was born to parents who, indifferent to the poverty in which they lived, continued unperturbed to churn out babies whom they then left to crawl around in the dirt with the scrawny chickens; Osiel invented his own world, as far away as possible from the chaos that surrounded him. By age fourteen he was working as a mechanic's assistant in the morning, and at a *maquiladora,* or factory, in the afternoon, where he, along with two hundred other people, assembled vacuum cleaners that some Yankee housewife would use a few miles to the north.

Osiel met a girl at the *maquiladora*—smart, with pearls for eyes—but Osiel was ashamed whenever he asked her out, because he couldn't afford a car to go pick her up, or dinner in even a modest restaurant. He started dealing. Quick, profitable, risky enough to provide an adrenaline high. For pushers just starting out, whoever is the most unscrupulous usually takes the lead. Cruelty is essential; without it you might appear weak, and your adversaries will take advantage of you. It's like with dogs: Whichever one growls the loudest becomes the head of the pack.

He was arrested for the first time in 1989, when he was twenty-one, for homicide, but the charge didn't stick. When he was twenty-five he was arrested in Brownsville, Texas, and accused of drug trafficking; he was in possession of 2 kilos of cocaine. Sentenced to five years in prison, he got lucky again; thanks to a prisoner exchange between Mexico and the United States, he was sent back to his own country. In 1995, after just one year behind bars, Osiel was free again.

Great criminal leaders often have in common the desire to create an aura for themselves, the desire to enchant, seduce. It matters little whether the objective is a woman to bed or a rival dealer to eliminate by convincing your accomplices that the bastard has it coming to him. Once you find the right opening, the way to a person's will, you've won. Osiel knew he could cut off hands, threaten family members, or burn down warehouses, but he also knew that the fastest way to get what he wanted was to touch the right chord. Those who didn't fear him adored him. Acting as a *madrina*, or informer, Osiel infiltrated the Federal Judicial Police, gradually acquiring the protection that allowed him to move about freely. Now he could control both fronts and network with the Gulf cartel men in the meantime. He knew Salvador Gómez Herrera, alias El Chava, who became the Gulf cartel leader after Juan García Ábrego was arrested. El Chava too told Osiel the story of El Padrino raising his glass to toast Ábrego's receiving the Matamoros corridor.

In the second half of the 1990s the Gulf cartel faced a war of succession. Plenty of people were ready to write off the organization that only a few years earlier—after El Padrino's arrest and after the Golden Age of García Ábrego as leader—had been one of Mexico's most powerful cartels. But now it had the police on its back, as well as the FBI and rival cartels. Founded in the 1970s by a man with the high-sounding name of Juan Nepomuceno Guerra, who had smuggled alcohol into the United States during Prohibition, the cartel's days now seemed numbered. The new leaders fell one by one. García Ábrego fell, arrested by the Mexican authorities and then extradited to the United States, where he is serving eleven life sentences. García Ábrego's brother Humberto failed: too weak. Sergio "El Checo" Gómez fell, betrayed by a conspiracy orchestrated by his partners and his bodyguards. Óscar Malherbe de León fell, arrested immediately after he took command. Hugo Baldomero Medina Garza, the Lord of the Trailers, fell too: His arrest put a stop to the tons of cocaine he'd been shipping to the United States every month, hidden in crates of vegetables or bags of seafood. The police celebrated, but in the meantime, El Chava and Osiel became friends and accomplices. They seemed inseparable, helped each other out, and amassed power and money. Not enough, though, at least for Osiel. You can't wield power as part of a pair, as he'd always say to whoever insisted on pulling out that El Padrino story: "If you can have the whole world, why be satisfied with just a piece?" And so, after they were arrested together, and after they bribed the prison guards to escape, Osiel killed El Chava. On that day in 1998 he obtained two things: absolute control of the Gulf cartel and a nickname, El Mata Amigos, or Friend Killer.

You're someone who kills your friends. If you don't have any ties, what is there to fear? If you're bright, you have a radiant future ahead of you. El Mata Amigos restructured the organization and brought it into the twenty-first century. Protection was guaranteed through bribes. Even the Twenty-first Motorized Cavalry Regiment of Nuevo Laredo was in his pay. It was good theater: The authorities would receive a report that a shipment of cocaine was hidden in the warehouses of an abandoned factory on the edge of the desert. They'd rush to the site in force, followed by a host of obliging journalists: a rapid, bloodless raid, no one there, just some white powder. But never an arrest. Photos, handshakes, smiles. A good, clean job.

Meanwhile, the frontier between Mexico and the United States was being violated day after day, hour after hour. But other organizations also wanted the sinuous tongue of Tamaulipas, which licks America's ass it is said, and they declared war on the Gulf cartel. The Valencia brothers, together with the Tijuana cartel, Vicente Carrillo Fuentes's Juárez cartel, and even Los Negros, the death squad in the service of Sinaloa—they all challenged the Gulf cartel. A real war. Cities such as Nuevo Laredo, Reynosa, and Matamoros became battlegrounds. There wasn't an hour day or night when executions and kidnappings weren't taking place; it wasn't unusual to find bodies on the street, hacked to pieces and stuffed into plastic bags.

The escalation of violence and deaths increased national and international pressure for the capture of Osiel Cárdenas Guillén. He was finally arrested and four years later was extradited to the United States. The cartel subsequently decentralized, with two drug lords sharing control: Osiel's brother Antonio Ezequiel Cárdenas Guillén, alias Tony Tormenta (killed by the Mexican army in Matamoros on November 5,

2010), and Jorge Eduardo Costilla Sánchez, alias El Coss (arrested by
the Mexican navy in Tampico on September 12, 2012), leaders who
proved unable to put an end to the internal feuds devouring the cartel.
And soon enough, once their suns had set, it was Mario Armando
Ramírez Treviño's turn. But Mario, known as El Pelón, Baldy, or X20,
was arrested in Reynosa on August 17, 2013. So now who? The DEA
bet on one of three men: Luis Alberto Trinidad Cerón, known as El
Guicho, Juan Francisco Carrizales, known as El 98, and Juan Alberto
de la Cruz Álvarez, known as El Juanillo. But there would also be room
for another of Osiel's brothers, Homero Cárdenas Guillén, known as El
Majadero, or Stupid. Some say he sits atop the Gulf command structure; others say he died of a heart attack in March 2014.

Today the Gulf cartel continues to take advantage of its proximity to
the U.S. border. It is an efficient money-making machine, using an
unbelievable variety of means to transport cocaine north, including underground tunnels, which are also used for human trafficking. These
humans are the new drug mailmen: In exchange for the mirage of a
new life beyond the border, they carry up to half a million dollars of
drugs on them. Or they use the buses on I-35, which goes from the
border city of Laredo, Texas, all the way to Minnesota, or I-25, which
you can pick up twenty-five miles from El Paso, Texas, and take all the
way to Wyoming. Buses are the perfect mode of transport for narcos,
because they're not usually X-rayed. But the Gulf cartel doesn't disdain
more creative options either, such as trains or submarines: fast, safe, and
capable of carrying astronomical quantities of cocaine.


"In the heart of every man is a desperate desire for a battle to fight, an
adventure to live, and a beauty to rescue." Nazario Moreno González,
one of the most powerful bosses of The Michoacán Family, often
quoted these words, by writer and Christian activist John Eldredge.
Moreno González preached the divine right to eliminate his enemies
and was never without his "bible" of teachings. "It is better to die fight-

ing face to face than to live your whole life humiliated and on your knees," Moreno wrote, taking his cue from the sayings of the Mexican revolutionary Emiliano Zapata.

For some he was El Chayo, for others El Más Loco, the Craziest One. But everyone remembers him as the Mexican boss who died twice. In December 2010, the Mexican authorities declared that the boss of The Michoacán Family had been killed by the Federal Police of Apatzingán. Even the then president, Felipe Calderón, went out of his way to explain that the forces of order had surprised Nazario Moreno González during a party organized by some La Familia members, and that he had been killed during the ensuing shoot-out. His body was never found, but no one doubted the official version: It had been taken away by La Familia members. Not until October 2011, that is, almost a year later, when Mario Buenrostro Quiroz, the leader of Los Aboytes, a group of kidnappers with ties to The Michoacán Family, was arrested. Under interrogation Buenrostro revealed that El Chayo was alive and had become the head of the Knights Templar cartel, which had broken away from The Michoacán Family. Rumors started flying. Confirmation came on March 9, 2014, when marine and army special forces killed a man who had forcefully resisted arrest during a shootout in Tumbiscatío, Michoacán. Fingerprints and a DNA test left no room for doubt this time: It was Nazario Moreno González, who had officially been dead for more than three years. During those dead years he'd been able to command undisturbed from his stronghold in Michoacán, without even having to worry about being arrested: No one hunts down a dead man.

Michoacán is on the Pacific coast. This was where the Sinaloa *gomeros* had moved with their opium poppies, and they were the ones who taught the campesinos how to cultivate them. Michoacán-Sinaloa-United States: For years this was the route.

The Michoacán Family claimed to be born to oppose violence and protect and defend the weak. For several years the Gulf cartel, which was expanding in those areas, relied on La Familia for paramilitary support. But La Familia ultimately became an independent cartel specializing in methamphetamine trafficking, and it became the principal supplier of meth for the United States. This area, with its hills—a natural refuge—and Pacific shoreline—that facilitates transportation—and above all with the vast stretches of fertile terrain in the so-called Tierra Caliente, or Hot Land—perfect for growing marijuana—has attracted traffickers for decades. But today it is dotted with meth labs. According to Michael Braun, former DEA chief of operations, La Familia has specialized laboratories that can produce up to 50 kilos of methamphetamine in eight hours. La Familia also has very strict rules about selling it: never to its own members; never to Mexicans. The cartel hangs banners in its territories: "We are against the use of drugs and we say no to the exploitation of women and children."

La Familia cartel celebrated its entry into the world of Mexican drug trafficking in high style: On the night of September 6, 2006, twenty men dressed in black, their faces covered with ski masks, burst into the discotheque Sol y Sombra in Uruapan, some sixty miles from Morelia, the capital of Michoacán. Armed to the teeth, they fired into the air and shouted at the public and the girls dancing on cubes to get down on the floor. Amid general panic, they raced up to the second level, opened black plastic trash bags, and rolled five decapitated heads across the dance floor. On their way out the hit men left a note on the floor, next to the severed heads: "La Familia doesn't kill for money, it doesn't kill women, it doesn't kill innocent people. The only ones who die are those who deserve it. Let it be known by all: this is divine justice." The Michoacán Family had introduced itself to Mexico.

The organization's members view their territory as sacred and will not tolerate it being sullied by drugs or disease. This makes them quite similar to Italian mafias, which stop and punish whoever deals in their territory. The Michoacán Family has a sui generis welfare system. They fight drug addiction in an unusual, martial fashion: They go to the rehab clinics and encourage the addicts to come clean in every way possible, including through the help of prayer. Then they make them work for the cartel. If they refuse, they are killed. Prayer meetings play an important role in the organization; one's career depends on them. The cartel lavishes money on peasants, businesses, schools, and churches, and it promotes itself in the local papers in order to gain public support. In an ad in *La Voz de Michoacán* in November 2006, La Familia announced: "Our strategies may be aggressive at times, but this is the only way to impose order in the state. Some people might not understand our actions right now, but we know that in the hardest hit zones they do, because it is possible to fight these delinquents, who have come here from other states, and we're not going to let them come to Michoacán and commit crimes." La Familia is like a parallel state within the state of Michoacán. It finances community projects, controls petty crime, resolves local disputes. And it demands protection money from businesses: a hundred pesos a month for a stall at the local market; thirty thousand for a car dealership. Businesses are often forced to close and turn operations over to the organization, which then uses them for money laundering.

"We want President Felipe Calderón to know that we are not his enemies, that we admire him. We are open to dialogue. We do not want Los Zetas in Michoacán. What we want is peace and tranquillity. We know we are a necessary evil. . . . We want to reach an agreement, we want to establish a national pact." This was the voice of Servando Gómez Martínez, alias La Tuta, speaking in a phone call to the show *Voz y Solución*, hosted by the journalist Marcos Knapp on a local channel of Michoacán CB Televisión. Gómez, a high-ranking member of the cartel and one of Moreno González's associates, was proposing nothing less than an alliance with President Calderón to eliminate their most feared competitors, but the government refused to negotiate. Nevertheless, La Familia has been one of the fastest-growing cartels during the years of Mexico's war on drugs. Its power has spread from Michoacán to the neighboring states of Guerrero, Queretaro, and México. And also into the United States: In October 2009, federal authorities released the findings of a four-year investigation—known as Project

Coronado—on La Familia's activities in the United States. It led to one of the biggest operations against Mexican drug cartels operating in U.S. territory. More than three thousand agents took part in just one raid, which lasted two days and involved local, state, and federal authorities: 303 men were arrested in nineteen different U.S. states; 62 kilos of cocaine, 330 kilos of methamphetamine, 440 kilos of marijuana, 144 weapons, 109 vehicles, and 2 drug labs were seized, along with $3.4 million in cash. In November 2010 La Familia proposed another pact: It offered to dismantle its own cartel on the condition that the state, the federal government, and the federal police guarantee Michoacán's security. The proposal appeared on flyers slipped under the doors of homes and shops, in phone booths, on cartel banners hung across streets, in letters sent to blogs, radio stations, newspapers, and national and international press agencies. It claimed that La Familia was created to make up for the government's failure to provide for the safety of its citizens, and that it was composed of Michoacán men and women who were prepared to give their lives to defend the state. But once again Felipe Calderón, who was born in Michoacán, refused to negotiate with the cartel.

The conflict between La Familia and Los Zetas reduced Michoacán to a war zone. What is considered to be the first act of narco-terrorism in Mexican history took place in Morelia, Michoacán's capital city, on September 15, 2008, the eve of Mexico's Independence Day. Shortly after Governor Leonel Godoy rang the Independence bell and declared three times "*¡Viva Mexico!*" two frag grenades exploded in the crowded square, killing eight people and wounding over a hundred, all of them innocent civilians. Even the innocent are victims in the narcos' war. The authorities pointed a finger at La Familia, which in turn hung banners blaming Los Zetas: "'Coward' is the correct term for those who undermine the peace and tranquillity of the country. Mexico and Michoacán are not alone. Thank you, Zetas, for your contemptible acts."

The Morelia attack marked a turning point, a shift from El Chapo's methods to those of Los Zetas and La Familia. Before there were rules.

If you betrayed El Chapo, you were simply put to death, period. No macabre or gruesome scenes. Today ferocity is theatrically displayed. Extreme violence is compounded by public humiliation. El Chapo understood the shift immediately. The day after the attack he sent around a prounouncement via e-mail denying responsibility for this and similar attacks that was signed by El Mayo as well. "We of Sinaloa have always defended the people, we have always respected the families of capos and the crew, we have always respected the government, we have always respected women and children. When the Sinaloa cartel ruled all over Mexico, there were no executions, and do you know why? Because we know how to do our job, and we have feelings. Soon you will see more Sinaloans in Michoacán (we will take back all the territory that was snatched from us and kill all those who have offended the Sinaloa family), and neither the government nor the cartels will be able to stop us."

The new cartels flaunt their ferocity, which serves as a sort of ambassador. Sinaloa resorts to ferocity only when necessary. It is a confrontation between postmodernism and modernism. Between screams and silence. The rules of the game have changed. The number of players has increased. New cartels spring up quickly, devouring territories and entire regions. It's crazy making, all these new cartels. More flexible structures, faster responses, familiarity with new technology, ostentatiously lurid killings, and obscure, pseudoreligious philosophies. It is altogether a new level of frenzy.

A residential neighborhood in Cancún. A small van, left parked for days, started attracting people's attention, so they called the police: "That van stinks of rotting meat." When the police opened the door they discovered three bodies, handcuffed, with plastic bags over their heads. A note next to them: "We are the new group Mata Zetas. We are against kidnapping and extortion, and we will fight against them in every state, for a cleaner Mexico." Signed: "Cártel de Jalisco Nueva Generación (Los Mata Zetas)." It was later discovered that before being killed the three were interrogated by men with ski masks and assault rifles. A video was posted on YouTube. This was how the Cártel de Jalisco Nueva Generación—Los Mata Zetas, the Zetas Killers—introduced itself.

The cartel traces its inception to the death on July 29, 2010, of Ignacio Coronel Villarreal, the leader of the Sinaloa cartel in the state of Jalisco, one of El Chapo's trusted collaborators, and uncle of Emma Coronel, El Chapo's current wife. He was killed in a shoot-out with the Mexican army in Zapopan, in the state of Jalisco. His followers suspected he was betrayed by his own cartel, so they decided to break away and form a new one. Among the founders of Jalisco New Generation were Nemesio Oseguera Ramos, alias El Mencho; Erick Valencia; El 85; and Martín Arzola, El 53, all former members of the Millennium cartel, then a branch of Sinaloa. So began a waltz of alliances and ruptures. In early 2011 the Jalisco New Generation cartel decided to take possession of Guadalajara, the capital city of Jalisco. A free-for-all broke out. But only a few months later they allied with Sinaloa again. Since then they have been fighting against Los Zetas for control of Guadalajara and Veracruz, but they are also active in the states of Colima, Guanajuato, Nayarit, and Michoacán.

Los Zetas and Jalisco face off openly. On September 20, 2011, right in the center of Veracruz, thirty-five bodies—twenty-three men and twelve women—were found in two trucks, in plain daylight. The victims showed signs of torture, their hands tied, some with bags over their heads. All were Los Zetas members. A video was posted on the Internet after the massacre: five men with ski masks sitting at a table with a tablecloth, small bottles of water in front of them, just like at a press conference. Which is what it was, a press conference to claim responsibility for the crime: "We want the armed forces to believe us when we say that our only objective is to put an end to Los Zetas. We are anonymous, faceless warriors, but proud to be Mexican." A few days later the lifeless bodies of thirty-six people were found in three different houses in Boca del Río, also in the state of Veracruz. On

November 24, a few days before the inauguration of the International Book Fair in Guadalajara, the police discovered twenty-six bodies inside three vans, dead of asphyxiation and blows to the head. On December 22, in the early hours of the morning, three public buses were attacked by drug traffickers on Highway 105 in Veracruz: sixteen dead, including three U.S. citizens from Texas who were in Mexico for Christmas vacation. The next day, in Tampico Alto, Veracruz, ten bodies were found: tortured, handcuffed, almost all decapitated. On Christmas Day near Tampico, in Tamaulipas on the Veracruz state border, army soldiers performing a routine patrol discovered thirteen cadavers in a trailer truck. They also found drug cartel banners on the scene with messages that referred to feuds among rival groups.

July 1, 2012. Mexico has just elected a new president, Enrique Peña Nieto. The war on drug trafficking is one of his priorities. Twenty-four hours after his election a group of about forty killers stops four kids between the ages of fifteen and sixteen who are dealing drugs for the Familia Michoacana, at ten in the morning in Zacazonapan in central Mexico. Other Familia members show up. Shooting breaks out. An hour of confusion and terror. Schools suspend classes until the army and police arrive, who confirm the number of dead: at least eight.

The forty killers belong to the Knights Templar cartel, founded just over a year earlier in yet another upheaval in the murderous madness that contemporary Mexico has been condemned to by drug trafficking. The Knights Templar are exiles from La Familia Michoacana, which, they feel, has lost sight of its principles and now regularly practices theft, kidnapping, extortion. The Knights Templar, on the other hand, maintains a very rigid honor code. Its members are required to fight against materialism, injustice, and tyranny. They are waging an ideological war to defend ethical social values. They swear to protect the oppressed, widows, and orphans. It is forbidden to abuse women and minors or to use their power to deceive them. Kidnapping for money is strictly prohibited. Authorization to kill is required, since no one should take a life for money or for the fun of it: You first have to investigate, find out if there is sufficient motive, and only then can you proceed. A Knight Templar must not fall prey to sectarianism or pettiness. He must promote patriotism and show pride in his country. He must be humble and respectable. The use of drugs is forbidden. The Knight Templar must be an example of chivalry for all. And he must always seek the truth, because God is Truth. Whoever betrays or breaks the code of silence will be punished with death, his family will suffer the same fate, and his property will be confiscated.

This clearly insane parody masks a very young, very aggressive group at war with its original cartel—now grown weak—whose territory it intends to seize, perhaps along with some neighboring areas. Its members feel omnipotent enough to declare war on Los Zetas. Like the original Knights Templar—the medieval order of chivalry founded in Jerusalem after the First Crusade to protect pilgrims to the Holy Land—these new knights claim to have been charged with a divine mission. Members are elected by a council of more experienced brothers, and once they join they can never abandon the "cause"; they take a vow that they must honor at the cost of their own lives. They must participate in ceremonies in which they dress like the Templars from whom they take their name: helmets, white tunics, and red crosses on their chests. In the countryside, the cartel distributes a manual outlining its principles, which are all linked to their fundamental aim to "protect the inhabitants of the free, sovereign, and secular state of Michoacán." The cartel flaunts its purifying intentions while it organizes an army so as to dominate the amphetamine business. The Knights Templar are well equipped and are not afraid of openly challenging the authorities.

Blood calls for blood. It's not just an expression. The history of Mexican cartels shows that all attempts to fight violence with violence have only led to more killings. Under President Vicente Fox, from 2000 to 2006, no decisive initiatives were taken against drug trafficking. The troops sent to the U.S. border to hinder cartel operations were insufficient and poorly equipped. The turning point came on December 11, 2006. President Felipe Calderón, who had just installed himself in Los Pinos, the Mexican White House, sent 6,500 soldiers to the state of Michoacán. It was a historic date, destined to end up in Mexican schoolbooks: a declaration of war between two opposing states, Mexico and the "narco-state." The narco-state has an unlimited appetite, and Calderón knew it, which is why he launched the war on drugs. He couldn't let a parasite state dictate the law. More than 45,000 soldiers have been involved in the war, in addition to the regular local and federal police forces. But blood calls for blood, and the threatened cartels have responded with worsening brutality. To judge from the numbers, Calderón's war has not been won: The Mexican government's official drug war bulletin of January 11, 2012, noted 47,515 people killed by violence associated with organized crime between December 11, 2006, and September 30, 2011. What's worse is that the number of deaths increased exponentially: In 2007 there were 2,826 deaths connected to drug trafficking; in 2008 the number rose to 6,838; in 2009 it reached 9,614; in 2010, 15,273; and by the end of September 2011 it had already reached 12,903, with three months still to go before the end of the year. The new minister of the interior under Peña Nieto, Miguel Ángel Osorio Chong, declared in mid-February 2013 that Mexican drug war deaths would reach around 70,000 during Felipe Calderón's six-year term, adding that it is impossible to provide a precise official figure because "at the end of the previous legislature they stopped keeping official accounts" of drug war victims, just as there is no register of missing persons or unidentified bodies at the morgue. But some hold that the number of deaths in this dirty war is much higher. Death accounting is an imprecise science, and a few canceled lives always slip through the cracks. How many victims were dumped in *narcofosas*, or mass graves? How many bodies dissolved in acid? How many cadavers burned, and thus missing forever? Politicians at every level—local, regional, and national—are victims: In the first six years of the Mexican drug war, thirty-one Mexican mayors were killed, thirteen of them in

2010 alone. Honest people are now afraid to run for office; they know that sooner or later the cartels will arrive and try to replace them with a more welcome candidate. Amnesty International published a report in May 2014 stating that the number of victims between December 2006 and November 2012 (that is, during Calderon's six-year term) was 136,100 (and not the 70,000 official Mexican sources say). Associations such as the Movement for Peace with Justice and Dignity, founded by poet and activist Javier Sicilia after his son was killed by narcos, maintain that the total is much higher.

Numbers and figures. All I see is blood and money.

# COKE #3

Take a rubber band and stretch it. At first there's almost no resistance. You can make it longer, no problem. Until it reaches its full extension, beyond which the elastic will break. Today's economy works like your elastic: All merchandise has to submit to the rules of the elastic. All but one. Cocaine. No market in the world brings in more revenue than the cocaine market. No financial investment in the world gives better returns than cocaine. Not even the record upward trends on the stock exchange are comparable to the "interest" coke offers. In 2012, the year the iPhone 5 and the iPad mini were launched, Apple became the most valuable company in terms of market capitalization ever listed on the New York Stock Exchange. Apple shares shot up by 67 percent in just one year. If you had invested €1,000 in Apple stock in the beginning of 2012, you would have €1,670 in a year. Not bad. But if you had invested €1,000 in cocaine at the beginning of 2012, after a year you would have €182,000.

Cocaine is a safe asset. Cocaine is an anticyclical asset. Cocaine is the asset that fears neither resource shortages nor market inflation. There are plenty of corners of the planet where people live without hospitals, without the web, without running water. But not without cocaine. According to the UN, in 2009, 21 tons of it were consumed in Africa, 14 in Asia, 2 in Oceania. More than a 101 in Latin America and the Caribbean. Everyone wants it, everyone does it, everyone who starts using it needs it. The costs are minimal; you can place it immediately, and the profit margin is extremely high. Cocaine is easier to sell than gold, and the revenue from it can exceed that of petroleum. Gold requires mediators and bargaining time; petroleum needs oil wells, refineries, pipelines. You could discover an oil well in your backyard, or inherit a coltan mine and supply all the cell phones in the world, but you wouldn't go from nothing to villas on the Costa Smeralda on Sardinia as quickly as you would with cocaine. From the streets to the stars with a nuts-and-bolts factory? From poverty to prosperity selling cars? A hundred years ago maybe. Today even the big multinationals that produce primary assets, or the last remaining colossal car manufacturers, all they can do is hang in there. Lower costs. Beat the far reaches of the planet in an attempt to increase exports, which is proving to be less and less feasible.

The most reckless licit investment, the most forward-looking speculation, the fastest movements of vast sums of money—which affect living conditions on entire continents—none can compare with cocaine's multiplication of value. Whoever bets on cocaine accumulates in just a few years the sort of wealth that it takes big holding companies decades to achieve through investments and financial speculation. If an entrepreneurial group manages to get its hands on coke, it holds a form of power impossible to achieve in any other way. Which is why, whenever coke is traded, there is always a violent, ferocious clash. With cocaine there's no mediation. It's all or nothing. And all doesn't last long. When you traffic in cocaine, you can't have unions and industrial plans, government assistance or rules subject to court appeal. If you're the strongest, the cleverest, the most organized, the most armed, you win. The more you stretch the elastic, the more you assert yourself on the market—that's true for any business. Only the law can break the elastic. But even when the law traces the criminal roots and tries to eradicate them, it probably won't be able to track down all the legal activities, real estate investments, and bank accounts acquired thanks to the extraordinary tautness white powder allows.

Cocaine is a complicated asset. Behind cocaine's candor hides millions of people's work. But only those at the right point on the chain of production are getting rich. The Rockefellers of cocaine know how their product is created, every step. They know that in June you sow and in August you reap. That the sowing must be done with seeds from plants at least three years old, and that harvest is three times a year. That the harvested leaves have to be laid out to dry within twenty-four hours; otherwise they're ruined and you can't sell them. That the next step is to dig two holes in the ground. In the first, along with the dried leaves, you have to put in potassium carbonate and kerosene. That you have to pound this mix really well, so as to obtain a sort of greenish dishwater—cocaine carbonate—which, once filtered, is transferred to the second hole. That the next ingredient is concentrated sulfuric acid. That is how you get cocaine sulfate, the base paste, an off-white paste that then needs to be dried. That the final steps call for acetone, hydrochloric acid, and pure alcohol. That you have to filter it over and over, and then let it dry again. They know that's how you obtain cocaine hydrochloride, commonly known as cocaine. The Rockefellers of cocaine know that to obtain more or less half a kilo of pure cocaine, you need 300 kilos of leaves and a handful of full-time workers. The cocaine entrepreneurs know all this, just as any company head would. But more than anything, they know that the majority of the peasants, dealers, and transporters who have found jobs that pay a little better than those they could hope to get somewhere else still have both feet firmly planted in poverty. It's unskilled labor, a sea of interchangeable subjects, that perpetuates a system of exploitation of the many and enrichment of a few. Those few at the top of the heap are the ones who had the foresight to realize that, in cocaine's long journey from the leaves of Colombia to the nostrils of the casual consumer, the real money is made through sales, resale, and price management. Because if it's true that a kilo of cocaine in Colombia is sold for $1,500, in Mexico for $12,000 to $16,000, in the United States for $27,000, in Spain for $45,000, in Holland for $47,000, in Italy for $54,000, and in the UK for $77,000; if it's true that the price per gram varies from $61 in Portugal to $166 in Luxembourg, going for $80 in France, $87 in Germany, $96 in Switzerland, and $97 in Ireland; if it's true that on average 1 kilo of pure cocaine is cut to make 3 kilos that are then sold in single-gram doses; if all this is true, it's also true that whoever controls the entire chain of production is one of the richest men in the world.

Cocaine traffic today is managed by a new middle class of mafiosi. They use distribution to gain control of the territory where it is sold. A game of Risk on a planetary scale. On one side are the areas where cocaine is produced, which become fiefdoms where nothing but poverty and violence grow, areas the mafias keep under control by generously doling out charity and alms, which they pass off as rights. No development, only profits. If someone wants to better himself, he demands riches, not rights. Riches that he needs to know how to grab. In this way only one model of success is perpetuated, of which violence is merely a vehicle and a tool. What is established is power. On the other side are countries where you plant your little flags to mark your presence: Italy, England, Russia, China. Everywhere. For the most powerful families coke works as easily as an ATM machine. You need to buy a shopping center? Import some coke, and after a month you'll have enough money to close the deal. You need to sway an election? Import some coke, and you'll be ready in a few weeks. Cocaine is the universal answer to the need for liquidity.

# 6

# FEROCITY IS LEARNED

For years I've been asking myself what the point is of dealing with shootings and death. Is it really worth it? Why? Are you going to be called in as a consultant? Do a six-week teaching stint in some university, the more prestigious the better? Throw yourself into the battle against evil, believing you are the good? Wear the hero's crown for a few months? Will you profit if people read what you write? Will they hate you, the people who said these things before you did but were ignored? And what about those who didn't say them, or said them poorly, will they hate you too? Sometimes I think I'm obsessed. Other times I'm convinced these stories are a way of measuring the truth. Maybe that's the secret. Not for others. Secret for me. Hidden from myself. Left out of my public pronouncements. Tracking the paths of drug trafficking and money laundering makes you feel you can measure the truth of things, understand the fate of an election, a government's fall. It's no longer enough to listen to the official statements. While the world is clearly heading in one direction, everything seems focused on something else, something banal even, superficial. Some government minister's statement, some tiny, insignificant event, some piece of gossip. But everything is really being decided by something else. This intuition is at the base of every romantic choice. Every journalist, novelist, and director would like to tell things the way they are, the way they really are. To say to his reader or viewer: It's not how you thought it was, *this* is how it is. I'm going to open the wound for you, so you can glimpse the ultimate truth. But no one ever succeeds completely. The danger is in believing that reality—that real, pulsating, decisive reality—is completely hidden. If you trip and fall into it, you start thinking everything's a conspiracy—secret meetings, Masonic lodges, spies. Reporters are full of this sort of idiocy. To square the circle of the world in your own interpretations is the onset of shortsightedness in an eye that thinks it has perfect vision. But it's not that simple. The complexity lies precisely in not believing that everything is hidden or decided in secret chambers. The world is more interesting than a conspiracy between sects and secret agents. Criminal power is a mixture of many elements.

When you do figure out how to make the story gripping, when you hit on the exact doses of style and truth, when your words finally rise from your chest and begin to resonate, you will be the first to be disgusted by them. The first to hate yourself, with your entire being. And you won't be the only one. Those who listen will hate you too, the very people who choose to listen, without being coerced, because you make them face this abomination. Because they'll always feel you're holding up a mirror to them: Why didn't I do it? Why didn't I say it? Why didn't I understand? It hurts. A wounded animal usually attacks: He's the one who's lying, he's doing it to throw people off, because he's corrupt, because he wants fame, or money.

Maybe you think that dealing with all this is a way of redeeming the world. Of reestablishing justice. And maybe it is, in part. But maybe you also have to accept the burden of being a tiny superhero without a shred of power. Of being, in the end, a pathetic human being who has overestimated his strength merely because he's never run up against its limits before. The truth is that there's really only one reason for deciding to stay inside these stories of drug traffickers, criminal entrepreneurs, massacres. To know that what you find out won't make you feel better. Yet you keep trying. And you start to develop a disdain for things. By things I mean objects, stuff. You come to know how things are made, where they come from, how they all end up.

And even if you feel bad, you convince yourself that you can really understand this world only if you decide to stay inside these stories. You may be good at what you do, but that doesn't necessarily mean you want your calling in life to be to stay inside these stories forever. Being inside means they consume you, compel you, corrode your daily life. Being inside means you carry city maps in your head, maps marked with construction sites, open-air drug markets, places where pacts were sealed and where "excellent" homicides were carried out. You're not inside them just because you're on the street or you infiltrate a clan for six years, like FBI undercover agent Joe Pistone. You're inside because these stories are what give meaning to your being in the world. I decided to stay inside them years ago. Not only because I grew up in a place where the clans decided everything and I'd seen those opposed to their power die, not only because defamation dissolves all desire to oppose criminal power. Being inside cocaine trafficking was the only way I could fully understand things. To look at human weakness, the physiology of power, the frailty of relationships, the inconsistency of bonds, the appalling power of money and ferocity. The absolute impotence of all those teachings about beauty and justice I'd been raised on. I realized that the axis around which everything turns is cocaine. There was only one name for the wound.

"The Serbs. Precise, ruthless, meticulous torturers."

"Bullshit. The Chechens. They have such sharp knives, you bleed to death before you even know you've been cut."

"Amateurs compared to the Liberians. They rip your heart out when you're still alive and eat it."

It's one of the oldest games in the world. The ranking of cruelty, the top ten of Earth's most ferocious people.

"What about the Albanians? They're not satisfied just eliminating you; they wipe out your future generations as well. They cancel everything out. Forever."

"The Romanians put a bag over your head, tie your wrists to your neck, and let time do its work."

"The Croatians nail your feet down, and all you can do is pray that death comes as soon as possible."

The escalation of blood, terror, and sadism goes on for quite a while, eventually getting to the inevitable list of special forces: France's Foreign Legion, Spain's El Tercio, Brazil's BOPE.

I'm sitting at a round table. One by one the men around me, all soldiers, share their experiences and catalog the cultural distinctions of the people they know best, having been on peacekeeping missions in various territories. It's a ritual, this sadistic and slightly racist game, but like all rituals, it's necessary. It's the only way they have of saying that the worst is over, they survived, it's real life from here on in. A better life.

I keep quiet. Like an anthropologist I try to interfere as little as possible, so that the ritual will unfold without any hitches. The guys' faces are serious. When their turn comes to talk, they all avoid looking at the guy across the table or the one who just finished talking. Each one tells his own story as if he were in an empty room talking to himself.

I've heard dozens of these classifications over the years, in meetings, conferences, dinners, over a plate of pasta, or in court. Usually they're just lists of acts of increasingly inhuman brutality, but as these episodes gradually accumulated in my mind, a common denominator surfaced, a cultural element that recurred with stubborn insistence. Cruelty is awarded a place of honor in the genetic patrimony of a people. Making the mistake of equating acts of ferocity or war with an entire population, drafting lists of this sort becomes the equivalent of showing off one's sculpted muscles after endless hours in the gym.

Ferocity is learned. You're not born with it. As much as one may be born with certain inclinations, or have inherited rancor and violence from his family, ferocity is taught, it is learned. Ferocity is passed down from teacher to pupil. The impulse isn't enough; it has to be channeled and trained. You teach a body to empty out its soul, even if you don't believe in the soul, even if you think it's religious nonsense, a flight of fancy, even if for you it's all muscle fibers and nerves and veins and lactic acid. Yet something's there. Otherwise, how do you explain the brake that, right at the last minute, keeps you from going all the way? Conscience. Soul. It has a lot of names, but regardless of what you call it, you can compromise it. It's convenient to think that ferocity is inherent to the human condition, handy for anyone who wants to cleanse his conscience without first coming to terms with things.

When one soldier finishes his story, the guy next to him starts immediately. Everyone seems to agree that some populations just have that impulse, it's in their blood, there's no way around it, we're born with it. A soldier to my right seems particularly eager for his turn to speak. He fidgets in his plastic chair, making it squeak slightly. He's obviously not some undisciplined novice: His long beard suits his face, and the insignia on his uniform make it clear that he's faced quite a few dangerous situations. He shakes his head. I think I even glimpse a scornful smile on his face. It's distracting, so now I'm eager for his turn too. I don't have to wait long, because halfway through a graphic description of someone's nails being removed by some secret service in Eastern Europe, the man silences the discussion.

"You haven't understood a damn thing. You don't know what the fuck you're talking about. All you do is read the tabloids, watch the eight o'clock news; you don't know shit."

Then he rummages in his pants pockets—military fatigues—and takes out a smartphone, scrolls his finger nervously down the screen until a map appears. He zooms in, blows it up, zooms in more, and finally shows the others a slice of Earth. "Here, these guys are the worst." His finger points to a place in Central America. Guatemala.

"Guatemala?"

The veteran utters just one word, unfamiliar to most of them: "Kaibil."

I'd heard that name in depositions from the 1970s, but no one remembered it anymore.

"Eight weeks," the bearded soldier starts up again. "Eight weeks and everything human about a human being is gone. The Kaibiles have a way of annulling one's conscience. In two months they can extract from a human's body everything that distinguishes him from a beast, what allows him to tell good from evil, to know moderation. They could turn Saint Francis into a killer in eight weeks, capable of biting animals to death, of drinking piss to survive and eliminating masses of people without worrying how old they are. All it takes is eight weeks."

Silence. I've just witnessed a heresy, the paradigm of innate savagery has been shot down. I have to meet a Kaibil. I start reading. I learn that the Kaibiles are the Guatemalan army's elite counterinsurgency force. They were formed in 1974, when the Commando School, which would later become the Kaibil training center for special operations, was established. A civil war was raging in Guatemala at the time, and government and paramilitary forces, backed by the United States, had to face first disorganized guerrilla fighters and then the rebel group Unidad Revolucionaria Nacional Guatemalteca, or Guatemalan National Revolutionary Unity. A relentless struggle. Students, workers, professionals, opposing party politicians—anybody and everybody—were caught in the Kaibiles' net. Mayan villages were razed to the ground, peasants slaughtered, their bodies left to rot. In 1996, after thirty-six years and over 200,000 deaths, 36,000 *desaparecidos,* and 626 confirmed massacres, the civil war in Guatemala finally ended. A peace treaty was signed. The first president after the war, Álvaro Arzú, decided, at the request of the United States, to transform Guatemala's counterrevolutionary army, considered to be the best anti-insurgency force in Latin America, into an efficient weapon against drug trafficking. On October 1, 2003, a counterterrorism platoon of Kaibil special forces was officially created.

By their own definition, Kaibiles are "killing machines." They are
put through gruesome tests, their courage challenged constantly, day
after day, horror after horror. Drinking the blood of an animal he has
just killed and eaten raw makes a Kaibil grow stronger. Guatemala's
Historical Clarification Commission has been taking an interest in
these practices and drafted a document entitled "Memory of Silence." It
states that 93 percent of documented crimes in Guatemala in the
thirty-six years of civil war were committed by law enforcement or
paramilitary groups, in particular the Patrullas de Autodefensa Civil
and the Kaibil special forces. The report also states that Kaibiles committed acts of genocide.

One of the most brutal slaughters took place in Las Dos Erres, a
village in the department of Petén, which was razed to the ground. On
December 6, 1982 forty Kaibiles entered the village to take back nineteen rifles lost in a previous guerrilla ambush. No one was spared: They
killed men, women, and children; raped young girls; kicked and beat
pregnant women with their rifle butts, jumping on their stomachs until
they aborted; threw live children into wells or beat them to death with
clubs, even buried some alive. The youngest were smashed against walls
or trees. The bodies were thrown into wells or left to rot in the fields.
There is talk of more than 250 deaths: 201 deaths have been documented, 70 of them children less than seven years old. When they left
the village the soldiers took with them two girls, ages fourteen and sixteen. They made them dress as soldiers and held them for three days, rap-
ing them repeatedly. When they got tired of them, they strangled them.


It's not hard to meet a Kaibil, as it turns out. They are proud of who
they are. After I heard that soldier talk I started asking around, looking
to meet a Kaibil fighter. I was directed first to a household servant who
works for a Milanese entrepreneur's family. He's pleasant; we arrange a
time and meet on the street.

He tells me he used to be a journalist; he keeps copies of some of his articles in his wallet. He rereads them every now and then, or maybe just saves them as proof of his former life. He knows a Kaibil.

"I know him. It's hard for a Kaibil to become an ex-Kaibil, but this one has done some not good things."

He doesn't want to explain what those not good things are.

"You won't believe a word he tells you. I don't believe him either, because if what he says is true, I wouldn't be able to sleep. . . ."

Then he winks at me. "I know it's true, but I hope it's not exactly completely true."

He gives me a phone number. I say good-bye to the journalist-servant and dial the number. The voice that answers is cold but flattered by my interest. We arrange to meet, in a public place. Ángel Miguel arrives. Short, Mayan eyes, elegantly dressed, as if for the cameras. All I have is a notebook, which he doesn't like, but he decides to stay any-way. His cold telephone voice has given way to a studied manner of speaking. The whole time we talk, he never lowers his gaze and never makes a gesture that is not strictly necessary.

"I'm glad you're a fag," he starts out.

"I'm not a fag."

"Impossible, I can prove it. You're a fag, no need to be ashamed."

"If I were gay I wouldn't be ashamed, that's for sure. But what are we talking about?"

"You're a fag, because you didn't even notice all this."

Without ever taking his eyes off mine he rotates his neck a few de-grees to the left, and that instant, as if in response to some call, a girl steps forward. It's true; I hadn't noticed her. I was concentrating on the Kaibil.

"If you don't notice even her, you're a fag."

Very blond, her dress like a second skin, vertiginous heels. Despite her outfit, not even a hint of makeup, maybe she decided that her fair eyes, with their golden specks, light up her face enough. His girlfriend. She introduces herself; she's Italian and happy to be there with this man whom she probably thinks is some sort of war hero.

"You have to become *cuas*. If you're not *cuas*, you don't know what brotherhood in battle means."

Ángel Miguel, I realize, doesn't like to waste time. He's declared me a homosexual and introduced me to his girlfriend. For him that's enough; now he can begin his story. I read somewhere that in Q'eqchi' *cuas* means brother. But now I realize that it's not a biological relationship. *Cuas* is not the brother you meet when you're born; *cuas* is the brother who is chosen for you.

"Once, during training, I asked some Kaibiles to leave me a bit of food. My *cuas* went white, like a dead man. The Kaibiles threw their food on the ground and started stomping on it. Then they tied us up and said, 'Start pecking, hens.' If we stretched out our tongues too far, they'd kick and shout: 'Don't graze, chickens, peck!'

"If either *cuas* makes a mistake during training, both are punished; if one of them does well, they both get plenty to eat and both get a bed. You're practically engaged to your *cuas*. Once my *cuas* and I were in our tent, and at nighttime my *hermano* started touching my dick. It bothered me at first, but then I realized we had to share everything . . . solitude and pleasure . . . but we never fucked . . . just touched. . . ."

He barely breathes as he talks, as if he had to deliver his speech, prepared in advance, in the shortest time possible. His girlfriend nods proudly. The gold specks in her eyes shine more brightly now. I would like to interrupt and point out that just a few minutes before he'd been calling me a fag, but I decide it's best not to interfere with his thought process.

"You learn what a combat brother is there. You share rations, you huddle close when it's cold, you beat each other bloody to keep your nerve up."

To stop being a man, with all his honeyed qualities and imperfect defects. To become a Kaibil. To move through the world hating.

"There's an inscription at the entrance to the Kaibil training camp in Poptún, in the department of Petén: 'Welcome to hell.' But I bet only a few people read the second inscription there: 'If I advance, follow me. If I stop, urge me on. If I retreat, kill me.'"

My contact rattles off the foreigners who have helped train young Kaibiles since the 1980s: Green Berets, Vietnam Rangers, Peruvian and Chilean commandos. During the civil war in Guatemala it was said that the Kaibiles' distinguishing signature was decapitation, even though some people were convinced it was only a legend, like their war song: "*Kaibil, Kaibil, Kaibil! Mata, mata, mata! Qué mata Kaibil? Guerrillero subversivo! Qué come Kaibil? Guerrillero subversivo!*" "Kaibil, Kaibil, Kaibil! Kill, kill, kill! What does a Kaibil kill? Guerrilla insurgents! What does a Kaibil eat? Guerrilla insurgents!"

"The first training phase lasts twenty-one days," Ángel Miguel says, "followed by the second, twenty-eight days. In the jungle. Rivers, swamps, minefields. This is the Kaibil's home. And just like you love your home, the Kaibil loves his. The last week finally arrives. The last step in becoming a real Kaibil. You learn to eat whatever there is, whatever you can find. Cockroaches, snakes. You learn to conquer enemy terrain, annihilate it, take possession of it.

"To complete the training you have to go without sleep for two days, in a river up to your neck. They'd given my *cuas* and me a puppy, a mongrel with watery eyes. They told us to take care of it, it was part of our brotherhood. We had to take it with us everywhere, and feed it. We gave it a name and were starting to grow fond of it when our chief told us we had to kill it. A knife to its belly, one blow from each of us. By that point we were nearing the end of our training and didn't ask a lot of questions. Then the chief told us we had to eat it and drink its blood. To show him how brave we were. Even this order we carried out, it was all so natural by then.

"The Kaibil knows that you don't need to drink or eat or sleep in order to survive. What you need is a good rifle and ammunition. We were soldiers, we were perfect. We didn't fight because we were ordered to, that wouldn't have been enough. We had a sense of belonging, which is stronger than any command. Only a third of us made it to the end. The others either ran off or were thrown out. Some others got sick, and some died."

The Kaibiles' world is above all a symbolic world. Fear, terror, brotherhood, solidarity with your *cuas*. It all can and must be flaunted through a clever game of codes and cross-references, through the invention of acrostics. Starting with the word *cuas*: C = comradeship, U = unity, A = adherence, S = safety. Or through the Kaibil motto, which expresses their philosophy: "The Kaibil is a killing machine for when extraneous powers or doctrines attack the country or the army." The Kaibil must never—not for any reason in the world—be parted from his maroon beret, which bears their coat of arms: a mountaineering carabiner, which represents unity and strength; a dagger, symbolizing honor, with five notches in the handle, which represent the five senses; and the word "Kaibil" in capital yellow letters. "Kaibil" in the Mam language means "he who has the strength and cunning of two tigers." The name comes from the great Kaibil Balam, the Mam king who in the sixteenth century courageously held out against the Spanish conquistadors, against Gonzalo de Alvarado's men. Yet the very troops who bear the symbolic name of the Mayan king and his fierce resistance against the conquistadors became a tool for exterminating their own people. The legend has been so distorted that now the word connotes terror.

"At the end of the eight weeks there's a dinner. Huge, smoking grills, the fire fed constantly, and alligator, iguana, and deer steaks thrown on it all night long. There's also a tradition of grabbing the Guatemalan minister of defense and throwing him in a pond with crocodiles (they're far away, but those government guys are real wimps!). After the dinner, you can finally wear the Kaibiles' emblem: the dagger on a blue and black background. Blue for day: The Kaibil operates in the sea and sky. Black for silence in nighttime operations. Running diagonal is a rope, for terrestrial missions. And rising up from the dagger is a flame that burns eternally. Liberty."

Ángel Miguel suddenly raises his hand and spreads out his fingers.

"Smell. Hearing. Touch. Sight. Taste."

The five senses, which the perfect Kaibil must develop and always keep sharp.

"Unity and strength."

I look at Ángel Miguel. He's no longer a Kaibil, but he still has that hollow look in his eyes. When you meet a Kaibil you come face-to-face with absence. He's barely five feet four inches, but Ángel Miguel looks me up and down. All that talk about training and brotherhood has fed his pride, and he lords it over me and his girlfriend somehow. I have a question, and this could be the time to ask it.

"What can you tell me about the Kaibiles and narco-trafficking?"

Amnesty International began noting this phenomenon in 2003, in a report denouncing dozens of cases of military and police participation in drug-trafficking networks, as well as illegal activities such as car theft, trafficking in children for illegal adoptions, and "social cleansing" operations. In the same year, Washington included Guatemala on the list of "decertified" countries, because between 2000 and 2002 the Guatemalan government seized only a fifth of the cocaine seized three years earlier.

If Ángel Miguel is annoyed, he certainly doesn't show it. So I look to see his girlfriend's reaction, but she too remains immobile, except for shifting her weight slightly from one high heel to the other. I'm sure she had to pass some sort of training too, before she could be with him. Finally, Ángel Miguel opens his mouth. "Unity and strength," he repeats, and falls silent.

"Is it true that some former combatants have had successful careers in Mexican cartels?"

For several years Mexican authorities have been reporting a growing number of former Kaibil and Guatemalan soldiers being recruited by local criminal organizations. Former soldiers are a real plus for these organizations, who save time and money by enlisting young men who are already trained and experienced. A former Kaibil, who knows how to handle a weapon and operate in mountains and woods, can be very useful to the cartels. A former Kaibil knows how to survive in extremely difficult conditions and can maneuver just as well in southern Mexico as in northern Guatemala, regions with similar climates. The situation is made even more worrisome by the demobilization of the Guatemalan army, which in recent years has dropped from thirty thousand to fifteen thousand soldiers. Many soldiers were discharged and found themselves out of work. Some joined private security agencies and were sent abroad as mercenaries, to Iraq, for instance. But others ended up expanding the ranks of criminal cells.

Ángel Miguel is rubbing his thumb and index finger together, as if rolling an invisible cigarette, and there are tiny wrinkles, which I hadn't noticed before, at the corners of his eyes. His girlfriend looks around and curls her lips nervously.

On the phone, before he agreed to meet me, Ángel Miguel had given me a list of rules that at the time I had taken for pure propaganda, but which, in his sustained silence, I now realize I hadn't respected. A Kaibil must "earn the trust of his subordinates, direct their efforts, clarify objectives, inspire safety, create team unity, be an example of moderation at all times, keep hope alive, sacrifice himself for victory." With two simple questions about Kaibiles past and present I had broken the spell. Our conversation was over.

## 7.

# Z

Ángel Miguel left me wanting more. He had painted a picture of his apprenticeship to violence, but he was merely playing a part: the retired combatant reminiscing about the glory days of his training. But it's not enough. I have to see it in action, to go back to where the savagery took root and grew into an instrument of power. I have to go back to Mexico. To Osiel Cárdenas Guillén, the boss of the Gulf cartel.

Osiel is famous for never making mistakes and never forgiving those who do. But even he finally made one, and with the wrong people. In November 1999, Joe DuBois, a DEA agent, and Daniel Fuentes, an FBI agent, were in a Ford Bronco with diplomatic plates, a Gulf cartel informer sleeping in the backseat, his head pressed against the window. The informer was taking the two agents on a tour of Gulf cartel bosses' houses and hangouts in Matamoros. He didn't wake up even when the Ford Bronco slammed on the brakes and voices—all too familiar—were heard. "That guy's ours, gringos!" Several vehicles surrounded the agents' Bronco, and a dozen or so cartel members hopped out, AK-47s pointed. Osiel got out of his Jeep Cherokee, went over to the Bronco, and stuck a gun in one of the agents' faces. So the Americans flashed their badges, revealing their identities. But Osiel didn't give a damn who they were. It was the first time he had exposed himself like that; he knew it was risky, but he didn't have a choice; he couldn't let the informer talk. Time froze; the players faced off but without showing too much muscle—one wrong move and what seemed like a negotiation could quickly become a bloodbath. The FBI agent took a chance: "If you don't let us go, the United States government will hunt you all the way to your grave." Osiel caved. He shouted at the gringos: This is his territory, they can't control it, and don't ever show your faces around here again. Then he ordered his men to reverse. The FBI and DEA agents gave a sigh of relief.

It was the beginning of the end. The American authorities put a price of $2 million on Osiel's head, and he began to get paranoid. He started seeing enemies everywhere; even his most trusted collaborators could be *madrinas*—godmothers, as informers are called. He needed to increase his firepower, and decided to buy himself an army. He didn't want to be imprudent and so chose corrupt defectors from GAFE (Grupo Aeromóvil de Fuerzas Especiales or Special Forces Airmobile Group), the Mexican army's elite corps. Ironically, GAFE's role was to flush out criminals like him. GAFE men are tough: They're modeled on U.S. special forces and trained by Israeli and French specialists. Among these Mexican Rambos was Lieutenant Arturo Guzmán Decena. Guzmán and Osiel had some traits in common: Both were cynical, ambitious, ruthless. Arturo, along with thirty other deserters, was put on Osiel's payroll. So troops that had been paid to fight drug trafficking now swore loyalty to the very man who was, until recently, the enemy to take out. But the Friend Killer paid more than the Mexican government. That is how Osiel's private army was born, and why it was baptized Los Zetas: Z was the code letter the GAFE soldiers used to communicate with one another via radio. Lieutenant Arturo Guzmán Decena became Z1.

Violence is self-absorbing; it voluntarily degrades itself in order to renew itself. In the tortured territory of Mexico, Los Zetas are like a cell that annihilates itself in order to grow stronger, more powerful, more destructive. The escalation of atrocity increased national and international pressure to get Osiel Cárdenas. On March 14, 2003, after a shoot-out in Matamoros, the Mexican army arrested him. Osiel was locked up in the La Palma maximum security prison. But being behind bars didn't undermine his leadership; in fact, the alliance between the Gulf and Tijuana cartels was born in that prison. But although Osiel might have been able to issue orders from his cell, he couldn't control his men, particularly Los Zetas, who were showing increasingly clear signs of wanting to be independent. Los Zetas are attracted to the most ruthless aspects of organized crime: They have absorbed the worst from the paramilitary forces, the worst from the Mafia, the worst from the drug traffickers.

From a military point of view, it's hard to compete with Los Zetas: They have bulletproof vests and Kevlar helmets, and their arsenal includes: AR-15 assault rifles; thousands of *cuernos de chivo* (or goat's horns, as they call AK-47s); MP5 submachine guns; grenade launchers; frag grenades like those used in Vietnam; surface-to-air missiles; gas masks; night-vision goggles; dynamite; and helicopters. A February 2008 army raid on the El Mezquito, one of Los Zetas' farms near the city of Miguel Alemán, about sixty miles west of Reynosa, uncovered 89 assault rifles, 83,355 ammunition cartridges, and enough explosives to blow several buildings sky-high. Los Zetas members are highly professional; they use a modern phone-tapping system, encrypted radio signals, and Skype instead of regular telephones to elude surveillance.

Their internal hierarchy is rigid. Every *plaza* has its own capo and bookkeeper, who manages the finances for the criminal cell, which, in addition to drugs, exploits various niches of the criminal economy: theft, extortions, kidnappings. According to Mexican and American sources, there is a precise division of duties within Los Zetas, each with its own name:

—Las Ventanas, the Windows: kids who sound the alarm when
    they spot police officers sticking their noses into drug-dealing
    zones;
—Los Halcons, the Falcons: who take care of distribution;
—Los Leopardos, the Leopards: prostitutes trained to extort pre-
    cious information from clients;
—Los Mañosos, the Clever Ones: in charge of weapons;
—La Dirección, the Command: the brains of the operation.


Ángel Miguel may not have known Osiel's story, but he certainly would
have known that relations between Los Zetas and the Kaibiles were
very tight. The Guatemalans had trained GAFE soldiers who then became Los Zetas. Then, once they were independent, Los Zetas started
recruiting Kaibiles, their former teachers.

If there is one thing the Guatemalans did not need to teach it was
the uses of the video recorder. Type in "Los Zetas Execution Video" on
YouTube and a list of videos uploaded directly by group members pops
up (or better yet, don't). Savagery works if it spreads like an infection,
from mouth to mouth, person to person. Decapitations, suffocations,
and flayings are their marketing strategy, videos of bestiality their press
releases. Los Zetas are particularly fond of electric saws, and the heads
they brandish are their calling card. They want their victims to scream,
and they really know how to make them do it. Their cries have to be
heard everywhere; they have to be the ambassadors for Los Zetas
throughout Mexico and the world. One characteristic in particular
distinguishes Los Zetas from other cartels: They don't have a territory
of their own, no physical place, no geographical roots. A postmodern
army that has to produce an image that creates outposts. Terror must
conquer the country. The mujahedin realized that decapitations could
be a trademark of atrocity before they did, but Los Zetas didn't take
long to adopt the same technique.

The web is their preferred platform, but Los Zetas don't disdain old methods either, such as the banners they hang in Mexican cities and towns. "The operating group Los Zetas wants you, soldier or former soldier. We offer good pay, food, and protection for your family. Stop suffering from abuse, stop suffering from hunger." These so-called narco-banners promise benefits and money to soldiers who decide to enlist in Los Zetas; they deliver messages directly to the people; and they aim to intimidate enemies and governments. "They will not be able to stop us, even with the support of the United States government, because here Los Zetas rule. Calderón's government must reach an agreement with us, because if he doesn't, we will be forced to topple him and take power by force."

Los Zetas' enemy cartels started using them too. In February 2010 La Familia Michoacana hung a banner announcing the creation of a resistance front to fight Los Zetas and inviting the people to join in: "A polite invitation to all Mexicans to unite in a common front in order to put an end to Los Zetas. We are already taking action against Los Zetas. Let's join forces against these evil beasts."


Resortito and El Bigotito are two clowns. Jokes, water pranks, imitations, tricks. They know that the kids are expecting them on the buses that run the Cárdenas-Comalcalco-Villahermosa route.The kids laugh and snort and always get home a little later because these guys are really good. Resortito and El Bigotito collect a few coins every time, nothing much, but it's better than begging. And besides, the kids' clear laughter makes them feel good, appreciated.

A misunderstanding, a cruel joke that spun out of control, or a deliberate, studied attack. It's a mystery, but the fact remains that a rumor started going around. A false rumor, maybe. "Army informers hide under the clowns' wigs." On January 2, 2011, the clowns' lifeless bodies were found on the edge of a country road. They'd been tortured and then shot to death. Near their bodies, a piece of paper with a brief message claiming responsibility: "This happened to me because I was a spy and thought that SEDENA would protect me." SEDENA is the Mexican Secretariat of National Defense. An acronym identified those responsible: FEZ, or Los Zetas special forces.

There's no end to Los Zetas' brutality: Cadavers swing from city bridges in broad daylight, for children to see; bodies are decapitated and hacked to pieces, then abandoned along the side of the road, their pants often pulled down for one final humiliation; mass graves are discovered in the countryside, dozens of bodies are heaped on top of one another. Cities have become war zones.

Violence. It always comes back to violence. A word that smacks of instinct, primitivism, yet which Los Zetas—like the Kaibiles—knew how to write into education. Rosalío Reta was one of their pupils. Born in Texas with the dream of becoming Superman, at age thirteen Rosalío ended up in a Los Zetas military training camp, on a ranch in the state of Tamaulipas. At first it seemed like a game.

"Here's your super weapon, a laser."

"But Superman doesn't use lasers."

"That's okay. Just point it, press, and everybody in front of you will disappear."

That's how Rosalío got his first pistol, and after six months of training he was ready for a loyalty test: In one of the cartel's safe houses a man waited, tied to a chair. Rosalío didn't know anything about him, didn't know why he was condemned. Rosalío didn't ask questions. He was handed a pistol, .38 caliber, just like the one he had fired at cardboard targets for six months. All he had to do was pull the trigger. The adrenaline rush was electrifying. Rosalío felt invincible, like Superman. He can fly, he can stop speeding bullets, "leap tall buildings at a single bound." He can kill. "I thought I was Superman," he later confessed to the court judges in Laredo, Texas, after he was arrested: "I liked doing it, killing that man. Then they tried to take my pistol away, but it was like trying to take candy from a child."

A couple of years after his initiation, Rosalío—along with Gabriel and Jessie, two kids his age—arrived in Los Zetas' Never-Never Land:

a nice house that the cartel rented for them in Laredo; every type of pill imaginable; a console hooked up to a plasma TV. In the beginning the aim was simply to kill liquid crystal men. Days and days with the game pad, pretending to drive a car that zooms through imaginary American cities. In that virtual reality you can do whatever you want. Kill whomever you want, no consequences, no remorse. The worst that can happen is, your eyes get bloodshot. For Rosalío and his friends the reality of the game superimposed itself on real life: Everything became possible, and fear disappeared. Los Niños Zetas were ready. The deal was clear: Five hundred dollars a week for stakeouts and odd jobs, but the real money was in special jobs. Some men had to be eliminated, but it wasn't enough just to kill them; you had to slit their throats. That's where the money got good, a fifty-thousand-dollar bonus for every hit. When Rosalío was arrested four years and twenty murders later, the police officers who interrogated him never noticed any fear or remorse in him. The only time a shadow even crossed his face was when he talked about a mission to San Nicolás de los Garza. He missed his target and caused a massacre, four people dead and twenty-five wounded, none of them with any ties to organized crime. "I made a mistake," Rosalío said, "and now they're going to make me pay." "They" were his old teachers, Los Zetas.


In 2002, a year before Osiel's imprisonment, Arturo Guzmán Decena, El Z1, was killed in a restaurant in Matamoros. A crown of flowers was placed on his tomb with the message: "You will always be in our hearts. From your family: Los Zetas." After his death Heriberto Lazcano Lazcano took over. Lazcano, alias El Lazca, born on Christmas Day 1974, was also from the army special forces and was wanted by the federal authorities in the United States and Mexico for drug trafficking and multiple homicides. Mexico offered a reward of 30 million pesos for anyone who could provide information leading to his arrest. The U.S. Department of State offered $5 million.

El Lazca was famous for his favorite method of killing: He'd lock his victim in a cell and then watch him starve to death. Death is patient, and so was El Lazca. Following in Guzmán Decena's footsteps, he reinforced and expanded the group, setting up training camps for fifteen- to eighteen-year-olds and for former local, state, and federal police, and he recruited former Kaibiles.

Under El Lazca's leadership Los Zetas gradually went from being merely the armed branch of the Gulf cartel to more independent roles. Los Zetas were feeling strong; they wanted their independence. And in February 2010, after a series of shoot-outs and murders, their break from the Gulf cartel was decisive. Los Zetas, now an independent cartel, sided against the Gulf cartel, their former employers, and aligned themselves with the Beltrán Leyva brothers and the Tijuana and Juárez cartels.

El Lazca was a young boss, but he was already a myth, and his legend was amplified by his death. In October 2012 an anonymous tip arrived at the Mexican navy: El Lazca was watching a baseball game in a stadium in Progreso, in the state of Coahuila, right this minute. An unexpected gift. El Lazca, the most wanted drug trafficker after El Chapo, was killed during the police siege. It was a great coup.

Less than twenty-four hours later the triumph was soured when a group of Los Zetas commandos stole their boss's body from the morgue before forensics had finished with it. Fingerprints were a match, but they still had other tests to run, including the decisive one: DNA. But now the body had disappeared. Los Zetas had another incredible story to tell, at any rate.

Miguel Ángel Treviño Morales, alias El Z40, became the next Los Zetas leader. He had been rising through the ranks since the group's founding, and was known for his "stewing" technique: He'd stuff his adversary in an oil barrel and then set it on fire. But Miguel Ángel Treviño Morales's rule didn't last long. He was arrested in Nuevo Laredo on July 15, 2013. The baton passed to his younger brother Omar, close to him because of his nickname; El Z42. However, Miguel

Ángel's subordinates apparently did not trust Omar Treviño Morales, who was wanted in Mexico and the United States on charges of drug and arms trafficking, murder and kidnap. The Mexican government offered a 30 million peso reward and the United States up to $5 million for information leading to his arrest. On March, 4, 2015, Omar was arrested in a luxury home in San Pedro Garza García, Nuevo León. His neighbors, who were interviewed by Mexican newspapers, said the house had been bought about six months earlier by a quiet family, which did not mingle with other residents. Omar's capture was possible thanks to a joint operation by the federal police and the army. They seized the Zetas' chief without a shot being fired, but there was little time to celebrate: The hunt for a new boss was on.

Los Zetas' epicenter of economic power is the border city of Nuevo Laredo. But they've spread throughout the country, into the states of Oaxaca, Guerrero, and Michoacán on the Pacific coast, in Mexico City, in Chiapas, and in the states of Yucatán, Quintana Roo, and Tabasco along the Gulf coast. In Nuevo Laredo they have total control, with sentries posted all along the main traffic routes in the city and roadblocks near the area bus stations and airports, the better to know who is leaving, but what is more important, who and what is arriving.

Los Zetas is a criminal dictatorship whose laws are based on extortion, whose decrees are kidnappings and torture, and whose constitution is founded on decapitations and dismemberments. Its targets are often politicians and police, with the aim of intimidating the government and dissuading people from accepting institutional roles in opposition to Los Zetas' interests.

It was two in the afternoon on June 8, 2005, when Alejandro Domínguez Coello, a former typographer, fifty-six years old, took over as chief of police in the city of Nuevo Laredo. "I'm not tied to anyone," he declared. "My only obligation is to the citizens of this city." Six hours later, as he was getting into his pickup, a Los Zetas commando unloaded thirty large-caliber bullets into him. His body wasn't identified right away because his face had been completely obliterated.

On July 29, 2009, at five in the morning, two cars stopped in front of Veracruz and Boca del Río deputy police chief Jesús Antonio Romero Vázquez's home: About ten Zetas men, armed with AK-47s and grenade launchers, got out and stormed the house. It took them a few minutes to kill Romero Vázquez, his wife (also a police officer), and their seven-year-old son. Then they set the house on fire, killing his three daughters as well, the oldest of whom was fifteen.

Rodolfo Torre Cantú, a gubernatorial candidate in the state of Tamaulipas with the Partido Revolucionario Institucional, or PRI (Institutional Revolutionary Party), was killed on June 28, 2010, six days before the election. His killers, armed with AK-47s, attacked his car on the way to the airport in Ciudad Victoria, the capital of Tamaulipas. He had been planning on going to Matamoros to wind up his campaign. Four people traveling with him were also killed, and four others wounded. According to witnesses, the killers' vehicle—a 4 x 4—had an unmistakable Z painted on the windows. But after their statements appeared in the papers, a man who identified himself as the "Los Zetas press officer" contacted several local papers to say that Los Zetas were not responsible for Torre Cantú's murder. Investigations are still under way, but Los Zetas are among the primary suspects.

When they carry out operations, Los Zetas wear dark clothes, paint their faces black, drive stolen SUVs, and often put on federal police uniforms. In Acapulco in early 2007 they disguised themselves as soldiers and killed five police officers and two administrative assistants. On April 16, 2007, in Reynosa, six men dressed as Tamaulipas ministerial police—maybe Zetas men in disguise or maybe corrupt police officers in the pay of the cartel—aboard five SUVs and carrying R-15 rifles, which are used exclusively by the armed forces, stopped four AFI agents (Agencia Federal de Investigación, the Mexican equivalent of

FBI agents until July 2012, when they were replaced by the new PFM, Policía Federal Ministerial) whom the Los Zetas cartel accused of having ties to a "rival gang." In fact, a few days earlier the agents had burst into the El Cincuenta y Siete discotheque in Reynosa, right before the singer Gloria Trevi's show was to begin, and handcuffed and removed seven hit men who were in the service of the Zetas. The fake ministerial police made the AFI agents get into an SUV. They beat them and took them to China, a small town in the state of Nuevo León, a known Zetas stronghold, intending to kill them. They didn't realize that one of the agents, Luis Solís, had a cell phone in his pocket. While his kidnappers were momentarily distracted, Solís took out his cell and dialed Commander Puma at AFI headquarters: "We've been kidnapped by Los Zetas, they're taking us to China, they're going to kill us." The message was received. Meanwhile, the four agents were transferred to a *casa de seguridad*, one of the places the Zetas use to torture their victims before finishing them off. Here the agents were kicked and beaten, including by the illustrious El Hummer, head of the Zetas in the Reynosa area. The kidnappers were convinced that the agents were in the service of a rival cartel and wanted to make them confess. But the agents didn't talk, so they were drugged and taken to another safe house—for electric shock treatment. But when Los Zetas got wind of the fact that federal agents were searching everywhere for their men, they decided to rid themselves of the agents, and let them go. "We survived by the hand of God," the agents allegedly said after they were freed.

When Los Zetas kill their enemies, they are sadistic, their revenge exemplary: They burn bodies, stuff them into barrels filled with diesel oil, dismember them. In January 2008 in San Luis Potosí, during a roundup that led to the arrest of Héctor Izar Castro, alias El Teto, considered the leader of the local Zetas cell, weapons of all sorts were found, along with three paddles with a raised letter Z on them: This way, when they beat their victims their mark is imprinted on their skin. To terrify their rivals they often cut off their victims' genitals and stuff them in their mouths, and hang headless bodies from bridges. In early January 2010 Hugo Hernández, thirty-six years old, was kidnapped in the state of Sonora, taken to Los Mochis in nearby Sinaloa, killed, and cut into seven pieces by men from a rival cartel. The victim's face was skinned, fixed to a soccer ball, and left in a plastic bag near city hall with a note: "Have a Happy New Year, because this one will be your last." Other body parts were found in two plastic barrels: in one his torso; in the other his arms, legs, and faceless skull. Dismemberment is the language of Los Zetas. They make bodies disappear inside already occupied tombs, or bury them in clandestine cemeteries within their strongholds, or dump them in mass graves. They often bury their victims alive. Or dissolve them in acid.

Los Zetas are bloodthirsty assassins, yet they have one characteristic in common with normal kids thousands of miles away: They love television, that dangerous teacher. Violent films and reality shows are cultural reference points. One day in San Fernando, a village about eighty-five miles from the U.S.-Mexico border, Los Zetas stopped several buses traveling along Highway 101 and made the passengers get off and fight like gladiators, armed with clubs and knives. Whoever survived was guaranteed a place with Los Zetas. Whoever succumbed was buried in a mass grave. In spring 2011, such a grave was discovered in San Fernando; it contained 193 corpses, the victims all killed with powerful blows to the head.

And this sadistic carnage occurred just a few months after what has become known as the First San Fernando Massacre. More innocent victims, more mass graves: August 24, 2010. More than seventy illegal immigrants from South and Central America were trying to cross the U.S. border at Tamaulipas. We know about them from a man from Ecuador who survived. In San Fernando he and his companions were joined by a group of Mexicans claiming to be Los Zetas. They herded the immigrants onto a farm and started beating them up. One by one. They either hadn't paid the "toll" for crossing the border into Los Zetas territory or—more likely—they hadn't accepted the Zetas' "request" that they work for them. Los Zetas don't take no for an answer. They shot the immigrants in the head. The Ecuadorian was wounded in the neck and played dead, but later he managed to escape and miraculously reached a roadblock manned by the Mexican army. The soldiers, following his directions, went to the farm and had a shoot-out with Los Zetas. When it was over they found the seventy-two bodies: fifty-eight men and fourteen women, all piled in a heap.

Los Zetas are notoriously the masters of violence, but they're learning at their own expense that they can be surpassed by their pupils. Some of Los Zetas' rival cartels began to not just cut their enemies' heads off but to replace them with pigs' heads and—of course—post the video on the Internet.

Ferocity is learned. Ferocity works by its own rules. Ferocity spreads, like an invading army. Los Zetas and Ángel Miguel know this. Now I know it too.

# COKE #4

Like something sacred, whose name cannot be uttered,

like a secret lover you hold close in your thoughts,

like an empty surface where every word can be written,

such is the one you seek, evoke, call out to in a thousand ways.

Her every name is a desire and a driving force,

a metaphor, an ironic illusion.

She'll make you joyful and desperate, she's the one you want

at all times, all places, all ways.

In America, you can call her *24/7*,

like your neighborhood drugstore,

or *Aspirin*, like that effervescent

that makes you feel better, and in Italy *Vitamin C*

because it's how you cure your cold.

C is her letter—

you can simply call her that—

or *Charlie,*

the C all pilots and radio operators know.

Or at the take-away of desires,

order *Number 3,* the third letter,

punch in *C-game, C-dust,* or call her *Caine,*

her second syllable, which sounds like Cain.

Choose any female name with C:

*Corinne Connie Cora Cory* or most common of all *Carrie,*

the girl who grabs you and carries you away.

She's a *Cadillac,* a *Viaje,* a voyage.

In Turkish a line is *Otoban,* highway,

*la Veloce, Svelta;* Ускоритель, uskoritel', the accelerator,

Энергия, pure energy, *Dynamite.*

She loves B, explosive and sensual.

She's *Blast, Bomb, Boost,*

she's *Bonza, Bubbazza, Binge, Bouncing Powder,*

in Spanish you'll *Bailar* till dawn.

And when you're too paranoid to speak,

dial *256* on your cell—

it's the same as BLO or *Blow* or snort.

She makes you feel good,

she's *Big Bloke, Big C, Big Flake, Big Rush.*

She'll make you feel like a god,

so *Dios* is what she's called in Latin America,

but she's also *Diablo*, *Diablito* too, Little Devil.

*Devil's Dandruff* is cocaine powder,

while crack is *Devil's Drug*, you smoke it

with the *Devil's Dick*.

Regular coke can be *Monster*,

*Cat Piss*, *A Visit to the House of Horrors*,

but that's not what you're looking for,

what you want is the exact opposite:

*Paradise*, *Alas de Angel*, *Polvere di Stelle*,

*Polvo Feliz*, *Polvo de Oro*, *Star-Spangled Powder*,

*Heaven Dust* or *Haven Dust*, an inhalable oasis of peace.

*Happy Powder*, *Happy Dust*, *Happy Trail*.

She's a *Dream*, a *Beam*, a ray of light.

She's *Aire*, she'll make you feel so light.

She's *Breath*, *Soffio*, *Soplo*,

Or simply *Sobre*, with her you're always on.

Call her *Angie*, your most angelic friend,

or *Aunt Nora*, your aunt who bakes cakes.

In Brazil she's *Gulosa*,

so sweet, those sweets kids go crazy for:

*Icing* on the top of a cake,

*Jelly* and *Jam*, those secret jars of marmalade,

*Candy* and *Candy C*, *Bubble Gum*, *Double Bubble*,

—you can blow double with the best chewing gum—

*Granita, Mandorlata, Cubaita, Dolcetto,*

*California Cornflakes, Bernie's Cornflakes,* or *Cereal.*

Cornflakes, snow *Flakes,*

Cocaine is always snow.

*Snow*                              *Snö*

*Schnee*            Снег             *Sne*

*Neige*

*Nieve*


Wherever snow falls, coke is snow,

but you can also call it *Florida Snow,*

as miraculous as a Miami snowfall.

It's Свежий—svezhij, fresh

but it can turn to *Ice,* and make your veins run cold.

She is *Snow White,* the fairest of them all—

but you don't envy her because you lay her down

on the mirror of your desires.

Or simply *Bianca*

*Blanca*

*Blanche,*

*Branca* and *Branquinha* in Brazil

*Beyaz Ten,* white skin in Turkey

in Russia белая лошадь—Belaja loshadj, white horse

*White Girl, White Tornado, White Lady,*

*White Dragon, White Ghost, White Boy, White Powder*

*Polvere Bianca, Polvo Blanca, Poudre, Pudra* in Turkish

Whatever looks like *Sugar*

*Azúcar, Toz şeker,* that powder Turkish Delight is coated in.

But she looks like flour too,

Мука, Mukà, in Russian or 白粉—Bai fen in China.

And whatever sounds like her,

*Cocco, Coconut, Coco* in French, кокос—kokos

or Кекс—Keks, the Russian tea cake, but above all Кокс—

*Koks* in German and Swedish as well.

That ancient name means nothing now

though she's still there to warm you,

those old coal stoves no longer exist

so now when you say *Coke* (in English or French)

you no longer think of fuel for the poor.

Now she's *Coke* like Coca-Cola,

though it's Coca-Cola that took her name.

So she adopted all sorts of ways of referring

to that famous pop: *Cola* in Danish,

*Kola* in Swedish and Turkish,

Кока in Serbia and Russia.

And then, sometimes, I don't know why, she turns into an animal.

You can call her *Coniglio,* maybe because she's magic

like the rabbit that gets pulled out of the hat, or *Krava,* cow, in Croatian,

in Spanish *Perico* or *Perica,* parrot,

maybe because she makes you more loquacious,

or the *Gato* who makes you purr.

*Farlopa*—her most common slang—

or *Calcetin*, sock, or *Cama*, bed,

because she makes you dream, or *Tierra*, the ground under your feet.

If you blow the cheapest stuff

she'll be your old friend *Paco*, in Italy *Fefè*,

while in Russia you can call her коля, Kolja,

in the United States she's *Bernie*, but also *Cecil*,

a more haughty name, or you can call her *Henry VIII*

the great English king.

You can make a fuss over her,

call her *Baby* or *Bebé*.

But more than any other drug,

it's a *Love Affair* with a beautiful lady,

*Fast White Lady, Lady, Lady C,*

*Lady Caine, Lady Snow, Peruvian Lady,*

she's the *Dama Blanca*, the *Mujer*,

the woman par excellence,

she's *Girl* and *Girlfriend*,

your *Novia*, your fiancée.

There's no one like her,

so you can even call her *Mama Coca*;

or simply say *She* or *Her*,

she's pure, purely herself.

She consumes her names like she consumes her lovers

So this list is nothing but a taste,

so call her any way you want,

No matter what name you choose, she'll come when you call.

# 8

# THE PUSHER

"It's bitter on the tongue, and you'll feel like you've just been given novacaine."

It's the most common way of consuming coke in the Andes. Strip the central veins from a few leaves, put them in your mouth, and chew them slowly, wetting them with saliva and mashing them into a ball. Then add a pinch of ash—slightly alkaline—from the burned plants. It goes by various names, *tocra* and *llipta* being the most common.

"If you do *basuco* it means you're really in a bad way, because *basuco*'s the waste product from the extraction process, and it's made with harmful chemical substances."

*Basuco* is what prison inmates use, because it's really cheap. It often makes its way behind bars on the wings of a homing pigeon. Somebody on the outside paper clips a little bag under the bird's wings and trains the bird to fly to a window, where a prisoner will be delighted to receive it, either for himself or to sell. Sometimes the pigeon's wings are so loaded with the stuff that it crashes into the prison wall. *Basuco* is made with the worst quality ingredients: brick dust, acetone, insecticide, lead, amphetamine, and red gas. It's an intermediate product. The leaves are cut, then the paste is extracted from them. *Basuco's* the by-product of the second phase of production, the crude product, but some people don't seem to mind.

"If you do snow, you have to add hydrochloric acid to the paste and treat it with acetone or ethanol."

Snow is cocaine hydrochloride. Whitish, bitter-tasting flakes that are ground into white powder. You snort it, or at most shoot it up, usually twenty, thirty, even fifty milligrams, though regulars might get up to a hundred milligrams a hit.

"If you do crack you have to add to snow a watery solution, made up of ammonia and sodium hydroxide or sodium bicarbonate, basic substances in other words, and then you filter the whole thing."

Crack is smoked in a special pipe, usually made of glass; it heats up and then you inhale the vapors. Or, more often, it's smoked together with other substances, such as marijuana, tobacco, or phencyclidine— angel dust—but you have to mix it really well first. It works fast, in just a few seconds, and it's highly addictive: The drug dealer's dream and the drug addict's nightmare, is what they say about crack.

"To freebase, you have to dissolve the mixture with ether or other volatile solvents, but then you have to wait till the solvent evaporates."

As with crack, you need a special pipe, a water pipe or *narguile* (hookah). Freebase, which is also called "rock," takes effect immediately; you start feeling euphoric as soon as it reaches your brain, but a little later you become irritable, partly because the effect wears off in a few minutes, making you want to get high again.

"*Erythroxylaceae.* That's what the primary material is called. I'll give you fifty euros if you can say it without stuttering."

The unpronounceable Latin name of this family of plants is the common denominator for all forms of cocaine consumption. This plant family has more than 250 species, but two in particular interest me, because they're where cocaine comes from: *Erythroxylum coca* and *Erythroxylum novogranatense.* The leaves of these plants contain from 0.3 percent to 1.4 percent alkaloids, including the tropane alkaloids that produce the effects of cocaine on your brain. *Erythroxylum coca* is native to the Peruvian Andes, but it now flourishes even in the tropical zones of eastern Peru, Ecuador, and Bolivia. Its main variety—which is also the most common one—is *Huánuco*, Bolivian coca. It's also the most prized: Its leaves are big and firm, dark green with yellowish tips. The second species, *Erythroxylum novogranatense*, comes from the mountainous regions of Colombia, the Caribbean, and northern Peru, areas that are drier, more arid. *Erythroxylum novogranatense* has two principal varieties: Colombian coca and Peruvian coca, the latter is called *Truxillo*; its leaves are smaller and more tapering than *Huánuco's*, light green with grayish tips. But you don't need fancy lab tests to identify these two species. Just put a bit in your mouth and chew: If you feel a slight numbing effect, you've got a good one, one that contains alkaloid. *Huánuco* and *Truxillo*, the protagonists of global commerce.

So many names to say the same thing: cocaine. Cocaine, which travels from producer to consumer, which goes from leaves to the white powder, which is passed deftly from hand to hand. From chemicals to street life. From the Andean farmer to a pusher who, once he'd explained his products, talked business to me:

"The target. Walk around Milan, Rome, New York, Sydney, and you have to slalom your way among men who are packaged in suits selected by fashion managers—that's what people who know these things call them—they choose quality fabrics, how many stripes, how much space between them, their initials monogrammed on their fashionable business shirts. One hand in their pocket, the other clutching their iPhone, eyes focused six feet ahead so as not to trip, or step in dog shit. If you don't get out of their way, they'll run right into you, but they can't say 'excuse me' or even gesture courteously, because then they'd lose the flow, and everything would go to hell. Eventually you learn to weave around them, like in those old video games where you swing your spaceship around with a touch of the joystick to avoid getting hit by the asteroids that are flying at you. Same thing: You rotate your chest and your shoulders follow, turning sideways, and you slip past, barely brushing the guy's cashmere jacket, and your gaze lands on his sleeve; he's missing a button, and he sees that you noticed it and thinks you think he forgot and that he's not a true gentleman, but I know that an open buttonhole is one of the characteristics of custom-made menswear, the sign that you're part of an elite. I dodge him and then lengthen my stride, and he keeps walking straight ahead, talking the whole time, and the word I keep hearing is 'target.' The target has to be identified, chosen, hit, bombarded, made to surface."

That's how the pusher talked to me. He's sold a lot. And not on some street corner, either. A pusher's almost never the way you imagine he'll be. That's what I keep saying, when I write or when I talk to someone about this stuff: It's not the way you imagine. Pushers are seismographs of taste. They know how and where to sell. The better the pusher is, the easier he moves up and down the social ladder. There's no such thing as a pusher for everyone. There's the pusher who sells on the street, with a monthly paycheck and an assigned zone, who deals to strangers. There's the pusher who delivers right to your door; all you have to do is text him. There are kid pushers. Nigerians, Slavs, Maghrebs, Latinos. Just as an aristocratic lady would never step foot in a discount store on the outskirts of town, there are pushers for every type of customer, pushers for gentlemen and pushers for down-and-outs, for rich students and day laborers, for wallflowers and extroverts, for space cadets and scaredy-cats.

There are pushers who get their goods from a "base," which is usually made up of four or five people. Bases are independent cells with strong ties to organized crime, because that's where the drugs come from. Bases are intermediaries between criminal organizations and street pushers; they're the ones who supply the stuff already cut, ready for retail, and they're an insurance of sorts for the organizations: If the base fails or its members get arrested, the next level up doesn't feel the effects, because those down below don't know enough about them.

The bourgeois pusher, on the other hand, has a direct relationship with an organization affiliate, but he doesn't get a regular paycheck. He has a sort of deposit account instead. The more he sells, the more he earns. And it's rare that he ends up with any unsold goods. The bourgeois pusher's strength lies in the fact that he can create his own personal workforce over time. He uses fake names with his clients, or if he's already known, he's selective about who he sells to. When he can he prefers to hire people who have their own circle. The circle is made up of people whose day jobs are something other than dealing: The pusher supplies them, and they use their own contacts to create a regular clientele, usually made up of friends, girlfriends, lovers. The bourgeois pusher's workers never sell coke to someone new. It's a layered organization in which the pusher knows only the people closest to him and can never grasp the whole chain. That way, if someone were to talk, only one person would pay. That's the way it always is in the world of cocaine. You want to know as little as possible.

At the bottom distribution level is the retailer, the one at the train station or on the street corner. He's like a gas station. He often keeps balls of coke in his mouth, wrapped in plastic or tinfoil. If the police arrive, he swallows them. Some dealers won't risk having the plastic break and their stomachs becoming a painful sore, so they keep the balls in their pocket. Retailers make their fortunes on weekends, Valentine's Day, or when the local team wins. The more there is to celebrate, the more they sell. Like wine bars and pubs.

The pusher who taught me how to choose a target thought of himself as a pharmacist rather than a cocaine dealer:

"Every business has its target; the formula for success is in finding the right one, and once you do, you have to unleash all your firepower on it, drop the napalm and swallow up needs and desires, that's the goal of the modern man who dresses according to the canons of the fashion manager. It's exhausting dealing with a fragmented market, where the niches keep multiplying; they come and go in the space of a week, replaced by others that maybe last even less, and you have to anticipate them, prepare your weapons in time; if not, you risk firing your precious napalm on empty territory. I attract my target. Targets, rather—plural—because, even though there's only one product, the needs are many. So a woman came to see me this morning, she was probably pretty cute years ago, but now she's all skin and bones, she doesn't look so healthy; I wouldn't fuck her even if she paid me; the only signs of life on her are her veins, they bulge out all along her forearms, her calves, her neck, but underneath she's all flabby; it's like she has chicken skin. She told me her name is Laura, a fake name, obviously, but she's got nice, high, round cheekbones that light up her face, I really like cheekbones; they're the sentinels of the face; they either let you in or repel you, it depends. In the case of Laura, they invite familiarity, and in fact, she told me once that at her gym she heard there's this quick, easy, and—all things considered—fairly risk-free way to lose weight. It's true, I said; why go buying those sci-fi gadgets for your abs, or running in the evening, and then eating only protein because some French luminary decided that's the way it has to be? Laura's sentinel cheekbones relaxed and she smiled at me. I've seen her every week since then, and every time those beautiful cheekbones seem like they've been sanded, and now those sweet sentinels of her face are like menacing halberds.

"It was Laura who introduced me to the Connoisseur, one of those snobs with shabby clothes, his Moncler torn and full of burn marks, who when they greet you, even if it's for the first time, they pull you close, press their right shoulder up against your left, like some kind of tribal salute of belonging, then they pat you on the back, all very cool. He never wanted to tell me his name, not even a fake one, call me 'friend,' he says, as if we were in some alleyway in the Bronx. I nearly laugh in his face, but I control myself, and I have to even more when he tells me he wants some Pearl. The Connoisseur's referring to the most precious blow, 95 percent pure, maybe more: It's silky to the touch, creamy almost, and so white it shines like a pearl. I've never even seen it, some people say it doesn't exist, others that it's super rare because it's still made by hand by a small group of campesinos who use only two tools: time and patience. Time for the leaves to mature and patience to wait for the right moment to harvest them. But it doesn't end there, because then you have to press everything by hand, package it in virgin oil, no impurities or noxious substances, work it with acetone, ether, and ethanol, never with hydrochloric acid or ammonia; you don't want to risk damaging the active ingredient. If you do it right—ten days of work, sweat, and swearing—you get that pearly tone that's so sought after. Of course I have it, I say to the Connoisseur; I don't even try to steer him toward something more feasible, like Fish Scales; it's not as pure as Pearl, but it has come my way, and I can say that its shine really does remind you of a freshly caught fish, and I don't even dream of pushing him toward more crude varieties like Almond-flavored, or toward Stone—even though it is 80 percent pure—and I refuse even to take into consideration variants like Cat's Piss or Mariposa. Guys like the Connoisseur have granite wills and—luckily—zero expertise; if not, he wouldn't come back after I palm off some mediocre stuff cut with glass powder on him. It sparkled, he tells me every time, and I nod knowingly; I don't even have to pretend anymore, it's so natural now. Obviously I don't always say yes; I can't let word get around that you can always get everything from me. I'd risk inflation; I'd risk losing control of my targets, and then someone ends up having a heart attack."

Cocaine can be altered—cut, or stepped—with various substances, which get added to the drug either during production or, more simply, mixed with the final product, with the white powder. There are three kinds of cut: active cuts, done with substances that produce the same psychoactive effects as cocaine; cosmetic cuts, with substances that reproduce some of cocaine's collateral effects; and inert cuts, with products that increase volume without creating damaging effects. People may think they're snorting good quality stuff, but they're really paving their nostrils with concrete. Active cuts are made with amphetamines or other stimulants, such as caffeine, that enhance and prolong the effect of the drug, as in the case of Chalk—low quality cocaine that's dressed up with amphetamines. Cosmetic cuts use pharmaceuticals and local anesthetics, such as lidocaine and ephedrine, that reproduce some of the same collateral effects as coke. When you just want to increase the volume to get more doses and make more money, you use innocuous substances, such as flour and lactose. The most commonly used substance for inert cuts is mannitol, a laxative gentle enough for children and the elderly that, other than in appearance, has nothing in common with cocaine.

"One of my most loyal customers just got back from the United States. He says blow there's 30 percent."

"Thirty percent?"

"Yeah, the active ingredient is 30 percent. But I say it's a load of crock. I know places in Paris where it's 5 percent. And in Italy some pushers sell balls of coke where the active ingredient's practically nonexistent. But they're real cheats."

Over the years I've seen just about everything there is to see in drug distribution. In Europe the average ranges from 25 percent to 43 percent; some countries come in lower, Denmark at 18 percent and England and Wales at 20. But these figures could change at any time.

The cut is where the real money is made, because it's the cut that makes a line of coke precious, and it's the cut that ruins nostrils. In London some bourgeois pushers hide quality coke in garages to put on the market when drug seizures make for a shortage of goods and as a consequence everybody starts cutting it, lowering the quality. At that point you can sell the really good stuff for four times as much. In an economy in which supply and demand fluctuate so rapidly, the cut becomes the discriminating factor. The distributor can cut it, with the approval of the Mafia family. The base is allowed to cut only in extreme cases, and only with the authorization of the distributer. The pusher who cuts is a dead pusher.


"I took some courses; I crashed one of those clinics where people who want to quit are bullied with statistics, like 25 percent of heart attacks in people between the ages of eighteen and forty-five are caused by my product. If you ask me, these courses spew a lot of bullshit. But I did learn something. It acts on your neurons, makes your nervous system go haywire, and over time it damages it. In other words, it pisses your brain away. And that's not all: It's dangerous for your heart too; all it needs is an extra chaser to make it collapse, and if the product's washed down with a Long Island or a Negroni or a Jack Daniel's, or accompanied by little blue pills, well, then it's like stepping on the gas on a curve. You also have to consider that cocaine is a vasoconstrictor; it constricts your blood vessels, anesthetizes you. All these effects happen pretty much right away, depending on how you do it: If you shoot up, it starts taking effect before you even realize it; if you smoke crack or freebase, it's a little slower but still really fast; and if you snort, it hits you a second later."

I ask him about the good moments.

"The good moments? It wakes you up right away, raises your attention level, gives you energy, you're less tired, you don't even feel the need to sleep, eat, or drink. But that's not all: It improves your sense of self, you feel happy, you want to do things, you're euphoric, and any pain you might have disappears. And you lose your inhibitions, so it ups your sex drive, makes you more daring. And what's more, coke doesn't make you feel like a drug addict. A cocaine addict's nothing like a heroin addict. People who snort cocaine are users, not junkies. They satisfy a need and then get on with life."

But then he starts right in on the bad moments.

"If you do it a lot, you heart goes crazy, you have panic attacks, it's easy to get depressed, you become irascible for no reason, even paranoid at times. Since you don't sleep or eat much, you tend to lose weight. If you snort a lot for several years, you risk fucking up your nostrils. I know people who had to get their nasal septum redone because they snorted so much. I also know people who died: One dose too many and you have a heart attack. It's common knowledge, after all; it's not like I discovered hot water or something, but when I heard them say that if

you use my product you can't get it up anymore, I was, I mean, it's not
like I have that sort of problem, but a good chunk of my customers
come to me precisely for this reason, and they all keep coming back;
they're really charged up, they tell me they fuck for hours, they have
orgasms that electrify them from their heads to their toes, they do
things they'd only ever seen in porn movies, things they'd never even
dreamed of doing—a whole tribe of horny customers who, before they
met me, would come after two minutes, and now they're really having
a grand time. I had to understand, but it's not like I could ask them flat
out, guys don't talk willingly about certain things, and so I asked a
woman friend of mine, she's real tough and asks me for a bit of blow
every now and then, but only because she's finishing up med school and
has to study all night, because she works as a cashier during the day to
pay the tuition. With me she calls herself Butterfly, because she has a
butterfly tattoo on one cheek; I asked her to show it to me, because I
didn't believe her, but she always refused. The fact remains that we
agree to meet at the usual place, and as usual, she's all elusive because
she has a million things to do, but I stop her, ask her how things are
going with her boyfriend, and then I wink, I feel like an idiot, but I
don't know how else to broach the subject, and luckily she understands
and asks me how come I want to know, what's it to me? I tell her I'm
just curious, that she's important to me, her pleasure's important, and I
wink again when I say pleasure, but this time I feel less idiotic, like I've
gotten her attention. What's on your mind? she says, and at that point
I tell her the situation, that I heard it said that my product isn't so good
for those kinds of things, and so I'm conducting a sort of market survey,
that's all. And she does something real strange: She takes my hand and
drags me to a bar, orders a couple of beers, and lights a cigarette. The
bartender sees her and tries to tell her she can't smoke, but she tells him
not to bust her balls, so he retreats behind the counter and goes back to
serving cappuccino. And she tells me about her boyfriend: At first it
was really fabulous, so good it was almost scary, he'd have these amazing erections, Guinness world book of records, sex that would make the

Italian Stallion jealous—but then it was all over. His dick, she says, is as flaccid as a sausage left to boil too long; it takes hours for him to get hard, and if she tries to touch him, it's like he doesn't even feel it; it's like the heat's gone and his blood vessels are pumping ice water. He's superdepressed about it; all he does is apologize; he can't even masturbate when he's alone. So now he's taking Viagra, a small dose at first, just twenty-five milligrams, then he upped it to a hundred, but it's no good; he still only gets half hard, and he can't come. There's just no way to make him come, and it's painful, all that built-up energy that can't explode, it hurts like hell, and fucking for hours, waiting for him to finally blow, isn't exactly fun for her either. He's being treated by an andrologist, he confessed to using my product, and the doctor didn't bat an eye; he said lots of people come to him with the same problem, and the only solution is to ditch my product, but it's not easy. Butterfly talks freely, and I start putting the pieces together, and I realize I'm raising an army of sexually depressed men who just keep upping their doses on the remote chance they'll get hard. Fuck, I wanted to shout, if it weren't such an inappropriate thing to say right then. And then Butterfly tells me that women use it too, for the same reason, because it gets you aroused, really revved up, but from the point of view of sex it's a disaster, because one of the product's side effects is that it's also an excellent anesthetic; it's one thing if you rub a bit on your wisdom tooth that's coming in, but if you stop reaching orgasm, which is already difficult enough under normal circumstances, well, that's a whole different story. Not to mention, Butterfly continues, the things you do and then regret, like that time her boyfriend confessed to her that he was a bit too high one evening and ended up with a trans, that he'd always fantasized about it but never had the courage to do it. The courage? I say, and Butterfly nods, then after a minute of silence I ask her if she'll let me see her tattoo this time, and she smiles and stands between the tables, unbuttons her pants, and lowers her underwear. What can I say? She wasn't lying.

"I didn't stop walking, elbowing my way among those men dressed according to the latest dictates of business fashion, and I didn't stop my targets from coming to see me, but I didn't stop learning what's behind my product either; I see new faces, and the old ones fade away and get lost, who knows where. It's a shitty job."

A shitty job that he knows how to do. He talks about it as if he has already weighed the pros and cons of his profession in his head and has decided to keep the cons to himself. Paranoia, for instance. There are pushers who change cell phones and SIM cards once a week. All it takes is one customer to be a little careless and you're screwed. There are pushers who live like cloistered nuns: no contact with the outside world except when absolutely necessary, and a drastic reduction of one's private life. Girlfriends are particularly dangerous; they can easily guess what your day job is and can easily take revenge by telling someone about it. Some pushers are even more angsted: They spend their free time erasing all traces of themselves—no credit cards or bank accounts, no ATM cards, and never a signature on a piece of paper. Angst and paranoia. Some pushers, in order to quell the anxiety, do the same blow they push, but only end up feeding their angst. And there are pushers, like the one I'm sitting with, who sound like stockbrokers: "I sell Ferraris, not economy cars. You crash sooner in an economy car; in a Ferrari you last a little longer."

There are street pushers who can earn $5,000 a month, and even get a bonus if they sell well. But bourgeois pushers can earn up to $25,000, $40,000 a month.

"The problem's not the amount of money you earn, though; it's that any other job seems impossible, because it would feel like a waste of time. You earn more just by brushing someone's hands than you would working for months and months, no matter what sort of job it is. And knowing that you'll be arrested isn't enough to make you change professions. Even if I were offered a job where I could earn as much as I do now, I don't think I'd take it, because it would undoubtedly take up more of my time. The same is true for those poor souls who deal on the streets. They'd have to put in a lot more time to earn the same amount of money."

I looked at him and asked if he could confirm a sensation I had while listening to his stories, which was that he despises his clients.

"Yes. I liked them at first, because they gave me what I needed. But over time you look at them and you begin to understand. You realize that you could be one of them. You see yourself from the outside, and you're repulsed. I dislike my clients because they remind me too much of myself, or what I would become if I decided to enjoy myself more. And not only does the idea repulse me, it scares me."

# 9

# BEAUTY AND THE MONKEY

Evolutionary transformation is fueled by vacuums. The story of drug trafficking in Colombia is one of vacuums, transformations, and capitalism.

Today what was once a vacuum is swarming, like a plot of ground under the entomologist's lens. Swarming with hundreds of microcartels. Armed organizations that give themselves names that sound like local sports teams. Communist guerrillas who increasingly play the paradoxical role of large landowners, of plantation and production managers. Each one develops his own specialty, carves out his own slice of the action: production, distribution, transportation. Each one defends his own little corner of jungle, mountain, coast, or border. It's all disconnected, parceled out, ground up. Today the doses of territory, and the spread of power and alliances, for which blood still flows, seem infinitesimal compared to the heyday of the big cartels.

But if the Colombia of drug trafficking today seems like the land of the Lilliputians to Gulliver, the problem is partly in the eye of the beholder. Or in his mind, rather; in his memory. Eyes see what they expect to see, or they gather in the remains. What they see is based on what they no longer see. So if there aren't any more big showdowns or massacres, if cartels no longer carry out attacks on presidential candidates or no longer finance presidential elections, if Colombia is no longer a narco-state, and if the big players are all dead or sentenced to life in the United States, you might think the war has been won. Well, maybe not completely won, but at least well on the way to victory.

Or your gaze might get stuck in the past: Since "cocaine" and "Colombia" are still synonymous—a denomination of origin as inherent as Scotch whiskey or Russian caviar—the imagination continues to picture Colombian drug lords as the most powerful, the richest, the most terrifying in the world. But no regular person knows the names of the big traffickers anymore, or of the major organizations operating in Colombia. And yet, despite decades spent battling the Colombian narcos, the market share the country has lost is much less than one might expect in this era of global commerce. This apparent paradox makes it extremely difficult to grasp the current reality, to see its actual dimensions.

The alleged Lilliputians are no longer the absolute lords of cocaine, but it's calculated that Colombia continues to produce around 60 percent of the cocaine consumed worldwide. And coca plants continue to take root in every cultivatable clod of Colombian soil.

How can this be? What does it mean?

The first answer is elementary, the basic principle of capitalism. If demand holds, if, in fact, it continues to grow, it would be absurd to cut off the supply, or even to reduce it significantly.

The second answer is that the decline of the Colombian cartels corresponded to the rise of the Mexican cartels and of all the new, powerful players in the criminal economy. Today the Sinaloa cartel directs the cultivation and production of coca plants, cocaine paste, and cocaine in Colombia just as multinational corporations direct the cultivation and processing of fruit.

But all this does not fully explain what happened in Colombia. It's important to understand, though. Important because Colombia represents a matrix of the criminal economy, and its transformations reveal the full adaptive capacity of a system that has one fixed constant: white powder. Men die, armies disintegrate, but coke remains. This, in short, is the story of Colombia.

In the beginning there was Pablo, Pablo Escobar. Before Pablo, the drug trade was on the rise in Colombia, with its ideal conditions for producing, storing, and transporting cocaine. But it was in the hands of "coke cowboys," who were too weak to impose their own rules and too scattered geographically to impose the law of the strongest. There was a vacuum, and Pablo filled it right away. The first evolutionary step in Colombian drug trafficking began with this ambitious young man, who was determined to become so rich that he'd have more influence than the president. Starting from nothing he accumulated wealth, gained respect, and conceived of the first cocaine distribution network, using small boats and single-engine planes. To safeguard his operation he relied on an old Colombian saying: *plata o plomo*, money or lead. If you were a police officer or a politician, you either accepted his bribe or you were dead. For Pablo, who became Medellín's godfather, the cocaine business was simple: All you had to do was take a walk in the poor barrios and enlist the kids, who were ready to do anything—bribe people here and there, or pay off a friendly banker to help you bring the money you laundered back in. He said as much himself: "Everybody has a price. The important thing is to figure out what it is." The vacuum filled quickly, and the Colombian system became a monopoly, its distribution network extending to the most important points on the American continent. Everything was done in high style: intercontinental flights crammed with cocaine; affable customs officers who let in thousands of containers of flowers full of white powder; submarines for really big shipments; even an ultramodern tunnel that ran from Ciudad Juárez to El Paso, Texas, the private property of a millionaire who lived more than twenty-five hundred miles away. Colombia ruled; Pablo

Escobar ruled. And the godfather of Medellín reached an agreement with the godfather of Guadalajara. Mexico looked, learned, pocketed its percentage, and waited its turn.

By the early 1980s Pablo was making half a million dollars a day; he had ten accountants. The Medellín cartel was spending twenty-five hundred dollars a month just on elastic bands to bundle its rolls of cash. This was capitalism at its beginning. Large concentrations of wealthy entrepreneurs were laying down the law and penetrating every fiber of society. It was a conservative capitalism, in which the captains of industry vied with one another in flaunting their power and their wealth, without skimping on gifts for the people. Pablo had four hundred public housing units built, and he opened a spectacular public zoo right on his estate, Hacienda Nápoles. Robin Hood capitalists—unscrupulous, bloodthirsty, ruthless spendthrifts. Capitalists in their infancy, though, at the top of rigid pyramidal structures. They felt like giants and considered themselves the incarnations of a sovereign power they'd earned with money and lead—the only legitimate form of power. Pablo even offered to eliminate all of Colombia's public debt, because the country was already his, because the government of Medellín was stronger and wealthier than that of Bogotá. So if the government caused them any trouble they felt justified in waging a head-on war: car bombs, killings, attacks on enemy politicians and judges. A presidential candidate—the front-runner—was assassinated. But Escobar and his faithful failed to realize that the very thing they believed to be a show of strength was actually their weak spot. A body rots once its head is cut off. When Pablo fell, his organization died, creating another vacuum.

The vacuum Pablo's death created was a warning sign: Colombian drug trafficking had to take another evolutionary step. Like capitalism itself, it had to adapt to changes, incorporate social and economic mutations, free itself of tradition, and cross the threshold of modernity. A new species of narco was ready; in fact, it had already begun to proliferate, colonizing more and more territory. Flanked by powerful natural allies, it didn't have to bleed itself dry in its battle to gain control. Pablo had been a real macho, a striking symbol of untamed sexuality. But now that dominant stereotype was broken, thanks to Hélmer "Pacho" Herrera, one of the bosses of the neohegemonic Cali cartel. Openly gay, Pacho wouldn't have been able to take two steps under Pablo. But for the Rodríguez Orejuela brothers who founded the Cali cartel, business is business, and if a homosexual can pave the way for Mexico, can plant distribution cells right in New York City, then who cares who he sleeps with. Even women were accepted. Medellín's old sayings fell out of use: People stopped saying that all women did was spend money and spoil business. Women knew how to do everything, and they did—from money laundering to important negotiations. "Ambition" was no longer a dirty word.

Another difference: Some of Pablo's associates were practically illiterate; they didn't even know who Gabriel García Márquez was, Colombia's greatest writer then living. They were proud that their power had been born of the people, and they needed to identify with them. Cali bosses, on the other hand, recited verses by Colombian poets and knew what an MBA was worth. The new narcos were capitalists just as Pablo's were, but they were more sophisticated. They were at home among the elite of the New World. They played at being honest businessmen, wore elegant clothes, knew how to behave in high circles, and moved about freely. No more bunkers and deluxe homes hidden away somewhere. The new narcos loved the light of day, because that's where they did their business.

The nature of trafficking changed too. Now you had to guarantee shipments, using fake companies or exploiting those legal channels in which it was easy to pass off illegal goods. And then there were the banks. First the Banco de los Trabajadores, then the First Interamericas Bank of Panama, prestigious and respected credit institutions that the new narcos used to launder money from the United States. The more territory they gained in the legal economy, the more maneuvering room they had to grow their cocaine business. Construction companies, factories, investment firms, radio stations, soccer teams, car dealerships, shopping centers. The symbol of this new mentality was a chain of American-style drugstores called Drogas la Rebaja, Discount Drugs.

Pablo's pyramid structure—a dinosaur that had been limping along— had been surpassed. Narco-businesses now established "production objectives," actual multiyear plans. The Cali cartel was divided into five strategic sectors: politics, security, finance, legal support, and drug trafficking.

Violence and terror were not done away with, though: *Plata o plomo* was still the order of the day, but while *plata* still flowed freely, *plomo* had to be weighed more carefully, applied more professionally and with more common sense. Before the hit men were youths yanked out of poverty; now they were former or corrupt soldiers. Well-trained mercenaries. Politics became one of the many sectors of society to finance. The money injected into the political system was like an anesthetic: It paralyzed Congress, making it incapable of mounting any threats while conditioning its actions. The last, weak link that tied drug traffickers to their lands was broken as well. To do business the country must be at peace, a fictitious, papier-mâché peace that needs shaking up every now and then—a warning to remind Colombians that those in charge are always there, even if they're unseen. Henry Loaiza Ceballos, alias the Scorpion, was a real pro in this regard. One day in April 1990 he ordered hundreds of campesinos to be chopped to pieces with chain saws: Under the leadership of Father Tiberio de Jesús Fernández Mafla, the Trujillo parish priest, they had organized a march to protest the armed conflict and call for better living conditions in the countryside. Father Tiberio's body was found—hacked to bits—in a bend in the River Cauca. Before death took him he was forced to witness the rape and murder of his niece. Then Scorpion Loaiza had the priest's fingers cut off and forced him to eat them, along with his toes and his genitals. Father Tiberio is buried in a park honoring the Trujillo victims. The inscription on his tomb—something he'd said during his last Easter mass—is prophetic: "If my blood can help a much-needed peace to be born and blossom in Trujillo, I will spill it gladly."

. . .

To their Italian partners, the use of violence in the New World still seemed excessive, but nonetheless, the Italians were quite happy to form a strong connection with Colombia, to get on well with their new suppliers. The Calabrese mafiosi were as tied to their land as the men of Medellín, yet they shared with the new men of Cali the most salient feature of their success: rule and prosper, without making too much noise. Don't challenge official power, but rather use it, drain it, manipulate it. It was as if they'd been traveling the same road together for a while.

The narco-state expanded and flexed its muscles. Rather than kill a presidential candidate it didn't like, it preferred to buy votes to elect one it did. It contaminated every corner of the country, infecting it like a cancer, mutating it in its own image. By now everybody, including the United States and the magistrates who had not been bribed, realized that Cali had become too bloated. Its fall seemed to obey a law of physics: When more growth was no longer possible, it didn't take much to implode, and Mexico, Colombia's North American cousin, started getting in on the action. The narco-state, presided over by the cartel, starts to vacillate, and then unravel.

The end of the Cali cartel was the last real revolution of Colombian drug lord capitalism. And with it went the whole colossal, systemically pervasive structure. It was like a beam of bright light penetrating the dark shadows for the first time, scattering cockroaches in all directions; friends became enemies, every man for himself. Some Cali cartel deserters joined the Norte del Valle cartel, which from the beginning was merely a pale imitation of the one that preceded it. Brutal without being charismatic, greedy without any particular business skills or inventiveness, incapable of keeping internal rivalries at bay, they were so scared of extradition and the betrayal of informers that they became paranoid. But times were different now. Times had changed because capitalism had changed, and the Colombians were the first to realize it.

The rest of the world was optimistic, euphoric even. It was heading toward the new millennium convinced that peace, democracy, and liberty were destined to conquer the globe. President Bill Clinton was reelected in November 1996, and a few months later Labour Party leader Tony Blair—who was convinced that a social democratic agenda must be coupled with greater free markets in order to keep step with modernity—was elected prime minister in the UK. On Wall Street, until early 1997, the Dow Jones Index climbed to levels never seen before, and the NASDAQ—the world's first electronic stock market, which is dedicated to tech stocks such as Microsoft, Yahoo!, Apple, and Google—was up big. What's more, Steve Jobs had just returned to the helm at Apple, confident he would be able to lead the company out of crisis, and, as we all know, he succeeded brilliantly.

In keeping with the spirit of the times, the euphoric West asked for more and more cocaine. Coke was a white stain on all the optimism. And coke was identified with Colombia. It was unacceptable that in this era of creative capitalism and commerce without borders, a nation could be so rich in resources but so oppressed by a criminal monoculture. The Cali cartel had been taken down, the narco-state had been crushed. Marxist guerrillas holed up with their hostages in the jungle or mountains were an anachronism; they no longer had any reason to exist. The superpower that defeated the world communist bloc thought that all it would take to return Colombia to the free world was a concentrated effort.

The United States didn't attach enough importance to what Mexico had become, right under their noses. Or rather, they realized it only in spurts, in individual daily reports that ended up on this or that desk, disjointed alarms about stability and public safety. Blinded by optimism, they couldn't or didn't want to see that what was emerging in Mexico was nothing other than the dark side of that same global capitalism they were proud to have opened every door to, to have loosened every restriction. Their gaze, also, was imprisoned in the past. Working off a borrowed plot, they wanted to write a happy ending for Colombia's story.

. . .

Latin American stories are complicated. They're not like those Holly-wood tales where the good are good and the bad are bad. Where if you're successful it's because you deserve it, because you earned it with your talent and your skill that, in the end, are nothing more than the fruit of your moral virtue. So it's easier to understand the transition that takes place in Colombia by tracing two success stories.

The first is the story of a woman. The prettiest and most popular girl in the whole country. The girl who all the men dream of having, the girl who all other girls dream of being. The exclusive model for a linge-rie brand and for Colombia's most popular beer. A line of beauty prod-ucts known all over Latin America named after her. Natalia Paris. A sweet face, golden locks, honey-colored skin. Girlishly petite but with explosive breasts and glutes. Feminine perfection in miniature. Natalia is the one who created a new model of beauty, that same mix of playful naïveté and supersexy seduction that Shakira—also short, blond, and Colombian—established all around the world, thanks to her powerful voice and wild wiggles, but Natalia's star rose first. The other story is about a man who as a boy was saddled with a nickname that doesn't do him justice: El Mono, the Monkey. He doesn't have the grotesque fea-tures of a howler or a spider monkey, the most common species in Colombia; at most, his slightly sunken eyes might make you think of a gorilla: There's something frightening in his fixed gaze. His mother is Colombian, his father an Italian who left the town of Sapri to make a better life for himself in the New World. El Mono is named after his father, Salvatore Mancuso, and he fulfilled his father's immigrant dream of integration and success, in his own way.

Both the Beauty and the Monkey were born in cities in the north, the most densely populated and developed part of the country, to fam-ilies that work hard to achieve the relative ease of the middle class. Natalia's father is a pilot who dies when she was only eight months old, but her mother is a woman of vigorous temperament and principles, and she's a lawyer, a career that has given her financial autonomy. Salvatore is the second of six children, his father an electrician who, after years of hard work, manages to open first an appliance repair shop, and then an auto repair shop.

Their parents save in order to send them to good schools, which is also a way of keeping them, as much as possible, away from bad company and street violence. Natalia attends a Catholic boarding school, goes to Boston to study, and enrolls in college with the idea of becoming an advertising agent. But in the meantime, her modeling career takes off. While still a teenager she lands her first important contract: Her radiant smile promotes a toothpaste made in the United States. Then she becomes the poster girl for Cristal Oro beer, a sunny presence in a tiny bikini who winks from the walls of houses, in magazines passed from one person to the next at the hairdresser's, on huge billboards along the highway. She is everywhere, admired and recognized in a way that had never happened to a Colombian model before. The most common dream of every attractive girl in Colombia was—and still is—to become a beauty queen. The long lead-up to the Miss Colombia pageant is sheer madness. A circus of glossy magazines lands on the Cartagena de Indias beach, and schoolchildren in Cartagena are given two weeks' vacation. A 24-carat, gold-plated crown with an emerald—the national gem—in the center is placed on the winner's head, and during her year as Miss Colombia she is received by the president of the republic.

But there are also hundreds of minor beauty pageants. Wherever they're held, the aspiring beauty queens are eagerly awaited. The hearts of the people of Colombia swell with the desire to make up for their tough daily lives, to forget the violence, the injustice, and the political scandals that seem as if they will never end. Colombians are a happy people, that vibrant happiness that develops as an antidote to fatalism.

But that's not enough to explain the proliferation of the phenomenon. In Latin America, and in particular in drug-trafficking countries, beauty pageants are also fairs where thoroughbreds already belonging to a particular stable are paraded. The contest is often fixed from the start: The girl who belongs to the most powerful owner wins. The best present you can give a woman is to buy her a beauty queen's crown, a gift that also makes the prestige of the man who chose her shine. That's how it went for Yovanna Guzmán, who was elected Chica Med when she was with Wílber "Soap" Varela, one of the leaders of the Norte del Valle cartel. But even when that's how it goes, the less fortunate girls can still hope to be noticed by other drug lords who flock to the pageant to choose a new lover, or try their luck in the next pageant.

But Natalia, who did not have to go through anything of the sort in her rise to stardom, suddenly finds herself more envied than Miss Colombia. Her mother would never have allowed her to exhibit herself in a setting where every courteous display of attention is tantamount to a risk. The people who hang around a set are easier to keep an eye on. She goes with Natalia to every appointment, and is her manager and guardian. And she gives her a breast enlargement—two sizes—for her eighteenth birthday, though she never imagines that this further investment in her daughter's already winning image will make her the forerunner of an epidemic that will soon become all the rage. Even girls from the poorest countryside and the most derelict barrios start prostituting themselves in order to scrape together enough money for breast implants—the prerequisite for getting into the good graces of some boss, which is the only chance they have to better themselves. This is the story the Colombian TV series *Sin tetas no hay paraíso* (*Without Breasts There Is No Paradise*) tells. Shown all over the world in toned-down versions, the original was based on Gustavo Bolívar Moreno's rigorous reportage about the southwestern department of Putumayo, a traditional coca-growing area.

Lucia Gaviria—Natalia's mother—is always on the lookout. The opportunity that fate has given her daughter must be cultivated fully for as long as it lasts, but it would be a grave error to depend on it. She too had posed for some fashion photo shoots in her youth, but without her law degree, who knows how she would have managed after she was widowed. You have to keep your head on your shoulders and your feet on the ground, aim for safe and solid goals. That beauty is an ephemeral asset, and that a Colombian woman must use other means to earn and to maintain control over her life, to be the author of her own destiny—of these lessons, Natalia's mother is the best teacher, because she is the perfect model. She has a new partner now, and a second child: a normal family, one that is proud to know that's what they are, especially in this time and place, which is overrun by such unbridled madness.

Colombia is the country of a thousand faces. One minute you're blinded by the sun reflecting off white walls, and the next you're hit with a sunset, the colors of which light the landscape on fire. If Colombia is disorienting, Montería is energized by its contradictions. A city on the banks of the Sinú River, it is the capital of the department of Córdoba. Simple cottages and skyscrapers burst through tropical trees, dozens of different ethnicities are jammed together in an often impossible cohabitation.

Montería is where Salvatore Mancuso Gómez is born and raised, in a house his father builds with his own hands. His sons, even as little boys, tag along when he goes hunting, fascinated by his treasure: a small arsenal they are never allowed to get near. Don Salvador—which, thanks to an error at immigration, is how he is known in the registrar's office—raises his children with a firm hand. To maintain their relative social and economic tranquillity, he sets down strict rules that are beyond question.

But in the end his severity pays off. Monkey's recklessness is limited to his youth, when he is the little boss of the neighborhood, and the other children, in homage to the fuzz that sprouts on his body before any does on theirs, give him that nickname. Or during motocross season in the 1980s, when he wins the national championship and turns the Bianchi brothers, his Italian compatriots who run a Yamaha dealership in Montería, into sales champions.

Like Natalia's mother, Don Salvador knows that a boy needs gratification, needs such moments of fleeting glory, as long as they don't risk derailing his life. Salvatore is a good son. He finishes high school and goes to study in the United States; if he fails to graduate from the University of Pittsburgh, it's not because he lacks the will to study but because he's too homesick. Especially for Martha, whom he married before he was even eighteen, and little Gianluigi, just a few months old. Don Salvador insists he really wants his tenacious son to build a life for himself in the United States, but he can't help but yield to the reasoning of a young father. Salvatore returns to Colombia, and he and Martha move to Bogotá, so he can finish his studies there.

Once again the second-born son's plans diverge from those of his father, and once again his father will not be able to stop him: Salvatore doesn't want to become an engineer; he wants to become a farmer and animal breeder, a real old-fashioned Colombian. It also seems that he plans to avenge his father, who, after thirty years of sacrifice, had finally managed to buy some land but was forced to sell his beloved *finca* when he refused to give in to the guerrillas' extortions. What can you say to a son who stubbornly wants to finish what you couldn't? That it's too dangerous, too hard? The Mancusos are proud people, and in the end Salvatore takes a degree in agrarian studies, returns to Montería, and settles with his family on the Campamento farm that Martha has just inherited from her father. The soil is rich, the farmhouse a jewel to be treasured. Don Salvador backs the loan his son needs to transform his business into a lucrative, exquisite dream. It means getting up at dawn and toiling as much as—even more than—the campesinos. Putting his father's philosophy into practice is hard work. Two years go by, and the hacienda Campamento arouses the admiration not only of the other farmers but of the guerrilla fighters as well, whose appetites are ravenous.

In the early 1990s, the country where Salvatore is starting to make a

name for himself is like a gangrenous Wild West. For years now it has
been impossible to keep track of all the guerrilla violence in the department of Córdoba: extortions; executions; cattle rustling; kidnapping of
innocent people, women and children included. The guerrillas take advantage of the lack of political leadership and the inability of the police
to control the situation. A decade earlier the farmers and breeders of the
department of Antioquia gathered for the first time, in Medellín, to try
to find a solution to the problem. The Association of Middle Magda-
lena Ranchers and Farmers (ACDEGAM) was born. Nothing revolutionary, they were simply acting on a 1965 decree that gave farmers the
right to take up arms in self-defense, with the help of the authorities.
Soldiers and farmers arm in arm in an all-out war, where what counts
is not the monopoly of force that characterizes every modern state but
the identification of a common enemy to annihilate. Yet the situation
for farmers in Antioquia and Córdoba remained alarming, the worth of
their lands and livestock having fallen to one-fifth its previous value.

Salvatore Mancuso knows all this far too well, just as he knows of
the acronyms, manpower, and locations of the insurgents. For years he
has listened to the stories of oppression and assembled all the examples
he could of people confronting those parasitic bandits who fatten on the
fruits of honest people's labor. He is ready. If an immigrant electrician,
worn down by a lifetime of work, didn't cave, then neither will his son,
in the prime of his life and prepared to die for his land and his men. Let
them try something, if they dare.

It's just past dawn, the sun's slanting rays speckle the ground ochre.
Three shadows, lit from behind, approach Salvatore. Emerging into the
light, they take on the appearance of guerrillas. Salvatore grabs his rifle
and without thinking twice, points it at them. They tell him that their
boss wants to see him, but Salvatore refuses to go with them.

Parrita works on Salvatore's *finca*. He's a sharp kid, barely twelve
years old, not afraid of anything. The men tease him, tell him he'll be
afraid once he grows up, that Colombia teaches you respect for those
who are stronger than you. But Parrita just shrugs his shoulders. He's a

cocky kid, and Salvatore likes him. Salvatore sends for him, gives him a two-way radio, and tells him to follow the three guerrillas, to find their base, and to lie in ambush, awaiting further orders. In the meantime, Salvatore starts organizing; he convinces the colonel of the Junín battalion of Montería to lend him some men and, following Parrita's directions, he flushes out the three guerrillas and kills them.

Salvatore Mancuso has taken his destiny into his own hands. There's no going back now unless he wants to lose everything he has built for himself. Word spreads from farm to farm about the young *haciendero* who defied the terrorist thugs in a way no one had ever dared to do before. Not even Pablo Escobar, who, when the daughter of Don Fabio Ochoa Restrepo, a big horse breeder and primogenitor of a high-ranking criminal family in the Medellín cartel, was kidnapped, founded a group called MAS, Muerte a Secuestradores (Death to Kidnappers) in keeping with his theatrical bent. The most powerful man in Colombia shouted threateningly and loaded the avengers with money and weapons. But an immigrant's son, rather than sending others to do the job, silently took the law into his own hands. Salvatore himself, rather than his farm, became the example to follow. The Montería soldiers get him the permissions he needs to turn his estate into an armed fort and provide him with bodyguards. They're galvanized as well, and start calling Salvatore *cacique*, because he's a chief now, a leader, recognized by the local community. One man in particular bonds like a brother with Salvatore: Major Walter Fratini, vice commander of the battalion that came to his aid during his first retaliation against the guerrillas. They're both of Italian descent, and they share a love of guns and good wine.

Together they devise a military plan. They divide up the region on a map, assigning surveillance and patrol duties for each area. The farmers communicate via radio, so they can report suspicious presences and have military escorts whenever they make a move. Their experiment in self-defense takes off, and Salvatore's prestige grows even more.

But he never loses sight of the larger goal. His work follows him home every evening. And one evening he gets some bad news: While defending a group of *contras* under attack, Major Fratini's helicopter was shot down, and Fratini was kidnapped by the EPL—the Popular Liberation Army—one of the many Colombian guerrilla groups. His body is found the next day: He'd been tortured to death. Unforgettable images. Images that deepen the ruts in Salvatore Mancuso's path.

The very blond girl who appears on bars of soap and school notebooks all over Colombia has become, now more than ever, a friendly presence in her hometown, offering gaiety and comfort. To the rest of the world it seems that Medellín has lost the one person who had made it famous—Pablo Escobar. But for those who live there, Natalia's shining star attests to all things good and beautiful and eases the anxiety created by the death of Colombia's lord and master. Yes, because if on the one hand there's a sense of relief, on the other there's a sense of fear. Fear of a vacuum. Not of the vacuum itself, but rather of who and how many will step forward to fill it. Pablo Escobar was killed in the same year as Major Fratini, Monkey's fraternal friend. Now that the king is dead, all those who were his enemy can try to elbow their way in. The guerrillas come forward, Cali gains ground, and a vigilante group calling itself Los Pepes, for Perseguidos por Pablo Escobar, or People Persecuted by Pablo Escobar—which seems like a sarcastic response to MAS—puffs out its chest. The rival Cali cartel had bribed Los Pepes to get rid of Escobar, and Los Pepes' members had sown terror primarily in his own fiefdom. Now what will they do, these men trained and equipped for killing? Will they leave? Will they want a slice of territory to manage? The only thing people know for sure is that there's no hoping Los Pepes will simply fade away. Irregular armies don't simply dismantle themselves.

The government shares the people's concern. The state's major antagonist is dead, but the breeding grounds of conflict are multiplying, which is a problem. A problem for the Colombian people, naturally, but also for a leadership hoping for an image boost after the demise of the country's most famous antihero. Instead it looks as if civil war might break out again, worse than before. Colombia's presidents, one after another, are aware of the limits of their own power. The best they can do is aim for a balance of forces. They need the counterrevolutionaries to check the guerrillas, but the vigilantes need to be curbed somehow as well. They think they've finally hit on the right strategy with Salvatore Mancuso's approach, which a growing number of *haciENDeros* are imitating. Self-defense needs to be legalized further so that even those groups born as armed wings of cartels—the most ferocious and best equipped formations—will be interested in banding together. So, in 1994, a decree is issued to regulate private vigilante groups and their collaboration with the army, extending the military's exclusive use of certain weapons to groups that now call themselves CONVIVIR— Cooperativas de Vigilancia y Seguridad Privada, or Special Vigilance and Private Security Services. Mancuso is the head of the Convivir Horizonte, expanding the original cadre by ten or so men armed with pistols, rifles, and machine guns.

Now that he has the full right to do so, Salvatore wants to prove his worth and to avenge the friend who initiated him into the use of weapons. Accompanied by an army battalion he walks in the forest for thirty days, surviving on canned goods so as to avoid lighting a fire and alerting his enemies. In the tract of Cordillera that separates Córdoba from the northern tongue of Antioquia they come upon a mountain. The overhanging rock cliffs terrify the men, many of whom turn back. But, urged on by the Monkey, enough of them make it to the top to make a surprise attack on the region's FARC stronghold. Shooting breaks out, but Salvatore and his men come out alive.

A private army is operating in the same area as Mancuso, the Autodefensas Campesinas de Córdoba y Urabá, or the Peasant Self-Defense Forces of Córdoba and Urabá. The army renamed itself in light of the law on CONVIVIR forces, so as to legally provide armed protection to farmers and breeders. It belongs to the Castaño brothers, who have a long history of implacable hatred for guerrilla fighters and who were born into money. Wealth is what has defined their lives. The sons of Don Jesús, a breeder so highly regarded as a politician and so convinced of landowners' rights to rule that he was one of the first men whom the FARC came after on his *finca*, in order to teach him a lesson. It seems like centuries have passed since that day thirteen years ago, since that interminable wait, till that moment when the brothers finally knew for sure that, despite the ransom they'd paid, their father would never come home again. The black hole of their existence. They've been at war ever since, a war that—on principle—takes no prisoners. They fought on their own, hiring a hundred or so men willing to do anything. They sent them into the area where Don Jesús had been held hostage and had them kill, impale, and chop to pieces every human being they could find there to teach the people who supported those villains a lesson. They developed a good relationship with Pablo Escobar, and had Carlos, the youngest Castaño brother, join MAS, which educated him in every conceivable method of dirty war.

But then the Castaño brothers broke with Escobar, who, in his megalomaniac paranoia, had had some of their friends killed. Realizing that he planned to have them killed as well, they accepted the invitation of the Rodríguez Orejuela brothers of the Cali cartel and formed Los Pepes. They became the pack of dogs in the hunting party out to get their former ally, whose partners and relatives they murdered. So now they're practically right back where they started: a vigilante group bigger and wealthier than the others.

In the last decade the Castaño brothers have grown even wealthier. The cocaine lords have paid them extremely well. They've also paid their enemies well. The Castaño brothers would have already crushed FARC and all the other communist bastards, would have already destroyed all their support networks, if the guerrillas' anticapitalist insurrection had not been financed by cocaine money. But it costs money to maintain a permanent war, and that's why the insurgents have entered the drug business as well.

When the Castaño brothers invite Salvatore to join forces, he takes his time in answering. He'd prefer to just carry on as before, knowing, perhaps, of their long-standing ties with drug trafficking. But then one day, on his way home with his wife, his first-born, Gianluigi, and his second son, who is barely two years old, he runs into a roadblock between Montería and his estate: a FARC ambush, a kidnapping attempt. He hides his agitation so as not to scare his children even more, but a few days later he tells Martha that he can't keep going it alone. He agrees to merge with the Castaños. And then, when his first arrest warrant for murder arrives, he leaves Campamento for good. From that day in 1996 he stops being Salvatore Mancuso. Now he is only El Mono, the Monkey, El Cacique, Santander Lozada, Triple Cero, and all his other adopted battle names. He is no longer a rice grower and horse breeder but an underground warlord.

When the Monkey, now about thirty, is making the third decisive move of his life, beautiful Natalia is just over twenty. When her mother sees her in bed, in her knit pajamas and surrounded by her stuffed animals, when she wakes her up to get her ready for school or to take her to a morning meeting and watches her, still sleepy, stumble sulkily to the bathroom, she tells herself that she still seems like a little girl. Because Natalia will always be her little girl, just like for every mother. But also because nature has been kind to Natalia, passing on her mother's genes, giving her a body that resists time. A lighthearted girl, naïve and happy. And this is because Lucia Gaviria knows how to protect her daughter's other nature—her inner nature—from the fangs of time. The money she has earned has made her even more lighthearted, which is as it should be, even though it doesn't always work that way. To the sea of stuffed animals has been added a closet, overflowing with shoes, clothes, creams, perfumes, and some jewelry.

By now Natalia Paris has gotten used to being a star as soon as she steps out her front door. Used to seeing an army of girls who could be her clones on the streets of Colombia. Used to the paparazzi's flash-bulbs around the corner, used to rebuffing advances with a no that is as sweet as it is firm. Not one of the boys she goes out with has ever made her lose her focus, let alone her head.

Lucia Gaviria's fears begin to wane. You can breathe more easily in Medellín now than you could a few years ago. It no longer happens that she has to go to a funeral because her best friend's daughter has been ripped apart by a car bomb and for a while afterward she can't find the courage to call her because her own daughter is still alive. It no longer happens that Natalia asks to go to a disco with her school friends and comes home talking about how shooting broke out when they were on the dance floor. Natalia is still frightened, sure, but not nearly as much now. When you grow up in certain places, you end up adapting to the reality around you. Doña Lucia realizes that bell jars are pathetically fragile.

It's also true that those early days, when sudden success threatened to upset an adolescent's precarious balance, are gone. In fact, Natalia's celebrity was precisely what helped her. A star enjoys less freedom of movement than a normal person. In order to make her life bearable she frequents the same places where, mainly, people learn to pretend not to notice her, to treat her normally.

And so, a gray area worms its way into Lucia Gaviria's vigilance. The gym. Keeping in shape is a professional necessity for Natalia, and besides, she really loves physical activity. For the most part she takes classes for women: aerobics and Latin American dance, activities that take the place of evenings at the disco, which, with all the attention she received, had become too exhausting. But now she wants to learn how to scuba dive. Her gym offers a one-week class in Santa Marta, the famous Caribbean tourist city. It's not the tropical fish that frighten Doña Lucia, or the breathing apparatus and tanks. Sea sharks are far less dangerous than land sharks.

It must have been an almost mystical experience to watch Natalia remove her mask and fins and peel off her wet suit with a decisive tug.

And yet she seemed oblivious to the way everyone looked at her. There was a man in the group who had had the same effect on her, though, ever since their first dive. He took off his equipment, stowed it, and then dove off the edge of the dinghy. She wanted to dive in after him, but didn't dare. She waited for him to make a move, even the smallest sign, some joke, or a plea for help. He was already an expert diver, already had his instructor's license, in fact. He'd gotten it in California, where he'd lived for work. The class her gym offered was merely a way for him to get back into his favorite sport.

This is what he tells her a few evenings later when he takes her to a romantic bistro. Medellín is not like Los Angeles, where, to recharge your batteries, you can ride the waves on your surfboard, go running on the beach, or swim out to the horizon and back. "I'm really tied to my family and my city," he says, "but I miss the ocean and being outside."

Natalia is already deeply in love. But now she's convinced that Julio is the most extraordinary man she'll ever meet. She's comfortable pressing against him in the boat, kissing him, or clinging to him in the water. Love is a triumph that must be flaunted.

At first Lucia merely thinks that the vacation did her daughter good. But she soon senses that Natalia's irrepressible happiness can't be simply the positive effect of the Caribbean sun. There's clearly a budding romance. It must be a special sort of crush, though, because, oddly, her daughter doesn't talk to her about it. She feels a pang of anxiety, but represses it immediately. Natalia has always been impulsive, enthusiastic. She's a Leo, a passionate sign, but sooner or later the fire goes out. It's better to wait, to trust her. Lucia thinks she knows her daughter well enough to know that she'll be the one to talk about it first.

And, in fact, Natalia doesn't keep quiet for long. When she tells her mother about Julio, how handsome he is, how athletic, how attentive and elegant, her face lights up so much that her mother has to take a deep breath before she can begin asking questions. She is truly sorry to tumble her off the cloud she's floating on.

"How old is he?"

"I don't know. Thirty, thirty-five . . ."

"Are you sure he's not married?"

"What are you saying, Mami? He was in Los Angeles, he came back to help his family, I think."

"And what exactly was he doing in Los Angeles?"

"I didn't ask."

"So you have no idea what it is he does, this Julio of yours?"

"Oh, business of some sort. But he's rich, family money. He has a fabulous house and some other properties too, a hotel maybe, or a country estate."

"Maybe. But you don't know how he got rich. Or how his family got rich."

"No, Mami, and I don't care! You can't always think like this, calculating everything all the time, planning. Those things don't matter at all when you're in love!"

Natalia starts to cry and locks herself in her room. Lucia Gaviria stays sitting in the kitchen, devastated. She has an awful feeling; she can barely breathe. To calm down she pours herself a glass of water and finishes up some mindless house chores.

The only question she dares ask the next day is the last name of Natalia's beau. She tries to sound casual, but she knows Natalia's not fooled. With that piece of information she heads to court, as she does every morning. Off to face her tragedy.

Julio César Correa. A drug trafficker. He got his start as a hit man at Pablo Escobar's side. His new last name, which replaces his original one, reflects his status as a killer: Fierro, Julio Fierro. All over Latin America *fierro*—as in Italy, *ferro*—literally meaning "iron," means "gun." In this new era Julio established his independence as a professional killer and got involved directly in the cocaine business, becoming a *traqueto*, a trafficker. Doña Lucia wonders if he went to the United States because of Don Pablo's death, to make himself scarce. But now he's back. Back in time to make Natalia lose her head. She simply won't listen to reason. She confesses that Julio carries a pistol around town, but then screams: "What's wrong with that, everybody else does!"

Whenever she addresses her mother now, Natalia always shouts.

Doña Lucia establishes peremptory rules and strict curfews, much stricter than when Natalia was under age. But when she's alone, waiting for her daughter to return, Lucia Gaviria takes to brooding and blaming herself. Why did she let her take that damned diving course?

The years pass. Natalia's mother is done in by the war she is fighting in vain. More and more she has long crying fits that are only in part a way of emotionally blackmailing her daughter. Julio tries to soften her up whenever possible, reassure her how deeply in love he is, swears that he will always have the utmost respect for Natalia and those dear to her. And he does seem sincere and polite, quite different from the ugly, vulgar *traquetos* she comes across in court. But Doña Lucia remains coldly courteous. She must resist; she must break their bond.

But her daughter is still as crazy for Julio as she was that very first day. And everything Doña Lucia does—cry, threaten, argue furiously— merely pushes her daughter further away. Further into Julio's arms.

One morning Natalia comes into the kitchen with a frighteningly serious look on her face, her eyes puffy and red. She's been even more nervous lately, and has been sleeping poorly. She doesn't open her mouth until her stepfather, Doña Lucia's companion who has acted as Natalia's father since she was little, arrives.

"Natalia wants to tell you something."

"I'm pregnant, Mami. I'm in my fourth month."

It's a catastrophe, and Lucia Gaviria is the last in the family to know. She doesn't speak to her daughter for a week.

But she doesn't hold out for long. She senses that for the first time in all these years Natalia is frightened as well. She no longer lives in a fairyland. Fairy tales don't exist in Medellín, and Doña Lucia can't abandon her now. So one day she buys her a pair of sneakers, so she'll be more comfortable in the months to come, when the baby in her womb starts to weigh on her. She leaves the box on Natalia's bed with a note that says "God bless you." They both weep that evening, Natalia in her bedroom, her mother in the living room. But the door is too thin for them not to hear each other's sobs.

Natalia is under contract with Cristal Oro for their new ad campaign, but she'll be in her seventh month by the time the shooting starts. Is Lucia Gaviria supposed to cancel? What excuse can she give them?

She is more furious with Julio than ever, even though he does everything one could expect from a Colombian man. He says he wants to marry Natalia, that having a baby with her is the most wonderful thing that has ever happened to him, that everything will be fine. And her daughter goes along with everything he says. But at a certain point, Natalia's happiness no longer seems like the other side of fear. She starts sleeping better, and gradually looks more radiant. Doña Lucia attributes the difference to hormonal changes related to her condition, until her daughter talks with her again.

"It's all resolved, Mami. We're going to go live in the United States soon; we're going to start a new life there!"

A new life? In the United States?

The United States is every drug trafficker's nightmare, so much so that in the 1980s a popular saying among the Colombian narcos was: "Better a tomb in Colombia than a prison cell in the United States." What's more, in 1997 Colombia, backed into a tight corner by the United States, altered its constitution so as to reintroduce extradition. Sometimes her daughter is so naïve she seems stupid.

And yet everything Natalia told her turns out to be true.

Not even a month goes by before Natalia leaves for Florida. All she had to do was pack her suitcase. Julio took care of everything else: the villa on the beach, their visas, all the other paperwork necessary for settling in the United States. Or rather, his new Yankee contacts took care of most of it. They're not cocaine importers, though. In fact, they're the cocaine importers' antagonists par excellence: the Miami DEA.

Julio César Correa is one of the first Colombian narcos to negotiate something that officially never existed. Precisely because his case is intended to motivate others, he's one of the luckiest ones: not a single day in jail; no more trials hanging over his head for having flooded the streets of North America with cocaine. In exchange for millions of narco-dollars deposited in U.S. coffers and—more important—precious information.

The Miami DEA's undertaking seems like a wild shot. How can the "world's policeman" allow someone guilty of serious crimes under its own jurisdiction have his sentence eliminated?

Beyond that, how would it make contact with a drug lord and propose something of the sort to him? He would be the first to suspect he was being screwed. The contact person might never come back. The DEA's office needs a more sophisticated intermediary.


Baruch Vega is a Colombian fashion photographer living in Miami. He has worked for Armani, Gucci, Valentino, Chanel, Hermès, all the major fashion houses and cosmetics companies. The second of eleven children of a trumpet player from Bogotá who relocated to Bucaramanga, a plateau in the middle of the mountains in northeast Colombia, Baruch won a Kodak competition when he was fifteen. He immortalized a bird as it emerged from a lake with a fish in its beak. But his parents make him study engineering. At the University of Santander he is recruited by the CIA and sent to Chile: Salvador Allende's government is about to fall.

Baruch Vega hates his job. To make his escape he dusts off his skill as a photographer. He arrives in New York in the 1970s and photographs the very first top models, the likes of Lauren Hutton and Christie Brinkley. He manages to get what matters most where he comes from: success, money, and women. Earning them in the United States increases his prestige. Every time Vega goes back to Colombia he shows up with a slew of cover girls. They're his business card. And that's how, in the course of his double career as photographer and undercover agent, he got to know many of the big Colombian cartel bosses and frequented the homes of important drug lords, such as the Ochoa brothers, Escobar's associates in the Medellín cartel.

His first encounter with Julio Fierro is in a hotel in Cartagena, during the Miss Colombia pageant, not coincidentally. Vega plays his part. He says he knows some DEA agents you could make a deal with. All you have to do is pay: the gringo cops' assistance, plus a percentage for his services.

For a drug lord, if you don't have to pay, it's not credible. The higher the price, the more trustworthy it seems. Baruch Vega is the best guarantee on the bargaining table. What could a man like him, who makes money in an enviable profession, want? More money. A man who risks his life for more money is a man who deserves respect. Respect and trust. As proof of his reliability, Vega organizes trips to Miami with his "private plane," which will later turn out to be paid for by the DEA. The presence onboard of an antidrug agent guarantees that there will be other friendly cops at the airport ready to walk the drug traffickers— several of them on the top of the DEA's most wanted list—through passport control without a visa. Just a little outing—to take their girlfriends to the hottest restaurants, shower them with gifts, and then back home. Next time, their farewell to Colombia and drug trafficking will be final.

Julio Fierro proves to be very useful to Vega and his friends at the DEA, whose initiative makes a qualitative leap. In Panama they organize the first of many big meetings between drug traffickers and antidrug agents. A summit of sorts, or a convention. In fact, that's exactly what they call them. Julio arrives from Florida with Baruch Vega and the men from the DEA. Vega has taken care of everything, down to the last detail. He has filled the plane with the usual bevy of beauties, booked suites at the Intercontinental Hotel; he even makes sure that, after their trying day, they can catch some R&R at just the right club, with agents and drug traffickers emptying champagne bottles together, surrounded by willing women.

But Julio holds the trump card. He takes out a Colombian passport and passes it around to his former rivals and allies. The gringos have given him a new identity and a regular visa. Thanks to the United States, Julio Fierro no longer needs to hope for a tomb in Colombia. His gesture sets off a chain reaction that will change everything. But the big news in Natalia's life is something else: Mariana, born in Miami, is a U.S. citizen.

These negotiations between the DEA and the drug lords—which sound like something right out of a novel—are less unbelievable than they first seem. The situation in Colombia is extremely complicated. The government's credibility is lower than ever, incapable of holding any sway at home or of representing it abroad. In some respects, the United States takes advantage of this weakness. During the last year of President Ernesto Samper Pizano's term, he was under investigation for having been elected through Cali cartel support, and Article 35 of the constitution is altered so as to reintroduce the long-awaited—or feared—policy of extradition. The Colombian president knows he has nothing more to lose.

For the moment, that's all the United States can obtain through official channels. Unless they're considered in this new juridical context the "under the counter" meetings the DEA promoted don't make much sense. The concrete threat of extradition with no possible sentence reduction all of a sudden makes the alternative of near impunity in exchange for collaboration and the restitution of large sums of illegal money quite attractive. The DEA's real objective is to corrode the trafficking organizations from within, to use the information obtained to prepare the decisive blow and to foster a climate of suspicion that generates exhausting internal feuds. Giovanni Falcone, the Italian judge killed by the Mafia in 1992, noted that *pentiti*, or criminals turned informers, were the legal weapon the Mafia feared most. In Italy it was possible, albeit with notable resistance, to strictly regulate the way criminals turned informers were handled. But for the United States the problems are many: Its widespread *Law & Order* culture; its international hegemony, which cannot be openly compromised; the very fact of approaching non-U.S. citizens; and finally, the urgent need to do something to reduce the power of cocaine, which, despite the dismemberment of Colombia's drug-trafficking dinosaurs, continues to grow. The DEA targets every exponent of real power: bosses who still control the old cartels; high-ranking members of rising clans; and narcos for all seasons, such as Julio Fierro. But also members of Mancuso's and the Castaño brothers' Autodefensas, who are becoming an increasingly formidable threat.

After the Cali cartel's fall, paramilitary groups started receiving many more requests for their protection services from emerging groups, such as the Norte del Valle cartel. But their own involvement in drug trafficking is reaching a level of systematic autonomy in direct relation to the increase in their territorial dominance. By now they manage every step, from cultivation to transportation routes to negotiations with buyers. Half the department of Córdoba *cocaleros* are under their control, half under the control of leftist guerrillas. They can now take each other on with the force of two opposing armies. In 1997 the self-defense groups formed a federation, the Autodefensas Unidas de Colombia (United Self-Defense Forces of Colombia), or AUC, headed by Carlos Castaño. The Monkey was a cofounder, in command of AUC's largest military formation, the Bloque Catatumbo, which would come to include forty-five hundred men.

The conflict is becoming less of an ideological clash and more of a full-blown war of conquest. Once the outer shells of extreme right nationalism and revolutionary Marxism are removed, events in Colombia prefigure the current postmodern barbarity in Mexico. The AUCs are the "founding fathers" of the Familia Michoacana and the Knights Templar, and they increasingly descend on villages in areas controlled by the guerrillas, wiping out the inhabitants. They use primitive tools, such as machetes and chain saws, to behead and chop peasants to pieces,

but they plan their operations with cold military calculation, flying
military planes hundreds of miles to the place of action and then flying
out once the killing is done.

The situation has become intolerable. Public opinion no longer buys
the rationalization for the killings, which merely repeats the same old
story about the victims having supported the guerrillas. The strategy of
balancing opposing forces has proven to be a disaster: Just over six
months after the AUC is founded, the Colombian constitutional court
declares the part of the decree that regulates surveillance and private
safety co-ops illegal. Paramilitary groups are supposed to hand over the
military weapons they've been issued and to respect human rights.

But it's too late. Carlos Castaño has more than thirty thousand men
under his command, and the income from cocaine trafficking is more
than enough to supply them with all sorts of military equipment.
Declaring them outlaws has only made them more ferocious. In old
Hollywood westerns the pistol-carrying hero never turns into a ruthless
outlaw. But in the land of coke, that and much worse happens. The
Monkey has mutated into one of Colombia's principal strategists of
horror.

El Aro is a tiny village of sixty houses, which are more like shacks
than homes, with zinc roofs and rotting doors. Compared to his fellow
villagers, Marco Aurelio Areiza, who owns two grocer's shops, is a rich
man. But because El Aro is in FARC-controlled territory, he also risks
his life every day. Because Marco Aurelio also sells food to the guerrillas. He'd be crazy to refuse: Who would ever dream of saying no to
armed men who emerge from the forest? In the tormented land of
Colombia there's an unwritten law: Collaborate with whoever is holding a gun, regardless of what uniform they're wearing. In fact, Marco
Aurelio also collaborates with Salvatore Mancuso's army, which comes
and accuses him of supporting the guerrillas. It's a bogus interrogation,
because the village and its inhabitants had already been condemned to
death days before. El Aro is like a bridgehead, an outpost that must be

conquered in order to get to FARC-controlled areas. Its fate is also meant to serve as a warning to all the other villages.

The 150 men of Mancuso's Bloque Catatumbo torture and kill 17 people, burn down forty-three houses, steal twelve hundred head of cattle, and force 702 villagers to leave their homes. Marco Aurelio is tortured, his body broken. When the police arrive they find his wife, Rosa María Posada, sitting vigil over her husband's body. She doesn't want their children to see his mangled flesh.

Everyone is convinced that drastic change is needed in Colombia. An election campaign is starting up, reigniting the hopes within the country as well as in the White House. One candidate's résumé boasts not only of his defeat in the previous election because of the handful of votes the Cali cartel bought, but of his miraculous survival—he was kidnapped in the late 1980s while running for mayor of Bogotá, a post he held after his liberation. This politician, so unpopular with the drug lords, seems to be just the man to lead the country.

Andrés Pastrana promises pacification and tight collaboration with the United States. When he wins he opens the doors to the Great Alliance for Change, inviting congressmen from all parties to participate. The wave of optimism and grand negotiations has finally reached Colombia.

As promised, the new president negotiates simultaneously with FARC and the United States. That this does not generate immediate opposition in Washington is probably due not so much to the Democratic Clinton administration as to the global receptivity to negotiations. In war-torn Bosnia-Herzegovina the 1995 Dayton Accords are put into effect. The peace process between Israel and Palestine is slowly picking up again, in the wake of the Oslo Accords. But the most encouraging example is probably that of the United Kingdom: Opposing governments are successfully negotiating a permanent truce and IRA disarmament. The end of the lengthy and devastating conflict in Northern

Ireland is close at hand. "Peace" is a word that now flows freely from people's lips.

And yet Colombia's ambitious plans will all fail miserably. Because it's not only a question of men with opposing political objectives ruling illegally; those men can be eliminated in various ways. But cocaine dies hard. Pastrana's experiment to allow the guerrillas a demilitarized zone—the so-called distension zone—twice the size of New Jersey—turns out to be an ill-considered risk from the get-go. The FARC does as it pleases in its assigned territory and doesn't even dream of entering upon serious negotiations: It grants no truce; in fact it intensifies its military activity. Kidnappings, whether politically or financially motivated; urban raids; control of cocaine: It's all the same as before. Disappointment beats down the president's popularity. When in 2002 the guerrillas go so far as to hijack a plane—a regularly scheduled flight—to kidnap a senator, Pastrana realizes that the moment has come to declare an end to the peace talks. War breaks out again: The distention zone must be reclaimed immediately. Three days later FARC forces abduct Ingrid Betancourt, a presidential candidate for the Partido Verde Oxígeno in the upcoming elections. Convinced that an armed conflict should not deprive citizens of their fundamental rights, Betancourt wanted to bring her platform to the Colombians in that area. But her captivity will last until July 2, 2008—2,321 days—when she is liberated by the Colombian armed forces.

According to the new president, Álvaro Uribe, the approach to take is that of an iron fist. The state must show its muscle and take back the country. Besides, the world is no longer what it once was. In one day the Twin Towers and the world's optimism collapsed. The only possible response now is war, it seems. In Colombia the war on terror coincides with the war on drugs. There can be no victory without a victory over drug trafficking.

And so, despite their differences, Álvaro Uribe will maintain one of his predecessor's key efforts: Plan Colombia, the major pact with the United States to end the production and sale of cocaine. Pastrana had announced emphatically, shortly after his election in 1998, that he was negotiating a Marshall Plan for Colombia with the United States. As in postwar Europe, billions of dollars were supposed to pour in to revive the country, help Colombians free it of cocaine, and support those campesinos who agreed to convert their fields back to far less profitable but legal crops. But the actual plan, signed by Bill Clinton in 2000 and reconfirmed by George W. Bush until the end of his term, takes a different direction. A slow and costly social and economic transformation suddenly seems like a utopia. There's not enough money, trust, or consensus. There's not enough time. Funding depends on being able to show results. So everything rests on the quickest option, that of force.

The use of force translates, first of all, into a war on cocaine. Victory will be declared only when not a single leaf of cocaine is left growing in Colombia. Plants are uprooted, fields carpet-bombed with fumigation planes, lands made barren with aggressive weed-killer treatments. From an environmental point of view, the cost is extremely high. The ecosystem of the country's virgin forests is compromised; the ground and aquifers are filled with toxins; Colombia's land is burned or polluted, incapable of producing anything of value in the short term. From a societal point of view, the consequences are equally grave. The peasants, lacking alternatives, abandon the devastated areas en masse and start growing coca in more inaccessible zones. The dispersed cultivation and the displaced campesinos' vulnerability work in the drug lords' favor. What's more, the narcos invest in methods to make the fields more fertile, which allows them to double the number of annual harvests.

The result is that after years of a literal scorched-earth policy, Colombian cocaine still represents more than half of all the cocaine consumed worldwide.

The other part of Plan Colombia's use of force is directed toward individual criminals. The U.S. military bolsters the Colombian army's actions against drug lords and narco-terrorism: logistics, arms and equipment, special forces, intelligence, training. On the eve of the attack on the Twin Towers, AUCs were included on the White House's blacklist of terrorist organizations, but that wasn't enough to ruin long-standing good relations with the Colombian military machine, let alone with part of the political and economic establishment. President Uribe, who is respected by the paramilitaries, negotiates the demobilization and disarmament of the Autodefensas, but the success is merely superficial. Most groups have no intention of laying down their arms, or of renouncing drug trafficking, and they continue controlling the cocaine business and spreading terror under new names.

Even though it led to significant disarmament and killed off the primary FARC leaders, one after another, the brutal war against the guerrillas was not able to get to the root of the problem either. Today FARC still has nine thousand members and ELN—Ejército de Liberación Nacional (National Liberation Army), Colombia's second-largest guerrilla army—three thousand, but more important, they still control a conspicuous part of the cocaine production, having become increasingly involved in processing in addition to cultivation. While it's true that Plan Colombia, with its use of military force, helped to weaken FARC, paradoxically, precisely because of the fragmentation and dislocation of cocaine cultivation, their role as one of the major players in Colombian drug trafficking was confirmed.

In short, if Colombia today is no longer the extremely dangerous country it was ten or twenty years ago, international antidrug policies in South America can take the credit only if one also accepts that, in part thanks to those policies, the conflict was shifted farther north, to Mexico.

But to better understand what exactly went wrong, you have to go back to those confusing times of transition, torn between hope and uncertainty, times in which the fates of the Beauty and the Monkey collided.

Natalia is living happily in Miami, taking care of her newborn baby girl. Her only sadness is that her mother keeps trying to convince her to leave her husband. She takes little interest in what Julio does or why; every now and then he has to leave suddenly for some trip. Now he too deals with the big fish of the drug world who are floating to the surface, in order to negotiate a surrender with the United States, especially since a coordinated DEA and Colombian police investigation resulted in the biggest roundup since the days of the narco-state—thirty or so arrests, including that of Fabio Ochoa, an important, historic member of the Medellín cartel, who was trafficking in cocaine with his new partners. The investigation's code name, Operation Millennium, says a lot about the exemplary value assigned to it. The United States is already looking to the future, to Plan Colombia's ratification. Encouraged by the extradition agreement and the collaboration with the new Colombian presidential administration of Andrés Pastrana, they've sent a signal they want everyone to hear, even the Mexican traffickers, whom the antidrug agency has begun to recognize as a growing threat. In fact, the operation also involves Mexican authorities. And it is then that the arrest warrant for Armando Valencia, alias Maradona, is issued. Maradona, who, together with Alejandro Bernal, a Colombian from Medellín who had been like a brother to Amado Carrillo Fuentes, the Lord of the Skies, was managing a new and important cocaine import alliance.

The evil must be eliminated at its source, in other words, in Colombia. This is the fundamental error at the base of the United States' efforts. You can rip up a plant, but you can't uproot the desire for well-being that leads to addiction, any more than you can eradicate greed. Cocaine is the fruit not of the earth but of man.

But the United States, convinced that the war on cocaine is the same as the war on Colombian cartels, waves an initial victory flag. Fabio Ochoa is the big trophy, flaunted on the front page, but there were other bosses in their sights too who'd escaped capture by a hair's breadth. How was that possible? The DEA's office that coordinated Operation Millennium is not in touch with the group in Miami. Nevertheless, Baruch Vega is contacted to find out if there are any moles working for the drug lords. The ubiquitous photographer sets up a meeting on neutral ground in Central America with his new informers: one is Julio Fierro and the other an AUC member who trafficked for Carlos Castaño.

The official policy of the stick is complemented by the unofficial policy of the carrot. There's a line of people interested in understanding how the Narcotics Traffickers Rehabilitation Program, as the Miami DEA agents called it, not without some bureaucratic irony, works. At the same time, the certainty that more and more prominent figures are turning traitors sows discord among the traffickers, in particular within the Norte del Valle cartel and in the tight ranks of the Autodefensas.

Right at the peak of this feverish, underground agitation, Natalia Paris receives a fabulous offer. She's invited to be a special guest on Colombiamoda, the most important fashion event in the country. She dons a little white number that could be a wedding dress if not for the enormous silk wings on the back. A crown of flowers graces her flowing hair. She's twenty-eight and has a daughter who is learning to walk, but she still looks like a young girl. Her hazel eyes roam the audience as if to embrace these Colombians who had welcomed her back so warmly, but in truth she's searching for one person in particular. Julio had promised to join her there so she wouldn't have to endure other men's longing gazes on her own. They also planned on taking advantage of his clandestine return to have Mariana baptized. But Julio Correa, aka Fierro, has vanished into thin air.

Natalia spends months at the public prosecutor's, between interrogations and attempts to identify her husband in the photos of dead bodies, sometimes mere masses of butchered flesh, that they place before her. But in vain. Each time it's not him she feels a moment of relief, an absurd, stabbing hope. It's obvious by now that he's been kidnapped, but he might still be alive. She has to keep hoping, praying, hugging her child, casting out every negative thought about what the child's father may have suffered.

Julio César Correa's properties in Colombia are sequestered. Natalia Paris's U.S. visa is revoked. Her ad contracts are canceled. It's the end.

Her mother had warned her, she who knows all too well what it means to end up alone with an eight-month-old baby girl. Doña Lucia was right after all.

It's at that point that Natalia discovers her own maternal instinct. She has to act; she can't lose heart. Shortly before her world collapsed she had launched her own suntan lotion. Now she travels the country promoting it, signing autographs, making deals to get it on supermarket shelves. It's the first step in her comeback. Little by little she reclaims her position, which she still holds to this day: an icon in Colombia and a sex symbol throughout Latin America. But starting with that moment, she also became her own person. A businesswoman who knows she must manage the passing of time. She has a fit if someone draws attention to her age, and the older she gets the younger she claims to be. Her body is her business, and she can't risk obsolescence.

Julio Fierro's body has never been found.

The mystery of his disappearance gave rise to a sea of inferences about who could have eliminated him. Suspicion fell primarily on the Norte del Valle cartel because it had a terrible reputation and because it was one of the United States' main targets, with whom Julio was collaborating. Only very recently has the truth regarding his death surfaced.

According to the revelations of various AUC collaborators, once it was learned that Fierro was in Colombia, Carlos Castaño, El Mono, and a boss named Daniel Mejía, known as Danielito, decided to get together. At the end of their meeting Castaño gave orders to abduct the traitor from his hiding place near Medellín and take him by helicopter to somewhere in the department of Córdoba. There he was tortured, for various purposes, including to get him to hand over some of his property to his kidnappers. When he was finally killed (some say with a chain saw, after having been brought back to Medellín), Danielito had the job of dealing with the body. Danielito was not a casual choice.

Daniel Mejía belonged to the military bloc in the area. More important, however, he was also charged with putting into effect the Autodefensas' new method of concealing the number of murders that could be ascribed to them. Despite the ceaseless killings, the AUCs still had a reputation as authentic Colombian patriots rather than simple criminals devoid of any scruples. The spokesman for the Autodefensas' honor was Carlos Castaño. Every time someone branded his men narcos, he would fly into a rage and respond with indignant denials. Obviously he denied all the rest too. "We have never killed innocent people. We are only out to get the guerrillas, not people whose ideas are different than ours. We do not use chain saws."

This was not just cynical hypocrisy. As often happens with authoritarian individuals, Carlos Castaño lived in a parallel universe manipulated to satisfy his whims, and he did his best to defend it from anything that contradicted it. What rankled him most was to be accused of conniving with narco-trafficking. That may seem strange, because his brothers had almost always rounded out their earnings with cocaine. But that was precisely what provided the foundation for his house of lies: Coke was merely the means, not the end—the same justification the insurgents used.

And yet the increasing force of his organization blew like a gale-force wind against that unrealistic construction. In some regions it was becoming impossible to distinguish between narcos and paramilitaries. The area around Medellín was one such region. Daniel Mejía was now the right-hand man of the bloodthirsty Don Berna, who, in grabbing up the remains of Escobar's empire, had joined with the AUCs, to his clear advantage. Danielito was slotted to take over as boss of the new cartel Oficina de Envigado, or Office of Envigado. Together they killed, as in any drug war, in order to subjugate people by terror and to eliminate competition.

It was urgent that all be kept hidden, so a new method was devised. Danielito set to work building crematoriums. Up to twenty bodies a week would be burned in them. According to some former AUC soldiers, even Julio Fierro was incinerated in one of those ovens. And, a fitting twist, Daniel Mejía himself ended up in one, after being killed by the other ex-paramilitary with whom he had assumed command of the Office of Envigado.

At any rate, it's around the time of Julio's abduction and murder that Carlos Castaño's unease begins to wear away at him. Without ever attending any of the meetings Baruch Vega organized, those circlings of the wagons, he contacted the Miami lawyer involved in the DEA negotiations, the same lawyer who later will defend El Mono. He too now has a young wife and a baby girl, born with a rare genetic disease. The only hope for treatment is in the United States.

Carlos Castaño wants to save his family, but at what cost? On September 10, 2001, he bore the shame of being identified as the head of a terroristic organization by a country he had always greatly admired. Terrorist and drug trafficker. He must remove that unbearable blot, from himself and his Autodefensas. So, in early 2002, he summons a hundred or so commanders from every corner of the country. He prepares his remarks carefully and is counting on his prestige and charisma. After what happened in New York and Washington, the Yankees will hunt us down like rats. We can't keep on killing. We can't keep on trafficking cocaine. It's the only way to safeguard our association's honor and survival.

The silence that greets his words is not that of dumbstruck approval. The commander in chief realizes that many of them have no intention of following his path. A defeat so humiliating that he steps down from running the AUCs. Carlos Castaño is like a wounded jaguar in the Colombian jungle now. He lashes out left, right, and center; he resorts to the Internet to expose his former underlings, giving first and last names and declaring that they are "irresponsibly involved in drug-trafficking activities" and adding that "the penetration of drug trafficking in some self-defense groups is unbearable and is known to the U.S. and Colombian intelligence agencies."

A time bomb, a deadly threat.

He declares that from now on he wants to dedicate himself to his family, but he's lying. Or rather, he's telling only half the truth, for the great Carlos Castaño does not stoop to lying. The Miami lawyer comes to see him more often. He's negotiating his surrender, his betrayal.

In April 2004 Carlos Castaño disappears. Legends circulate regarding his whereabouts, the foreign destination where he took refuge in order to make a new life for himself, as well as speculations about who could have wanted to eliminate him. His remains weren't found until two and a half years later, in the most banal of places. He was buried on the Las Tangas *finca* where he and his brother Fidel had launched the first paramilitary counterrevolutionary group. That *finca* was the beginning and the end for Carlos Castaño. His death warrant had been issued by none other than his brother Vicente.

Carlos Castaño's exit favors the further rise of El Mono. Not only is he second in command of the Autodefensas, he's also the most clearheaded, the most capable. He doesn't seem rattled in the least by the extradition request that now hangs over his head too. He doesn't let himself be infected by the poisonous rage with which, after their commander's resignation, many other bosses spit on the name of Carlos Castaño. It's important to stay cool headed, to remember the larger picture, the organization and his men. This means not hiding problems but resolving them in other ways.

El Mono is the one who opens negotiations with the Uribe administration. He sends his spiritual adviser, the bishop of Montería, who has known him since he was a boy, to initiate contact and to serve as ambassador. The first agreement is reached in July 2003. The AUCs will demobilize completely, cease all hostilities, and cooperate with investigations. In return, the Colombian government will offer huge legal concessions. Many pending cases are dismissed, most of the investigations of AUC members are dropped, and sentences for crimes such as drug trafficking and human rights violations, for which one normally risks life in jail, are reduced to a mere few years.

El Mono is also an excellent press officer. A few days after the agreement is reached he grants *Semana*, Colombia's most important weekly, an interview, during which he explains why the AUCs agreed to negotiate only now: "For the first time a government is trying to strengthen democracy and state institutions. We have always demanded the presence of the state, called it to responsibility. We have wielded guns because the state failed in its responsibility. It was up to us to step in, to take its place in the various regions we controlled and where we acted as the de facto authorities."

He's also astute in handling the delicate topic of drug trafficking. He doesn't try to deny it but insists that his men do nothing more than collect protection money on cocaine, just like everyone else. In truth, even in this he's a much more ambitious and able leader. His Italian origins, greatly looked down upon at first, turn out to be useful to him. Mancuso oversees negotiations with the Calabrians, the biggest and most trustworthy buyers on the Colombian market since the days of Don Pablo Escobar.

So for the moment everything seems the same as before. Better, in fact. After years of living in hiding Salvatore can now return to Martha and his children, the youngest of whom don't even recognize him. But Salvatore has trouble recognizing Gianluigi, who is all grown up and soon to make him a grandfather. He's even received in parliament, where, dressed in a dark suit and red tie with diagonal white stripes— the picture of Italian elegance—he pleads the historic role of the Auto-defensas.

El Mono chooses a place under his control on the border of Venezuela for himself and the men under his direct command to turn over their weapons. It is a solemn, moving moment and sets the tone for his speech: "My soul awash with humility, I ask forgiveness of the people of Colombia, I ask forgiveness of the countries of this world, including the United States, if I have offended them by my actions or omissions. I ask forgiveness of every mother and of all those whom I have made suffer. I take responsibility for my role as leader, for what I could have done better, for what I could have done and did not do, errors surely caused by my limitations as a human being and by my lack of a calling for war."

Then, nearly two years later, he has his bodyguards accompany him to the police station in Montería, to turn himself in. In the meantime, some of the legal benefits of negotiating with the government are declared unconstitutional, but El Mono is not afraid of Colombia's law or its prisons. In fact, he still leads his troops and manages his affairs from within the maximum security prison in Itagüí, almost on a par with Escobar during his years of imprisonment.

Even so, the AUCs officially disband. Some—including mere narcos who pass themselves off as military bosses—turn themselves in, still hoping to benefit from the agreements. The others, the paramilitaries and narcos feeling orphaned by the big cartel, regroup into different organizations: Águilas Negras, or Black Eagles, headed by the fratricidal Vicente Castaño; Oficina de Envigado; Ejército Revolucionario Popular Antiterrorista de Colombia (ERPAC); Rastrojos; Urabeños; Paisas. They join forces and they break apart—the only element unifying them is cocaine. A new Colombia is being born, the ferocious land of Lilliput. The days of El Mono are coming to an end.


The defendant Salvatore Mancuso Gómez shows up clean-shaven and wearing a pinstripe suit fit for a wedding or business meeting. It's January 15, 2007. Sitting in front of a prosecutor, with a microphone and tape recorder in front of him, he takes out a laptop, places it on the table, and turns it on. He starts to read. The room fills with names, rattled off one after another, with professional detachment. When he is done, he has listed at least three hundred names, in strict chronological order: the homicides for which he takes personal responsibility, either as killer or commander, some of which he'd already been absolved for.

Bewilderment in the courtroom. Why did he do it?

Why, after getting away with so much, reveal the massacres he ordered or helped plan?

La Granja: July 1996

Pichilín: December 1996

Mapiripán: July 1997

El Aro: October 1997

La Gabarra: three raids, May–August 1999

El Salado: February 2000

Tibú: April 2000

In all these attacks, the defendant Mancuso Gómez declares, we were not alone. High-ranking members of the military provided logistical support and entire units of soldiers. And there were political representatives—such as Senator Mario Uribe Escobar—whose support never wavered.

Why is he doing this? Why him, a man of his intelligence, with his leadership skills? That's what many of the people he named are wondering. Then he is extradited to the United States, a move that weakens his voice in Colombia but that does not silence it completely.

From now on, no one is spared.

Colombia's high circles did business and collaborated with the paramilitary organizations. Lawyers, politicians, police officers, army generals: some to profit from the cocaine market, some to insure votes and support. And that's not all. According to Mancuso's deposition, the oil business, the drinks industry, the wood industry, transportation companies, and multinational banana corporations also had ties to the Autodefensas. All—with no exceptions—paid huge sums of money to the paramilitaries in exchange for protection and the possibility of continuing to work in the area. For years the AUCs had a hand in every step of the process.

Mancuso appears on *60 Minutes*. Then the spotlights are turned off and the prisoner is led back to his cell inside the maximum security prison in Warsaw, Virginia. Colombian as well as U.S. justice awaits him. It is highly likely that he will spend the rest of his life behind bars.

# 10

# THE TREE IS THE WORLD

The tree is the world. The tree is the genealogy of families linked by dynastic relations and sealed in blood. The tree is knowledge.

But the tree is also real. In the story handed down in 'ndrangheta lore it is an oak tree on the island of Favignana, but the tree I encountered is in Calabria, a hearty chestnut with green leaves, though its massive gray trunk is as cracked and as concave as a grotto. At Christmastime that natural grotto often hosts a nativity scene, with the Three Kings who have arrived from the East and the Archangel Gabriel watching over all from above, perched on a surface root. For centuries, as storms raged in the mountains, this tree offered shelter to sheep and dogs and donkeys, who could at least stick their front paws and big heads in, and even to humans: shepherds, hunters, and brigands. That's what I was thinking as I crouched in its hollow, breathing in the smell of musk and earth, of resin and stagnant water. This tree has always been here, in this gorge near the crest of Aspromonte. Men came later, and they took on the tree's form and its meanings.

The 'ndrangheta tree covers nearly the whole world. Though not as mythologized as Sicily's Cosa Nostra, in part because it is much more

discreet, the Calabrian criminal tribe is arguably the most powerful
organized crime group in the world; its estimated annual revenue, €53
billion, is over 3 percent of Italy's GDP. We are in a new era of waxing
'ndrangheta power, invoked by three dates. In 2007: the August 15
massacre at Da Bruno restaurant in Duisburg, Germany, an extension
of the feud that broke out in Calabria, among San Luca families, during
Carnival celebrations in 1991. In 2008: the 'ndrangheta is added to the
White House's list of foreign narcotics kingpins, drug-trafficking organizations considered to be a threat to U.S. security and whose assets are
immediately blocked. In 2010: Operation Crimine-Infinito, coordinated
by the DDA (Antimafia District Directorate) of Milan and Reggio
Calabria. Over three hundred arrests. Circulation of two videos: one,
the meeting at the Giovanni Falcone and Paolo Borsellino Club in Paderno Dugnano, in the hinterlands of Milan, which documents Calabrian dominance in northern Italy; the second, the annual summit of
the major 'ndrangheta bosses at the Polsi sanctuary, in Calabria, which
reveals the rigid hierarchical structure of the entire organization.

But the truth is awkward for many Italians. One day, leafing through
the papers, I let out a short, scornful laugh, as when you suddenly realize you're the butt of some awful joke, even though it somehow doesn't
surprise you. "Add your signature against Saviano, who calls northern-
ers mafiosi." It was mid-November 2010. A week earlier I had spoken
of 'ndrangheta transplants in northern Italy in comments on material
that had already been in the public domain for four months. There's
none so deaf as one who won't hear, I thought to myself. It occurred to
me that the Calabrian bosses could have found reassurance in that
proverb: Everything was still the same; no problem.

The 'ndrangheta owes as much to others' shortcomings as to its own
strengths for what it has become. One of its primary merits is the way
it cloaked its expansion so that only the occasional growth spurt was
noticed. Never the whole picture, never the full extension of the tree's
crown, even less its deep roots. For a good decade it disappeared from
sight even in Italy. The state seemed to have won on all fronts: It had

defeated terrorism, weakened the Sicilian Mafia after the season of bombs, occupied *manu militari* (with military aid) not only Sicily but Campania, Puglia, and Calabria, which was guilty of carrying out the killing of Judge Antonino Scopelliti, who was involved in the Palermo maxi-trial, the biggest trial ever against the Cosa Nostra, held in the second half of the eighties in Sicily. That "excellent cadaver" nevertheless fueled a dangerous misunderstanding: It appeared to be further proof of Calabrian subordination to the Sicilians, founders of the Mafia, the oldest and most notorious Italian criminal organization. What's more, in the collective imagination the 'ndrangheta still had no face, or if it did, it was still thought of as a primitive rural outfit that relied on kidnappings as the primary source of its organization's income, like the gangs of Anonymous Sardinian shepherds who dragged their hostages up onto the Gennargentu and treated them worse than their beasts, sending back severed ears in request for ransom money. They were beasts themselves, adding yet another element of terror to a country that in the 1970s was already far too bloody and unstable, but only by controlling areas that were totally backward. That was the idea that still stuck in people's minds, and no new one arrived to correct it.

It was an idea that proved useful to the 'ndrangheta. With the new Italian law introduced in 1982 that allowed for the freezing of mafia assets, the Sardinians were done in, and it was thought that the Calabrians were too. The mafiosi had stopped killing each other even in Reggio Calabria—peace seemed to be the right answer everywhere. But in Calabria it was a pax mafiosa. A strategic shift, a tactical withdrawal. The 'ndrangheta had decided to give up kidnapping, to stop letting Cosa Nostra get it mixed up in ineffective strategies against the state, and to keep from bleeding to death in fratricidal wars. The tree flourished in silence: Its roots continued to extend deeper into Calabrian soil through public works projects, such as the Salerno-Reggio Calabria highway, and its crown to reach into global trafficking, which now meant primarily cocaine.

The tree, which had long represented both the individual 'ndrina and the Onorata Società (the Honored Society, as the 'ndrangheta is called), also contained the answer to the growing need for cohesion and coordination. For a century more or less its symbolism had been handed down from father to son, from elderly boss to new affiliate. According to a 'ndrangheta code that came to light at Gioiosa Jonica in 1927, "the trunk represents the head of the society; the narrower part of the trunk the accountant and master of ceremonies; the branches the *camorristi* of blood and by crime, the twigs the rank and file; the flowers the young men of honor; the leaves the bastards and traitors who end up falling and rotting at the foot of the tree of knowledge." Oral transmission has generated many variants, but the substance is always the same. The bosses are the base of the trunk or the trunk itself, from which the other members of the hierarchy branch out, all the way out to the smallest and most fragile twigs.

The 'ndrangheta hierarchy was not an imitation of the Cosa Nostra's high command, as erroneously has been said; the Sicilian structure is that of a pyramid, the Calabrian tree can be simplified geometrically into its inverse: a downward pointing triangle, or a V, the sides of which can be extended and expanded into infinity.

And that was more or less what was happening. In Italy the Socialist and the Christian Democratic parties had crumbled, new governments came and went, rightist and leftist governments, and emergency governments, awkward coalitions of the two. There was Berlusconi and the Olive Tree Party, which was much more fragile than the 'ndrangheta tree. In Colombia, in the meantime, Pablo Escobar had been killed, and the Calabrians had redirected their middlemen toward Cali. Then the Cali cartel crumbled as well, and the 'ndrangheta had to do business with whoever was left, or whoever was starting to step in, secure in the knowledge that nothing was as immutable as their honored society, their tree.

Italy was forced to remember the existence of the 'ndrangheta in 2005, when Francesco Fortugno, vice president of the regional council of Calabria, was killed in the Calabrian town of Locri, and for the first time the area youth let out a collective cry: "Kill us all!" The shock didn't last long, though, as is always the case with news stories from southern Italy, which are considered manifestations of an endemic problem that is confined to those lands without hope and have nothing to do with the rest of the country.

The tree had become enormous. It wouldn't have been hard to notice it. It would have been enough to follow the news more regularly. It would even have been enough simply to reflect on a single story that made the national headlines. A story in which the tree reveals itself in its entirety. A leaf of the tree had fallen off and was gathered up by investigators before it could reach the ground. In and of itself the fallen leaf would not have constituted any risk. To date, the 'ndranghetisti who have decided to turn informers number less than one hundred, and you can count the bosses on two hands. It's tremendously difficult to turn your back on an organization that coincides with the family into which you were born or to which you're joined through marriage or baptism, and which almost everyone you have spent time with since you were a child belongs to. It's almost impossible to break away from a tree once you've become a branch. But this wasn't a branch, or even a twig. It was just a leaf, never anything more, what in the more elaborate versions of the myth are "contrasti onorati," those who support the organization without being members.


The leaf was named Bruno Fuduli.

Bruno was still a kid when he collected his inheritance and became the head of his family. The fate of the first born. In the 'ndrine dynastic succession based on seniority is one of those hard-and-fast laws that prevent a power struggle if a chief dies or ends up in jail. In a family business it's a widespread practice, and not only in Calabria or the South. The oldest son is the first to be brought into the business, to help out and to learn, and often to introduce new ideas, which younger generations can grasp more easily.

Bruno was just over twenty when his father died, leaving him his stone masonry business, the Filiberto Fuduli company in Nicotera, an ancient village that looks over the Tyrrhenian Sea and a famous stretch of long, white beach that fills with tourists in the summer. He also inherited half a billion lire of debt, but he was sure he'd be able to manage things if he revitalized the company, made it competitive.

Marble, granite, and all the other stones that his craftsman father had worked with were coming back in style. There was a demand for large stone surfaces in private homes, in addition to their timeless use in cemeteries. So Bruno throws himself into the fray: He updates his range of products, changes the name of the company and the corporation, and then opens two more companies, in partnership with his brother-in-law. But there are other obstacles Bruno has to face. Along with his father's debts, Bruno also inherited another aspect of his business: theft, vandalism, malice. An elastic response to such obstacles is usually what is expected in southern Italy, but Bruno stays true to the old Filiberto stubbornness. Instead of going to the right people to set things right, he goes to the police.

For the family who rules the entire province of Vibo Valentia, this sort of thing is a mild annoyance, like a fly that disturbs your postprandial nap on a muggy summer afternoon. The Mancuso family has been there forever. They can boast of a 1903 court sentence, when their great-grandfather Vincenzo was condemned for criminal conspiracy. By now they've got their hands in every sort of illegal activity and are on friendly terms with the 'ndrangheta families in the Gioia Tauro plain. The Piromalli family gang controls the territory where the port and the steel plant are being built, and the Mancuso family gang controls the quarries in Limbadi and environs, which supplied the building materials. The amount the young Fuduli refuses to cough up is nothing to them, small change. But he's setting a bad example with his arrogance. It's routine, standard practice, to repeat their requests for payment, something they do on principle, till the stubborn kid learns to lower his head. It's merely a question of time. Time is not only the best healer, it's also the best fee collector.

Debts. Bruno manages to keep them under control for years, even with all the expenses and additional losses inflicted on him by the forces he refuses to give in to. He practically works himself to death to pay the interest, but the sword of Damocles still hangs over his companies. It wouldn't take much to upset his precarious balance. All it would take is one more problem, a few more customers whose checks bounce, or who don't pay at all. Which is exactly what happens toward the end of the 1980s, a moment in which the entire country's economy starts slowing down, nudging Italy toward the financial crisis that will explode in 1992. So one day the bank tells Fuduli that, for want of guaranties, it is forced to close his credit line. Either he declares bankruptcy, or he finds some other way to survive. Those are his only options.

The people he contacts don't have a problem lending him money, but they charge 200 percent interest, even more. Loan sharks. The Mancuso family usurers are becoming more and more threatening. But suddenly a man with unlimited resources holds out a helping hand to him: Natale Scali, boss of the town of Marina di Gioiosa Jonica, an experienced drug trafficker. He needs a guy like Bruno: a young businessman toughened by years of training, during which he used every possible resource to defend his companies. Intelligent, dynamic, determined. Someone who knows how to behave, and who speaks Spanish well. His record is spotless; in fact, it's even adorned with repeated reports of extortion threats. Scali tells him so, quite openly. He doesn't push, doesn't rush. He flatters him, telling him each time they meet that he needs someone like him, someone clean. And for a sum that no bank would ever lend him—1.7 billion lire—Scali asks him for a favor, in the form of a plane trip. An arrest warrant has forced Scali to hole up in his bunker house in his hometown, but before, when he used to go to Bogotá himself, to take care of business, he'd live like a fat cat, the guest of a governor's brother. All Bruno has to do is go and renew Scali's old contacts. He can think of it as a vacation.

Natale Scali was a far-sighted businessman with lots of experience. The Aquino-Scali-Ursino 'ndrangheta families, like the other 'ndrangheta families on the Ionian coast, had become so specialized in importing cocaine from Colombia that they were allowed to have their own representative *in loco:* a man named Santo Scipione, who goes by the name of Papi, and who was sent directly from the town of San Luca, the 'ndrangheta stronghold, known as mamma, from whom all things come. She's the one who makes the rules, the one who slaps you, punishes you, caresses you, rewards you, the one with whom all problems must be discussed. If problems arise among 'ndrangheta sons anywhere in the world, mamma San Luca resolves them. Santo Scipione is in regular contact with Natale Scali, but his supply channel does not cover all of Scali's demand. He has settled in Montería, appealing because of its sizable Italian community, and because Salvatore Mancuso, El Mono, is there. Even though Mancuso is now officially a commander in hiding, he is becoming more and more crucial for Italo-Colombian relations. For every fugitive, home is home: the place where your family is; your people; the place you belong to and that belongs to you. The Calabrians have worked with the AUC since they were founded. So their decision to settle their representative right in the middle of AUC territory is a much appreciated gesture of respect, and good for business.

When he returns from Bogotá Bruno discovers that Scali has charged him 600 million lire in interest, to be paid with another trip, and then another. It's no longer a matter of calling on people on Scali's behalf. Now Bruno has to contact new suppliers. The deals he helps launch result in tons of cocaine being shipped to Calabria. Natale Scali had been right about Bruno. So when he offers to put an end to Bruno's debt problems by taking over his company and gets a "no, thank you" in response, each serenely goes his own way. It's not a problem for Scali, but it is for Bruno. This boss from Marina di Gioiosa Jonica has now joined the Mancuso family orbit of usurers, and has taken a personal interest.

Towns in Calabria are small, and the 'ndrangheta's branches are intertwined. There's a small branch on the big tree that needs to be tended to. Mancuso narco Vincenzo Barbieri has just been released from prison and has to serve the rest of his time under house arrest. In order to leave the house he needs to find a job that the police will find credible. The solution is so simple, and so near at hand. Diego Mancuso, a Vibo Valentia 'ndrina boss, steps in. He merely asks a favor, that Barbieri be given a job—to help with his rehabilitation—at Fuduli's company Lavormarmi. Maybe Bruno fools himself into thinking that he can keep up the facade with Barbieri and his partner, Francesco Ventrici, a guy with a clean record whom Barbieri brought along. Perhaps Bruno believes them when they insist they'd prefer not to have anything to do with the Mancuso family. Everything unfolds from there: Bruno ends up being outmaneuvered, and his companies, increasingly in the red, fall into the hands of the 'ndrangheta.

They make a strange couple, Vincenzo Barbieri and Francesco Ventrici, not exactly blood brothers loyal to the Onorata Società or 'ndrangheta, but something akin to that, anyway. Ventrici, the younger of the two, may not even be ritually affiliated with the organization but merely close to it, in part because he's always close—very close—to Barbieri. They're like one of those inseparable couples that sometimes form in small villages in southern Italy. Villages like San Calogero, buried in boredom, where all the men hang out at the bars, and where permission to enter them is already a rite of passage of sorts. Where certain kids cling to the most admired character, so that when they grow up, their untiring reverence and emulation is cemented into a real bond. Ventrici marries one of Barbieri's cousins, and then they become family for real—they're godfathers to each other's children. Which is how Fuduli's unrequested partners introduce themselves when they're in San Calogero. Barbieri is the official owner of a company that makes living room furniture, and his well-kept, bourgeois look earns him the nickname U Ragioniere or Accountant. Ventrici is a big kid with narrow eyes and a double chin, whose usual nickname, El Gordo—Fatty— must have been pinned on him by one of Barbieri's Colombian friends. The trafficking they engage in through Fuduli's companies and the service their owner provides make theirs a most productive friendship.

Bruno is still the pivot on which everything turns. Bruno, who now finds himself the servant of two masters and prey to many more. Bruno, who continues to fly across the ocean, to negotiate or mediate for Scali and the Vibo Valentia 'ndrina, to consider new contacts, new routes, new transportation methods, all the while winning more of his South American interlocutors' trust. He meets them in Cuba, Panama, Venezuela, and Ecuador, but also in Italy and Spain. He's growing more sure of himself, more confident, precise, and organized. A friendly partner, a pleasure to work with. If they talk on the phone about parties and the number of guests as codes for shipments and quantities of cocaine, it doesn't mean they don't invite him to parties for real.

All those business trips are exhausting, though. If you are in a certain line of work, Colombia can be a deadly forest, even when you stay in the best hotels in the capital or are a guest in the most luxurious villas. And after the collapse of the Cali and Medellín cartels, those that offer the best prices are also the most dangerous: AUC, FARC. Bitter enemies united by the production and wholesale marketing of cocaine, but also by the fact that they can nab you and make you disappear whenever they feel like it. At that point the only thing you can do is pray to the Maronna 'ra Muntagna—the Madonna of the Mountain— and ask her to make sure your guys over in Calabria get the overdue payments there in time. But Bruno learns on his own how proud his compatriots are to be the only customers the Colombians don't ask a percentage from in advance. They are men of honor, men of their word. Their word, sure, but there has to be a down payment in flesh and blood, withheld until the last drug dollar is credited. His turn could be next.

Bruno has been living this life for years now. Negotiate, oversee the process by which the blocks of marble, of *piedra muñeca*, are turned into something that looks like Swiss cheese, except they're square: pierced with cylindrical holes that are then filled with plastic tubes stuffed with cocaine and sealed with a paste made of marble dust. Then contact the Colombian exporters—front businesses—to pick up the goods, which are to be shipped to one of his companies. And finally, go back to Calabria, take delivery of the shipment once it has cleared customs at Gioia Tauro, and get it transported to a quarry near San Calogero. That's probably the critical moment. The moment when he stands before those blocks of marble weighing twenty tons, which, had they been left untouched, once they'd been cut and polished, would have revealed all their splendor: golden in color, rich with veins, so similar to travertine. Instead, Bruno, the former owner of Lavormarmi and now the owner on paper of Marmo Imeffe, he who accepts delivery of those marble blocks, now must teach complicit workers how to remove the cylinders without even scratching them. Salvage the cocaine. Reuse merely the scraps of those earthly treasures that take geologic eras to form and now are worth the same as an empty tin can. He prefers it when the cocaine ends up in flowers, or stinking leather skins, or cans of tuna fish. But when that's the case, the coke isn't unloaded in Italy, not right before his eyes anyway.

When Barbieri or Ventrici tells him he can leave because nothing that happens afterward has anything to do with him, Bruno, driving home, tumbles into darkness. This is not the life he wants. Not the life he's willing to land in jail or be killed for. He feels old. He's almost forty and doesn't feel all that different from those blocks of marble filled with holes: a failed marriage, one business already lost, and the others he can't seem to salvage. If he thinks back on how he was able to stand his ground with the Mancuso family: he was just a kid with a small business then, his turnover ridiculously small. Yet he had resisted the Mancusos for years. Then they crushed him for no reason, just for the sake of trying to squeeze him like an orange picked on the Rosarno plain. And now he's letting himself be squeezed, like the lowliest illegal immigrant.

But he's not a lowly illegal immigrant. This is not who he is. If he wasn't afraid as a kid, he shouldn't be afraid now either, now that he has learned that everyone, whether in Calabria or Colombia, has a hand on his head that can crush him at any time, either in punishment, by mistake, of just for the heck of it. Who knows how long he would have harbored such thoughts, brooding over them ad nauseam. The fact is, one day Bruno makes up his mind. He goes to the Carabinieri again, this time not to report a threat but to turn himself in: his role, his trips, his marble shipments, and what they really contained. They're incredulous at first. They need the assessment of a higher authority. But on the basis of investigations already under way, ROS, the Carabinieri's Special Operations Group, realizes that Fuduli's statements are true. For two years he acts as a confidential source. Then he takes a further leap: He becomes a government witness. A secret witness. An inconceivable figure in the heart of 'ndrangheta territory. An infiltrator.

The investigation Fuduli contributed to was called Operation Decollo (Takeoff), and to this day it is still considered the mother of all transnational drug-trafficking investigations of Calabrian families. The leaf has fallen, the tree is more visible now. Visible doesn't mean uprooted, though. In terms of its economic and operational repurcussions, Operation Decollo, which involved police and investigators from Italy, Holland, Spain, Germany, and France, together with the DEA and Colombian, Venezuelan, and Australian magistrates, and which led to arrests in Lombardy, Piedmont, Liguria, Emilia Romagna, Tuscany, and Campania, as well as the seizure of five and a half tons of cocaine, was merely a scratch on the tree's bark. The primary worth of the investigation was informational. Seizures are data points, proof that shipments left from one country and arrived in another, sometimes with stopovers and transfers along the way. They provide a reliable measurement of the tree, or at least of some of its main branches.

Early in 2000, three containers that left Barranquilla, Colombia, aboard ships owned by the Danish company Maersk Sealand pass through the port of Gioia Tauro. All on their way to Fuduli's companies, all filled with marble blocks that contain 220, 434, and 870 kilos of cocaine, respectively. In March 2000 another container with 434 kilos of cocaine stashed in marble blocks is shipped from Barranquilla to Australia, to Nicola Ciconte, a man with Calabrian roots but born in Wonthaggi, a farming town southwest of Melbourne. It arrives in the port of Adelaide in August. The Australian police eventually track down about two thirds of it, which a Calabrian has already put in storage. Then they start to strike in Italy, but with strategic prudence. It's not the amount of cocaine seized that matters but rather the fact that another mode of transport has been uncovered, and even more, that it leads directly to another branch of the tree, the Lombard branch. On January 23 and March 17, 2001, at Milan Malpensa Airport, 12.1 and 18.5 kilos of cocaine are seized on two different commercial flights from Caracas, Venezuela. A SEA employee, the company that manages the airport, is there to remove the bags in which the goods are stashed from the luggage carousel. He is from San Calogero. The Mancuso and Pesce of Rosarno clans are set up to speedily restock the Milan drug market, where the demand for coke is inexhaustible. Almost a whole year goes by before they touch another ship. January 10, 2002: At the port of Vigo in Galicia, a container from Ecuador is searched. Inside are found 1,698 kilos of cocaine, stashed in cans of tuna in olive oil and destined for the Conserva Nueva in Madrid. Bruno Fuduli, who negotiated the deal with the Colombians, the Vibo Valentians, and the Spanish, had kept the investigators informed.

April 3, 2002, is an important date. The first real big action in Italy. The shipment was supposed to arrive at Gioia Tauro, but it ends up by mistake at the port of Salerno, where it is seized. This time the container left from La Guaira, Venezuela, and the 541 kilos of cocaine are stuffed in the loading pallets for the granite blocks being sent to Fuduli's Marmo Imeffe.

Another year of waiting, and of apparent calm. Then comes the most important blow, just beyond Europe's main port of entry for cocaine. During the night of June 3-4, 2003, Spanish authorities intercept the trawler *Alexandra* off the Canary Islands, with 2,591 kilos of cocaine onboard. It was probably loaded off the coast of West Africa, in Togo or Benin perhaps, where the 'ndrine have storage and transportation facilities.

But it's not over. The next action covers the entire Atlantic, right up to where it becomes the North Sea. On October 29, 2003, a shipment from Manaus, Brazil, that has come through Rijeka, Croatia, is stopped at the port of Hamburg: 255 kilos of cocaine are hidden in a load of plastic ceiling panels. Stopovers make drug trafficking easier, since the number of the container is changed every time. The one that arrived in Hamburg was supposed to be delivered to San Lazzaro di Savena, to a company called Ventrans, owned by Francesco Ventrici, which a road haulage portal elected "company of the month" in 2002 for its "seriousness, reliability, and precision." Mancuso's man was held up as a model businessman in the town near Bologna where he had taken up residence.

It's not until January 28, 2004, three years later, that the port of Gioia Tauro is hit. A shipment of 242 kilos of cocaine hidden in blocks of *piedra muñeca* that sailed from Cartagena for Marmo Imeffe is seized. It's the final act, the moment when the investigators remove their masks. Arrests are under way. Operation Decollo is over.

Colombia, Venezuela, Brazil, Spain, Germany, Croatia, Italy, Africa, Australia. The first points to mark for sure on the map. They're not the only ones, though; they couldn't be. When the investigators insist that they only manage to confiscate 10 percent of the cocaine destined for the European market, which amounts to a typical business risk— less than the percentage of goods stolen from a supermarket or checks bounced in a small business—they're merely revealing publicly what they can of the bitter truth. It's extremely difficult, of course, to find the eggs smuggled inside the body or the lots hidden with increasingly sophisticated methods, to intercept ships that sail the high seas and anchor for the night off the coast, wherever they choose. It's difficult even when they've gathered detailed information. The narco-traffickers often manage to get away with it right under the noses of those trailing them. But there's also another, more complicated aspect. The state not only needs to get cocaine off the streets; it also needs to block and possibly break up the organizations that sell it. But these two objectives conflict. If you keep hitting the same port, the traffickers will know for sure that you've got them in your sights, so they will alter their routes and cover-up cargo, dock in unpredictable places, in ports under less surveillance. In the case of Operation Decollo, the investigators had an extraordinary hidden card to play: an infiltrator who informed them in real time about new shipments and destinations. But this isn't usually the case. They may resort to extensive wiretapping, but precautions on the other side make it extremely tricky to identify routes and unloading points. One risks losing the trail, and with it the entire investigation, which necessarily depends on such confirmations.

Even when, as in this case, the investigators know almost everything, every move has to be weighed carefully. Pretend. Pretend it was all just a lucky strike. It doesn't mean your opponents won't smell a rat. But what matters most in this secret poker game between cops and robbers is to not raise the level of alarm too high. Or for too long. The investigators can always be sure of one thing: Narco-traffickers may fold a hand, but they never cash in their chips. Sometimes you win, sometimes you lose. Given the market needs, the calculation of risk becomes relative.

Who knows how much Bruno Fuduli pondered the choice he was about to make that day when he decided to walk into police headquarters in Vibo Valentia. Never enough. He thought he could escape the loan sharks who would have strangled him and the increasing probability of

ending up in jail for a long time. Once he turned informer and eventually accomplice to the criminal investigation police, taking the code
name Sandro, he knew he would receive protection and assistance in
order to create a new life for himself, far from where people considered
him a rat, a leaf destined to rot at the foot of a tree. One thing he knew
for sure—if they discover that it's me, they'll kill me. If they only find
out later—after I've made a new life for myself—who it was who betrayed them, they'll never give up searching for me. Clear thinking, but
too generic, too abstract. He simply couldn't imagine in advance the
anxiety that would assail him, day after day, as a leaf in the hands of
those who were starting to interfere with the flow of sap. A choice always transcends the calculation behind it; it is made powerful and inescapable by its blind spot. You never know how much it will cost you.
You don't know how you will manage to hold to it, day after day. You
really don't understand what you're doing, what you've already done.
That's the conclusion I came to as well, over almost nine years. It often
wakes me up and crushes me, like a punch in the chest. Then I get up,
try to breathe, and tell myself: In the end, this is the way it has to be.

In reality, Bruno already starts to realize the tribulations that await
him the morning after the first shipment (the only one that comes off
smoothly, even with an exchange of hostages between Calabria and
Colombia) when his two bosses, Natale Scali and Vincenzo Barbieri,
end up arguing over the price of the cocaine, and start threatening each
other. The second shipment is a dud: cocaine that has already been cut,
stuff no one in Calabria buys. The Australian shipment would have
been the most profitable—the market price down under is pretty
high—if most of it hadn't been seized. At first the traffickers think
they've been screwed. Then, when they learn more about the bust from
the Internet , they insist that they were responsible for the goods only
until they cleared customs in port, which they had done. Bruno scram-
bles, irons things out, negotiates discounts. But then, incredible as it
may seem, debts start threatening the marble and cocaine imports as
well. And since Fuduli is already in hock with the loan sharks, Barbieri

and Ventrici send him to contract more loans, with people even closer to the Mancusos and their vassal families. The lords of the province, kept out of his company by the gates, now appear at the windows.

All it would have taken to set things right was for the 870 kilos that arrived in Gioia Tauro in May-June 2000 and sold in bulk to the powerful Platì boss Pasquale Marando not to cause any more problems. But instead the shipment causes a frenzy. A frenzy born in a mini Colombian cartel, which infects the one established by Ventrici and Barbieri. The coke for that shipment was supplied by a family business, three or four brothers. But two of them hate each other. Felipe, in charge of sales and transportation, harbors deep rancor toward Daniel, who runs the production side and can be considered the head of the company. Colombians have a saying: "More people die in Colombia of envy than of cancer," Bruno will say when telling the magistrates the story, which leaves them dumbfounded. Envy pierces and devours them, but profit holds them together, like the most poisonous glue. Felipe is kept at a distance with tasks that let him vent and even put to good use his violent nature and restless swagger. But envy merely waits for a soft landing to climb out of the crevice where it is hiding. It comes in the form of the two men from Vibo Valentia, with their lack of experience and their unflinching desire to hang on to the billions they've already pocketed from selling the shipment to Pasquale Marando. Felipe demands a small share of the payment for himself, saying he intends to ruin his brother and promising that he'll be the one to deal with him. Ventrici, who unlike Barbieri can travel to meetings, is the first to give in. "Let's pay the six million and let them sort it out," he says to his partner. But for Daniel things aren't adding up. He wants his share, he doesn't care in the least about the money his brother got. He wants his own.

Daniel finds a way to make himself heard even while staying "in the kitchens" hidden in Colombia. He sends armed ambassadors to Ventrici with an ultimatum. Even worse, he personally sends him a fax from Colombia with a photograph of Ventrici's house, followed by a second fax in which he informs him that he's going to give $2 million to his ETA (the armed Basque organization) friends to blow it up with him inside. Fatty Ventrici, who was insolent up to that moment, is now terrified. He asks Bruno to meet with the narco he's on most familiar terms with in Cuba—a guy named Ramiro—who reassures him that while Daniel sells coke to the Basque terrorists, it's out of the question that ETA would mobilize to collect the debt.

Things calm down. All this has probably had a strange effect on Bruno. He's seen the man who took his company out from under him shit his pants—for reasons he knows all too well. And he's gotten further confirmation that in the narcos' hierarchies of respect, he's on a higher rung than the two men who think they can control him like a puppet. Now Ventrici and Barbieri know it too, they know that Calabria, compared to Colombia, is like a kids' playground. It's easy to feel like a man when you have the organization backing you up. Easy when you're grabbing on to the tree as if it were your mommy's apron strings, or when you merely give them an adolescent tug. In the end it's always the tree that controls each and every leaf that moves. But Bruno decided not to let the tree control him anymore.

In fact, hostilities only die down because the big branches intervene. Natale Scali and Pasquale Marando guarantee the Colombian brothers against insolvency. In other words, they take on Ventrici and Barbieri's debt in Colombia. Holding them by the balls for a mere $6 million means the bosses can avoid a whole slew of hassles nobody really needs. They've got plenty of other more pressing matters to deal with. In Colombia, for example, Santo "Papi" Scipione is running into the usual snags when it comes to payments. The experience and authority he's already acquired in the field aren't enough to prevent the paramilitaries, who nabbed his most trusty narco the month before, from wanting to get even with him. There are enormous advantages to bargaining with AUC, but all it takes is one hitch, which for normal traffickers would become the object of a tranquil discussion, and you seriously risk ending up in a ditch. Santo Scipione waits for them to come get him.

"Because I don't have anywhere to flee to, nowhere," he sighs anxiously to Natale Scali, whose phone has already been tapped. The boss of Gioiosa Jonica wants to save Scipione: "A Calabrian's life is worth more than a debt with these people, who don't even know how to keep their word. They ask you for two but then they expect to get four." Even the paramilitaries trust Scali's word and, above all, his solvency. The hostages return home. But this time the veteran Calabrian narco has had the living daylight scared out of him.

Relying too much on past experience can sometimes betray you. You lean too much on what worked well before and have trouble evaluating anything new. This may partly explain why, curiously, the Aquino and Coluccio families of Marina di Gioiosa Jonica went into business with the Gulf cartel—to be precise, with Los Zetas, which, when the Italians first started dealing with them, was still the military arm of Friend Killer Osiel Cárdenas. What's more, they did it from New York, after the Mexican narcos had already become the United States' Enemy Number 2, when even direct imports of Taliban heroin could get into Europe more easily than a small shipment of cocaine from the heart of North America. It's not as if the Calabrians didn't try to be prudent. They shipped only microscopic lots, small enough at times to be sent by priority mail, and they never set foot outside the Big Apple when negotiating. But they still ended up with the DEA hard on their heels. The arrests started in 2008, and the substance of the huge investigation called Operation Reckoning (which in Italy was coordinated by the DDA of Reggio Calabria and was called Operazione Solare) became public. The United States punished the 'ndrangheta immediately by putting it on its Office of Foreign Assets Control blacklist, as a Specially Designated Narcotics Trafficker. A tough blow. Excessive, from the Calabrians' point of view. Their prudence wasn't merely aimed at avoiding trouble with the DEA but with their new partners as well. They weren't looking for some big business opening but were merely testing a new, alternative supply channel that opened up, to supplement the Colombian one.

The Colombians have never been interested in or able to manage the European drug markets on their own, which is why the Calabrians preferred to cultivate their role as direct importers. But they find themselves in competition with the Mexicans. The strength of both lies in their handling the entire narco trafficking distribution chain, cocaine *in primis*. And both knew how to take advantage of Colombia's growing weakness. But now the fragmentation of the Colombia cartels and their increasing subordination to the Mexicans was making 'ndrangheta business dealings more complicated and uncertain. Which is why it needed to find a way to adapt to the new economic reality but without running too many risks. What the Calabrians fear most is that the Mexicans will land in Europe and invade their markets. The apparent absurdity of importing through the United States seemed to reflect this fear. The 'ndragheta's nightmare was not the Mexican cartels' military but rather their commercial aggressiveness. Yet it wasn't wholly indifferent to this other aspect either, perhaps because it believes itself to be an expression of a saner, more civilized Old World than the Mexicans, or because dealing with people capable of such incalculable ferocity increases the risks associated with their business. Yet the 'ndrangheta had worked with the Colombians, for whom mass killings were standard practice, and that collaboration had been successful for years. So it may be that, when the leaders in Marina di Gioiosa Jonica approved the New York experiment, the comparison between AUC and Zetas played a role, especially as Los Zetas had not yet become an independent and powerful cartel.


I look for the photos of the tree near the Polsi sanctuary. I'm sorry I didn't study it longer, didn't observe closely what the top was like, the tips of the branches. I was with my Carabinieri bodyguards and a Calabrian carabiniere who was acting as guide. "Special tour in the land of the 'ndrangheta" he said to me. I had time to take some pictures with my phone, step inside the tree trunk, and linger a while longer, but then we had to move on to our next stop. I was a specialist tourist, and my guide was someone who usually came to these places to arrest someone, carry out a search, or look for underground hideouts. I couldn't wander off on my own and contemplate the tree like some crazy poet in search of inspiration. To tell the truth, it didn't even occur to me. After years of spending entire days with my escort I don't even realize anymore how much I adapt my behavior to conform to the rules of the group. But that's only normal. All of us have our rules, not just the Carabinieri or the 'ndrangheta.

Looking at a photo of myself inside the tree, I'm reminded of Santo Scipione, who left Aspromonte in order to become the 'ndrine agent in Colombia. He's in jail now, but there are plenty of others like him in Latin America, western Africa, and in who knows how many other parts of the world where illegal commerce hasn't been put on the map yet. Dreadful, dangerous places where you go to live only for business. I suspect that Santo Scipione would tell me there's no difference whatsoever between what he was doing for the Onorata Società and what the heads of multinational corporations were doing when they paid AUC so as to obtain the best working conditions, as his wholesaler Salvatore Mancuso confirmed from prison in Warsaw. The only risk you have to reduce is your business risk. Your personal risk is compensated for with money. If, alas, things go poorly for you, if, for example, you happen to be at the petrol plant that Islamic terrorists storm and you end up dead, the company will always find someone who will go and replace you for the right price. But it's not like these poor people could pick up the phone and talk with their boss, I can imagine Papi saying. The 'ndrangheta isn't just some company with a head office and various businesses scattered about. It is a tree where the outer branches communicate with the trunk, which is welcoming, protective.

.   .   .

Bruno Fuduli was becoming more and more indispensable for the tree
he never wanted to be part of. That is what's so absurd about his story.
Even Natale Scali enlists his services again, because he realizes how
good he is. And since he's not concerned about his two accomplices, the
last person he thinks he needs to fear is their puppet. So while investigations are under way, Bruno is leading not a double but in fact a triple
life. In Calabria he's nothing more than a useful cog in the wheel. But
in Colombia his esteem continues to grow with the people who really
count. He's not dealing just with narcos anymore but directly with the
upper ranks of AUC. He would be wise to take to heart the Colombian
proverb about more people dying from envy than from cancer. He
needs to be more careful, he realizes, about revealing his contacts in
Colombia—so as not to make the Calabrians jealous—than about
concealing his unspeakable secret. Only to the Carabinieri and the
judges can and must he report everything, word for word. Fuduli is
revealing a new world to them, in all its detail. He's the first person in
Italy, and most likely not just there, to put a face on the new world of
drug trafficking. He tells of a FARC guerrilla who lives in the jungle
on the border with Ecuador, and who comes to Bogotá exclusively to
traffic cocaine and procure materials to make explosives. He describes
a paramilitary who handles cocaine for AUC and calls himself Rambo.
He talks about narcos not as Colombian drug lords but as small businessmen, coerced and consumed by subservient relationships far worse
than the ones he himself is caught in. He remembers the stories his
friend Ramiro confided in him, from fleeing Cali with all his family
after the hegemony of the cartel ended, when his offering to the new
arrivals wasn't enough to placate them, to the last time he had to high-
tail it out of there because they hadn't "set things right" with AUC for
managing the "kitchens." *Cocinas, cocinero, negocio.* Kitchens, cook,
business. Bruno borrows from Spanish an untranslatable vocabulary,
words that ooze toil and rivalry.

The Italian investigators are treading on virgin territory. They have trouble following Bruno into a reality so different from the one they know: the Medellín cartel, the Cali cartel. But it doesn't mean a thing now if you come from Medellín or Cali: For the power system that orbits around cocaine, what matters most is if you're a paramilitary or a guerrilla. Fuduli has been going to Colombia since 1996. His confidential relationship begins one year before the United States declares AUC a terrorist organization, whose ties to narco-trafficking are merely strongly suspected. FARC, though long a target of massive military aid, still passes for a subversive army funded by robbery and kidnappings.

It's not surprising therefore, that the first time Fuduli names Castaño and Mancuso in his statements to the magistrates there's a fair amount of confusion. In the end it is impossible to decide whether Fuduli, together with Ramiro and his brother, had been summoned "to the jungle" by the supreme commander and his number two or if the narcos negotiated the *nulla osta* for the shipment that was later stopped in Salerno with a lieutenant whose nom de guerre is Boyaco. Sure, the transcription is even more confusing than the recording of Fuduli's interview with the magistrates, rambling on as he does about paramilitaries in general and about Carlos Castaño, who "by this point . . . has incriminated himself and has been completely condemned." Yet the transcription does seem to preserve some trace of the kinds of misunderstandings that arise when one party alludes to information that the other party doesn't know anything about. Fuduli probably expected to be asked more than merely "Mancuso who?" to which he responds with a laconic "Mancuso Colombian." I certainly would have liked to delve deeper into his story, to know more about such an anomalous witness's experience, even if it weren't directly related to the investigation. The fact remains that Operation Decollo verified the connection between AUC and the 'ndrangheta, and was the first to do so. But Fuduli's words have a different taste than the phone calls between Santo Scipione and Natale Scali. A strange, ancient taste. Not the taste of tales of those who went in search of treasure or explored uncharted lands but of one who has ended up there because someone else willed it. They often reminded me of the accounts of the first missionaries sent to the American continent.

There's one point in particular the investigators linger over, circle back to, even though Fuduli can't provide them with any other essential information. He alleges that Felipe, toward the end of 2000, proposed he meet a narco-trafficker who had access to ships that could deliver supplies right off the Ionian coast—huge shipments, from both the guerrillas and the paramilitaries. The idea even enticed Natale Scali, and he sent one of his men, along with Bruno and a cousin of Francesco Ventrici, to represent him. The meeting didn't take place in Colombia, nor in the bordering countries of Venezuela, Ecuador, Brazil, or Panama. The Calabrians were instead taken by tourist charter to Cancún, from there to Mexico City, and finally to Guadalajara. They were met at the airport and taken by car to a *finca* in the countryside. There they awaited the arrival of someone whom Felipe introduced merely as "my godfather."

Fuduli cannot tell the investigators the godfather's name or nickname. He doesn't know if he is Mexican or Colombian. He's been told he is in hiding, but he doesn't know the country he's wanted in. Felipe is the unreliable type, with delusions of grandeur that will reveal themselves later. So when he passes his "godfather" off as "one of the biggest in Mexico," there's no reason to believe him. But Ramiro, who is much more trustworthy, confirms to Bruno that every fifteen days he prepares a shipment and readies the runway so that Felipe can fly 400 kilos of cocaine to a private landing strip in Mexico. He also tells him that the reason those low-flying flights are made only every two weeks is simply that all the Colombian family cartels together aren't able to fill the plane every week.

The Italian magistrates must not have found sufficient proof of the deals with the "godfather living in Mexico," even though a Mexican citizen figures among those condemned in the first round of the trial that followed the investigation. But in light of what has transpired in the more than ten years that have passed since these reports were transcribed, in light of the information that the Reckoning and Solare investigations provided, Fuduli's story seems in fact to be the chronicle of the Calabrians' first landing in Mexico.

When I think about Bruno, when I recall his words, I ask myself what it means to encounter your destiny by mistake rather than by chance. The difference between fate and accident depends on your point of view, on the stories you tell—or don't tell—yourself about the meaning of your life. The error of accepting Natale Scali's proposal. The error he decided to try and erase by collaborating with the law. But Bruno Fuduli continued to dwell in that error for nearly ten years. He wasn't an independent broker, and he wasn't affiliated with a clan. He'd get on planes and go to tropical borderlands, to no man's lands brimming with mines, fear, and poverty. And right at the end he found himself locked up for two weeks in a hut in the Bogotá savannah, altitude 11,500 feet, guarded day and night by paramilitaries armed to the teeth. The problem, that time, was the Vibo Valentia guys' shipment seized in Hamburg, valued at $3 million. The Colombians wanted to be paid, they wanted to collect on what they'd sent. The Calabrians didn't want to hear it, though; they wanted to pay only for the goods they received. Natale Scali couldn't step in anymore. He'd been arrested in Marina di Gioiosa Jonica. Pasquale Marando couldn't either—he was killed, but there's no trace of his body. Right before the end the double game was turning into Russian roulette, with more than one bullet in the barrel. Bruno lost twenty pounds; all they gave him was water. He got sick. They moved him to an apartment in the capital, fearing for the life of their hostage. From there, instead of calling his counterparts in Calabria, he came up with a way to alert the Carabinieri. The Special Operations Group (ROS) collaborated with the Colombian police, who on January 12, 2004, managed to rescue him without firing a single shot. Later the AUC came for Ramiro. They stuffed him in the same hole of a hut Bruno'd been in until Ventrici and Barbieri finally settled their bill. Bruno's double life as an infiltrator was about to end.


Even the judicial inquiries draw on the tree metaphor, and they propagate like branches. After Operation Decollo will come Decollo bis, Decollo ter, and Decollo Money, each of which will become intertwined with still other investigations. Follow the money: That was Giovanni Falcone's pioneering investigative strategy and his lesson to magistrates who came after him. Yet this remains the hardest thing for investigators to do. It's the fault of inadequate laws and tools, widespread complicity, and a lack of awareness and therefore of public pressure about the matter. It's the fruit of a certain media logic, in which a drug seizure is worth at least ten lines in the paper, while the seizure of a property or business barely gets a mention in the local news, even though the economic aspects of Mafia activities are getting more attention in Italy. The information arrives, but it isn't seen. The money even less.

Money isn't merely that abstract entity, almost mystical for its volatility, infinite quantities of which can be moved from one end of the planet to the other with a mere click of a keyboard. Invested in the most cryptic funds, in the most high-risk stocks. At least not for the 'ndrangheta, or for mafias in general. For them, money is money. Cash, wads of it, suitcases crammed full of it, secret stashes. Their money has substance, weight—you can count it on your fingers. And the moldy smell it has isn't lost even when it lands in the most unreachable bank accounts. 'Ndrangheta money is the fruit of their labor, the fruit of the tree. Which is why the 'ndrangheta does not disdain any method of cleaning it, reinvesting it, making the fruit of their labor bear more fruit. So their grand laundering schemes through finance companies that fit together like Chinese nesting boxes sit alongside the simple purchase of some two-room apartment or plot of farmland.

Operation Decollo's first money trail discovery was incredible, both because of the amount involved and for the sheer simplicity of the laundering method. The Vibonesi bought themselves a SuperEnalotto lottery ticket. In May 2003 there was a 5+1 jackpot. The winning ticket turned out to have been sold at the Poker bar in Locri, which belonged to the father-in-law of a young man named Nicola Lucà, who laundered money for the Mancuso family. He contacted the winner right away and offered him more than €8 million for the ticket. Then he opened new accounts at the UniCredit banks of Milan and Soverato, so that the National Lottery—the Italian state, that is—could credit him the money. For Nicola Lucà the easy money marked the moment of greatest media notoriety, whereas his ascent in the 'ndrangheta hierarchy passed unobserved. He moved to northern Italy, where he became the accountant for the "local"—a 'ndrangheta cell—of Cormano, near Milan, which elected him to represent it at the summit in Lombardy: The video recording of Lucà toasting along with the other heads of the Lombard locals at the Giovanni Falcone and Paolo Bordellino Club in Paderno Dugnano, ten miles outside of Milan, during an October 2009 meeting, became the most clicked-on report on the web about the Crimine-Infinito investigation. Not a summit among bosses in 'ndrangheta territory—in Platì, Rosarno, or Gioiosa Jonica, or some Calabrian forest. This summit took place twelve hundred kilometers away, in Lombardy, Italy's wealthiest and most advanced region, which—despite a number of investigations that have proved otherwise—had always considered itself immune to the cancer of the 'ndrangheta and of organized crime in general.

Another way that the 'ndrangheta hides is through affiliation density, which in Calabria reaches about 30 percent—and more than double that in the heart of Aspromonte—and with a capillary diffusion beyond their home turf. For anyone who doesn't deal with the 'ndrangheta professionally, there are simply far too many of them to memorize who and where they are, and what they do. The tree's shape is covered by its lush foliage, the branches of which are too fine and intricate to trace.

We find Nicola Ciconte—the Australian-born affiliate with Calabrian roots involved in the Decollo investigation—ten thousand miles from the base of the tree. Italy has been asking for his extradition since 2004. The most recent request is from 2012, a sentence in which he was condemned to twenty-five years. For now he tranquilly makes the rounds of the bars on the Gold Coast, the world's surfing paradise, where he settled after making his way up the east coast from Melbourne. Since shipping Fuduli's marble to the port of Adelaide, Ciconte has served time in Australia for fraud, swindled an ex-girlfriend, and driven a real estate agency into bankruptcy. Compared to what he did for the country he is most deeply tied to, these are minor things.

Australia—like Canada— has become such a 'ndrangheta colony that an independent Crimine has been established there, divided into six *mandamenti*, or districts, that coordinate directly with the Polsi Crimine, taking part in their decisions. Even the codes for affiliation and promotion to higher ranks have made their way to Australia. The illegal activities it engages in change over time, but the codes remain the same, regardless of where they are. Its strength, which allows it to take full advantage of globalization, rests on a double tie: on the one hand blood and homeland, on the other disciplined by immaterial bonds of rules and rites.

The 'ndrine began arriving in Australia, along with honest immigrants, in the early 1900s, then in earnest after World War II. They set about reinvesting dirty money from Italy in legal activities, and began cultivating cannabis, for which there was an endless amount of space, fertile terrain, and favorable climactic conditions. Then cocaine arrived, and all the families there—originally from Platì, and as well as from Sinopoli and Siderno, which are tied to the powerful Canadian branch—got in on the business.

Nicola Ciconte kept up his close contact with Vincenzo Barbieri, who, according to investigations, sent him another 500 kilos of cocaine, this time from Italy. But mostly he laundered money. For most of his life his official job has been as a broker, a financial broker. So Barbieri turned to him not only to get cocaine into the Southern Hemisphere, but also—and more important—money. Ciconte, who was not always reliable, was another contact who often caused problems for U Ragioniere. But in the end he allegedly bounced the money through Hong Kong and some other offshore channels so as to launder and deposit it clean in Australian, and even New Zealand, banks. The Calabrian tree doesn't seem to touch the minor Pacific islands. Maybe because there are so few banks there.

Vincenzo Barbieri was killed in March 2011, in a classic mafia ambush. A gray Audi A3 pulled up alongside him late one afternoon, right as he stepped out of a tobacco shop. Two killers, their faces covered, got out of the car and unloaded a 7.65 caliber and a sawed-off shotgun into him. The shotgun wasn't to kill, but rather to tear the victim's flesh apart in a sign of contempt. They shot him in the head and got back in the car, the motor still running. Panicked shopkeepers lowered their shutters; passersby ducked into coffee shops as much to avoid the danger of seeing too much as to escape the shooting. A well-oiled response, a primitive instinct, even though there hadn't been any executions in San Calogero for quite a while. Barbieri hadn't lived there for years, yet they killed him in the center of his hometown, right in those narrow, twisting alleyways, without worrying about the people on the street or the video cameras trained on them. The burned-out car was found four days later, a few miles away.

Who wanted Barbieri dead? Or who more than anybody else? Why right then? For the 'ndrangheta, U Ragioniere had committed plenty of errors. Cocaine importation, through Fuduli and his companies, had already been marred by fuckups and foul play. But whenever possible, "men of honor" prefer to solve conflicts with money, which is much quieter and more useful than lead. The answer lies in Barbieri's expansion, with the help of his accomplice Francesco "Fatty" Ventrici, into another wealthy region in northern Italy, the Emilia Romagna.

Business deals are easier to negotiate there, and the lifestyle is much more free and relaxed. Nobody there objects if you build a big rustic villa for your family, hold meetings in your rec room, or enjoy the garish luxury of your living room, watched over and blessed by a huge oil

painting of your father. When evening comes you drive the half hour
from the new development in the countryside to the old town to satisfy
the rules of your house arrest. Which is what Ventrici does. They don't
even scowl at you if you register your fleet of Porsches, Mercedeses, and
Maseratis in someone else's name, or if you prefer to live right in the
center of Bologna, in a fancy penthouse on Via Saffi. Which is what
Barbieri does. When the place is searched in June 2009 and he's found
with €118,295 in cash, he is arrested for illegal financial transactions.
It's the first stumbling block in many years. It reminds the Bologna
magistrates of Barbieri's first arrest in Emilia. While under judicial
supervision he had spent several months in room 115 of the Grand
Hotel Baglioni, the only five-star hotel in the capital of Emilia
Romagna.

Barbieri played the wealthy southern Italian gentleman, taking advantage of the trust he inspired, while Ventrici played the complemen-
tary figure of the nouveau riche who is still a hard worker, a simple man
at heart. Neither one fit the stereotype of the mafioso. Besides, it's not
all that remarkable, even in Emilia, that all sorts of people turn out to
be loaded. So the two of them went on buying, buying, buying, hatch-
ing ever more ambitious expansion projects. Ventrici controled the
Futur Program, a real estate agency in San Lazzaro di Savena affiliated
with Gabetti (a major real estate chain). Barbieri, without even talking
price, invested in the King Rose Hotel in Granarolo, a three-star hotel
with fifty-five rooms conveniently located near the Bologna convention
center. Then shares in the clothing company Cherri Fashion, the Montecarlo café in Via Ugo Bassi, real estate, land.

Even though they were much better off far from Calabria and its
rules, above all that unspoken rule that—as in Colombia—envy is more
deadly than cancer, they always maintained their ties to the homeland.
It wasn't a question of nostalgia but of business. Francesco Ventrici controlled M5, a construction company he employed in Emilia as well, the
Union Frigo Transport Logistic, and the VM Trans (which had replaced Ventrans after it was confiscated thanks to Operation Decollo).

All registered in Calabria, even though the road haulage company had a branch in Castel San Pietro, in the province of Bologna. His trucks meant he was still a force to contend with. Ventrans had an exclusive deal with Lidl, a multinational deep-discount supermarket company in Calabria. The confiscation of the company did not prevent VM Trans from taking over that contract. But in 2009 a problem arose. Lidl decided to use other carriers as well—a question of costs. "It's either us or them," Ventrici screamed, and halted pickups and deliveries. Police reports started piling up, fast and furious. Drivers beaten up, verbal abuse that went from broken legs to death threats. "You're not unloading this truck, your boss has to come do it, that way we'll burn him alive . . . your coworkers have already been warned . . ."

The first company turned down the job. Lidl tried again with an Umbrian company, paying armed guards to accompany the drivers to Calabria. But the violence didn't stop. In the end, as Decollo ter revealed, the Lidl managers met with the owner of VM Trans in Massa Lombarda, in the province of Ravenna. Ventrici, playing the part of the big boss, declared, "You want a war, but in Calabria not even the pope would win a war." And in case his words weren't enough, that same day the drivers supplying a supermarket in Taurianova were attacked by armed assailants. The two pistol-wielding ambassadors fled as soon as they saw security guards arrive. But Lidl Italia had had enough. Too many complications, too many losses. So they reestablished an exclusive relationship with Ventrici until he was indicted for this story as well. According to the magistrates, the criminal businessman was able to break Lidl, forcing it, through the use of the violent behavior and threats described above, "to reconsider its organizational strategies, and to renounce the assured economic advantages, including those of competitive prices, that would have resulted from using multiple carriers to transport goods to Calabria."

Fatty enjoyed making sensational, exaggerated statements during more important negotiations as well. He works with a family, he's not a gypsy, and in twenty years of trafficking cocaine, he's never once paid

€30,000 a kilo. This is the substance of his retort to the Colombians who came to see him in his rustic villa in Emilia Romagna to talk about the differences of opinion blocking 1,500 kilos of cocaine in Ecuador. The German pilot, Michael Kramer, who had already pocketed a €100,000 advance, refused at the last minute to take the load to Lubiana, Slovenia. Ventrici shit his pants again, fearing that his about-face was a sign that he'd somehow hired a DEA infiltrator. Then Barbieri was killed, and Ventrici decided to interrupt his first big drug deal organized without U Ragioniere. The magistrature took care of the rest: From January to August 2011 it bombarded him with arrest warrants and seizure orders, from Catanzaro to Bologna.

Vincenzo Barbieri, like his accomplice or ex-accomplice, had organized an import circuit with close relatives and personally recruited accomplices. He wanted to do things in style, and even got himself an agent in Colombia, a young man who'd already started a family and had opened a restaurant. In the department of Meta, where many cocaine fields and "kitchens" had moved, the restaurant's name—La Calabrisella—which evokes not only a popular folk song but also the marijuana grown in Calabria—has a bitter, sarcastic taste. But things didn't go smoothly for him this time either. In September 2010 a load of 400 kilos was seized in Colombia, and in November the same thing happened to an entire ton that had landed in Gioia Tauro, inside agricultural trailer frames. Barbieri, who was varying the cover-up methods he'd tried out with Fuduli, had another 1,200 kilos of pure cocaine sent from Brazil in cans of palm hearts. The container was seized at the port of Livorno on April 8, 2011, by which date the buyer was already dead.

U Ragioniere managed to set off a scandal of unprecedented proportions even from the grave. It was the first time his name echoed all over the media without disappearing quickly into the burial mound of mafia news. The DDA of Catanzaro opened a new line of inquiry within the mother investigation, Decollo Money. The public learned about it on July 29, 2011. In December 2010, Vincenzo Barbieri allegedly summoned the manager of a San Marino bank to the King

Rose Hotel in Granarolo and gave him two suitcases filled with cash: €1.3 million ended up in an account in his name at the Credito Sammarinese bank, and a comparable amount was subsequently deposited in an account in the name of one of Barbieri's relatives, transferred thanks to the mediation of some notable individuals in the Calabrian town of Nicotera. But that's not all. Thanks to the economic crisis the bank was facing serious liquidity problems, and so was up for sale for the sum of €15 million. Credito Sammarinese was already negotiating with a Brazilian bank, but U Ragioniere allegedly promised to put up the same amount, thus raising the prospect of a 'ndrangheta takeover. The public prosecutor, assisted in his investigation by San Marino magistrates, asked for the indictment of former manager Valter Vendemini, the president and founder Lucio Amati, as well as the Calabrian middlemen and the holders of the still active accounts. In the end, Credito Sammarinese was forced into receivership.

A suspicious activity report, or SAR, was sent, but too late: on January 31, 2011, five days after the Catanzaro magistrates had Barbieri arrested again in the context of Decollo ter.

Barbieri was ambushed just before he was able to return to Bologna. It's thought that they feared he would expose the whole tree, in particular the Mancuso 'ndrina, that all the newspapers and TV news dragged in every time there was a story that had to do with him. The sensational seizure in Gioia Tauro in November 2010, which could not fail to trigger inquiries, severely shook the entire organization's business serenity. Moreover, it is not unlikely that in Calabria they knew about his San Marino bank plot and thought it a huge mistake to open an account in one's own name in an offshore paradise just sixty miles from home.

The press painted Vincenzo Barbieri and Francesco Ventrici in increasingly superlative terms: superpowerful bosses, top narco-trafficking brokers, incredibly dangerous criminals. Sure, they imported tons of drugs. But from close up they look pretty insignificant. Greedy bunglers with only average intelligence. Duped by their own victim. It was merely the use of violence that gave them strength. That and—much more important—cocaine. Cocaine money. Cocaine money ready to buy up failing banks. Cocaine money transformed into trucks, ready to supply an entire supermarket chain, and thus be turned into millions more in profit. With money laundering you keep on earning. It's not that complicated.

What hurts me the most, though, is knowing that their mediocre affairs found more space, filled more pages, than other stories. Extraordinary stories like Bruno Fuduli's. When Operation Decollo went public there were only a few passing mentions in the Italian press of an unnamed infiltrator. Then, years later, a few more lines when El Mono made news with his disclosures from a United States prison. Nothing more. Invisible. Invisible, like almost everyone who pays with silence for words offered in the name of justice. Who pays for the affront they caused that tree watered by fear and fed by business deals? Them. Not the others. Not men like Ventrici and Barbieri, who move in and out of prison as if playing a real-life game of Snakes and Ladders. And who then serve most of their time in their own homes, in the place where they chose to live, surrounded by their loved ones, integrated into society. With the chance to cultivate their interests, legal and illegal, with oodles of money to invest or spend for whatever they desire or need. Only killers and those bosses condemned to a special regime or forced to reconcile commanding and living in hiding are worse off than those who helped to denounce them.

But they have respect.

Respect. A word tainted by the use mafias all around the world make of it. Aped by the most disastrous, ferocious youth gangs. *Respecto*. The maras in Central America shout it when they beat a new affiliate bloody. *Respect*. Fat gansta rappers loaded with gold chains and surrounded by girls wiggling their hips utter it. *Respect*, brother. Yet this desecrated and ridiculed word continues to mean something essential.

The certainty of possessing—by right—a place in the world, a place among other people, wherever you are. Even in the void of an underground hole or the vacuum of solitary confinement.

Yet those who choose to side with the law often lose even that certainty. And then what's left? Can the decision to choose liberty turn into the most radical solitude? Can an act of justice be repaid with unhappiness? Informers become invisible. Like ghosts. Like the shades of Lake Averno, the mythical entrance to the underworld. I think about it a lot when I try to come to terms with those in Italy who accuse me of having received too much public attention. Nothing replaces the friends lost along the way, the cities left behind, the colors, tastes, voices, the use of a body that can move freely, walk, sit on a wall and stare at the sea, feel the wind through its clothes. Public attention can weigh on you like a prison. But it is also related to respect. Attention lets you know that your existence counts for other people. It tells you you exist.

Bruno Fuduli testifies at the trial. He shows his face to his loan sharks and the business partners imposed on him, but also to the Colombian narcos with whom he had become friends. Then he returns to the shadows. He is invited to appear on an investigative TV program on the port of Gioia Tauro. The appointment is at the Salerno train station, chosen at random because they can't reveal where he lives or film his face. They stop to do the interview along the waterfront. Bruno is wearing pants and a white, raw linen shirt. He looks like a burly giant compared to the reporter and the girl in sneakers who accompanies him. He has a deep voice, like a baritone, and he appears calm the whole time. He doesn't lose his composure when he reveals he's afraid and suffers from insomnia. He doesn't betray the least emotion as he talks about the ten men armed with pistols and machine guns who watched over him when he was held hostage in Colombia. Finally, as if mentioning an inescapable fact, he says that something will happen to him someday. They will look for him, if they aren't doing so already, and sooner or later, they'll kill him. The 'ndrangheta may wait fifteen or even twenty years, but it doesn't forget. Just a few minutes to sum up a life. A body without a face on the screen. And then, once again, nothing. Until two years later.

In early December 2010, the DDA of Catanzaro launched Operation Overloading, which would have brought to an end a drug-trafficking investigation like so many others were it not for the fact that it happened to involve some anomalous figures: a Carabinieri colonel in service in Bolzano and a young, very wealthy real estate agent in Rome who is called Pupone, or Big Baby, like Totti, in the wiretappings. The first was involved in picking up some suitcases at Fiumicino Airport and then delivering them to their addressees in Rome. The second, of helping to finance loads of cocaine, thanks to his friendship with Antonio Pelle, nephew of the recently deceased boss 'Ntoni Gambazza.

The first customers for that round of imports were two allied 'ndrine on the Tyrrhenian side of the province of Cosenza—minor families, despite how formidable they were. Their initial objective was to supply their own zones and still have enough of a surplus to sell in the north. But they wanted to do things right. So they hired Bruno Pizzata, the best narco in San Luca. Pizzata, a real pro, insisted that for the moment it was too slow, too complicated, and too inefficient to send the lots by ship. So he decided on air delivery from Venezuela and Brazil to Amsterdam, Rome, or Spain, making use of "mules" who swallow drug-filled pellets or carry false-bottomed suitcases. Pizzata was constantly traveling between South America, Spain, Holland, and Germany. He'd spent a good part of his life in Germany, and that was where he took refuge after having escaped arrest during Overloading; until February 2011, when they found him eating in the pizzeria La Cucina in Oberhausen, a city very close to Duisburg, the 2007 site of the 'ndrangheta massacre.

Pizzata was too busy, his life too complicated, for him to take care of everything. So he delegated the bulk of the coordination in Italy to Francesco Strangio. Then he found out that the Bellocco family of Rosarno were allegedly about to meet with a Colombian agent in Italy who could get his hands on enormous quantities of "material," as cocaine is called over the phone. So toward the end of 2008 the two groups decided to form a business alliance. The man who provided that precious contact for the San Luca and Rosarno families was none other than Bruno Fuduli.

Bruno was arrested for drug trafficking and condemned to eighteen years of imprisonment on May 16, 2012. How was that possible? How was it possible that the leaf destined to rot on the ground found its way back onto the branches of the tree? How was it possible that in late October 2008, he declared on a TV program that they would track him down and kill him, and then, not long after, he got in contact with his old Colombian acquaintances and 'ndrangheta clients again? Despite Bruno's previous collaboration, the judges did not grant him a sentence reduction.

To try and understand it I consulted the court records. They reconstruct the facts, the dates, and the evidence; they trace in great detail the events as they unfold, but they can't reveal a person's soul—even less that of a person so apt at hiding his intentions without even lying. The records say that Bruno managed again to make fun of the state. He met with the narcos' middleman, even put him up in his home in Calabria, accompanied him to near where his appointments with Pizzata or Francesco Strangio were, almost always near the Central Station in Milan. When he was placed under police protection they made him live in Fiorenzuola d'Arda near Piacenza, not far away from Milan. But the San Luca and Rosarno men never saw him. He became a director and secret organizer. He evaluated costs and routes, came up with transportation systems, ironed out problems, calmed people down. All he needed was one person willing to act as an interface with the buyers. Probably an old acquaintance in this case as well: Joseph Bruzzese, a marble cutter by trade but whose résumé qualifies him for the Calabrian families. He was the one who proposed the new route to a Bellocco lieutenant. So the mechanism Fuduli thought up was set in motion.

No one, other than a few Calabrian newspapers, even noticed the incredible evolution of Bruno Fuduli's story. They talk about a "return to his old love, crime," and "to his first passion, cocaine." They're loaded with quotation marks for words like "infiltrator," "songbird," "deep throat," "rat." They all use the same vocabulary, full of ambiguous ironies, and they ooze contentment because the "supercollaborator is still in jail. In solitary confinement." They even feign indignation at the infidelity of a man who had turned himself in, so as to water down the real reason for the scandal: The infiltrator had succeeded in insinuating himself with the upper echelon of the 'ndrangheta. Yet these are the same papers that had dedicated a lot of attention to another episode, the only documentable one in the period of Fuduli's life between the end of the trial and the beginning of his return to drug trafficking.

The morning of May 21, 2007, an antimafia demonstration marched through the center of Vibo Valentia. That day was chosen because it coincided with the opening of the new eyewear store of Nello Ruello, the shopkeeper who, after enduring ten years of extortion and usury, decided to report his oppressors and turned government witness. Onstage, along with the other authorities, were the mayor and the prefect, an undersecretary of the interior, the president of the Antimafia Commission, Francesco Forgione, and Don Luigi Ciotti, the founder of Libera, an association on the front line in the battle against the mafia. Before them were gathered a hundred or so students, union and antimafia association militants, a few townspeople, and even fewer shopkeepers. A typical demonstration in mafia territories, unfortunately. Yet during the closing rally a small incident occurred. A man climbed onto the barriers enclosing Piazza Municipio and started shouting. "Where's my money? Where's my 5,000 kilos of cocaine?" The local papers took photos, and they printed the image of Bruno shouting and raising his left arm defiantly while being restrained by the police. He was wearing a new, light-colored linen suit, this time with a jacket, only his eyes are hidden behind a pair of sunglasses. Later on he was interviewed.

Fuduli said that he'd applied for the financial assistance provided to victims of rackets and usury, which he needed to start a new enterprise, two years before, but he still hadn't seen a cent. He explained that he came to Vibo Valentia with his mother and brother because he'd decided to leave the protection program. One interview in particular is chilling, starting with the title: "Don't collaborate with the law, they'll screw you." It opens with a statement Fuduli made: "Thanks to me, 140 people went to jail, I uncovered five tons of cocaine and the trafficking between Calabria and Colombia, but now I told them all to go to hell. . . ."

The rest of what he says is just as unequivocal. The state ruined his life, Fuduli claims. It gives him less than €1,000 a month. He's starving, he's being evicted from his apartment, he has a sister who suffers seriously from stress, an elderly mother. He's so desperate he decided to expose himself right in the center of Vibo Valentia. When asked if he ever thought about going to the other side, he replies: "Yes, I've thought about it, and I regret not having done it, given what my collaboration with the law has brought me." In the space of ten days he is granted the economic assistance he'd requested as well as a mortgage to start a new commercial enterprise. But perhaps it's already too late. The former double agent had announced in no uncertain terms his intention to betray the state. Bruno Fuduli never lacked determination or courage. It's only fair that he pay for his choice.

In a conversation the DDA of Milan intercepted in the context of its next inquiry, Pizzata remembers an episode from his trips to Colombia. He tells of a narco nicknamed Lo Zio, or Uncle, who allegedly cut off the hands of someone who had stolen material. "Mamma mia," his brother-in-law Francesco Strangio responds. "We're more flexible about those sorts of things. When has anything like that happened in our territory? Never. A shooting maybe, but not that sort of torture."

Maybe Bruno Fuduli gambled on the range of possibility that could open up between that hoped-for flexibility and the bullet he was already expecting. Maybe he wasn't going merely for narco dollars but for something much higher: to prove himself in the long run as able and trustworthy as he used to be at high-level trafficking. Perhaps he might even have risked coming out into the open at that point. Maybe Fuduli was trying to ransom his own life with cocaine. We'll never know if he succeeded.

COKE #5

It's the most vexing mathematical equation you'll ever have to solve. More difficult than the twin prime conjecture or Landau's Problems. And more mysterious than crop circles. All things considered, you're really only being asked a simple question: the ratio of cocaine seized to cocaine produced. A fraction. Grammar school stuff. Well, let's collect the data, you might say. Okay. Where do we start? With the 2012 United Nations Office on Drugs and Crime's "World Drug Report"? Okay, take a look at the graph. The difference between the amount of cocaine seized in 2010 and 2009 is 38 tons: 694 as opposed to 732. A mountain of cocaine but substantially irrelevant in the ocean of world drug trade. So you might deduce that cocaine seizures in recent years have not varied significantly. Go back a bit further. Look at the stats for 2001 to 2005. Do you see how seizures are on a rise then, reaching a peak in 2005? Interesting, isn't it? Maybe something happened after 2005. Maybe the drug traffickers wised up, maybe they came up with new ways of exporting cocaine. Maybe. But there's another variable: In recent years cocaine's purity has decreased. Again according to the "World Drug Report": The purity rate of cocaine seized in the United States over the four-year period 2006 to 2010 dropped from 85 percent to 73 percent. People are snorting tons of shit. But this consideration doesn't throw off your calculations. Newly produced cocaine is 100 percent pure, but the stuff that ends up on the street outside your house is far less so. How do you compare the two? How can you have a fraction where the numerator refers to one thing and the denominator another? Can't you just hear your teacher saying: "You can't compare apples to oranges"? In other words, "You can't compare pure coke with coke that's been cut." And besides, how much cocaine is actually being produced annually? Keep reading the report. The range varies from 788 tons to 1,060 tons. A pretty sizable difference, don't you think? The difference corresponds to the total production of an entire country. And the purity percentage of seized cocaine isn't always declared. I could also mention that some figures may in fact be doubled, the result of more than one police force being involved in an operation leading to the seizure's being counted twice. If you're okay with ignoring these last variables and do your own calculation, by using 694 tons of cocaine seized (knowing nothing about its purity) as your numerator and a figure that oscillates between 788 tons and 1,060 tons as your denominator, you'll come up with between 65 percent and 88 percent. Isn't a 23-point difference a bit too high to be reliable? I agree. Not that you're the first to try such a calculation. The "World Drug Report" tried it in 2011. The result? From 46 percent to 60 percent. "Only" 14 points of uncertainty! But go back two more years and the percentage finally has a leg to stand on, and the number is 41.5 percent. How did they come up with that? you ask. By inventing an average purity index for street cocaine of 58 percent. Is it reliable? Maybe. Or maybe not, as many, including the antimafia organization Libera, maintain. They focused on a year—2004—and did some calculations not unlike the ones you're doing right now. World cocaine production that year came to 937 tons. Subtract from that the tons seized (490) and consumed (450) in the Americas. Then subtract the 99 tons of cocaine seized in the rest of the world. The result? A negative number: -102 tons. But Europeans snort cocaine too, lots of it, about 300 tons in fact. After some quick arithmetic it turns out that in 2004 a little over 400 tons are somehow missing, at least according to the data. Disappeared without a trace. One of the world's many mysteries, along with the Loch Ness monster.

Now you know what you need to know. Now it's up to you. I'm sure you'll figure it out.

11.

# THE WEIGHT OF MONEY

There are two kinds of wealthy people: those who count their money and those who weigh it. If you don't belong to the latter category, you don't really know what power is. I learned that from the narco-traffickers. I also learned that narcos are turning into citizens of the world, but no matter where they are, their gestures, their moves, their thoughts are the same as if they'd never left home. Live wherever you want, even in the middle of Wall Street, but don't abandon the rules of your hometown. Old-fashioned rules that help you survive in today's world without getting lost. It's sticking to those rules that gives Italian organizations the upper hand when dealing with South American narcos and Mexican cartels, that lets them purchase tons of drugs with just a promise.

Calabrian drug traffickers may have shed the look of shepherds from Aspromonte, but Aspromonte's rules, the rules of blood and earth, still provide their moral coordinates, still guide their actions. Except that now they also know the rules of economics and know how to move in the world so as to guarantee an annual turnover of billions of euros. Which is why it's hard to describe the men who govern the world's narco-traffic. If you handed the material to a screenwriter, you'd get characters who go from bespoke pinstriped suits to gutter street dialect, from marble palaces to stinking streets, characters whose ambiguity is charming, whose paradoxes are worrisome. But all that's fiction. In reality the drug-trafficking bourgeoisie is on the whole more solid and serene than the average industrial bourgeois family. Mafia families are used to closing ranks, to suffering and responding to setbacks—for them absence and distance are the norm. To cover or conceal things that shouldn't be known isn't tantamount to a fragile respectability but rather a fundamental necessity. They're prepared for pain, loss, and betrayal, and it makes them stronger. They don't deny the savagery of living in this world.

When I ask myself who the archetypical cocaine manager would be, two names emerge, like opposing poles of a magnetic field. North and South. The man from the North is the prototype of a self-made entrepreneur, trusting only in his own strengths and business sense. The man from the South is a bourgeois from the capital who had a taste of what it would be like to go beyond the secure existence of a government employee and went for it. Neither feels beholden to any political or moral position. If they need to be democratic and transgressive, they know how to do that. And if it's better to seem like strict conservatives, they're fine with that too. Businessmen capable of tempting upright, moral individuals by taking advantage of microscopic fissures, imperceptible weaknesses. They corrupt without ever letting the corrupted one feel as if he's sinning, and pass off corruption as normal, a swift and weightless procedure, something that everybody does, after all.

The man from the North conveys first of all solidity and determination; the man from the South seems more vivacious and worldly, but both come across as middle-aged and middle-class gentlemen. This is clear even from their nicknames, which are banal, even slightly ridiculous. Who would ever suspect Bebè and Mario?

The younger one was born sixty-three years ago, in Almenno San Bartolomeo, a village in Lombardy. Bergamo's not too far away, but it takes even less time to cross the Brembo River and head into the Val Brembana, the valley that even for Lombards is the epitomy of provincial backwardness. He's named Pasquale—probably in memory of his grandfather from Brindisi—Claudio, so he has a more modern name too. His last name is Locatelli, like just about everyone else around there. He becomes Mario later, again like everyone else.

Pasquale Claudio Locatelli is twenty when he starts making forays into the wealthy part of Lombardy, between Milan and Verona, to steal cars with powerful engines. He works with guys from Milan who grew up in the *ligéra*, the old criminal underworld still celebrated in popular songs in the local dialect, although the Bar del Giambellino and the Palo della Banda dell'Ortica described in those ballads now belong to a more innocent past. Milan has become a war zone: Political subversion is mistaken for and at times intertwined with common criminality, and the number of armed robberies and kidnappings is rising precipitously. Homicides average a 150 a year. Those criminals who don't become stars, such as Renato Vallanzasca, Francis "Angel Face" Turatello, and his former second in command, Angelo Epaminonda, those who aren't serving a life sentence for murder or other serious crimes, can carry on tranquilly.

Locatelli understands this; he understands that the crime that pays is not that of the fanatics of the 1970s. He goes from car theft to supplying all the services that a seller of stolen cars needs; he forms a network of contacts from Austria to France, studies foreign languages, eventually mastering four of them. He's already thinking like an international-level entrepreneur. Illegal business is a business just like any other: What matters are reliability and foresight. A deceptive peace is settling over Milan, something that is both bubbly and creamy, like the food and drink that are so in fashion. The man who goes by the name of Mario but will also be called "Diabolik" understands that wherever there's more money and a desire to have fun, that's where new markets spring up. Fashion and design, private TV channels, young entrepreneurs, and lots of daddy's boys and girls walking around, swinging their hips. Here in Italy's richest city and region more people can indulge in the vice of cocaine than elsewhere. Locatelli throws himself decisively into the business. He's under house arrest for a past offense, and it's this restriction on his movements that leads him to go into hiding. He tries to better his luck in a place where he knows he can easily find new clients, the Côte d'Azur. He moves into a villa in Saint-Raphaël, which is more sedate than nearby Saint-Tropez. People there, who know him as Italo Salomone, mind their own business, as wealthy homeowners usually do. They don't know that the French police have been hunting him ever since they seized a false-bottomed suitcase from Colombia stuffed with cocaine at the Nice airport. Pasquale Locatelli has already been convicted twice for drug trafficking, in two French courts, and has been sentenced to twenty and ten years in absentia. Italo Salomone seems to be an ordinary Italian, enjoying the mild climate and carefree life. Till the day when, after three years of searching, the *flics* arrest him in his villa, where they find a stash of Colombian cocaine—41 kilos.

It's 1989.

During this same period Bebè is restoring an old farmhouse in Valsecca, at the foot of the Bergamo Alps, half an hour from Brembate di Sopra, Locatelli's last Italian residence. Bebè didn't choose that spot for the peacefulness or the mountain air. He chose it in order to turn it into a refinery for white heroin—the rarest, most prized kind—for which there is still a niche market in the United States, so as to be able to trade it with the Colombian drug lords. According to police informer Saverio Morabito, the notorious former boss of the Milan 'ndrangheta, at the end of the 1980s the Colombians were trading 25 kilos of the purest Colombian cocaine for 1 kilo of white Bergamo heroin.

Bebè is Roberto Pannunzi, a Roman with a Calabrian mother, a former Alitalia employee now past sixty-five who emigrated to Canada when he was young, as many southerners did back then. The Calabrians there worked hard: construction, transportation, trash removal, restaurants. But the massive presence of Italian immigrants was exploited, not just by Canadian employers, but by the lords of Siderno. U Zi, or "Uncle" Antonio Macrì, had quickly gained control of drug trafficking in Canada and also established excellent relations with the American Cosa Nostra. His murder in Calabria in 1975 set off the first 'ndrangheta war, but the entrepreneurial empire he'd constructed overseas remained untouched. Macrì had created or bought all sorts of commercial activities, in particular export-import businesses, which helped him establish excellent contacts in the most important ports. In the 1980s the Canadian police considered the organization he left his heirs to be the most powerful 'ndrangheta presence in all of Canada. In Toronto, Roberto Pannunzi rediscovers his maternal roots, thanks to Antonio Macrì. Zi' 'Ntoni likes this kid with thick black hair, a round face, and a proud gaze. Roberto is respectful, and—more important—he's loyal. Roberto sticks close to Macrì and learns. He's ambitious and obedient—not like a servant, but because he's convinced he can learn by obeying. He keeps his mouth shut and his head down, because when he grows up he wants to command. About the same time he meets Salvatore Miceli in Toronto: a Sicilian, and the point man for Cosa Nostra's drug trade. The two become friends, and then accomplices.

Through Miceli, Pannunzi receives from Cosa Nostra heroin refined in Palermo; he has it transported to Siderno, where it is then shipped to Toronto, hidden among ceramic tiles, and picked up by Vincenzo and Salvatore Macrì, Zi' 'Ntoni's nephews.

Pannunzi is getting good. He's not happy with the stuff his first contacts pass off on him. He wants the best price-quality ratio, and he gets it, that's why people like him. Through Macrì's friends he meets the major suppliers, who trust him precisely because of his connection with Macrì. By himself he never would have been able to get anywhere near the leading figures of the heroin trade, but he learns how to use Macrì's contacts in ports around the globe. If a group can't find a contact, Roberto comes up with one. He makes himself available to everyone, organizes shipments, even to parts of the world where heroin had never reached before. And when groups ask him for better quality stuff at a lower price, he gets in touch with specialists who know how to solve the problem. He's the one who arranges a meeting between the Sicilian Alberti and the Marseilles clans, who send one of their chemists to Palermo to set up a heroin lab.

And when Platì boss Pasquale Marando, in charge of drug trafficking in northern Italy, has to go into hiding, Pannunzi offers to mediate between the families of Marina di Gioiosa Jonica and Platì, in the heart of the 'ndrangheta region in the Aspromonte. Pannunzi unites rather than divides. That is his aim.

To bond even more with his financiers, when Bebè returns to Italy he marries Adriana Diano, who belongs to one of the most prominent families in Siderno. Even though they separate soon afterward, marriage and the mingling of blood are always more binding than a mere contract. Officially Roberto manages a clothing store in Rome. He also has a sense of irony and calls the shop Il Papavero or Poppy, in homage to his collaboration with the most important traffickers of Turkish heroin. In reality, he's at the Calabrian clans' disposal. The money the 'ndrangheta used to make from kidnappings must now be raised through drug trafficking. Roberto is ready. He knows where it's best to invest.

The man from the South and the man from the North travel on parallel lines without seemingly ever intersecting in time or space. Locatelli is slightly ahead of Pannunzi, not so much because he started his career closer to Milan, which is still the best cocaine market in Italy. A minor geographical advantage doesn't matter much when you're playing on a global chessboard. No, Locatelli's better sense of timing is more likely due to the fact that he is his own boss, is free to make new investments, is the only one to shoulder the risk. Pannunzi, on the other hand, is more like a top manager for a big holding company. New markets have to be conquered prudently, without letting the old, dependable ones lag behind, without risking a penny of their vast holdings. The idea of applying Calabrian expertise in heroin to cocaine production, thus increasing potential gains, is the typical stroke of inspiration any good manager would come up with to impress his superiors. Pannunzi

then puts his idea into practice: in order to find a farmhouse, he contacts Morabito as well as a 'ndrina ensconced in Lombardy, the Sergi of
Plati. Then he brings in the best chemists from France, two men of the
Marseilles clan who've already worked for Cosa Nostra and can guarantee excellent results.

While Pannunzi is laying the groundwork for a joint cocaine venture, Locatelli is on trial for international drug trafficking, and is sentenced to ten years' prison in Grasse, the world capital of perfume. All
he can see from jail is a scrap of that pleasing landscape which extends
below the old town; the sea at Cannes is something he can only sense.
But he doesn't need the sea view: Diabolik/Locatelli is swift in thought
and deed. He breaks his arm. He needs to be hospitalized, but the
French are not so naïve; they suspect that it might not have been an
accident. As a safeguard, they send him not to Nice but to Lyon, far—
more than three hundred miles—from the coast he knows every inch
of. The prisoner gets out of the police van and heads toward the hospital. After only a few steps, three masked and armed men appear, disarm
his police escort, and vanish with the prisoner. It's the end of an era.
Locatelli crosses the border into Spain. He becomes Mario, Mario
from Madrid: the point man for Colombian traffickers in Europe, the
owner of a fleet of ships for international cocaine traffic.


The entrepreneur and the manager converge in the figure of the broker.
They're pioneers, the men who create out of nothing this figure who
hadn't existed previously in the drug-trafficking economy. They connect
all the corners of the world. Istanbul, Athens, Málaga, Madrid, Amsterdam, Zagreb, Cyprus, the United States, Canada, Colombia, Venezuela, Bolivia, Australia, Africa, Milan, Rome, Sicily, Puglia, Calabria.
They create perpetual motion within a tight, intricate net that reveals
the motion of their merchandise only to the attentive eye. They become
fabulously rich, and make those who turn to them rich as well. Always
on the go, they need to find new channels all the time. Their lives come

to resemble ever more closely the game of connect the dots, which we played as kids in those rare moments when our parents put down their crossword puzzles and let us have the pen: You could only appreciate the image at the end, once you'd connected all the dots. The same is true with Pasquale Locatelli and Roberto Pannunzi. The picture of their trafficking only becomes clear when we connect all the dots that they have drawn.

No one deliberately designed an innovation that, had it been proposed in abstract terms, would have been rejected. No criminal organization would have said it was willing to share a significant part of its profits with someone outside the organization. It happens gradually; the qualitative leap is made simply because it happens at a certain point.

Mario from Madrid gains the Colombians' trust when they are still at the height of their power. He travels with a bodyguard and a personal secretary, has learned from Pablo Escobar never to stay more than two nights in the same place, and changes cell phones as frequently as anyone else changes socks. But he's not part of the Medellín or Cali cartels. And this turns out to be an advantage not only for himself, but also for the cocaine monopolists in Colombia, who start warring ruthlessly among themselves, a sign of their slow decline.

Bebè Pannunzi is tied to the Siderno and Platì families, linked by blood and lineage, but he never affiliates himself with any clan. He's not an 'ndranghetista, a *camorrista,* or a mafioso. He unites different groups into a single investment company: Calabrians, Sicilians, groups based in the Salento, along with others. He creates a joint venture for drugs, capable of increasing contacts and contractual power beyond what any one clan could do: a stratified organization with strong membership bonds and a clear division between commanders and subordinates. Pannunzi is a skillful broker who constructs enormous financial operations with ease and moves quantities of drugs that would prove unmanageable for a single clan. Without this new figure, a broker, cocaine acquisition would have kept on functioning the old way: The mafia family sends a representative to South America, pays for part of the

load in advance, leaves its trusted man—who risks getting killed if anything goes wrong or if the final payment is delayed—in the narcos'
hands as a guarantee, and then contacts an intermediary to arrange for
shipment.

Pannunzi reshuffles the cards. He moves to Colombia. He's learned
what there is to learn through close contact with the 'ndrine, and knows
the time has come to pass on his example and teachings. He brings his
son, Alessandro, into the business, who marries the daughter of a Medellín boss. On the telephone he speaks Spanish and calls him "Miguel,"
to throw off any unwelcome listeners. His daughter, Simona, gets engaged to Francesco Bumbaca, who becomes his father-in-law's right-
hand man. They nickname Francesco Joe Pesci and Il Finocchietto
("Little Faggot"). In the early 1990s, Pannunzi takes advantage of the
power of the Colombian cartels, who have punctuated the jungle with
private airports. The 'ndrangheta could use a cargo plane for intercontinental trips, so Bebè gets them one.

He can afford a whole fleet of planes for moving the white merchandise. He collects millions and millions of euros from the various organizations. He acts as his own guarantor with the cartels in order to
obtain enormous discounts for bulk purchases. He guarantees the
transport and arrival of shipments to the ports. He also knows who will
handle the cocaine once it reaches its destination. The more investors
he has, the lower the price per kilo. He spreads out the losses caused by
raids. He monitors the quality. He travels, creates contacts, meets clients. He seeks out financial backers and capital, but he's the one to
decide where and how to purchase. He looks for good carriers, safe
coastlines, storage towns.

Locatelli's actions mirror Pannunzi's. He's closer to his suppliers, so
he keeps his base in Europe in order to maintain more dynamic relationship with his clients. He deals with everyone: the Bagheria and
Gela families, the San Luca and Platì 'ndrine, the most powerful clans
from the area north of Naples. And, true to his entrepreneurial instinct,
he deals in everything: cocaine and—increasingly—recycling are his

core businesses, but it would be stupid not to take advantage of the nearness of North Africa, transporting hashish across the Strait of Gibraltar, which is one of his naval strongholds. Drawing on old relationships and past experience, he also sets up an international sales network for stolen cars. But events in a country farther from the Iberian Peninsula are what allow Mario to make yet another leap. He is one of the first to grasp the immense potential that the tensions and then the war in the former Yugoslavia present. Drugs, weapons, money—he creates a business triangulation based on these three elements, bouncing them from Spain to America, from America to the Balkans.

The man from Bergamo structures his business like a family firm, allowing himself only a few trusted collaborators. Close relations and people in his pay who are kept constantly under pressure and controlled, rigid hierarchies, a conspiracy of silence. Despite not having any historical ties to the mafia, the Bergamo enterprise absorbs more and more of its characteristics, thereby acquiring its winning impermeability as well. But the mafias' operational model is nothing other than a distinctive inflection of Italy's dominant business model. The intertwining of affection and business risks becoming an Achilles's heel, just as it does for real mafiosi. In 1991 the Carabinieri discover that when Locatelli is in Italy, he lives with his girlfriend, Loredana Ferraro, in Nigoline di Corte Franca, a village near Brescia. They're just about to spring the trap when Diabolik gets in a car and speeds away, eluding capture and turning the Franciacorta vineyards into a new version of a Hollywood high-speed chase scene. He and Loredana stay together and she, like their two sons, shares his interests and his fate: Ten years later she too will be arrested in Spain, the last of Mario's network to be brought to justice.

Men like Bebè and Mario, but also those bosses who drank the ancestral family rules with their mothers' milk, often turn out to be vulnerable because of a relationship with a woman. It's not the ones they buy for a night who put them at risk, women who to them are no different from other expensive luxury goods. It's the women they bond

with, with whom they form a relationship of trust. The pawn who
seems at one point to point to Pannunzi is named Caterina. She's not
just any girl, susceptible to the charms and power of an older businessman, nor would Bebè have wanted to really share the actual substance
of his life had she not been able to offer all the necessary guarantees to
become his true accomplice. Caterina Palermo has a reassuring pedi-
gree: She's the sister of a mafioso from the same clan as Miceli. The
investigators find out that she has booked a flight from Madrid to
Caracas, so they trail her. After landing in the Venezuelan capital
Caterina heads to a town on the Colombian border, where her companion is then living. They'd agreed to an amorous appointment there, but
Pannunzi, tipped off by some unknown informer, doesn't show. The
woman and the policemen return to Italy, for once sharing the same
feeling: disappointment.

The broker from the North and the broker from the South are the
Copernicus and Galileo of the cocaine business. With them the model
changes. Before it was cocaine that rotated around money. Now it's
money that has entered cocaine's orbit, sucked into its gravitational
field. When I follow their trails I feel as though I'm leafing through a
textbook on how to be a successful broker: First of all, vast available
funds—the prerequisite for being able to dictate the terms of a deal.
Formidable organizational skills. A broad vision combined with precision in defining every detail. They excel at mediation and have learned
how to solve problems. They guarantee provisions to anyone who gets
in their good graces and can pay. They know it's better to keep their
distance from politics, and from violence. All they want to do is move
the white stuff, and to do that, all they need is money and good connections. Criminal groups, even rivals, allow them this freedom, because
thanks to Mario and Bebè, they make money.

Last, they have intuition, a quality you can't buy and can't learn; it is priceless. It's something you're born with, and they were both born with far greater than average doses. Intuition is above all empathy, knowing how to put yourself in someone else's shoes, sniffing out his habits, his weak points, his resistance. For Bebè and Mario, a client is an open book. They know how to get to him, how to convince him. They know that if he hesitates, that's the moment to insist; if he seems too sure of himself, that's the time to make him understand who holds the purse strings. They switch easily from one language to another, from one culture to another; they know how to be sponges, how to transform themselves, to belong to whatever part of the world they happen to be in. They know how to appear as humble intermediaries and when to unleash their authority, sympathy, charm. That's what intuition is: knowing human nature and knowing how to manipulate it.

But intuition is also foresight. If financial brokers had learned from cocaine brokers, they probably wouldn't have crashed into the cement wall of economic crises. Pannunzi and Locatelli intuited that the mass market for heroin was coming to an end. They understood this even while the world continued to consume heroin by the ton and while the Italian mafias were still investing everything in it. Cocaine was about to invade the world, and it would prove more pervasive, and more difficult to check. And Pannunzi and Locatelli were there early.

The police nab them a couple of times, but the two brokers always find a way to resolve the problem. They don't order any killings. They have a lot of money; they know how to defend themselves, how not to leave clues. They don't draw media attention; very few journalists have heard of them; only a tight group of people in the know are aware of how important they are. When they get out of jail, there's no public uproar.

The year 1994 might have been their *annus horribilis,* but the cyclone that strikes them isn't strong enough to uproot them. In January Pannunzi is arrested in Medellín, where he's been living for four years. And the million dollars he offers the police to let him go isn't enough.

Shockingly, they won't play along. Pannunzi remains locked in a Colombian prison, awaiting extradition to Italy, where he's transferred in December.

Meanwhile, the final phase of a maxi-operation, subtly named Operation Dinero, which international police forces and the DEA and FBI have coordinated, is coming to a head. According to the DEA, the two-year investigation led to 116 arrests in Italy, Spain, the United States, and Canada. All in all, including two continents, around $90 million in cash and a huge quantity of cocaine—nine tons—were seized. On September 6, 1994, Locatelli is having dinner at Adriano, a well-known restaurant in Madrid, surrounded by his inner circle: his Swiss secretary, Heidi, who, like him, travels with fake documents; and his right-hand man in Italy, the Pugliese lawyer Pasquale Ciola. Domenico Catenacci, the deputy public prosecutor of Brindisi, is also there. Recently he'd thought of running for public office, but at the last minute he changed his mind and moved to Como. Later Catenacci is accused of having ties to organized crime and is suspended, but when put on trial he is able prove that he had no idea who Pasquale Locatelli was, and is acquitted. Mario is arrested and sent to jail in Madrid. He loses four of his ships in addition to his liberty, which were already loaded with drugs and weapons and ready to sail for Croatia, as well as many other pieces of his empire.

Operation Dinero is a huge success, and the head of the DEA and the Italian interior minister boast about it in press conferences on their respective sides of the ocean. Two years of investigations and top-secret operations. Infiltrators on two continents, and then the big bait: a bank opened in Anguilla for laundering narco-dollars. A real bank, duly registered, with elegant offices and highly qualified and extremely competent employees who welcome clients in various languages. Yet the whole thing is controlled by the DEA. The RHM Trust Bank offers dream interest rates, especially to wealthy clients. The Colombians grow greedy. One of the DEA's financial consultants manages to establish a rapport with Carlos Alberto Mejía, alias Pipe, a narco-trafficker linked

to the Cali cartel who organizes shipments to the United States and
Europe, by showing him the RHM Trust Bank's credentials. The bank
is located in a British fiscal paradise and guarantees seriousness, ease of
access, and extremely advantageous rates. The narcos are used to a life
of luxury and money that comes and goes like a tropical rainstorm.
Mejía loves to spend money on one of his country's abiding passions:
horses. Paso Fino horses are native to Colombia, dating back to the
arrival of Spanish conquistadores astride mysterious, gigantic beasts
that the terrified *indios* thought were gods. During the era of the cocaine kings the handsomest and most famous horse is Terremoto de
Manizales, a sorrel belonging to Pablo Escobar's brother. But just at
the time that the DEA infiltrator was getting close to Carlos Alberto
Mejía an enemy group kidnapped Terremoto, killing his jockey. They
abandoned the horse a few days later on a Medellín street, castrated.
They knew that this mutilation would hurt more than killing many
men and would be a serious blow to the Escobar family's image. There's
a legend in Colombia that Terremoto was used to produce an identical
horse sixteen years after his castration, cloned by a specialist firm in the
United States.

Mejía too owns a stable of prized Paso Fino horses, as well as an art
collection, which he seems less attached to. He decides to entrust the
bank's intermediaries with three paintings: a Picasso, a Rubens, and a
Reynolds. Experts estimated their value at $15 million. But money
laundering is the real business for the bank. Mejía starts with almost
$2.5 million, from narco-trafficking in Italy, to be reinvested, money
that arrives through a trusted colleague of Mejía's Italian partner who
operates in Spain and Italy.

Which is how the DEA agents suddenly and unexpectedly find
themselves on the trail of Pasquale Locatelli. Their plan had been to
hit the strongest narco-trafficking organization in the world at that
time, the Cali cartel. Mario from Madrid appears practically out of
nowhere. He and his organization turn out to be incredibly difficult to
get their hooks into. Never a call from a traceable phone. Money-

laundering schemes so swift that no one can keep up with the transfers. Precisely because of the Italian partner, the investigation comes to a dead end. The team decides to put an undercover agent on him, a very special agent. An inspector in the anti-crime unit of the Italian police whose financial expertise has been honed by years of investigations but who has never done an undercover mission. Young, not even twenty-seven years old, but very presentable, an impeccable presence. Fluent in several languages and familiar with sophisticated money-laundering methods. And a woman.

It seems like another plot twist in a Hollywood action movie. Out there in the real world beautiful young women who are also capable of taking on a new identity without the least slipup rarely exist. The Americans are skeptical, and even the Italians have their doubts, but in the end everyone is convinced of the advantages she offers as an undercover agent. And so, after some accelerated personalized training by the DEA, Maria Monti is born: an expert in international finance who exudes a vivacious femininity and an ambition as ravenous as it is innocent. Like many young women, she's more talented than the men and extremely eager to prove herself. Everyone who comes in contact with her finds that working with her is a pleasure.

Maria is catapulted into a whirlwind of business-class flights, taxis and limousines, hotels and restaurants for the happy few. The unreality of it all calms her anxiety. There's the risk of enjoying it too much, of letting her guard down, of growing distracted by all the novelty and luxury. But that doesn't happen. She handles it all as if she is used to such things. The infiltrator doesn't forget for a second that she's merely the vanguard of a team following her signal via the GPS hidden in her overnight bag, standing by and ready to come to her rescue if necessary. The risk she's taking is quite real, however. The first people she has to establish contact with are the narcos.

Miami's port is immense; it's called the cruise capital of the world. Moored in the shadow of Carnival and Royal Caribbean ships seven stories high are yachts that only seem small compared to the vast tonnage of those floating monsters. Maria was supposed to wrap up the deal in a more crowded place, but her South American clients don't show. So someone takes her to the port, has her board a yacht, and hoists anchor. She ends up in the middle of the ocean. The agent waiting for her on the wharf can't help her now; she has only herself to rely on. Well, this is all fantastic, she says, but I came here *for business, not for fun;* apologies if I'm not in the mood.

Mario from Madrid also brings Maria aboard a yacht the first time he meets her, off the Costa del Sol near Marbella, where he was living with Loredana. Locatelli wants to carefully study this girl who has made her way into his Colombian partners' good graces. Maria realizes what he's up to, and for a moment she feels naked, but then she summons up all her coolness. She talks about taxes and interest rates, stocks, investment funds. She discusses the risks and potential of betting on the new economy and suggests a couple of profitable transactions involving currency exchange. It works. The boss believes she's the real thing; the flow of money to the Antilles bank can continue.

And yet the moments of terror are hardly over. The day Maria receives a briefcase containing $2 million she realizes that she's being followed. She can't run the risk of being robbed, or—worse yet—recognized, as she gets into her colleague's car, as planned. She has no idea if the man behind her is some mysterious mugger or a shadow sent to check on her. She flags down a taxi and drives around the city for hours, from one end to the other.

Paradoxically, it's in Italy that she's most afraid. In Rome the meetings are always arranged in busy places: the Jolly Hotel, the Palombini Bar in the EUR neighborhood. What if someone recognizes her, calls out to her, uses her real name? They'd trained her for that too: act as if it's a mistake. A quick hard look, a second of perplexity, nothing more. But Maria isn't sure she can keep her cool. At times a more subtle anxiety writhes inside her: She can't rule out the possibility that one of her contacts might leak some information about her. She has to negotiate with Roberto Severa, Locatelli's right-hand man in Rome, a prominent

figure in the criminal organization known as the Banda della Magliana, to whom Locatelli has entrusted massive reinvestments in a supermarket chain and other activities in the capital city. He's the one who
floods Maria with money to be laundered as quickly as possible in the
Caribbean: £671.8 million plus $50,000, and then another two chunks
of £398.350 million and £369.450 million lire, all within a month and
a half.

Yet the really pivotal figure in Locatelli's business in Italy is Pasquale
Ciola, who has the reassuring look of a country lawyer. Like Bebè Pannunzi, Mario from Madrid at some point also rediscovers his maternal
roots and their advantages. Thanks to Ciola, who is on the board of
directors, he can make use of an entire bank, the Cassa Rurale e Arti-
giana in Ostuni. And given his growing interest in the Balkans, he's
also finalizing the purchase of a bank in Zagreb, the ACP, through his
Brindisi lawyer. Puglia is the region of Italy closest to the other shore of
the Adriatic. Pasquale Ciola has learned to do everything with utmost
prudence. To get to Spain to see Locatelli, he turns the trip into an
innocent family vacation. He piles his son and ex-wife into his Mer-
cedes, and staying in the best hotels along the way, they cross the Iberian Peninsula hitting one tourist spot after another: Málaga, the Costa
del Sol, Alicante. Only after four days of touring does he take the highway for Madrid, arriving in time for dinner at the Adriano restaurant.

This is where Maria's mission ends. This is the moment they've
been waiting for after trailing him for so long. Locatelli himself arrives,
carrying a suitcase containing £130 million in cash. The bust goes
down, but once the day they're all hailed as heroes on every newscast
has past, as soon as their adrenaline rush yields to exhaustion and they
return to normal, the Italian police officers begin asking themselves
just how decisive a blow they've really dealt Locatelli. They know he
still owns at least five large ships in Croatia, Gibraltar, and Cyprus,
property that turned out to be untouchable. His total wealth remains
incalculable. From prison in Madrid he continues to telephone right
and left, quietly managing his business affairs and exemplifying what

Camorra boss Maurizio Prestieri quipped about another Spanish jail: "It was like a Valtur vacation village" (Valtur is a chain of Italian vacation resorts). The only thing that might cause his empire to crumble is an imprisonment system where he would truly be cut off from the world.

Once again, Locatelli's and Pannunzi's lives mirror each other's. By a strange twist of fate, both men manage to elude Italian jail, the most rigorous penal system in all of Europe for mafiosi and drug dealers. Bebè, after being transferred to Italy, ends up being released: The legal limit for the duration of his pretrial custody had expired. In 1999 he's arrested again for "mafia association," and while under house arrest, granted for health reasons, he does what Diabolik did ten years earlier: He escapes from a Roman clinic without even the help of an armed commando unit. Like Mario, he chooses Spain for his hiding place: Spain, which at the time is in the midst of a huge real estate boom, the ideal place for drug traffickers to gather, and to buy.

In Italy Bebè maintains a tight network that in Rome centers around Stefano De Pascale, who in the past was linked to the Banda della Magliana, as was Locatelli's Roman contact. I think of him every time I'm on Via Nazionale, because right here, at the Top Rate Change agency, an accomplice would exchange into dollars and other currencies the hundreds of millions of lire that De Pascale managed for Pannunzi. As Pannunzi's consigliere, De Pascale didn't simply carry out orders, he also offered suggestions and opinions, in addition to keeping accounts and handling relations between clients and suppliers. The man I knew primarily as Spaghetto was Bebè's *longa manus* in Rome, the one to whom the Calabrian clans doing business with Pannunzi could always turn.

In January 2001, Bebè, hounded by an international arrest warrant, returns to Colombia, where he buys a grand villa. He contacts some narco-traffickers and ventures out into the countryside where coca grows, to visit the refineries. He never lets his guard down and selects his collaborators with utmost care. He knows from experience that it's a small world, and there's nowhere left where he can allow himself even the slightest imprudence.

Pannunzi's strength lies in the absolute impenetrability of his system. His entire criminal network maintains a level of stealth that make investigators bang their heads against the wall. As one official Italian inquest put it, Bebè "never makes a mistake, never a 'wrong move,' never a real name, an address, a meeting place in any comprehensible way over the course of countless conversations; it's all wordplay, metaphors, similes, and code names to refer to friends, times, meetings. The utmost prudence and attention, above all in the back and forth of phone numbers that are essential for maintaining contact: Those under investigation thought up secret codes with private keys—never a cell phone number stated openly, always a string of apparently meaningless ciphers."

In order to get to know who Roberto Pannunzi is you first have to immerse yourself in the inextricable tangle of his language. His men's names are always fake nicknames: the Youngster, the Blond, the Bookkeeper, the Nephew, Lupin, Longlegs, the Clockmaker, the Little Old Man, the Puppydog, the Dyer, Big Hat, the Mouse, Uncle, Uncle's Relative, the Parent's Brother, Auntie, the Halfwit, the Godfather, Blood, Alberto Sordi, the Girl, the Roly-poly Brothers, the Kid, Miguel, Pal, Throat, the Gentleman, Shorty, the Surveyor. Small mirrors that reflect slices of a distorted reality. He knows his phone is tapped, so he gives names, addresses, and phone numbers in the most cryptic way possible.

"21.14—8.22.81.33—73.7.15. They're initials, three initials, got it?"

"New line, dash: 18.11.33.—K  8.22.22.16—7.22.42.81.22. K.11.9.14.22.23.—: 18.81.33.9.22.8.23.25,14.11.11.25—(+6) (+6) is the number."

"Then 11.21.23.25.22.14.9.11.21.11 again. That's the city."

"New line, the office number: +1, -2 (I don't know if you need the zero or not) -3, -7, =, -7, +6, -3, +5, +3, +4."

Such extreme prudence makes it difficult at times for even his associates to understand the messages. But it's a necessary precaution. A total of six fugitives are part of the network: Roberto Pannunzi; his son, Alessandro; Pasquale Marando; Stefano "lo Spaghetto" De Pascale; Tonino Montalto, and Salvatore Miceli, the Trapani accomplice.

Phone numbers are communicated through prearranged alphanumeric sequences, and calls are made from phone booths or with a different phone card every time. They never go to a meeting in a car that's registered in their name. Cocaine is referred to as "bank documents," "checks," "invoices," "loans," "furniture," "the lion in the cage." And to find out how many kilos were ordered? Just talk about the "hours of work." Pannunzi's secret, shadowy world is boundless. A whirlpool it's easy to get sucked into. There's nothing to grab on to, and the few handholds that do seem to surface crumble immediately, replaced by even more cryptic ones. Only some anomalous disturbance can give shape to the shapeless, some error that lets you dispel the fog just long enough to glimpse a handhold. Once you've grabbed it, cling to it, don't let go.

The disturbance that arrives is named Shorty: His real name is Paolo Sergi, a prominent figure in the Platì 'ndrine. Shorty makes a thoughtless mistake: He uses his own cell phone, which the investigators intercept. A fatal carelessness, because it's what allows the Counter-Narcotics Group of the Catanzaro Finance Guard to break into the network. Paolo Sergi becomes the skeleton key, and he's the one who gives the Italian antimafia investigation its name: "Igres" is simply "Sergi" spelled backward.

Thanks to Shorty's carelessness the fog lifts to reveal a logical system. The blind alleyways and smoke screens the investigators had stumbled through could now be seen for what they were: smoke in their eyes. Distorted fragments begin to recompose into coherent images. What emerges is a gigantic economic force. From the wiretappings, investigators can trace the entire picture: a complex organization divided into two main branches, one in Calabria, the other in Sicily.

Pannunzi, whom the investigators characterize as "charismatic and never to be contradicted," takes care of everything from acquisition to distribution, and he procures enormous quantities of cocaine for Italy. His principal supplier in Colombia is the narco-trafficker known as Barba, or Beard. Beard and Pannunzi have a gentlemen's agreement, which seems incredible given that it's standard practice to ask for flesh and blood as well as financial guarantees. But Pannunzi is admired and respected in Bogotá, and the 'ndrina he works for is itelf a guarantee: The Marando-Trimboli families' resources are so huge that at times Pannunzi himself is amazed at the sums the Calabrian bosses keep coming up with to finance their business.

Roberto gives orders to his son, Alessandro, from Colombia. Salvatore Miceli and the Mariano Agate clan organize transport from South America and the transfer of goods off the coast of the Aegadian Islands, where boats from the Sicilian town of Mazara del Vallo, which have the advantage of being able to blend in with the rest of the fishing fleet, are ready to take delivery. The Sicilians' presence means there will be local mafia backing when the drugs are unloaded along the Trapani coast, which they control.

Rosario Marando and Rocco Trimboli handle distribution to the Rome and Milan drug markets. They call the buyers and establish the terms of purchase using a language rich in soccer metaphors. On the phone the two Platì bosses ask their interlocutors if they want to "reserve a field for the game." Sometimes the buyer says he'd like to "play," but "the rest of the team is away from Rome," meaning that his usual purchasing partners are out of town at the moment. So he asks if they can move the "soccer game" to the following Monday.

Every ten days Rocco Trimboli organizes a car trip to his sales point, a "home delivery" of sorts. The cocaine, usually about 10 kilos each time, is divided into blocks and hidden in the false bottom of his car. Francesco and Giuseppe Piromalli, the so-called Roly-poly brothers who act as representatives in Rome, are so powerful that they're allowed to return the merchandise if it doesn't meet their expectations. One time Francesco Piromalli complained to Rosario Marando that "there was too much sauce on the pasta," "too much oil in the pickles"—in other words, the coke had been cut too much. When Piromalli returned the merchandise he couldn't refrain from remarking scornfully: "If I'd wanted Neapolitan crap, I could have bought it right next door, instead of going all the way to Calabria."* Neapolitan crap is what you find in the area known as Scampia, the coke the Camorra cartels import to the biggest open-air drug market in Europe. But it's inferior to what the Calabrians sell. In Scampia they cut it with the idea of selling wholesale amounts; it's the only place where this happens without needing a go-between. You show up and place your order, and you can come away with even a kilo of reasonable quality coke at a good price. Direct sale. Anywhere else, for anything over single doses, or maybe a bit more, you need a contact high up in the trafficking structure, if not in the criminal leadership itself.

Aside from these minor drawbacks, the organization for acquiring, transporting, repackaging, and distributing coke is a well-oiled machine, rigid in its hierarchy but flexible when it comes to adapting to the unexpected.

Like in the adventure of *Mirage II.* A ship is needed to carry a load of Colombian cocaine across the ocean. A ship owner is needed. They find one, a Greek master mariner named Antonios Gofas, nicknamed the Gentleman. Back in the 1980s he transported heroin to Sicily to be refined, but the Gentleman has now switched to cocaine. He owns a merchant vessel, the *Muzak.* It costs too much for the Sicilians, but the Calabrians don't think twice about shelling out £2.5 billion. Now they have the vessel they need. But they change its name: The *Muzak* becomes *Mirage II,* which sounds more melodious to Italian ears. Gofas is good, and he has a reliable crew.

The *Mirage II* has to drop anchor in Colombia, take on the cocaine, circumnavigate the South American continent so as to avoid rigorous inspections at the Panama Canal, and then set sail for Sicily, where the

* Later, in 2007, Piromalli was acquitted of drug trafficking charges.

shipment would then be loaded onto fishing boats off the coast of Trapani. A huge vessel that plows the ocean waves, ports that await containers: It was all decided on March 2, 2001, in a hotel in Fiumicino,
near Rome, the Hotel Roma. Details are worked out: the route to take
from Colombia; the precise strip of sea where the merchandise will be
picked up; the modes of transfer from the mother ship to the Mazara
fishing boats; the code names and the radio frequencies to be used.
After almost a year and a half of negotiations and preparations, the
*Mirage II* can finally hoist anchor.

Before it gets to Colombia, however, the ship has engine trouble and
goes down off the coast of Peru, near Paita. The captain describes the
tragedy, goes crazy over the engine failure, doesn't know what to do.
Pannunzi, who has been following the whole operation from afar, immediately smells a rat: Did the Greek Gentleman deliberately sink the
ship? Pannunzi doesn't believe in fate. For him chance can't do much
when there's commitment and money involved. Chance is something
you confront.

The problem is that the Gentleman, true to his nickname, sent the
suppliers one of his own men as a guarantee. Now he's the drug traffickers' hostage. What's more, the ship sank *before* its precious cargo
was loaded into the hold. These factors, which would seem to suggest a
blameless accident, only increase Pannunzi's doubts. He suspects that
the captain calculated with cynical cunning the risk of cheating his
fearsome associates in order to pocket the insurance on the *Mirage II*.
For the money he would make, the hostage in Colombia could be sacrificed. If that's the case, Pannunzi is sure he'll be able to verify it.
Which, for a shipowner in the cocaine business, would mean the end of
his career and probable death.

But for the moment he has to put a good face on things so that he
can get the insurance money to his investors while simultaneously
arranging another voyage. The Sicilians, represented by Miceli, hire
the Turkish Paul Eduard Waridel, known as the Turk, who had a
history of getting Turkish heroin into Sicily. Waridel has good contacts

in Greece too, and knows who can arrange sea transport for any kind of merchandise. Now, as gangsters say, "It's a three-way job": Three containers set out from Barranquilla to Athens, with a port of call in Venezuela. About 900 kilos are concealed among the cover cargo of sacks of rice: enough to amortize the loss of the *Mirage II* and guarantee a considerable profit.

But the Greek police intercept one of the three containers as soon as it arrives in Piraeus and seize 220 kilos of pure cocaine hidden among the rice. Mysteriously, they don't notice the other two containers, which remain in port, waiting to clear customs. The Colombian suppliers once again find themselves without a cent, because the drugs are usually paid for when they're delivered to the Calabrians. Holding Gofas's right-hand man hostage isn't enough; they realize his life might not be worth anything. So they kidnap Salvatore Miceli, the Cosa Nostra representative responsible for the transport and final distribution to the 'ndrine.

Cosa Nostra is in trouble. The most watched criminal organization in the world, the one most talked about, seems incapable of handling the situation. The Trapani clan doesn't have the money. The Turkish wheeler-dealer had let them know it would take four hundred thousand dollars to get the two containers through customs and the goods to Italy. Pannunzi intervenes. He moves swiftly to save his accomplice and get the ball rolling again. He sends two representatives from his group to Lugano to hand deliver the money to Waridel, who in turn is supposed to take it to Athens. But the Turk, like the Greek shipowner before him, is playing dirty. Maybe he wants to get his hands on the cocaine as well, or maybe he just wants to keep the money that's supposed to be for getting the container through customs. After pocketing the cash he says that the remaining cocaine has disappeared from Piraeus and is now in an unspecified location in Africa, where a trustworthy fellow countryman is holding it. On the phone he uses an unintentionally poetic expression to refer to Africa: "on the other side of the bulls"; in other words, facing Spain.

The Calabrians and the Sicilians realize that Waridel is swindling them. But revenge has to wait—business first. They organize yet another trip, this time from Namibia to Sicily. In late September 2002, the ship carrying the cocaine is off the coast of the Aegadian Islands, but there's no sign of the Sicilian fishing boats that are supposed to do the pickup. A whole day goes by without the commander getting a reply signal. A second night, but all's still quiet. The commander waits until the third night. He tries to make contact, following the established procedures, but still nothing. In the end it turns out that the fishing boats from Trapani were using a different radio frequency. Incredible. They had misunderstood. Pannunzi can't check on every step. He's merely a broker, not a mafia boss: And when he makes a mistake, it's because someone else made a mistake in carrying out his orders.

Salavatore Miceli is scared. The Colombians no longer trust him. The excuses the Italians offer are worth less than nothing. When Pannunzi says he'll vouch for the deal, Miceli is finally freed. But Bebè is disappointed in his friend, who risked his reputation too. The 'ndrangheta bosses are even more furious. They hold the Sicilian partly responsible for the mess that threatens to blow the entire operation sky-high, the mess they've had to pay millions of dollars to extricate him from. At this point the Sicilians are excluded. Cosa Nostra is out. Pannunzi takes full control of the situation and decides that the shipment should be delivered to Spain. No problem: He's got connections there; for example Massimiliano Avesani, known as the Prince. The Prince is a wealthy Roman with ties to Pannunzi and the Calabrian 'ndrine. For several years he's been the respected owner of a shipyard in Málaga. Pannunzi knows that police forces around the world have managed to identify his shipment and are trying to trace its route. But this time the Calabrians and their accomplices don't make mistakes: They use extremely cryptic language and change phone numbers frequently. The investigators lose the scent. On October 15, 2002, the ship arrives in Spain and the cocaine's troubled voyage ends in Avesani's sure hands.

Meanwhile, the Catanzaro Finance Guard agents have discovered another possible pretext. Although phone communication between Italy and Colombia has been maniacally prudent, they've traced a number of calls to one particular landline. But it's a Holland number. It turns out to belong to an Amsterdam law firm, that of Leon Van Kleef. He and his partners are so well known, they were featured in the popular weekly magazine *Nieuwe Revu*. As usual, the link is Pannunzi, who builds his credibility through mutual acquaintances, not to mention his own savoir faire as a successful and worldly businessman. And so, in an elegant quarter of Amsterdam, in offices lined with contemporary art, a bunch of mafiosi, 'ndranghetas, and Colombian narcos come together to talk serenely about their business. In the investigation, reference is made to a shipment of 600 kilos or so of cocaine, which, according to Pannunzi is of a quality that's "never been seen before, something you dream about." They dub the enterprise the Flower Deal in homage to Holland's most famous export. If Bebè was the one to make up the name, he might have chosen it for the added pleasure of alluding to the tulip fever that swept across Holland in the seventeenth century, the first speculative bubble in history. Cocaine had become the same sort of exponential money multiplier that tulip bulbs had been back then, and it seems fitting that the place of negotiation is the same. Paolo Sergi and the Sicilian Giuseppe Palermo commute between Italy and Amsterdam to carry on the increasingly difficult negotiations. The lot is reduced to 200 kilos, but Alessandro Pannunzi phones his father, worried that they may not be able to cover the entire purchase with the cash they have on hand, and so may need to reduce the lot again by half. In the end, the Flower Deal crumbles, thanks to a banal hitch. Even though they have the money, the Marandos can't change it into dollars quickly enough. The Dutch won't accept any other currency, and since there's no shortage of interested buyers for such high-quality merchandise, they sell it to someone else.

The Italian antimafia unit investigated Leon Van Kleef but to no avail; he insisted that a lawyer with an international clientele can't be expected to know what the people waiting outside his office might be

discussing. He has his name to defend, as well as the twenty-year reputation of a law firm that the Dutch magazine describes as "the choice
of many leading criminals." On their elegant Web site the firm's lawyers let it be known that they specialize in homicide, manslaughter,
extortion, fraud, and money laundering, and that they are not prepared
to represent informers or whistle-blowers. Van Kleef, who specializes in
Spanish speakers, decided to stand by his client to the end. And Dutch
law has no provisions for such crimes as external support of a criminal
organization. Even the DDA of Reggio Calabria finally decided not to
press charges against him.

After the unfortunate dinner at the Adriano Restaurant in Madrid,
Pasquale Ciola continued to live peacefully in his house in Ostuni for
seventeen years, contesting sentence after sentence and trusting in the
slowness of the Italian judicial machine. The Supreme Court doesn't
hand down a definitive sentence until February 2011: seven years and
two months. Ciola, who was then nearly eighty years old, packed his
suitcase and was escorted to the regional jail.

Mario from Madrid, on the other hand, survives for years behind
bars, like an old-school mafia boss. From Spain he goes to Grasse, to
the same prison he'd escaped from almost a decade earlier. The French
are far more attentive this time, but in 2004 they have to extradite him
to Naples for one of his many trials. And in Italy the Supreme Court
orders him to be released. Mario doesn't waste a minute before disappearing again into the "land of bulls." He's arrested in Spain in 2006
with a passport and credit card belonging to a Slovenian citizen and
€77,000 in cash. The Spanish judges decide to release him on a technicality. Two months later he is arrested again, this time while passing
himself off as a Bulgarian, but once again he is released on a technicality.

Locatelli always seems to find a way to pick himself up when he
stumbles. His two sons, who stayed in Italy, are grown men now, capable of running a sizable, dynamic enterprise. The best thing for them to

do—their best cover—is to keep making dirty money, lots of it, while officially making clean money. The Locatelli family owns LOPAV S.p.A., a flooring company in Ponte San Pietro, a few miles from Brembate di Sopra. Their company has excellent credentials and has expanded significantly, thanks to its competitiveness and competence, and it contributes notably to the wealth of the territory. It's not their fault if their father, who left when they were young, turned out to be a rogue; they rolled up their sleeves and provided honest jobs to lots of people. That's how the locals, both ordinary and important folks, think of them. They don't ask where the financing came from to build the business to the point of dominating the industry nationally in less than ten years. Those Locatelli boys are enterprising; they're good, that's all. Everybody's good opinion of them is confirmed when LOPAV is awarded a five hundred thousand euro contract to build the undercoating and exterior floors for earthquake-proof housing in L'Aquila, as well as the flooring for a new shopping center in Mapello. Brembate and Ponte San Pietro have reason to be proud when the company's official Web site boasts that "the earthquake victims of L'Aquila will walk on 'Bergamasque ground.'"

But just as work in Abruzzo is about to begin, the Naples DDA issues an international arrest warrant for Pasquale Locatelli, once again accused of association with international drug trafficking. The link this time is the Mazzarella clan, Locatelli's clients in Campania, who get their cocaine and hashish through him. A joint operation coordinated by the Naples Finance Guard and involving Interpol and the Spanish police leads to his arrest at the Madrid airport in May 2010, after authorities trailed his son, who was on his way to Spain to see him. But people are even more bewildered when Patrizio and Massimiliano are also jailed five months later; wiretaps led to their being accused of playing a very active role in both money-laundering activities and the astronomical fees paid to drug traffickers. Pasquale Locatelli had built a mechanism that worked perfectly, even when he was in hiding or in prison. As much as they can try to stop him, he is the Galileo of cocaine. They can condemn him—and yet cocaine moves.

.   .   .

It seems impossible by this point, but on April 5, 2004, the Italian police flush out Roberto Pannunzi in an elegant Madrid neighborhood, along with his son Alessandro and his son-in-law Francesco Bumbaca. Once again he is sent to jail in Italy. And here he pulls off one of his typical magic tricks. For health reasons, on February 21, 2009, he's transferred to the Parma prison clinic, where he's kept under special surveillance. Then a heart ailment gets him house arrest for a year. The court indicates the Tor Vergata General Hospital for his treatment. But Pannunzi, after spending a few months at a clinic in Nemi, in the province of Rome, chooses Villa Sandra, a private clinic in the city. The media doesn't have its eye on him, public opinion doesn't know about him, so he's not considered a threat. Italian politics is distracted by completely different concerns. And thus, a couple of months before his house arrest is to end, Pannunzi escapes from a clinic a second time, leaving no trace. But what's even more incredible is that they only notice by chance that he's gone. On March 15, 2010, the Carabinieri make their usual rounds: Pannunzi's not there. His room wasn't guarded, and no one is sure exactly when he made his excape: He was supposed to be serving a sixteen-and-a-half-year sentence, and a first-level court had already sentenced him to an additional eighteen years. A man condemned to hard time but who wasn't even being guarded, who escapes easily, who buys himself silence and intercontinental plane tickets. The Italian state should not allow men with the unlimited financial resources of a Pannunzi to convalesce in private clinics. As Nicola Gratteri, the magistrate who has been following him for years, says: Roberto Pannunzi "is part of that class of people who don't count their money; they weigh it."

This is something drug traffickers know.

But Bebè's freedom doesn't last long. On July 5, 2013, he is arrested in a shopping center in Bogotá. In his pocket is a fake Venezuelan ID card, with the name Silvano Martino, which he shows to the police, denying that he is the narco-trafficker they're looking for. But the mug shots from the Italian authorities don't leave room for doubt. On the Colombian news that evening his face appears behind the journalists, who announce the arrest of "one of the most wanted drug lords in Europe." He had four arrest orders for drug trafficking and "mafia association" hanging over his head. Interpol had classified him as a "red alert." After the ritual photos, in which the Colombian agents show him off like a trophy, Pannunzi is put on a plane for Rome, via Madrid. He's not the only VIP on board: Raffaella Carrà is on the flight too, Italian television's most famous showgirl, who, like all the other passengers, is oblivious to the boss's presence. The photos of his arrival at Fiumicino airport show him wearing the same long-sleeved white polo shirt he'd had on in the video of his arrest in Colombia, the last shirt he put on as a free man. Pannunzi now has to serve twelve years, five months, and twenty-six days in jail. During his criminal career various epithets have been pinned on him— "prince of drug trafficking"; "the most wanted broker in Europe"; "the Italian Pablo Escobar"; "king of evasions"—but I prefer to call him "the Copernicus of cocaine," because he was the first to understand that it's not the world of cocaine that must orbit around the markets but the markets that must rotate around cocaine.

His arrest required the collaboration of the Italian security forces, the American DEA, and the Colombian police, as well as about two years of investigations coordinated by the public prosecutor's office in Reggio Calabria. Perhaps it's not a coincidence that only two days before his arrest, "il Principe," Prince Massimiliano Avesani, Bebè's contact in Spain, was arrested in Rome. He too had a fake ID in his pocket, a driver's license registered to a Giovanni Battista—who had a clean record—but after he was taken to police headquarters he had to admit his real identity. Avesani, who was considered the pivot between the Calabrian clans and the Roman criminal organizations, had been arrested in Montecarlo in 2011, but he went into hiding in order to avoid a fifteen-year sentence for international drug trafficking. He didn't go very far though: His hideout was an elegant apartment in the Torrino neighborhood in the south of Rome, where the police found other blank IDs that would have come in handy for his life as a fugitive. Apparently he congratulated the police officers who arrested him: "Bingo" he allegedly said. In truth, they were still one number shy of bingo, but it arrives two days later with the arrest of Bebè Pannunzi on the other side of the planet. Who knows, maybe it was Avesani himself who extracted the winning number from the tumbler. Pannunzi may have lost his protection once Avesani fell.

Some day I'd like to meet Roberto Pannunzi. To look him in the eye, but without asking him anything, because he wouldn't tell me anything other than empty chatter fit for a journalist who writes insubstantial fluff. There's something I'd really like to know, though: Where does he get his inner serenity? You can see he doesn't look tormented. He doesn't kill. He doesn't destroy people's lives. Like a good drug broker, all he does is move capital and cocaine around, without ever touching the latter. Just as others do with oil or plastic. Don't they cause car accidents, irreversible pollution all around the world, even wars that go on for decades? Do oil companyexecutives lose sleep over such things? Do plastic manufacturers? Or the heads of multinational IT companies, who surely know how their products are built, or that cornering the coltan market is the root of ongoing massacres in the Congo? I'm sure that's how Pannunzi rationalizes things. But I'd like to hear what sort of justifications he'd offer, one by one. What does he tell himself in order to say: "I'm just a broker. You give me the money and I'll give you the goods. Like everyone else." That's all. No better or worse.

# 12

# OPERATION MONEY LAUNDERING

How do you feel when, to enter your bank, you have to go through a security door that only lets one person in at a time? What runs through your head while you're waiting in line to make a money transfer, deposit a check, get some coins and small bills so you can make change for your customers at your bar or shop? When your father, who has a regular salary, has to sign in order for you to get a mortgage on a house, because both you and your wife make do with temp work? What concepts have you learned to associate with words like spread or rating, liquidity or deficit crises? Which of these terms are you familiar with: hedge fund, subprime, credit crunch, swap, blind trust? Can you explain what they mean? Are you too convinced that you belong to the 99 percent whose combined wealth does not even match that of the remaining 1 percent? That financial capitalism is primarily to blame for your increasingly difficult struggle to make ends meet? And do you too believe that the banks, which manage to get billions from the state—from you, in other words—and yet won't renew your credit, are a giant Moloch controlled by an invisible and untouchable clique of speculators and high-level executives? You're wrong, at least in part. There's no secret power trying to crush you, no specter with degrees from the best universities, dressed in expensive but understated outfits, and displaying calm, sober manners.

Banks and banking power are made up of people, just like everything else. If that power has proved to be deeply destructive, the fault lies not just with greedy cokehead brokers or that one corruptible employee, but with everyone: from the trader licensed to make high-risk deals, to the team of specialists that buys stocks on the global market that will flow into funds offered by the same bank, to the employee who suggests someone to manage your savings, right down to the teller at the window. All together they carry out the bank's directives, and almost all of them are honest. Honest not merely as in not doing anything illegal, but also in believing they're acting for the good of the bank without, however, acting for the ill of its clientele. Maybe a little less honest at times, but not because they decide on their own to look after their interests, but because they're doing what they've always done: carrying out tacit directives that are always in the bank's best interest. And this happens at all levels, high and low, and it forms a system. Which is how we arrive at that global mechanism that might seem to you like some kind of conspiracy but that really works much more along the lines of what has been called "the banality of evil."

But if the mechanism is made up of many loyal and banal individuals, a little grit can cause the gears to jam. For example, the man who, if it hadn't been for September 11, would have been kept waiting forever in a damp room at a London police station. The Twin Towers have just fallen and the United States is starting to recover. George W. Bush has introduced the PATRIOT Act, which among other things is supposed to identify and pursue international money laundering and funding for terrorism. The law establishes a series of special measures that U.S. banks are required to adopt when dealing with jurisdictions, institutions, or accounts they suspect are laundering dirty money; it provides greater transparency in financial activities and accountability, limitations on interbank operations, and tougher penalties for transgressors.

Four years later an Englishman with impertinent blond hair crosses the threshold of Wachovia Bank, one of the giants of the American credit system: a man named Martin Woods. He's just been hired as a senior money-laundering reporting officer in the bank's London office. Punctilious and precise, maniacal about order. Just the right person for a bank aiming to adhere scrupulously to the new money-laundering protocols. But Martin isn't merely a zealous employee who is good with numbers and loves double-entry bookkeeping. He is a former agent of the National Crime Squad. This gives him a huge advantage over his banking peers around the world: Martin understands people. He knows how to talk with them, how to read their gestures, how to weigh the nuances of their moods. Money is just one of the many variables, just one of the many color gradations, on his personal grid for evaluating people.

There are already three actors onstage in this drama: a wounded country that's reacting to attack; a measure that aims to stifle threats by fighting them on the financial front; and a man who wants to do his job. What's needed now is a fourth, a key character: a DC-9. The airplane lands in Ciudad del Carmen, in the state of Campeche; awaiting it are Mexican soldiers, who find onboard 128 black suitcases containing 5.5 tons of cocaine, worth about a $100 million. A phenomenal bust, a punch in the face of the narcotics trade. But the investigators' jaws really drop when they discover that the DC-9, which belongs to the Sinaloa cartel, was purchased with money laundered through one of the largest banks in the United States: Wachovia.

While investigators dig through the past of the DC-9 that landed in Mexico, Martin is already picking scrupulously through Wachovia's clients' records. That's what investigators and money-laundering reporting officers do. Stick their noses into piles of papers, poison themselves with numbers and dates, then put it all together and see if there are any discrepancies. Martin discovers that there's something not quite right about a bunch of traveler's checks issued in Mexico. A tourist couldn't possibly need that much money. Then his eyes fall on the numbers, which are strangely sequential. And the various signatures, why do they all look so much alike? He reports his suspicions to his superiors; many of the checks involve *casas de cambio,* Mexican currency exchange agencies. Martin spends hours on the phone, he sends e-mails, requests meetings to discuss the reports he keeps sending with stubborn determination. He smells a rat, and the news from Mexico and the United States only confirms his suspicion. The American authorities' constant scrutiny of the bank's activity pushes Wachovia to sever relations with some *casas de cambio,* and the ones that survive the cut decide to take a step back. Under fire from the outside, the banking giant vacillates at first, but then responds with a cleanup operation. Inside the bank, however, all is quiet. Silence and isolation are the most effective forms of "mobbing" (workplace bullying). Martin goes on writing new suspicious activity reports. When people point out that he'll never get a reply, and that he'll get himself in trouble if he keeps it up, he responds in his usual manner: He lowers his eyes and smiles. After his umpteenth report falls on deaf ears he receives an office communication: His most recent write-up was irregular, because his authorized range of action does not extend as far as the United States and Mexico. It's the beginning of the end for Martin's work: The spokes in his wheels multiply, office life is awful, he no longer has access to important files. The silent treatment his coworkers give him isn't enough: Wachovia is staging a counterattack; it has to do something to shut up this incorrigible busybody.

On the other side of the Atlantic the investigators looking into the DC-9 discover that since 2004 several billion dollars have moved from the Sinaloa cartel "cash box" to Wachovia bank accounts. It emerges that for three years the bank did not respect money-laundering protocols when transferring $378.4 billion. Of this at least $110 million were from drug trafficking, which had entered international banking circuits in this way. That's how it worked. The money entered through the *casas de cambio.* The world's richest cartel was sending money as if it were an army of *mamacitas* with their savings stitched into the lining of their clothes or of old men selling off a plot of land to help out their grand-children in the United States. Those same exchange agencies then opened accounts at a Miami branch of Wachovia Bank. Millions of dollars in cash were deposited in Mexico and then wired to Wachovia accounts in the United States to buy stocks or property. On numerous occasions the drug cartels themselves were the ones making the deposits. For example, about $13 million were deposited and transferred to Wachovia accounts to purchase airplanes for drug trafficking. More than twenty tons of cocaine were seized from these planes.

In English there's a lovely word for denouncing or exposing wrong-doing: whistle-blowing. Martin blew his whistle with all his might, and at a certain point Wachovia realized that if they wanted to silence the piper they'd have to muzzle him. The freeze-out at the office intensi-fies. Martin, close to a nervous breakdown, goes to see a psychiatrist. He's out of the game, but with his remaining strength he makes one last attempt. He finds out that there will be a meeting at Scotland Yard, where he hopes to find some colleagues open-minded enough to listen to him. He's sat at the same table with a representative from the Amer-ican DEA, a jovial type with a curious gaze. Martin doesn't think twice before pouring out his story to him. Putting all his trust in a total stranger, he pushes a rock down the escarpment in hopes of starting an avalanche. And the rock rolls. It rolls until March 16, 2010, when the vice president of Wachovia Bank signs a plea bargain in which the bank admits it provided banking services to twenty-two *casas de cambio* in Mexico, from which it accepted money in the form of wire transfers and traveler's checks.

More or less what Martin Woods had reported four years earlier, much to his detriment. Woods filed suit against the bank for retaliating against a whistle-blower. That lawsuit was finally settled by Woods' leaving the bank in exchange for an undisclosed sum and an agreement to keep the terms of the settlement confidential. A sad epilogue, at least until March 2010, a few days after Wachovia signed the plea bargain, when Martin at last gets some recognition. He receives a letter from

John Dugan, comptroller of the currency of the United States, who handles bank monitoring for the U.S. Treasury Department: "Not only did the information that you provided facilitate our investigation, but you demonstrated great personal courage and integrity by speaking up. Without the efforts of individuals like you, actions such as the ones taken against Wachovia would not be possible."

The authorities grant Wachovia Bank a deferred prosecution; that is, the charge is delayed till the end of a probation period: If the bank adheres to the law for a year and meets all its plea bargain obligations, the charges will be dropped. The authorities probably think they are acting responsibly. In such a delicate moment, with the country struggling to recover from the most serious financial crisis since 1929, they can't risk another big bank collapsing and disaster striking again. The probation period ends in March 2011: From that moment Wachovia is clean, everything's okay. They had to pay the government a $110 million forfeiture for accepting transactions linked to drug trafficking, and thus violating anti-money-laundering norms, plus a $50 million fine. An enormous sum but ridiculous compared to the earnings of a bank like Wachovia, which in 2009 were about $12.3 billion. Money laundering pays. Not one bank employee or director had to see the inside of a jail cell, even for a single day. No one is guilty; no one is responsible. Merely a scandal, which quickly sinks into oblivion.

We need to read between the lines, however, and go back to the story of Martin, who with his courageous stubbornness managed to obtain much more than what the sentence contains. The reticence of the authorities shows that there is a very tight link between the banks and the tens of thousands of deaths in the Mexican drug war. But that's not all. Martin stirred up troubled waters, he dirtied his hands with numbers in order to reactivate the American banking system's protections. A single lightning bolt in a cloudless sky. But there are thunder and lightning on the horizon. Controls grew very rigid after September 11, but with the financial crisis that exploded in the midst of Martin's investigation, the climate changed. Hence the verdicts that send the megaswindler Bernie Madoff to prison for 150 years, and the French trader Jérôme Kerviel for 5, along with repaying Société Générale nearly €5 billion, the amount he'd burned through. These men, who often describe themselves as sacrificial lambs of the system, nevertheless caused enormous harm to individuals, companies, and society as a whole. But the narco-dollars that flow into coffers don't seem to cause any damage; in fact, they provide that life-giving oxygen known as liquidity. So much so that in December 2009 Antonio Maria Costa, then head of the United Nations Office on Drugs and Crime, made a shocking statement: He had been able to ascertain that criminal organizations' earnings were the only liquid investment capital some banks had to keep from failing. The International Monetary Fund's data is grim: From January 2007 to September 2009 the total of toxic stocks and bad loans in the United States and Europe reached $1 trillion. And alongside these losses were the failures and temporary receiverships of credit institutions. By the second half of 2008 cash flow had become the banking system's principal problem. As Antonio Maria Costa emphasized, "That was the moment when the system was basically paralyzed because of the unwillingness of banks to lend money to one another." Only criminal organizations seemed to have enormous quantities of cash to invest, to launder.

No doubt by this point some of you are starting to think that I'm obsessed. The problem, you might say, isn't so much mafia money as it is the financial system. Money expands like gas. If that bubble bursts, the nebula will vanish so quickly that incoming narco-dollars will pale in comparison. Which is what happened on September 15, 2008, with the avalanche the Lehman Brothers bankruptcy set in motion, an avalanche that only billions in public funds managed to stop. But the mess I'm talking about—born amid the skyscrapers of Wall Street, and thus, to all appearances, far from simple Calabrian villages, the Colombian jungle, and even the perennially crumbling, blood-soaked towns along the Mexican border—in truth isn't a mess at all. It is well known that Lehman Brothers had invested vast sums in subprime mortgages, which were nothing other than a stroke of genius, a way of reselling mortgages that many signers could not possibly pay, as profitable investments. Profit derived from debt. When the rope snapped and the game ended, lots of people who bought homes this way ended up in the street. And above all, that time, it was decided that the bank bloated with hot air could fail too. No sooner were the catastrophic consequences of this decision unleashed than all the other banks and insurance companies that had more or less behaved like Lehman Brothers had to be saved. Yet U.S. government aid was only an emergency stopgap for a system based on those dynamics. The crux of the matter is that banks need to ingest a sufficient amount of solid food in order to produce the immense wealth that swells their bellies, which they have to be able to rid themselves of as soon as someone asks them for money, in whatever form. That is the problem with liquidity. The alchemy of contemporary finance is based on the transubstantiation of money from a solid to a liquid and gaseous state. But that solid/liquid mix proves systematically never to be enough. In the advanced West they've closed the factories, and consumption is nourished through forms of debt such as credit cards, leasing, installment payments, and financing. Who, on the other hand, earns the biggest profits from merchandise that must be paid for in full right away? Narco-traffickers. Real mafia money can make the difference to the survival of the financial system. That's the danger.

A recent study by Alejandro Gaviria and Daniel Mejía, two economists at the University of Bogotá, revealed that 97.4 percent of the revenue from narco-trafficking in Colombia is regularly laundered through banking circuits in the United States and Europe by means of a complex series of financial operations. Hundreds of billions of dollars. The laundering occurs through a shareholding system, like Chinese nesting boxes, in which cash is transformed into electronic stocks and transferred from one country to another. When it arrives on another continent the money's practically clean and—best of all—untraceable. So interbank loans have been systematically financed with funds from drug trafficking and other illicit activities. Some banks survived only because of this money. A huge portion of the estimated 352 billion narco-dollars was absorbed by the legal economic system, successfully recycled.

Three hundred and fifty-two billion dollars: narco-trafficking profits equal more than a third of the entire banking system's losses in 2009, according to the International Monetary Fund, and that's only the deducible tip of the iceberg we're sailing toward. The banks, which now own many people's existences and are capable of influencing the governments of even the richest and most democratic states, now find that they too risk being held ransom. Once again, the problem is no longer far away, in wretched countries such as Mexico and Colombia, or down in Sicily, Campania, and Calabria, a southern Italy that is both accomplice and victim of its ruin. I want to scream this loud enough so that people will know, so that they prepare themselves for the consequences.

As Martin, the Wachovia whistle-blower, did, even though the praise he earned from the American authorities did not simplify his life in the financial world. He had to go into business for himself, opening two consulting companies specializing in anti-money laundering: Woods M5 Associates, and then Hermes Forensic Solutions. But he wanted to work for an important credit institution again. He contacted the Royal Bank of Scotland, one of the ten largest banks in the world and the second in the UK—until the financial crisis of 2008, that is, when it became one of those banks to be saved at any cost. The British government temporarily held almost 70 percent, so the Scottish bank needed to do everything possible to regain investor confidence. Even, one might think, hiring a man like Martin Woods to show their intention to rigorously respect all the rules of fair play. And yet in July 2012 the Royal Bank of Scotland suddenly broke the contract they had entered into with him. No explanation. Had they learned of Martin's accusations against Wachovia? And just a few days later the LIBOR scandal broke, revealing that some leading banks, including the Royal Bank of Scotland, had for years been manipulating the London Interbank Offered Rate, the European reference rate for interbank loans.

Martin refused to give up; he sued them. He lost. The British judge agreed with the bank that an employer-employee relationship had not yet been established, and therefore Woods had no right to demand redress to an employment tribunal. In the meantime Martin began consulting about financial crime for the information giant Thomson Reuters. As of yet, no bank has been willing to hire him.

Today New York and London are the world's largest laundries for dirty money. No longer those fiscal paradises of the Cayman Islands or the Isle of Man, now it's Wall Street and the City of London. In the words of Jennifer Shasky Calvery, at that time chief of the Asset Forfeiture and Money Laundering Section of the Department of Justice, during a testimony before the American Congress on February 8, 2012: "Disguised in the trillions of dollars that is transferred between banks each day, banks in the U.S. are used to funnel massive amounts of illicit funds." The centers of world financial power have stayed afloat thanks to cocaine money. Calvery also noted, "As evidence of transnational organized crime's (TOC) global economic might, one need only consider the most recent estimates of the amount of money laundered in the global financial system—$1.6 trillion, of which an estimated $580 billion is related to drug trafficking and other TOC activities, according to the United Nations Office on Drugs and Crime's Research Report published in 2011. These staggering amounts of money in the hands of the worst criminal elements create a terrifyingly vicious cycle—money enables TOC to corrupt the economic and political systems in which they operate, thereby allowing them to consolidate and expand their power and influence, which gives rise to more opportunity to commit crime and generate revenue."

Lucy Edwards is a brilliant career woman. She is vice president of London's Bank of New York and is married to Peter Berlin, director of the British company Benex Worldwide. Lucy is invited to a two-day conference on financial services for Scandinavian, Eastern European, and Russian clients. She's perfect, because she, like her husband, was born in the former Soviet Union before becoming a naturalized Brit. She has no doubts about her speech, which she calls "Money Laundering: Latest Developments and Regulations." While Lucy is speaking to a rapt audience, the English authorities, who have been investigating Russian crime organizations for years, are informing their American cohorts that Benex is using a Bank of New York account to channel enormous sums of money. And Benex is linked to YBM Magnex, a front company belonging to one of the most powerful Russian mafia bosses, Semën Mogilevič.

The FBI discovers that Mogilevič washes billions of dirty dollars through the Bank of New York. A constant, quick flow of money in and out. This doesn't seem to trouble the bank much; it merely files a suspicious activity report. A river of money that also comes in handy to water some political campaigns in Russia. The New York district attorney's office realizes that the money-laundering operation involved the illicit transfer of $7 billion from Russia to American bank accounts and then to other accounts around the globe, through a series of cover companies.

In the Bank of New York case the only person who ends up in jail— for two weeks—is Svetlana Kudriavceva, a bank employee who lied to an FBI agent about being paid five hundred dollars a month by Peter Berlin and his wife. The bank gets off with a $38 million fine and a promise to respect money-laundering laws in the future.

The technique Mogilevič and his associates use is easily replicated in other contexts: Italy, for example. It's 1999, and the public prosecutor's office in Rimini is monitoring the accounts of two Ukrainians and a Russian who were, as the investigation records state, at the head of "a criminal organization that works to guarantee its control of the Emilia Romagna and Marche territories." Benex International—Bank of New York—Banca di Roma—Banca di credito cooperativo di

Ospedaletto in Emilia Romagna. More than a million dollars pass through these accounts. A million crisp dollar bills, ready to be used by the Russian mafia in Italy.

Lucy Edwards knows how to make even a boring topic like anti–money-laundering techniques fascinating. She's an excellent speaker, conveying just the right combination of confidence and seriousness. She even gets a laugh from her audience on more than one occasion. Lucy has just finished speaking. After the applause, lots of people, including the Bank of New York's most important clients, wait for her to step off the stage. They want to shake her hand and compliment her. She'd given a great talk.

Lucy Edwards had two months left before her bank has to fire her. She and her husband, Peter Berlin, helped recycle tons of money. She too would get off with a simple fine of $20,000 and six months of house arrest after being found guilty of money laundering, fraud, and other grave federal crimes. The woman who traveled the world explaining how to thwart money laundering had been doing it herself. I've often asked myself how she must have felt at the end of every speech she gave, and, once she'd been found out, if she tried to justify herself, to find some sense to her double game.

Who knows if Lucy still lectures on how to prevent money laundering, because she'd have lots of stories to tell. The control systems are leaking all over the place. In the distracted summer of 2012, when the Bank of Scotland slammed its doors in Martin's face, several leading American and European banks in the United States were being targeted, and one in particular, Bank of America, which, according to the FBI, the Zetas were using to launder their narco-dollars. On June 12, 2012, federal agents arrest seven people, including the big shot José Treviño Morales, the brother of Miguel, at that time the most prominent boss of Mexico's fiercest cartel. But in the United States he's known as a businessman devoted to an activity dear to the American South: He breeds winning racehorses. That's how he hides and reinvests dirty money. In order to arrive at such a remunerative and gratifying form of recycling, estimated to have been at a level of around $1 million a month, he first needs to get the money into an American bank account. Bank of America is willing to cooperate with the investigators and is not accused of any illegal activity. Up until now nothing has happened to it.

It's extremely difficult to expose money-laundering cases, or even to ascertain the scale and the degree of negligence. It's almost always like trying to squeeze sand in your fist: The grains just slip through your fingers. And if a few stay in your hand, it's more chance than will. Which is how it went for one shortsighted swindler, Barton Adams, officially a West Virginia doctor who specialized in pain therapy. He is found out while shifting hundreds of thousands of dollars—from systematic health-care fraud and tax evasion—between HSBC accounts in the United States and its branches in Canada, Hong Kong, and the Philippines. HSBC is a colossus: the fifth largest bank in the world in terms of market value, with branches in every village in the UK, and present in eighty-five foreign countries. Like Martin in the Wachovia affair, Barton rolls a stone downhill. But he does it unintentionally. On July 16, 2012, the U.S. Senate's Permanent Subcommittee on Investigations confirms rumors that had been circulating for months: HSBC and its American branch, HBUS, have exposed the American financial system to a wide range of risks of money laundering, drug trade financing, and terrorism. According to the subcommittee's report, HSBC used HBUS to link its branches around the world to the United States, thereby providing its clients services in dollars, movement of capital, currency exchange, and other monetary tools without fully respecting U.S. banking laws. Because of insufficient controls, HBUS allegedly allowed terrorist and Mexican drug money into American territory. Considering that HBUS provides twelve hundred accounts to other banks, including more than eighty HSBC branches, it's easy to see that without adequate anti–money-laundering policies, these services can become a superhighway for illegal capital to enter the United States.

The Senate subcommittee's investigation revealed that HBUS had

offered correspondent banking services to HSBC Mexico, treating it as
a low-risk client despite its being in a country with huge money-
laundering and drug-trafficking problems. Between 2007 and 2008 the
Mexican branch transferred $7 billion in cash to HBUS, exceeding all
other Mexican banks and sparking suspicions that part of this money
might be from drug sales in the United States. At the end of 2012,
HBUS declared that it was very sorry for what had happened and
agreed to pay a fine of almost $2 billion—less than a third of what
they'd taken in from Mexico alone.

It's not just the banks on Wall Street or in the City of London that
maintain privileged relations with drug lords. Banks that launder
money are scattered all across the globe, sometimes in rather disquiet-
ing places. Lebanon, for example, through which, according to the Catanzaro magistrates, the Australian Nicola Ciconte allegedly transferred
Vibo Valentia clan money. One of the biggest banks is the Lebanese
Canadian Bank of Beirut: branches spread throughout Lebanon; a liai-
son office in Montreal; more than six hundred employees. It offers a
wide range of financial services and correspondent accounts in banks
all over the world. On February 17, 2011, the U.S. Treasury Department declared that it had valid reason to consider the Lebanese Canadian Bank involved in money-laundering activities on behalf of the
Shiite group Hezbollah, and therefore subject to restrictive measures
prescribed by the PATRIOT Act. According to the Treasury Department the Lebanese bank, through insufficient controls and institutional
complicity, allegedly facilitated the money laundering of a criminal network trafficking drugs from South America through West Africa to
Europe and the Middle East, recycling $200 million a month through
Lebanese Canadian Bank accounts. Several conniving managers who
carried out the operations were identified. According to the Manhattan
district attorney's office and the DEA, the Lebanese Canadian Bank
allegedly took part in a scheme that transferred at least $248 million to
the United States between January 2007 and the beginning of 2011.
The money came from the drug trafficking and other criminal activities

of the Lebanon-based group led by the drug kingpin Ayman Joumaa and was used to purchase used cars in America. The cars were subsequently sold in western Africa, the declared revenue from which was greatly inflated so as to mask the amount of dirty money from Colombian and Mexican cartels that was added to the proceeds from the car sales. All this money was channeled toward exchange offices in Beirut, and from there to Lebanese Canadian Bank accounts, and also in part to accounts belonging to Hezbollah, which the United States considers a terrorist organization, one with increasing involvement in the drug trade.

Income from drugs and money laundering has not only sealed increasingly close alliances between terrorist and criminal organizations; it represents a more complex, pervasive, and even more dangerous connection to widespread corruption, making it one of the most elusive links to track. One case in particular illustrates quite sensationally the difficulties that beset financial investigations; the fact that it's dragged on for more than a decade only makes the point more clearly. On November 15, 1995, an elegant Mexican lady, Paulina Castañon, requests access to her safety deposit box at one of the oldest private banks in Geneva, Pictet Cie. Unfortunately there's a problem with the vault's security system, the highly presentable employees tell her. It's a way to gain time so that the Swiss police, tipped off by the DEA, can arrive with an arrest warrant. The client is the wife of Raúl Salinas de Gortari, brother of the former Mexican president, whose false passport is in her safety-deposit box. There are persistent rumors in Mexico that Raúl has maintained his contacts with all the leading figures of the Mexican and Colombian drug trade. First the DEA and then the Swiss attorney general, Carla Del Ponte, launch inquiries. Years earlier Del Ponte risked being killed along with Giovanni Falcone, with whom she was collaborating on the famous Pizza Connection investigation. Raúl Salinas is accused of having pocketed heavy transit taxes on cocaine shipments from just about everyone: the Medellín and Cali cartels; the Mexican cartels that emerged out of the territorial divisions decided on by El Padrino; and perhaps the Gulf cartel in particular. It's estimated that a total of $300 million ended up in overseas accounts, with about $90 million to $100 million going to Swiss accounts between 1992 and 1994. More specifically, funds were transferred through Citibank Mexico to private bank accounts in their London and Zurich branches, as well as the most prestigious Swiss banks, such as SBC, UBS, Banque Privée Edmond de Rothschild, Credit Suisse, and Julius Baer. The American giant allegedly helped Salinas with these transactions by making the money hard to trace. How? First of all by setting up an account in Salinas's name at its New York branch. Through Cititrust, an affiliate of Citicorp registered in the Cayman Islands, Citibank set up Trocca, an investment company also based in that fiscal paradise, where Salinas's patrimony could be kept. To further conceal Salinas's name, Citibank established another company, Tyler, which became Trocca's principal shareholder. Then it opened two investment accounts in Trocca's name, one at Citibank London and the other at Citibank Switzerland. What's more, Citibank not only allegedly neglected to obtain the client's bank references and compile a "know your customer" profile, it even let Raúl Salinas use another name when making transfers. No U.S. document names him as an owner or beneficiary of Trocca, nor does anything link him with the Trocca money that moved from Mexico to New York and on to London and Switzerland.

It was his wife, Paulina, who periodically made transfers from Mexico, and whom the vice president of Citibank's Mexico division had introduced to his Mexican colleagues as Patricia Ríos. Under that false name, Señora Salinas deposited checks drawn on at least five Mexican banks into her account, so they could be converted into American dollars and transferred to New York. There the money ended up in a so-called concentration account—a deposit account into which capital from various clients and bank branches flows before being sent on to numerous final destinations.

It seems rather ironic that the blow landed in Switzerland, the country most famous for its long tradition of banking secrecy, and where judicial proceedings against Salinas have been in progress for many years. They continued even after Carla Del Ponte became prosecutor for the International Criminal Tribunal for the former Yugoslavia at the Hague, where she investigated the crimes of Slobodan Milošević, and ended in a trial in which the Swiss judge ruled that the Mexican government structures were protecting drug trafficking and that the money could not have originated legally. In fact, it remained frozen in Swiss banks, waiting for the Mexican courts to issue a verdict on the connections between Salinas and the cartels. But there was insufficient proof on that crucial point, and the case was closed. And so, in 2008, Switzerland decided to hand over $74 million of it to the Mexican government, a sum that had grown to $130 million, and to return an additional percentage to third parties who had entrusted their money to Raúl Salinas. And it's not over yet, because on July 19, 2013, a Mexican federal judge absolved Salinas of the crime of illegal accumulation of wealth. The evidence was insufficient to prove that Salinas's fortune had been generated through illegal activities.

The problem that emerges from this interminable saga is the frequent lack both of tools of legal recourse and often of interest in going after dirty money, even when the accused is not a notorious member of some criminal organization but an exponent of that elite and that institutional apparatus that is needed to keep the machine of white profit running. Cocaine money first buys politicians and officials, and then, through them, the shelter of the banks.

## 13.

# THE CZARS CONQUER THE WORLD

"The Amalfi Coast, Sardinia, the Costa del Sol, Tuscany, Malta, Ibiza. It's all Russia!" The man who is speaking knows well the difference between Moscow's penetrating chill and Italy's refreshing warmth. A Russian like so many others who invade Italy when summer calls for bathing suits and sunscreen. The Russians are everywhere; you see them and automatically you think: Russians, Russian mafiosi. . . . As if all rich Russians were criminals. But the presence of the Russian mafia—the Mafija with a *j*—is as powerful as it is complex, difficult to understand and to learn about. We know it through clichés, through tales of jailbirds covered in barbaric tattoos, ex-boxers with broken noses, brutal ex-*specnaz,* hooligan pushers with eyes shot through with vodka and low-grade drugs. But the Mafija is something completely different. To get your bearings you have to look at the powerful families, observe their strength. Families bound not by blood but by the organization's common interests. And like all families, they have a photo album. Everything's in there: the color of the past; faces of distant relatives; snapshots of important moments; places of the heart.

It is not easy to leaf through a Russian Mafija family album, but I've tried to do that with the life of one quick-thinking boss, who is known as the Brainy Don. He's a way for me to understand how big business is linked to big crime. I imagine I saw him countless times in bars along the Italian coast, or drunk at dinner, with other mobsters. Hallucinations? Sometimes you have to go with your hallucinations, so I immerse myself in the story. I have a collection of the protagonists' photographs with me, a sort of album I've put together these past years; I need to start from something I can touch. The Brainy Don. He doesn't look like a mafioso. Like a Russian, yes, but he could also pass for American, German, Spanish, or Hungarian. At first glance he's just another elderly, obese gentleman. We tend to think that people who are that slow in their bodies must be so in their minds as well. Harmless. Innocuous. But that's not true; you have to take a closer look. In the most famous photograph of him he's holding a cigarette, caressing it with his chubby fingers. He's not looking at the camera but at some point above the photographer's head. His shirt and finely tailored vest barely contain his 290 pounds, which press against the fabric, creating pleats and wrinkles. Behind him, a fireplace framed in marble tiles; before him, a laptop and a pair of elegant reading glasses. To complete the picture, an office chair and a transparent ashtray, which suggests that the cigarette he's holding is not the first of the day. A businessman, rich and powerful, the head of numerous companies that operate in a wide range of sectors. Sure of himself, authoritarian, devoted to his work. With thousands of employees to oversee, budgets to review and approve, important decisions to make. The Brainy Don's name is Semën Judkovič Mogilevič. On January 20, 2011, *Time* magazine put him first on its list of Top 10 Real-Life Mob Bosses of all time, followed by Al Capone, Lucky Luciano, Pablo Escobar, and Totò Riina. American and European security agencies consider him one of the key Mafija leaders, the head of the Russian octopus, with tentacles all over the world.

Reconstructing his life story is a way to understand how the most violent crimes—extortion, murder, arms and drug trafficking, and prostitution rackets relate to the crimes committed by businessmen, politicians, and financiers. Tracing the rise of Don Semën, or Don Seva, as he's also known, lets me photograph a world in which borders have fallen and criminal energies are interwoven, converging on a goal of maximum profit.

Mogilevič was born in Kiev on June 30, 1946, to a Jewish Ukrainian family that was probably quite typical for the Soviet era: not religious, broadly speaking middle-class. He got a degree in economics at Lviv University, one of the oldest in Eastern Europe, then moved from Ukraine to Moscow, where he arranged funerals. Funerals are a winning business. People never stop dying, and mafias worldwide have their hands in the funeral trade. They're an excellent money-laundering tool and a fine cornerstone for building a fortune. Mafias never renounce concreteness. Tangible things. Earth, water, cement, hospitals, the dead. In the 1970s, Mogilevič joins a criminal group that deals in counterfeiting, petty fraud, and minor thefts. Small-time stuff compared to what he'll do later, but the street provides essential training in how to command, survive, build self-confidence. He spends his time in airports and train stations, exchanging rubles for dollars, hustling perfume and handbags to ladies who want to look Western, and selling "black" vodka to their husbands, who remain true to Russian traditions. Shortly thereafter he's arrested for one of the most common crimes: illegal currency exchange. He ends up in jail twice, for a total of seven years. Which turns out to be his lucky break. In prison he befriends some powerful Russian criminals, friendships that will last his whole life. The turning point in his criminal career comes when the Soviet government allows more than 150,000 Soviet Jews to emigrate to Israel. It's a race against the clock for these families. They can leave, but they have to go right away: Their precious relics, their earrings and necklaces passed down from generation to generation, have to be left behind. Mogilevič realizes that an occasion like this won't come around again. He'll take care of selling the emigrating Jews' possessions, then send the cash to them at their new address. Many believe him and entrust their possessions to him. But the money never reaches the legitimate owners: The fortune he accumulates will form the financial base of his criminal career.

Second page of the photo album, another famous photo. A man in three-quarter pose stares defiantly at the camera. He's bare-chested and looks surprised: his mouth slightly open; his nearly invisible eyebrows raised; his eyes like two crushed almonds. Vaguely Asiatic features; deep furrows across his forehead, from one temple to the other. But what's most striking are two identical tattoos at his collarbones. Two eight-pointed stars, with an eye at the center. The symbol of authority, of power. The photo is of Vjačeslav Kirillovič Ivan'kov, also known as Japončik, or Little Jap. He was born in Georgia in 1940, but his Russian parents soon decide to move to Moscow. In 1982 he's arrested for illegal firearms possession, robbery, and drug trafficking and is condemned to fourteen years imprisonment in Siberia. Years in which he rises to the rank of *vor*, just as the regime that marked their beginning is about to collapse. *Vor* is short for *vor v zakone*, literally "thief in law," in other words, a criminal who has earned himself the right to command according to the rules. He was supposed to remain behind bars until 1995, but the tentacles of the Mafija are long and reach everywhere, from politics to sports, from institutions to entertainment. In 1990 two popular figures, one a singer—the Russian Frank Sinatra, and with a similar collection of dangerous acquaintances—the other a former Greco-Roman wrestling champion who is using an association of retired athletes as a screen for Mafija interests, mount a campaign supported by numerous political, cultural, and sports celebrities: Ivan'kov has sufficiently expiated his guilt; it's time he is freed. Eventually even Semën Mogilevič offers a heavy helping hand: He generously pays off the judge on the case and involves a high-ranking Soviet functionary. The Little Jap goes free in 1991.

The Iron Curtain has fallen. The Soviet Union is crumbling. Russia is changing, its capital city is changing too. Feuds break out: Russians against Chechens. There's no end to the blood, but it flows more from business interests than ethnic hatred. Ivan'kov is an old-fashioned *vor*—he doesn't delegate, nor does he shy away from getting his own hands dirty. He starts eliminating Chechens and their business friends one by one. But it's an elementary rule that the more people you kill, the more likely it is that someone will return the favor. And that's not all. All that death and tumult leading up to it are starting to annoy the Mafija higher-ups, who decide to send Ivan'kov to the United States. Two birds with one stone: relative tranquillity at home and a business to build in the States. It's easy now that the borders are open. All you have to do is ask the American embassy in Moscow for a two-week visa. Vjačeslav Ivan'kov travels as a cinematographic consultant for a movie company headed by a Russian magnate who's lived in New York for years. Ivan'kov uses his real passport—just over a year after being released from jail in the USSR, which has only recently officially become part of the free world again. The Soviet Union had dissolved barely two and a half months earlier.

Ivan'kov arrives in New York, where everything's already been set up for him. Starting with money, which the Little Jap immediately invests to begin his new life. For a mere fifteen thousand dollars Ivan'kov buys a fake marriage with a Russian singer who is a U.S. resident. He settles in Brooklyn's Brighton Beach, where so many Soviet Jews had been coming since the 1970s that it's nicknamed Little Odessa. There's the ocean and beaches, but if you're thinking melting pot with fiddles and balalaikas, you've got the wrong idea. The most typical thing these immigrants brought with them to the trash-strewn brick tenements is the mafia, the Mafija with a *j*.

The third photo in the family album is of another neighborhood. Whoever snapped it was really good; he managed to soften the squalor with a play of chromatic reflections between the incendiary sunset and the chilly lake that laps at its shore. But not even the most gifted artist could do anything about the violent eruption of barracklike structures on the horizon. They pop up unexpectedly along Moscow's western periphery, in the middle of an immense park sliced brutally in half by four lanes of traffic. Seen from a distance they look like a bunch of rabbit hutches for giants, anonymous, stained by smog, and pathetic in their attempt to seem like a business district. This is Solncevo, a working-class neighborhood the Soviet authorities built in 1938. They had a sense of humor, those authorities. *Solnce* in Russian means "sun," but in Solncevo whatever light there is crashes into the buildings, so shadows reign unopposed. This is where Solncevskaja Bratva, the Solncevo Brotherhood, was born.

Sweat, bodies colliding: the very lymphatic fluid of Solncevskaja Bratva. The founder, Sergej Michajlov, also known as Michas, was born there. His youth was spent between odd jobs and petty swindles, for which he had a brush with jail. In the 1980s Michas makes the most of his love of fighting and gathers together all those who share this passion. Is this the beginning of a sports club? Or the nucleus of what will become an army?

Michas is arrested twice: once for extortion and once for murdering a casino owner. But he is never sentenced: insufficient proof. Meanwhile, the Solncevskaja Bratva, as Michas's handful of followers is now called, is expanding. Sweat and struggle. Violence and strength. The organization attracts other like-minded individuals: street fighters, hooligans, men ready for anything. They need to unite to defend themselves against other gangs, to pump up their muscles if they want to survive. They merge with other organizations, such as the Orechovskaja group, and within a few years Solncevskaja Bratva is powerful enough to extend its influence beyond the neighborhood, and to get involved in finance and business.

But their core business is protection, which in the 1990s takes on proportions that are nothing like Italy's idea of payoffs. According to the FBI, the Austrian shopping chain Julius Meinl has to pay fifty thousand dollars a month in order to manage its supermarkets in Russia. Coca-Cola announces that it is not its policy to give in to blackmail, and the next day its new factory near Moscow gets a visit from a machine gun and a grenade launcher—two security guards are seriously wounded. The company reported the assault to the Russian authorities, but the case remains unsolved. According to Interpol, other multinationals targeted are IBM, Philip Morris, and, curiously, Cadbury, Mars, and Hershey, as if there were some special sweetness in earnings extorted from chocolate factories.

The Russian Mafija came into being thanks to men who knew how to exploit new opportunities, but also because it draws on a history of structures and rules for how to dominate amid the great disorder. In my years of navigating the world's criminal sewers I've noted that mafias always flourish under such circumstances: a power void, weakness, something rotten in the state in comparison to an organization that offers and represents order. The resemblances between the most far-flung mafias are often striking. The Russian organizations were toughened up by Stalinist repression, which amassed thousands of delinquents and political dissidents in the gulags. That's where the *Vory v zakone* group was born, a society that within a few years was running every gulag in the USSR. An origin, therefore, that has nothing in common with Italian organizations, yet the principal characteristic that has allowed them to survive and prosper is the same: rules. Rules have many shades; they are made explicit through rituals and myths and made concrete through precepts that one must follow to the letter in order to be considered a worthy affiliate, that establish how to join and become part of the organization. Everything is codified and everything lives within the rules. What unites the *camorrista* and the *vor* are honor and loyalty, as well as the sacredness of certain gestures and the meting out of justice within the group. Even their rituals are similar. What grounds the ritual—the passage from one state to another—is common to both, since both share the desire to create an alternate reality, with different codes but equally coherent: *Camorrista* and *vor* are both baptized, punished if they step out of line, and rewarded if they obtain results. If in the past a *vor* was an ascetic who was averse to all earthly pleasure and every imposition, to the point of having his knees tattooed to signify that he would never bow down before authority, today luxury and ostentation are allowed. It's no longer a sin to live on the Côte d'Azur.

Russian bosses are swathed in designer gear, from their underwear to their luggage; they have political protection, control who gets appointed to public office, and throw megaparties without any police interference. The groups are becoming more and more organized: Every clan has an *obščak*, a kitty where a percentage of profits from crimes such as extortion and robbery are deposited, in order to cover the expenses of *vory* who end up in jail, or to pay off police and politicians. Soldiers, armies of lawyers, and highly skilled brokers are all on their payroll.

During the communist era the *vory* worked side by side with the Soviet elite, influencing every corner of the state apparatus. Under Brežnev they took advantage of the heavy stagnation of the communist economy and created an impressive black market: the Mafija could satisfy any desire as long as you could afford it. Shop and restaurants managers, heads of state agencies, government functionaries and politicians: They were all dealing in something. Every imaginable good was traded on the black market, from food to medicine. The *vory* tracked down whatever filthy capitalist goods the populace was forbidden in the name of socialism and introduced them into the homes of Party officials, thus forging an alliance between the nomenklatura and crime that was to have enormous consequences.

The fall of communism created an economic, moral, and social abyss that the Mafija was ready to fill. Generations of people out of work, penniless, often quite literally starving: The Russian organizations enrolled legions of unskilled workers. Police, soldiers, Afghan war veterans offered their services unreservedly. Former KGB members and Soviet officials placed their bank accounts and contacts in the service of organized criminal activities, including drug and arms trafficking. The transition to capitalism was armed with neither laws nor adequate infrastructure. The brotherhoods, on the other hand, had money, predatory swiftness, and intimidation tactics: Who could possibly oppose them? The so-called new Russians—those who were getting rich at dizzying speeds with the new market openings—found it was convenient to pay a "tax" that guaranteed protection from other groups as well as helped resolve problems with slow-paying customers or competitors. The small fish had no choice but to bow their heads: There was one extortionist who went around with a pair of scissors and a severed finger: "Pay up, or I'll cut yours off too." The West only caught the occasional echo of exaggerated violence; for the most part it was distracted and deluded. Even the funds the United States and European countries donated to reinforce post-Soviet civil society contributed indirectly to fattening the Mafija. NGOs were the preferred recipients, for fear that the money would be pocketed by ex-communists and used to reanimate the old regime and its old bureaucrats. But much of the aid was intercepted by criminal groups and never reached its destination.

With the intoduction of new banking laws, banks began to sprout up like mushrooms. Mafiosi no longer needed to corrupt the old institutions' executives. With their abundant cash flow and a few straw men, they could open a bank and staff it with friends and relatives, including some freshly out of jail. Then came the great plan for privatization, which was supposed to give all citizens a stake in Soviet enterprises, from colossal new energy companies to Moscow hotels. The value of the distributed stocks was low for those who already had money and power but huge for those who had trouble making ends meet. Poor people sold their shares, even below face value, to those who had the means to stockpile them, thus reinforcing the elite ranks of former Soviet managers and bureaucrats and mafiosi. The relationship between the Mafija and the government was symbiotic and long lasting, and it worked: Those envelopes stuffed with cash were handy for everyone, because everyone needed money to survive. The Mafija was everywhere. The Mafija had become the state.

In 1993, in Moscow alone there were fourteen hundred homicides linked to organized crime, as well as a shocking rise in kidnappings and explosions. Moscow was compared to Chicago in the 1920s. Businessmen, journalists, gang family members—no one was safe. People fought over the control of factories, mines, territory. Businesses and corporations were forced either to reach an agreement with the gangs or be eliminated. According to former FBI agent Robert Levinson, who also dealt with Italian American, Sicilian, and Colombian mafias, the Russian mafia is the most violent he's ever known. But there's something new here: Often the Russians have college degrees, speak several languages, and introduce themselves as engineers, economists, scientists, white-collar workers. When people abroad finally begin to realize that they're educated barbarians, it's too late. The Mafija didn't simply fill the power void in Russia. Its most formidable members are already operating far beyond Russia's borders, fashioning a new world according to their own ideas.

"Death is always after you," Sergej, one of Mogilevič's closest associates, loves to say. Sergej is an insignificant little man in rumpled clothes, and therefore very good at making himself invisible. Don Semën despises him but finds him useful: To be untouchable you can't be vulnerable to threats. And Sergej isn't. Everyone in Moscow knows he always carries a briefcase around with him. But only a few know what's inside. Mogilevič never talks about it, not even with his wife. Once Sergej was kidnapped by one of Mogilevič's rivals, a builder in the running for a public works contract from the city of Moscow. Sergej didn't put up any resistance; he let himself be dragged into the dark basement of some anonymous high-rise on the outskirts of Moscow: no pleas; no prayers to be let go; no hint of retaliation from his powerful boss. He simply opened his briefcase, and the next day—still in his threadbare suit, looking dazed and indifferent—he knocked at Mogilevič's door. "How did you do it?" his boss asked, actually glancing up from his laptop for once. Sergej went over to the desk and set his briefcase on it. *Click, click,* and with a swift move of the wrist he turned it 180 degrees. Mogilevič didn't bat an eye when he saw himself with Sergej on one of his rare vacations at the Black Sea. He hadn't remembered that Sergej had snapped that seemingly innocuous beach scene, which guarantees him that no one will dare touch a hair on his head. He smiled, closed the briefcase, and turned it another 180 degrees.

Perhaps it was Sergej's kidnapping, or the dangers of Moscow, now gripped by fear of gang warfare, that make Mogilevič think it might be better to get out of town. Money's not a problem; he's already accumulated several million dollars, which he's made in large part thanks to his most dangerous weapon: his acumen for financial affairs. As soon as perestroika opened the doors to private enterprise he quickly set up several companies, officially for fuel import-export, and registered far from the spires of Red Square, on one of the offshore islands in the English Channel. One company is called Arigon Ltd., the other, Arbat International, of which Mogilevič controls half the stock, the other half being divided between the Little Jap and the Solncevo bosses, Michajlov and Averin. With such good friendships now signed in ink, all Mogilevič has to do is pack his bags. In 1990 he decides to move to Israel, along with his most trusted men. They're the vanguard of the second wave of Soviet Jewish immigration, which is also the second wave of mafia importation, following that of the 1970s, which Mogilevič was so deft at exploiting. It wasn't only innocent victims of discrimination who emigrated but thousands of criminals whom the KGB was thrilled to be rid of. Many of them landed in the United States, colonizing Little Odessa, where Ivan'kov would settle in 1992; others ended up in different parts of the world. But they stayed on good terms, as part of a global network in which Don Semën and the Little Jap merely had to insert themselves, without ever losing touch with the Russian brotherhoods.

Mogilevič becomes an Israeli citizen and establishes ties with emerging Russian and Israeli groups who sense his talent for managing the complex workings of international finance. His empire expands, thanks to the money he makes from illegal activities—drugs, arms, prostitution. But it also grows through his reinvesting dirty money in legal enterprises, such as discothèques, art galleries, factories, and all sorts of businesses, including an international kosher catering service. According to an FBI document, he owns an Israeli bank with branches in Tel Aviv, Moscow, and Cyprus, which recycles money for Colombian and Russian criminal groups.

Yet the Promised Land is a tight fit for Don Semën: After one year there he marries a Hungarian woman, Katalin Papp, thus adding a Hungarian passport to his Ukrainian, Russian, and Israeli ones, and moves to Budapest. Officially he works as a wheat and grain dealer, but in reality he sets up a criminal organization that bears his name, with about 250 members and a hierarchical structure modeled on Italian mafias, to the point that many members are relatives of his. Budapest turns out to be a safe haven, and with the protection of corrupt politicians and policemen, his affairs prosper without too much interference. Mogilevič knows that tranquillity has a price, a price that money can't always pay.

In 1995 two colonels from the Russian Presidential Security Service pay him an undercover visit in Hungary, where, out of prudence, only one of Mogilevič's Israeli associates furnishes them with what they've come looking for: classified information to use in the Russian electoral campaign. The FBI's words are more eloquent than any image: "He also ingratiates himself with the police by providing information on other groups' activities, thus appearing to be a cooperative good citizen."

Don Semën has a few other tricks to help keep problems away; He never takes part in his group's day-to-day operations, never gets his own hands dirty, thereby making the work of the forces of order and justice trying to nail him extremely difficult. What's more, he pays Hungarian ex-cops to keep him informed of any police investigations involving him. Thanks to his managerial skills, his financial savvy, and his extremely talented staff, who are experts in cutting-edge computer technology, Mogilevič becomes one of the world's most powerful bosses. He creates his own private army, largely composed of *specnaz* and Afghan war veterans, who are famous for their brutality. To cover his prostitution business, he uses a chain of nightclubs, the Black and White Clubs, which he operates in partnership with Solncevskaja and

Uralmaševskaja, another Russian crime group. In 1992 Mogilevič organizes a strategic meeting with the leading Russian prostitution bosses
at Budapest's Atrium Hotel. He makes them a proposal: Invest $4 mil-
lion of prostitution profits to open more Black and White Clubs in
Eastern Europe. Don Semën recruits young women from the former
Soviet Union, gets them legitimate cover jobs, and puts them to work in
the new clubs. He even hires bodyguards to protect them. Business
thrives: The girls are beautiful and make tons of money. During the
same period Mogilevič contacts some Latin American organizations:
His girls are perfect for drug dealing. They're the ones who caress rich
gentlemen from East and West, who undress them and give them pleasure. And Don Semën, whom the girls call Pàpa, really does feel like a
father. From his viewpoint prostitution is a kind of welfare: His girls
don't fall into the hands of drunken brutes, and some of them even
manage to put something aside for the future.

But Pàpa has to get angry sometimes. There's another Russian,
Nikolaj Širokov, who's trying to move in on the Budapest prostitution
racket, and who goes about the city protected by his goons. He has a
weakness, though. Women aren't merely a business for him; he can
never get enough of them. Our brainy Don needs to find a woman with
real class, irresistibly gorgeous, wave her under Širokov's nose like a
jewel too precious to pass off to clients, and then wait for the right moment. At the end of 1993 Mogilevič strikes. Širokov is eliminated in
Budapest, along with two of his bodyguards. End of competition in the
capital city on the Danube.

Mogilevič doesn't enjoy using such brutal means, however, and is
always quite happy to leave the job to one of the groups he's associated
with. The Brainy Don prefers to speculate. As soon as the Berlin Wall
shows signs of crumbling, he starts changing rubles into hard currency,
into German marks.

In 1994 Mogilevič manages to infiltrate Inkombank, a Russian
banking colossus with a network of accounts in the biggest banks in the

world (Bank of New York, Bank of China, UBS, and Deutsche Bank), and to take control of it: This allows him to have direct access to the world financial system and to recycle proceeds from his illegal businesses easily. In 1998 Inkombank is dismantled for improper conduct on the part of its directors, violation of banking laws, and failure to honor its obligations toward its creditors. His business is booming, and Mogilevič becomes the object of several worldwide investigations, from Russia to Canada. But the *vor* recycles his identity just as he does his money: Seva Moguilevich, Semon Yudkovich Palagnyuk, Semen Yukovich Telesh, Simeon Mogilevitch, Semjon Mogilevcs, Shimon Makelwitsh, Shimon Makhelwitsch, Sergei Yurevich Schnaider, or simply "Don Seva." A ghost with the gift of ubiquity and a sense of irony.

As in the case of the Fabergé egg scam.

At the beginning of 1995, again in partnership with Solncevo, he acquires jewelry stores in Moscow and Budapest to cover his traffic in precious stones, antiquities, and artworks stolen from Russian churches and museums, including the Hermitage in St. Petersburg. But his project is far more ambitious and sophisticated, to the point of using the world's most prestigious auction house: Sotheby's. Mogilevič and his associates purchase a shed just outside Budapest and stock it with the most up-to-date equipment for restoring antique jewels and setting precious stones. Mogilevič watches the preparations from outside the building, arms crossed over his prominent paunch. Now he needs to find talented artists capable of replicating the most famous golden eggs of all time, Fabergé eggs. Don Semën activates his network of contacts and within a week he hires two internationally noted Russian sculptors. He promises them a lot of money and steady work. Sure, they'll have to remain in a shed on the outskirts of Budapest for the next few months, but it's still better than what they can find back home. Original Fabergé eggs in need of restoration arrive at the Budapest factory from collectors and museums all over the former Soviet zone. The two sculptors produce perfect copies, which are sent back to Russia. Meanwhile, the real eggs find their way to London and are sold by Sotheby's auction-eers, who unwittingly constitute the final link in the chain.

Mogilevič has always had a talent for swindles, and he's pulled off a few of gigantic proportions, such as the one where he stole billions of dollars from the public treasuries of three Central European states—the Czech Republic, Hungary, and Slovakia—by selling them gasoline disguised as heating oil, thus avoiding those states' extremely high taxes on auto fuel. Instead of being paid into those countries' coffers, the monies filled Don Seva's and his organization's pockets. When a Hungarian gangster involved in the deal started collaborating with investigators and named Don Seva, the response was unequivocal. A car bomb exploded in downtown Budapest, killing the canary, his lawyer, and two passersby, wounding another twenty-odd people, and reducing that popular tourist street to a scene of wartime devastation.

Mogilevič decides to stay in Budapest even after his wife's death in 1994. As for all the Mafija, one of the pillars of his fortune is arms trafficking. But now he makes an astonishing leap forward. He obtains a license to legally buy and sell arms, and thanks to his controlling a Hungarian weapons factory, Army Co-op, he manages to buy two more factories: Magnex 2000, which produces magnets, and Digep General Machine Works, a former state-owned factory, now privatized, that makes projectiles, mortars, and firearms. He is now in de facto control of the Hungarian military weapons industry. He sells arms to Afghanistan, Iraq, and Pakistan. He supplies Iran with material purloined from East German warehouses for several millions of dollars. Mogilevič is now the lord of war.

Another photo from the Russian album. Ivan'kov, the Little Jap, looks older now. Receding hairline, gray hair and beard, a little stoop shouldered even. He's put on a few pounds and looks tired. But his eyes, those two slits that earned him his nickname, are still the same. And his blue-tinted glasses can't hide their fury. Mogilevič has been busy, but Ivan'kov hasn't been wasting his time either. He's used his connections, reputation, and experience to set up international arms trafficking, gambling, prostitution, extortion, and fraud and money-laundering operations, with more sophisticated and modern methods than what the New York Russians were used to. He's established links to the Italian Mafia and the Colombian drug cartels. And to make sure he's protected, can fight, and intimidate, he formed an army of almost three hundred men, most of whom served in the Afghan war. He quickly gained control of the Russian Jewish mafia in New York, transforming it from a bunch of neighborhood shakedown artists into a multibillion-dollar criminal enterprise. And the old-school gangsters, frightened of him and his reputation, have to accept him. According to the American authorities he's the most powerful Russian mafioso in the United States. He's the one who expands Mafija business in Miami, where he supplies the Cali cartel with heroin and money-laundering services in exchange for cocaine, which he then sends to Russia. The former Soviet Union starts hungering after white powder, and the Little Jap wants to corner the market. And he doesn't hesitate to use whatever arms are necessary. Up till then Russia's cocaine trade was run by two criminals from the former Soviet Union: the Georgian *vor* Valeri "Globus" Glugeč and Sergej "Sylvester" Timofeev. The first was a pioneer drug importer in Moscow; the second, after a brief interlude with Solncevo, began collaborating with Ivan'kov. The Little Jap wanted their slices of the market. He kept trying to convince Globus and Sylvester that from then on he, the Little Jap, was the one in charge of the cocaine business. But in the end he was forced to kill them both: Globus was shot dead near one of his Moscow clubs, while Sylvester was blown to bits when he started his car.

The competition is over; Ivan'kov has won. His activities soon attract the attention of the FBI, who till then had mostly been used to dealing with the Italo American mafia and weren't really equipped to deal with the Russians yet. In 1995 Ivan'kov has an extortion on his hands, or rather "a debt collection" of $3.5 million. Aleksandr Volkov and Vladimir Vološin, two Russian businessmen with mysterious pasts working on Wall Street, founded Summit International, an investment company in New York in which the Chara Bank of Moscow invested, $3.5 million. But Volkov and Vološin's company is nothing but a gigantic Ponzi scheme: The two of them promise creditors, for the most part Russian immigrants, a 120 percent annual interest rate. But in truth they don't invest anything, spending the money instead on women, travel, and gambling. When the president of Chara Bank asks them to return the money they had "invested," the two managers refuse. So the Moscow bank asks Ivan'kov for help, and he takes it upon himself to get the money back. In June Ivan'kov and two of his thugs nab the two traders at the New York Hilton bar and take them to Troika, a Russian restaurant in New Jersey. They threaten them—if they don't agree to sign papers promising to give back the $3.5 million, they won't leave the restaurant alive. The traders agree—what else can they do?—and so they save their skins. The Little Jap has won again, or so he thinks; he doesn't yet know that the two kidnapped traders, once they are released, alert the FBI. A few days later, at dawn on June 8, 1995, they arrest Ivan'kov at Brighton Beach while he's asleep with his girlfriend. That same day several members of his organization are picked up, including his right-hand man. Even in handcuffs, even surrounded by FBI agents, the Little Jap is arrogant and cocky. He screams, curses, kicks.

He's found guilty of extortion and sentenced to nine years and eight months in the federal prison at Lewisburg, Pennsylvania. Four years go by, by which point it's clear that the Lewisburg jail isn't enough for someone like the Little Jap, who has no problem getting drugs delivered to him, and according to the FBI, sending orders to his men on the outside. The bars of the maximum security penitentiary in Allenwood await him.

At about the same time as Ivan'kov's arrest in the United States the forces of order in the Old World start getting serious about stifling the exuberance of certain Russian expatriates. On the evening of May 31, 1995, an endless stream of customers enters the U Holubů restaurant in Prague, for a special evening. No one notices the two big refrigerator trucks parked outside. They're all white, no signage, and anyone who looked at them more closely would have noticed that the tires show no trace of wear. But maybe the guests are in a hurry to get inside. It's a dinner in honor of a friend, and the Russian cabaret performer is supposed to be really hilarious. A few hours earlier, at the Czech Republic's organized crime squad headquarters, a diligent employee made a rather extravagant request: "I'm going to need a couple of refrigerated trucks, and I need them fast."

"May I ask what for?"

"Clean up. Very discreet."

Despite the fact that the squad is navigating in stormy financial waters, the request is granted. The operative gets on it and phones a cousin who owns a trucking company. Inside the restaurant the show was under way. Two hundred people guffaw at the cabaret performer's jokes, and he exits the stage to wild applause. Now it's time for the Russian chanteuse. While they wait, the customers chat merrily and clink glasses in endless toasts. The lights are dimmed, silence falls. Spotlights illuminate ropes being lowered from above, and some audience members rub their hands in anticipation of some seductive acrobatics. The first one to land on the stage is a brawny special forces agent. His machine gun pointed, his jaw drops when he manages to look around and realizes how many Mafija big shots are in the room. He quickly collects himself, and as soon as his partners arrive, he shouts at the top of his lungs—nobody move! They expect the restaurant to become a slaughterhouse any second, but no one opens fire, no one says a word or bats an eye. Those under arrest march silently out of the restaurant in an orderly and composed fashion. Among them are the girls from the Black and White. Only then does anyone notice the two big refrigerator trucks, even more resplendent and white under the full Moon. The special agents inside breathe a sigh of relief. They've got the

Solncevo heads as well as other leading Mafija figures, who will have to be released the next day, since they're not carrying weapons. But Mogilevič's not there. "My plane was late," he says during an interview, as impassive as a walrus. The interviewer isn't intimidated and asks if the girls at his clubs went to bed with the clients. Mogilevič stares at him as if he were addressing an idiot child: "There weren't any beds there. It was a standing bar, with tables."

By now the Brainy Don operates unopposed in Ukraine, the United Kingdom, Israel, Russia, Europe, and the United States, and he maintains relations with organizations in New Zealand, Japan, South America, and Pakistan. He has total control of Moscow's Sheremetyevo International Airport. From an FBI report it appears that one of his lieutenants, who is stationed in Los Angeles, met with two New York Russians linked to the Genovese crime family to develop a plan for shipping toxic American medical waste to Ukraine, to the area of Chernobyl, probably with kickbacks to local decontamination authorities. The Don's imagination knows no limits. It's 1997, and Mogilevič has several tons of enriched uranium on hand, apparently one of many gifts from the fall of the Berlin Wall. Warehouses are full of weapons; he just has to figure out how to be the first to claim them. The Brainy Don arranges a meeting at the Karlovy Vary spa; he loves that place. The buyers are seated across the table from him, distinguished Middle Eastern men. Everything seems to be going smoothly, but the Czech authorities blow the deal.

In 1998 an FBI report identifies money laundering as Don Semën's principal activity in the United States, and reveals both his and Solncevo's interest in YBM Magnex International, a Pennsylvania-based company with branches in Hungary and Great Britain, which officially produces industrial magnets. Valued at close to a billion dollars and quoted on the Toronto stock exchange, the company's principal stockholders include two women named Ljudmila: the wives of Sergej Michajlov and Viktor Averin, the two leaders of the Moscow brotherhood.* Mogilevič and his associates had noticed that the Canadian Stock Exchange is poorly regulated, so a company listed on the Toronto exchange would be a perfect cover for getting in and concealing illegal Mafija capital in their North American markets. In the space of just two years the value of YBM Magnex stock rose from a few cents to more than twenty dollars a share. On paper it seemed as if the investors were making vast sums, and the company was even listed among the three hundred most important securities on the Toronto Exchange. But in May 1998 the FBI pays a visit to the YBM offices in Newtown, Pennsylvania, and seizes everything: hard drives, faxes, invoices, shipping receipts. The stock price plummets in just a few hours, and Mogilevič is accused of defrauding American and Canadian investors. In practice the company conducted business through a series of front companies—boxes within boxes—empty containers that served only for moving money around. FBI suspicions were confirmed by the Newtown YBM office itself: A company that allegedly invoiced $20 million and had more than 150 employees couldn't possibly be headquartered in a small wing of a former schoolhouse. This gigantic fraud cost investors more than a $150 million.

YBM Magnex had received several million dollars from Arigon Ltd., which among its various activities sold fuel to the Ukrainian national railway system. Mogilevič is on very good terms with the Ukrainian minister of energy and the energy companies in his native country. Among other things, it was Arigon that owned Mogilevič's Black and White nightclub in Prague. Through Operation Sword, launched by Great Britain's National Criminal Intelligence Service, it emerges that Arigon Ltd. is actually an offshore company registered on one of the Channel Islands, as well as the pivot of Mogilevič's financial operations. According to investigators, it works like this: The dirty money that he and other Russian bosses make through their illegal activities in Eastern Europe flows into companies such as Arbat Interna-

---

* Michajlov was acquitted by a Swiss court for involvement in the Solncevo criminal group.

tional (owned by the Little Jap, Solncevo, and Mogilevič) and from there is transferred to Arigon, at times passing through Mogilevič's companies in Budapest. In turn, Arigon uses a number of checking accounts in Stockholm, London, New York, and Geneva to transfer funds to front companies around the globe, even in Los Angeles and San Diego, which are registered to Mogilevič's associates. The money is officially laundered through Arigon, and so it can enter the legal marketplace, flowing into other projects. Thanks to Operation Sword we know that of the more than £30 million that watered the London banks, £2 million were deposited with the Royal Bank of Scotland. The money, identified merely as having an unspecified origin in Russia, was destined for Arigon. Yet in the end Operation Sword came up empty-handed, because the Russian police either could not or would not furnish Scotland Yard with evidence that the money was the fruit of criminal activity. The accusations of money laundering were dropped. But there was still some backlash. I can only imagine Mogilevič's surprise when, a short while later, he opened a letter from the Bureau of Internal Affairs and read that he was no longer welcome in the United Kingdom.

Yet as Mogilevič's business gradually expanded, Arigon opened new branches and offices around the world. Prague, Budapest, the United States, Canada: extremely efficient launderers of dirty money.

"Why did you set up companies in the Channel Islands?" an interviewer asked Mogilevič.

"The problem was that I didn't know any other islands. When they taught us geography at school, I was sick that day."

Russia's story is one of men who knew how to profit from the transition after the fall of communism. Men who navigated without instruments during the 1990s. Men like Tarzan. Long hair, a fierce gaze, robust. Energy bursts from every pore in the photo I have in front of me and shows how apt his nickname is, even if it refers to something that happened years before it was taken. As a boy, to get attention, he jumped from the fourth story of the apartment building where he was living with his parents. They'd moved from Ukraine to Israel in the 1970s. He survived, but on that day Ludwig Fainberg became Tarzan.

He did his military service in the Israeli navy, but his height—six feet three inches—and pumped-up muscles weren't enough for him to pass the test and fulfill his big dream of becoming an officer.

In the early 1980s he moves to East Berlin. A contact of his offers to provide him with a diploma in medicine that would fool everybody. Tarzan ends up instead with a humble dental technician degree, but it takes more than a piece of paper to make dentures and braces, as many unlucky German dentists quickly discover. At that point all he can do is to join his fellow mafiosi, and he specializes in fraud and forgery. Then he moves to Brooklyn and opens a video rental store in Brighton Beach. He marries a "pure-blooded mafia girl," as they say in Russia: Her grandfather was a mafioso in Russia, and so was her first husband. In the United States Tarzan helps his childhood friend Griša "the Cannibal" Roizis, boss of a group of Russians in Brooklyn, to run some furniture stores that are really a front for international heroin trafficking, which also involves the Gambino and Genovese families. He also becomes friends with some higher-ups in the Colombo family. But when things in Brighton Beach start getting too shaky and several of his friends are killed, Tarzan decides to leave. In 1990 he moves to Miami, which has the second biggest group of Russian mafiosi in America. Since the 1970s many Russian immigrants there have been involved in extortion, drugs, gambling, prostitution, gem trading, and bank fraud. Tarzan starts several businesses in Florida, including Porky's, a strip club whose slogan is "Get lost in the land of love." In reality there's not much love going on there: The FBI, which was keeping a watch on Tarzan from a rooftop across the street, immortalize him on video while he beats up some of his dancers outside the club.

The dancers don't get a regular paycheck; they live on tips and percentages on drink orders, which are constantly being lowered. Tarzan

boasts that all he has to do is point at a woman in any adult magazine
for his agent to call her and bring her to the club, where Tarzan fucks
her till she drops.

Porky's becomes the place where—between slugs of vodka and a
striptease—Russians and Colombian narcos or their go-betweens
gather for meetings. Among Tarzan's many friends are guys like Fernando Birbragher, a Colombian on excellent terms with both the Cali
cartel, for which he recycled more than $50 million in the early 1980s,
and Pablo Escobar, for whom he purchased yachts and sports cars.
Then there's Juan Almeida, one of the biggest traffickers of Colombian
cocaine in Florida, who keeps in contact with the Colombian cartels
through a luxury car rental agency in Miami and other cover businesses.
Almeida and Tarzan live the good life aboard their yachts, and every
now and then they decide out of the blue to take a helicopter to Cancún
for lunch, to eat a plate of *mariscos*.*

Women, success, money. Tarzan has them, but the sea still calls to
him, the sea that since his childhood in Odessa has meant space, possibility. It still rankles him that he wasn't accepted into the naval
academy. Well, if the sea doesn't want him, he'll conquer the sea. His
plan: procure a Soviet Tango class submarine for the Colombian narcos.
Tarzan is a huge admirer of old Tango submarines. He's followed the
history of their construction from afar and knows they've made some
really amazing improvements: increased firepower and open ocean operation capacity. Sure, with time, even these supermodern subs were
surpassed. But Tarzan fell in love with them, and there's no ruling the
heart. The problem is that Tarzan is a boastful blabbermouth. One day
at the Babushka, another one of his restaurants in Miami, his friend
Griša Roizis introduces him to Aleksandr Jasevič, an arms dealer and
heroin trafficker who is actually an undercover DEA agent. Tarzan
doesn't know that his friend is also collaborating with the DEA. A
couple of courses and a few vodkas into their meal, he's already told

* Later, in 2003, an Atlanta court overturned Almeida's 1998 conviction for cocaine
conspiracy.

them about his ties to the Colombian narcos and the deals he's doing for them, including the submarine.

Cannibal Roizis would later become a reference point for penniless young Italian couples. Near Naples, where he moves following his collaboration with the DEA, he opens a furniture store whose selling point is super low prices: full kitchens and living rooms within everyone's means. There's a line outside his store: engaged couples ready to make the big leap who unknowingly help launder the Cannibal's dirty money while furnishing their future love nests. He's making deals with the Italian Mafia with one hand while he's still collaborating with the DEA with the other. Cannibal has always liked the smell of sawdust, so much so that he sets up his own office just a few yards from the loading dock where the Russians he'd brought with him unload furniture and appliances day and night. He's even had a desk made for himself out of simple plywood. Everyone who deals with him is fascinated by his tic: He rubs his palm voluptuously across the wooden surface and then holds his fingers to his nose. He tells his most loyal men that the intoxicating aroma reminds him of his childhood. Another thing he really enjoys is screwing over honest Russians working in Italy. He'll shake down plenty of Russian entrepreneurs until the Italian police manage to reconstruct his movements and nab him in Bologna, charging him with mafia association.

But to get back to the submarine deal: Tarzan's lawyer insists that his client is simply a braggart, someone who loves boasting about things that he couldn't possibly really do or provide. For the investigators, however, it was further proof of an alliance between criminal organizations of the former Soviet Union and the Colombian narcos: The narcos would supply the Russians with cocaine to transport to and distribute in Europe while the Russians would guarantee the Colombians arms and launder narco-dollars for them, especially in Miami, New York, and Puerto Rico. Tarzan's businesses were decisive in creating a link between the Mafija and the Colombian cartels. Though the submarine deal was never finalized, others during that same time were. Deals like the 100 kilos of cocaine hidden in crates of freeze-dried shrimp from Ecuador and destined for St. Petersburg, or the fleet of MI-8 Soviet army helicopters that Juan Almeida wanted so badly: Tarzan helped him acquire them for the modest price of $1 million each. "Escobar's men are going to fly these," Tarzan would apparently say. "So we had to gut the whole interior, get rid of the seats, find a thousand ways to stuff in as much coke as possible."

His criminal activities in Florida didn't show a lack of ambition. He owned immense cannabis fields in the Everglades, with an airstrip in the middle for landing loads of Jamaican marijuana.

Tarzan was charged with thirty counts, including criminal association, arms trafficking, and fraudulent data transmission. He risked spending the rest of his life behind bars but decided to negotiate with the American justice system. In exchange for testifying against Almeida and providing information about some Mafija big shots, all charges against him were dropped except for extortion. In the end he was only sentenced to thirty-three months in prison, after which he was extradited to Israel. All he had left was a few hundred dollars, a pale mirage of the vast fortune he had built in nearly two decades of life in America.

Tarzan's tale is the tip of the iceberg that is the story of the Mafija's growing interest in drug trafficking. Before the fall of communism the Soviet Union played only a marginal role in the distribution chain and in consumption. But in the years following it the demand for drugs in Russia grew consistently. What's so amazing is the speed with which it has grown, especially among the young. Because heroin is relatively affordable, consumption in Western Europe had always been associated with conditions of marginalization. But in Russia young people of all social classes began using it, not just the poor or down-and-out. It became an unstoppable wave that expanded the market to the most remote parts of the country. The variety of drugs expanded as well: to get high or to forget their problems, Russian users now had access to any and every substance, just like any American or European kid.

During the Soviet era, most of the drugs in Russia were locally produced cannabis or opium derivatives, products diverted from pharmaceutical factories and offered on the illegal drug market. In some parts of the country you couldn't even get a buzz except by sniffing toxic substances such as glue, acetone, or gas, or by using powerful anesthetics with hallucinogenic effects. When the Soviet regime collapsed, imports proliferated, prices dropped, and the drugs of the West—cocaine and ecstasy—finally made their way onto the market. At first cocaine use was limited to those Russians who could afford to spend the equivalent of three months' average salary. There was an invasion of substances that found fertile ground in part because of the breakup of neighboring states: wars, open borders, and an army of illegal immigrants unable to find work in the legal economy. For many of them—as in the rest of the world—drug dealing was the only way to earn a living. But the decisive step came with the opening toward the Western Hemisphere, first the United States and Canada, then Latin America and the Caribbean. That part of the world had a high demand for arms, and Russia a notable supply of Soviet military weapons. That part of the world had a massive supply of drugs and a need for money laundering, and Russia, a sizable demand for drugs and a significant supply of outlets for dirty capital. It's a done deal. At first it was merely a convergence, a symmetrical exchange between two sides of the ocean: Soviet arsenals were making organized crime in the former Soviet empire richer and more powerful, just as the white powder was doing for the Central and South American cartels. But business contacts with the narcos and the exponential growth of profits, combined with the shared necessity to reinvest and launder money, strengthened their bonds. In Latin America and the Caribbean especially, the Russians found the same conditions of governmental weakness that had favored the Mafija's growth: corruption, widespread illegality, porous banking systems, accommodating judges. Added to this was the ease with which Russian bosses could obtain citizenship, thanks to obliging governments.

The Russian organizations proved useful to the narcos looking for less risky money-laundering networks and methods—services for which they kept up to 30 percent of the earnings. The Russian mafiosi's other privileged activities in Latin America were prostitution, extortion, usury, kidnapping, fraud of every kind, counterfeiting, child pornography, and car theft. Solncevskaja, Izamailovskaja, Poldolskaja, Tambovskaja and Mazukinskaja are at home in Mexico, as are mafia cells from former Soviet bloc countries.

The multibillionaire Mogilevič was declared persona non grata in Hungary, the United Kingdom, the Czech Republic, and other Western countries. But their decisions could not undo what he and his associates had managed to create in those few decisive years of undisturbed freedom. It doesn't matter much that he returned to Russia, as did the Little Jap, who, after being released from a U.S. penitentiary, was extradited to stand trial for the murder of two Turks on the eve of his departure for America. After the trial, in which he was exonerated for lack of evidence, Ivan'kov was free to dive back into the streets of Moscow: All the witnesses swore they'd never seen his slanted eyes. He lived quietly, without drawing attention to himself, until July 2009, when a killer gunned him down in front of a Thai restaurant. A new feud had broken out, he'd chosen the wrong side, and this time he didn't get away with it. A thousand or so people joined in Orthodox chants and prayers at a cemetery, which was guarded on the outside by armed police fearing reprisal by the rival group. Brotherhoods from all over the former Soviet Union, from Georgia to Kazakhstan, laid wreaths, and *vory* from the entire country came to pay their final respects to one of their own, one of the last leaders of the old guard. But Mogilevič was missing. He'd only recently been released from jail and may have preferred to keep his distance from his old friends.

The fact that Mogilevič, after years of living so undisturbed that he even agreed to be interviewed by the BBC, was arrested in 2008 for tax fraud perpetrated through a chain of beauty supply shops, almost seems like a joke. If so, the one doing the laughing was the "world's policeman"—the Americans. In 2009 the FBI add Mogilevič to their ten most wanted list, alongside Mexican cartel killers, pedophiles, people who exterminated entire families. There are much more serious charges, such as criminal association, but the one given the most play is the YBM Magnex scam. It doesn't much matter what they use to nail him as long as the charge will hold up in court. It's the same technique that's been used since Al Capone's Chicago days; it works because the implacable U.S. prison regime is often more feared than the chance of death: The Colombian cartels started crumbling when narcos began being extradited to the United States. Mogilevič has already been jailed in Russia, but Russia and the United States do not have an extradition treaty. He's eventually released on bail, for once paying openly and legally. The spokesperson for the ministry of the interior declares that the accusation is not serious enough to prolong his arrest. About two years later the judges decide to drop all charges. Why was Semën Mogilevič held in a Moscow jail for a year and a half? There are lots of theories. The most delicate one has to do with the dispute over gas supplies between Russia and Ukraine, where in addition to Gazprom and Naftogaz Ukrainy—the energy giants controlled by their respective states—there's a third company, registered in Switzerland: RosUkrEnergo, 50 percent of which belongs to Gazprom while the other half can be traced to a Ukrainian oligarch, Dmitro Firtaš. RosUkrEnergo is the joker, in fact, the card that puts an end to the hostilities that in 2006 produced a brief shutdown in the flow of gas from Russia to Ukraine, which caused huge damages throughout Europe, since their energy supplies have to go through Ukraine's conduits. RosUkrEnergo meets Gazprom's price and then resells for a third of that in Ukraine. It manages to maintain this imbalance by buying Turkmen gas, which is cheaper, but also because it is licensed to sell on the world market without a fixed price. In 2008 Julija Timošenko, whose rise to prime minister is linked to her role in the Orange Revolution, adopts a tough stance with Vladimir Putin. One of her most stubbornly held objectives is the exclusion of RosUkrEnergo, since there is no need of an intermediary between Gazprom and Naftogaz. But the crisis hasn't yet reached its peak. In early January 2009, due to the Ukrainian energy company's debts to Gazprom and RosUkrEnergo, once again Russia stops the flow of gas to Ukraine and drastically reduces supplies to the rest of Europe, threatening to bring the economy of the entire continent to its knees and to let its people freeze in the dead of winter. Slovakia declares a state of emergency. The crisis lasts for over two weeks and starts to become worrisome even for those countries able to plug the leak through other channels. On January 17, after increasingly feverish discussions in Moscow involving leaders of the European Union, the Russian and Ukrainian prime ministers finally reach a ten-year agreement that, among other things, stipulates the exclusion of RosUkrEnergo. Yet it is precisely because of that agreement, which she fought for with such determination, that Julija Timošenko will stand trial in 2011 and be condemned to seven years imprisonment for abuse of office, an offense that the Ukrainian parliament decriminalizes in February 2014. Ex-president Viktor Janukovič, who was deposed during the popular revolt known as Euromaidan, and who had defeated Timošenko in the 2010 elections, would see that RosUkrEnergo received billions of dollars in compensation for supplies lost because of the Timošenko agreement.

Don Semën was in prison for nearly all of the most dramatic phase of the Russian-Ukrainian gas war. But what has he got to do with it? In 2006 Julija Timošenko had already told the BBC: "We have no doubt that Mogilevič is the person behind the entire RosUkrEnergo operation." Hers is one of the loudest among the many accusing voices that fell on deaf ears for years, until a document surfaced and caught the notice of public opinion in the West. It's one of the secret files published by WikiLeaks: a cable from Kiev dated December 10, 2008, from the American ambassador William Taylor. It refers to a meeting with Dmitro Firtaš, the Ukrainian oligarch behind RosUkrEnergo, in which he warned Taylor that Timošenko planned to eliminate his company both for personal interests and internal political conflicts, for which she was willing to make concessions to Putin, thus strengthening his influence in Europe. But then, as if to preemptively remove any weapon his opponent might have to discredit him, according to Taylor, the gas magnate goes on: "He [Firtaš] acknowledged ties to Russian organized crime figure Semën Mogilevič, stating he needed Mogilevič's approval to get into business in the first place. He was adamant that he had not committed a single crime when building his business empire and argued that outsiders still failed to understand the period of lawlessness that reigned in Ukraine after the collapse of the Soviet Union." Another cable, which predates their meeting, talks of potential ties between Firtaš and Mogilevič, suggested by their shared investment in certain offshore companies and the fact that they have the same lawyer. These ties had already been noted in a previous intermediary gas company, Eural Trans Gas. But that same lawyer sues the *Guardian* for publishing documents circulated by WikiLeaks's Julian Assange in an article by Luke Harding titled "WikiLeaks Cables Link Russian Mafia Boss to EU Gas Supplies." In the correction that the London paper was forced to print on December 9, 2010, "to clear up any subsequent mistranslation or misunderstanding of their meeting," Firtaš denies having any connection to Mogilevič other than a simple acquaintance.

The gas affair affects the vital interests of an entire continent. RosUkrEnergo's profits just from 2005 to 2006 came to almost $1.6 billion, little less than half of which ended up in the pockets of Firtaš and whoever else shared in his earnings. What does natural gas have to do with cocaine? At first glance, nothing. Except for one essential factor: dependency. Cocaine creates addiction, while there's no need to create an addiction for the gas to heat our homes. The business that those who've made real money bet on—money you can weigh, leaf through, smell—always originates from some irresistible need. And the Brainy Don, the specialist in scams and financial Chinese nesting boxes, knows this perfectly well.

Peter Kowenhoven, an FBI supervisory special agent, was asked to explain why they had put Mogilevič on their ten most dangerous criminals list, since he's not a violent criminal or psychopathic serial killer. "He has access to so much," he replied succinctly, ". . . that he can, with a telephone call and order, affect the global economy."

# 14.

# SEA ROUTES

I miss the sea. The overly crowded and dirty beaches where I spent my summers, echoing with shouts of vendors offering coconut slices, *taralli*, mozzarella, drinks, *granite*. Mothers shrieking for their children, wind-up radios broadcasting the soccer game and neomelodic Neapolitan songs, beach balls that either landed on my towel, spattering it with sand, or hit the wrong person on the head. Floating in the murky water, warm as a bath by this point, soaking myself for ages. I even miss the sunburn on my skin, the feel of the sheets, my shivers, which I tried to ignore, unable to fall asleep till very late. Nostalgia plays these sorts of tricks; it makes you yearn for things you'd really never want to experience again.

I miss even more the sea I'd later venture out on in a tiny fishing boat. I liked earning a little money that way, exhaling every time I saw the coast recede, nothing left but the expanse of azure, the smell of salt, the stink of nets and diesel. If the sea started to swell, I'd feel sick, and often vomited. But now even that is a precious memory, the proof that I really did travel by sea, proof I still carry in my gut.

I grew up on seafaring books. The catalog of ships in the *Iliad* fascinated me, and even as a boy I instinctively perceived that the *Odyssey* was about exploring the limits of human knowledge. A cunning and courageous man had circumscribed it in the beginning. I discovered and never stopped loving the typhoons and dead calms that put Joseph Conrad's captains to the test; I got lost in the obsessive hunt for Moby Dick, demon of the human soul incarnated in a sperm whale. At the time I sided with the great cetacean and identified with Ishmael, lone survivor of the wreck of the *Pequod,* saved to tell her tale. Now I know I have the same obsession as Captain Ahab. My White Whale is cocaine. It too is maddeningly elusive; it too sails every sea.

Sixty percent of the cocaine seized in the last ten years was confiscated on the high seas or in port. Sixty percent is a lot. Because all the other transportation routes are busy too, all the time. The Mexican border is a sieve through which cocaine flows constantly into the world's biggest consumer, the United States. Not one second passes without someone crossing over with coke stashed in the baby's diaper or in the cake Grandma baked for the kids. About twenty million people cross the U.S.-Mexican border every year, more than at any border on the planet. The United States manages to monitor at most a third of the more than nineteen hundred miles, even with three hundred miles of fencing, helicopters, and infrared vision systems. None of which can stop the flow of illegal aliens who risk dying in the desert, and who fatten up the *coyotes*—cartel-controlled human traffickers. In fact, it has created a double source of income for the *coyote*: If you don't have the fifteen hundred to two thousand dollars he demands, you can pay off your debt by carrying cocaine in your bag.

It's impossible to search every person, car, motorcycle, truck, and tour bus lined up at the forty-five official checkpoints; vehicles are prepared in the most sophisticated manner, as well as cans of coffee and jars of chili peppers, whose odors are strong enough to fool the sniffer dogs. Convinced that the best courier is the one who doesn't even know that's what he is, narcos use magnets to attach cocaine to the underside of cars with permits to cross the border in the fast lane. Once the cars cross the border they find a way to retrieve the stuff. Or they catapult it over the fence from the Sonora Desert into the Arizona desert, using modified Leonardo da Vinci machines. They fly it in at night on hang gliders painted black, like nightmarish bats or Batmobiles: two thousand dollars and possible death to the pilot if the cargo to be dropped across the border releases poorly and throws off the balance of his glider. A man was found, broken to bits, in a lettuce field near Yuma, Arizona. Half the cocaine he'd been carrying was still in the metal cage under one of the wings, so it was clear it wasn't some extreme sport accident.

The same is true with airplane transport. All over the world, every minute, some drug mule is boarding a commercial plane. And at that same moment dozens and dozens of containers purportedly filled with other merchandise are being loaded into the belly of a cargo plane.

Yet all this perpetual motion, all this ubiquitous, dusty frenzy, can't even begin to equal the amount of cocaine carried by sea. The percentage is even higher in Europe: 77 percent between 2008 and 2010. And the European market has almost reached U.S. levels. The sea is the sea. Oceans cover more than half the earth's surface: another world. If you want to work at sea, you have to accept its rules and those of seafaring men. "There's no bar in the middle of the sea," as they say where I come from. And no working cell phones, police stations, or emergency rooms. Nor are there jealous wives, anxious parents, girlfriends whose hopes you don't want to dash. Nobody. If you want to avoid becoming an accomplice, you learn to look the other way.

These are things that people who organize maritime drug transport know well. They know that there are seamen who are well paid yet eager to earn more, as well as a growing number who work under the table and are underpaid. But that's not the main reason that cocaine continues to travel primarily across the Atlantic. In order to move enormous quantities, up to ten or more tons in a single shipment, you need a huge ship. This makes it more affordable and lowers transportation costs by amortizing them, just as with any other export-import business, even though it increases the risks. Move the merchandise across the ocean in the safest way possible: that's the only rule of narco-trafficking by sea. Such a simple axiom in theory, yet in practice it sparks an incessant search for new means, new routes, new methods of unloading the goods, new cover merchandise.

The world is like a single body that needs to be bathed constantly in cocaine. If one channel becomes obstructed by stricter controls, another must be found right away. So while cocaine used to be shipped mostly from Colombia, in recent years more than half the ships bound for Europe have sailed from Venezuela, and then from the Caribbean, West Africa, and Brazil. The country that used to hold the monopoly on drugs has slipped to fifth place.

Spain is still the point of entry par excellence: Nearly half of all cocaine seized in 2009 was headed there. France has just barely surpassed Holland. Yet that statistic seems odd when you look at a map. It's based on seizures that for the most part occurred at sea, off the French Antilles or at some port of call along the African coast. In any case, once the routes toward the traditional northern European stronghold began to be controlled more rigorously, drug traffickers reacted immediately. They diverted traffic from the port of Rotterdam to that of Antwerp, which led to twice as many seizures in Belgium. In Italy, when the Gioia Tauro port came under tighter control, they fell back on Vado Ligure, Genoa, and Livorno, or rerouted shipments from Naples to Salerno. Transporting cocaine is like playing dominoes. If you move one tile, you have to rearrange all the others too.

The story of cocaine's journey starts at the end. It's the destination that determines both details and design. It's one thing if the cocaine lands on the continent after being transferred from the mother ship onto smaller, more agile craft that can dock anywhere, another if the ship has to unload its secret fruit in port, after going through customs controls. In the latter it's essential to hide it perfectly inside some other goods, whereas in the former you can choose some less sophisticated cargo as cover, or even do without. *Mother ship*: Drug trafficking revives the metaphorical force of maritime language. This is also true for the Spanish term, *tripulantes,* which means "crew" but which is derived from the verb *tripular,* which originally meant "to lead," or "to guide." Cocaine's *tripulantes* are men who guide it to a safe haven. At times they're corrupt sailors or crew members, at others they're cartel men who board an uncompromised ship in order to guard the hidden cargo.

Sometimes the traffickers purchase the mother ship outright, as in the case of the *Mirage II;* other times they simply lease it, purchasing only the complicity of the *tripulantes.* They also use cargo ships, as Fuduli did with the Maersk Sealand vessels, and cruise ships, whose owners, together with legal export companies—often big multinationals—are totally unaware of the precious parasite they're harboring inside the containers in the hold. In that case the shipments are called "blind loads."

A transfer at sea offers several advantages: greater flexibility; and less complex and often less expensive planning, which therefore is quicker to organize. The sooner the coke is put on the market, the quicker the investment starts turning a profit. This still seems to be the most widely used method of getting cocaine into Europe, judging by the drugs seized on their way to Spain or off the coast of West Africa. But keep in mind that, in general, these shipments are hidden less hermetically, and thus easier to intercept.

The Mexican cartels have come up with a transshipment variation that mirrors their baroque taste for destructive waste, but that's also an astute, effective tactic. Narco sea landings are, for a start, a speedy way to load cocaine without having to pass through heavily controlled ports. They take a car, stuff it full of coke, and take it for one last spin, to the top of a cliff, open the windows, and push it over the edge, into the sea. It could be a pickup or a jeep, one of their favorite makes, a Grand Marquis or a Cherokee. Both stay afloat just long enough for the cargo inside to be salvaged. Most of the packets, sealed in plastic, float to the surface, where they're easily collected by men who arrive on a rubber raft or motorboat. They either deliver the coke directly to its destination or transfer it to a larger vessel. But all this has to come off without a hitch. So the narcos resort to various roadblock techniques to prevent access to the area where it's happening. A *narcobloqueo* is often an act of spectacular violence that usually relates to a form of retaliation, ambush, or some other act of war. Armed commandos station themselves at various points along a road, or even a whole network of roads, where they hijack trailer trucks or force passengers off a bus. Then they position the vehicles sideways across the road, shoot out the tires, water them with gasoline, and set them on fire. This serves two purposes: They can get to the crash site without police or rival groups' interference, and they sow terror.

It usually takes far less effort to recover the crashed cargo, though. A moving roadblock is often enough, with cars speeding in the wrong direction, causing accidents or traffic jams on streets near the transfer point—the same tactic is used to cover a boss's escape route. In both cases the *narcobloqueo* creates a diversion, because the police have to try and reach the roadblock. In the meantime, the last packets of cocaine come floating to the surface undisturbed, and are scooped aboard.

The Mexican and Colombian cartels demonstrate their power through a mother ship that only they now use in any systematic way: the submarine. Every aspect of their power is summed up and symbolized by these vessels: economic and military power, as well as geopolitical control. It's difficult to imagine the number of submarines and semisubmersible vessels—drug subs—stuffed with tons of cocaine that are moving through the water of the Pacific Ocean, between Colombia and Mexico, as well as along the more frequented Caribbean routes off the coast of Florida. Semisubmersibles move through the water with only twenty-eight inches, or ten square feet, of hull exposed, and take in air for the diesel engine through a so-called snorkel pipe. They can travel up to three thousand miles. Actual submarines can travel the entire route at a depth of one hundred feet, surfacing only at night to recharge the engine. It takes from two to a dozen crew to operate a drug sub, but the job demands more than just specialized training. These vessels are called "coffins," after all. They're so low and narrow inside that they have to be steered lying down, and so hot that other nicknames come to mind, such as "nonstop tanning bed." But in truth, it's not unlikely that they turn into actual rather than merely metaphorical coffins. No one knows how many of them have sunk into the abyss along with their cargo and a handful of men mourned only by some South American sailors' women. On the other hand, they can carry up to ten tons of cocaine. Which is why American authorities are increasingly anxious. Submarines leave hardly a trace, other than perhaps a wake on the radar screen, which can never be attributed with certainty to an underwater vessel. What's more, the narcos' traditional means of transport— motorboats, fishing craft, fast ships—have only a tenth of a submarine's cargo capacity.

Intelligence and antidrug services fear that what's happening is something similar to when major airline companies renounced their old smaller planes for the new jumbo jets; the money and the need are both there. Submarines are becoming affordable enough for cartels, enough to form a fleet. Between 2005 and 2007 the Colombian navy confiscated eighteen of them off the Pacific coast, identified nearly thirty more, and estimated the existence of about a hundred. But their widespread use can't be reduced to simply a question of cost. It is a technological progress story whose pioneer was none other than Pablo Escobar, who boasted having two submarines in his immense naval fleet. Innovation is driven in part by the irrational desire to emulate some legendary figure, to prove that you're just as good because you can match or surpass him in power and riches. But the real tangible opportunities arrived when the Russian mafiosi began settling in Florida and offering to sell Soviet arsenals' pièces de résistance to the Colombians.

For nearly a decade it seemed to the Americans engaged in the war on drugs that the narcos' drug subs were like the Flying Dutchman: ghost ships, whose evanescent wake they could trail but which they could never capture, to the point of suspecting that they were nothing but legends, sailors' superstitions, marine myths. But in 2004 the Americans dealt a decisive blow to the Norte del Valle cartel, the organization that took over in Colombia after the decline of the Medellín and Cali cartels. They arrested about a hundred members and extradited the real big shots to the United States, starting with the godfather, Diego Montoya, known as the Cyclist. Agents confiscated millions of dollars in cash, gold ingots, luxury goods, and properties worth $100 million. And they finally get their hands on an actual submarine: a handmade, fiberglass drug sub capable of reaching the California coast. It's not clear whether the cartel men avoided interception by decrypting U.S. naval codes or if—more likely—they were tipped off by a Colombian admiral in their service.

Even today drug subs are being built in shipyards hidden in the South American jungle. No one knows how many the narcos have had made, or who and how many people it takes to assemble and test them, or which tributaries—or tributaries of tributaries—of the Amazon are used to get them to the ocean, or how many have been lost at sea along with their crews. No one knows how many have been sunk to avoid being confiscated, or how many managed to complete their voyage. But there's another incredible aspect to consider. All this expenditure of strength, means, and money is poured into the construction of something that's often treated as a maneuverable disposable. Or maybe it's better to say that the more modest drug subs are like those animal species whose lives span only a few reproductive cycles. After they've been lightened of their load a few times, they're left to sink. The crew flies back home by plane. Millions and millions of dollars, literally dumped into the sea.

The semisubmersible the Mexican navy recovered in the summer of 2008, in the waters of the Pacific near Salina Cruz in the state of Oaxaca, was worth about $2 million. The strange green splotch they'd sighted turned out to be a slender craft thirty-two feet long, loaded with nearly six tons of cocaine. The goods onboard were Colombian, as were the four crew members who came ashore without any resistance.

But the consignee was Mexican. Alberto Sánchez Hinojosa, known as El Tony, one of the Gulf cartel lieutenants after Osiel Cárdenas Guillén's capture, was arrested about two months later in the southern state of Tabasco.

More recent, sophisticated models are regular submarines, slightly larger and capable of reaching California from Central America with ease. So far only three have been captured, but the fact that all three were intercepted within a short space of time suggests that many more are being used.

The only known attempt so far to export the idea to the Mediterranean had a tragicomic ending. Two shady Spanish operators put up the money, and an "engineer" sets up a workshop where he can build a semisubmersible—nothing fancy, thirty feet long, needing only one person to navigate. All this in Galicia in 2006, the most popular place in Europe for cocaine transfers. The three manage to contact the right people, for whom they have a reverential fear: the Colombians. They sell their homemade creation for the modest sum of €100,000. The Colombians plan on using it for unloading a mother ship, so the engineer needs to deliver his jewel right after the trial run. But the sub starts yawing strangely and the sorcerer's apprentice panics. He's as terrified of suffocating to death in the Atlantic as he is of the clients to whom he's just sold a lemon. He figures that the only way to get off and to save his skin is to deliver the sub into the hands of the enemy—that way he can tell the Colombians that the police intercepted it. But the police don't play along. The investigators wait for the engineer and his associates to take delivery of some hashish to pay off their debt to the Colombians and then they arrest them. It turned out not to be so easy to imitate the pros, and the three Spaniards who tried it had to face the fact that they're inferior to the inhabitants of their former colony.

But Europe has already produced a new species of seafarers who are nothing like those pilots in the 1980s and 1990s, whose motorboats were loaded with cigarettes, hired hands of the Camorra or the United

Sacred Crown. In recent years the most common type of vessel on which cocaine has been found isn't the old merchant ship, container ship, fishing boat, or motorboat. It's a sailing vessel. Big catamarans, wooden yachts, sailboats that could compete with Giovanni Soldini's. Dream boats, anchored in the Caribbean, ready to take you island hopping, from one white beach to another, but more appropriate for those who really love the sea, who want the adventure of an ocean crossing. But those who pay the most for letting the skippers pursue their true vocation, displaying their ancient knowledge of currents and favorable winds, aren't interested in coming onboard. They're narco-traffic brokers and emissaries of organized crime. But not only: They're also friends of the summer, the privileged bourgeoisie who want to try going from easy use to easy money, squeezing cash, coke, and adrenaline out of the same exciting enterprise.

Today the *Blaus VII* is a school ship for the Portuguese military marines. A splendid, seventy-five-foot sailing vessel with two masts made entirely of wood, painted an elegant deep blue. It was intercepted in February 2007 a hundred miles northwest of the Madeira islands, which belong to Portugal but are closer to the coast of North Africa. The Portuguese navy and judicial police found two tons of cocaine that embarked in Venezuela, ready for delivery to Europe. They arrested the *tripulantes,* who this time were the entire crew: all Greeks except for the skipper, Mattia Voltan, from Padua. He wasn't yet twenty-eight years old, but the *Blaus VII,* worth about €850,000, was registered in his name. He'd been driven to Venice by Andrea, a guy his same age, where he caught a flight to Barcelona to join the ship and its crew, which were waiting for him in Portugal. Before they left Andrea's father showered them with advice: "Take a good look before you start wandering around," he admonished them on the phone from Dubrovnik, where he lives with his youngest son, Alessandro, and manages two companies he opened in Croatia. An Italian entrepreneur who, like so many others, migrated east. He also wanted to know if Mattia looked presentable, and Andrea, with that typical impatience kids show overanxious parents, reassured him: "Yes, he shaved, and I cut his hair. I went to the house myself to get the *rasp*."

The concerns that Andrea's father—Antonio Melato—has about the young skipper he'd hired are understandable, but it's not Mattia's fault that the *Blaus VII* is intercepted. After his release he goes back to Padua and tries to pick up his carefree existence. Andrea tells his father he's seen their friend Mattia around, and that he's an idiot. "You must be joking!" his father barks, getting right to the point: "That guy can't be trusted." But it's pointless for him to get so upset about somebody else, because the telephone being tapped is his own.

Melato is just one of the pieces in an investigation the ROS (the Special Operations Group of the Carabinieri) is carrying out in cooperation with the Milan DDA, which involves half of Europe, the Caribbean, and Georgia. He's arrested in June 2012, along with his sons and the other components of a network spread across Bulgaria, Spain, Holland, Slovenia, Romania, Croatia, Finland, and, in Italy, the Veneto, Piedmont, and Lombardy. About thirty people are taken into custody, six tons of cocaine seized, seven years of work. The name of the operation, Magna Charta, implies a good dose of irony. The archaic spelling of that document signed by King John Lackland now alludes to the fleet of *chartered* ships engaged in drug running.

But it all started far from the sea, with more ordinary questions regarding fighting the mafia. In 2005 the Turin Carabinieri discovered that the Bellocco 'ndrina and the other Rosarno families were supplying Piedmont through an unusual Bulgarian channel. The Bulgarians, headed by Evelin Banev—Brendo to his friends—an upstart forty-year-old *biznesman* who became a millionaire through financial speculation, set themselves up as brokers. But they'd entrusted the task of locating skippers and false-bottomed boats to ferry the cocaine from the Caribbean or to pick it up somewhere between Africa and Spain to various Italians: Antonio Melato and his sons and even more to Fabio and Lucio Cattelan, also originally from Padua but now living between

Turin and Milan. They're the ones who hired the crew of the *Oct Challenger*, the cargo ship sequestered by Spanish customs officials on the same day as the *Blaus VII*, with another three tons of coke onboard. And it was also the Cattelan brothers who contacted two expert skippers, Guido Massolino and Antonio D'Ercole, who set out from Turin for a Croatian port where the sailboat they were to bring back full of cocaine was waiting. Following the same route as Mattia, the two first made port in the Balearic Isles, then at Madeira. From there they were supposed to reach the mother ship. But she waited in vain in the middle of the ocean. Guido and Antonio vanished. Probably swept away by a storm, devoured by the waves along with their fragile boat. They may have decided not to send an SOS, not wanting to be discovered in some improbable spot in the Atlantic, or maybe they thought they'd manage somehow and waited until it was too late.

The two men from Turin, shipwrecked without a trace, were both over sixty.

Cocaine skippers usually aren't novices. For brokers, experience offers more of a guarantee, but even men who have lived their lives at sea seem to become more approachable as they grow older: the need to put aside some money so as to retire in style whenever they feel like it; the desire to live like the wealthy people they spend time with; a taste for adventure, for becoming importers of the same goods they—like everyone else—are already using. Where's the harm in that?

There's an ever-increasing number of sail and motorboat skippers whom narcos can turn to, and whoever hires them knows how to weigh the pros and cons. A small crew that can steer boats that are above suspicion, and that can slip into any little tourist port, is a profitable resource, even if it has to be paid well, and even if the skipper turns out to be more vulnerable than the more modest and less demanding *tripulantes*.

The *Mariposa*, the *Linnet*, and the *Kololo II*—these last two captured off the coast of Sardinia and escorted to port at Alghero—were carrying more than a ton of cocaine in total. The skipper and owner of the *Kololo II*, a forty-year-old Roman who'd set sail from the French Antilles and was heading straight for the ports nearest Rome, collapses under the weight of the nearly 300 kilos found in his boat. He collaborates in exchange for a reduction in his sentence. On the basis of his confessions, in July 2012 the Roman DDA calls for the arrest of another five accomplices, all of them residing in the Rome area. Some have police records, but none are mafiosi.

They sprout up in every corner of the continent, above all in areas without their own crime organizations. All of them are useful covers or sometimes just unsuspecting scapegoats, according to the investigators. Like the Italians—two from Bologna and the one from Livorno—who were arrested in 1995 because they were using the *Sirio,* the *Más que nada,* and a sailboat with the sarcastic name of *Overdose* to import cocaine from Brazil via Guadeloupe and the Canaries for a group of rich kids from good Bologna families. Or like the pilot of the Falcon *Sheldan,* a seventy-five-foot luxury yacht intercepted in September 2012 at the port of Imperia with three and a half tons of hashish. Or like the Croatian skipper living in Civitanova Marche, whom the DEA and the French, Croatian, and Italian police stop off the coast of Martinique in May 2012 with 200 kilos of cocaine on another sailboat. Or the Breton skipper Stéphane Colas, who was released in 2011 after being held for two years in Spain because the tanks for storing the drinking water for the voyage from Venezuela contained 400 liters of liquid cocaine. According to the investigations, all of them have highly useful covers. Their nationality doesn't matter, but it's best if their résumé, social class, and place of birth suggest a passion for sailing, so they can convince their eventual judges that they merely stumbled into being drug couriers by mistake. The accumulated evidence is often too weak to be upheld in legal battles devoid of specific legislation, and public opinion in the defendant's home country—as in the case of the Breton captain—accepts his professions of innocence. The secret register of *tripulantes* is spreading more rapidly than their sails in Atlantic winds.

. . .

And yet when I think about cocaine, the first thing I see isn't a swift boat wandering the oceans. It's something more compact, more omnipresent, more elementary. It's the merchandise, merchandise par excellence, which like a magnet attracts all the rest. Fruit of other fruits, the only parasite that multiplies a thousand fold the value of the flesh it burrows into, a protean vector of profit of every form of commerce. I can still see the expanse of containers in the port of Naples, yellow for MSC, gray for Cosco, Maersk's blue logo, green for Evergreen, red for the "K" Line, and all those other giant Lego blocks being stacked and restacked by the crane operators' claws into movable architecture. The pure geometry, the elementary chromatism that encloses and hides everything that can be bought, sold, or consumed. And everything, or almost everything, can become an involuntary or willing host to the white stuff.

It seems paradoxical but not even the most well-concealed merchandise can do without its own logo. Branding originated with heads of cattle being seared with symbols so as to distinguish them from other herds. In the same way, each block of cocaine is marked to certify its origin, as well as to direct each load to the right buyer when the big brokers organize megashipments headed to different customers. A cocaine logo is above all a symbol of quality. It's not some empty advertising slogan but serves a fundamental purpose: The brand ensures the integrity of every single block, how the narcos guarantee that the products they export are pure. The cartel's good name is important. More important, apparently, than the risk of being easily tracked down if a shipment were to fall into the wrong hands. A business risk, just like in any other. Nor is it by chance that the traffickers often decide to adopt the symbols of the most sought after, popular brands. Their anonymous merchandise is, after all, the product of voluptuary consumerism par excellence, and it's worth as much as all the other brands put together.

The blocks of cocaine La Spezia Finance Guard extracted from the false bottoms of ten cars in the village of Aulla, in the province of Massa Carrara, were stamped with either a scorpion or a checkerboard. The biggest drug bust ever in Italy, the fourth in all of Europe. The financial police started getting suspicious while inspecting several containers from Santo Domingo that had arrived at the port of La Spezia. In a single container they found a false wall that concealed 750 blocks. But they decided to close it up again and let the container pass through customs as bait. The identifying symbols are what tell them that this is only a small portion of a much larger shipment: The scorpion indicates the part bound for northern Europe, the checkerboard guides others toward central Europe. Because of this, or rather, because the scorpion symbol doesn't indicate the sender's signature but serves instead as sort of the buyer's zip code, it is one of the most common symbols found on blocks of cocaine today. Not only is this a huge deal, but it will turn out to have been arranged through one of the oldest and most tested partnerships: the Colombian cartel from Norte del Valle and the Gioia Tauro crime families. The Calabrians can't accept the loss of such a vast shipment, so they find out where it's being held in custody. The Finance Guard agents are tipped off. The coke can't stay where it is much longer. Fifteen patrols from La Spezia, bearing the yellow flames of the Finance Guard and the green berets of the Counterterrorism Rapid Response unit escort it to Ospedaletto, in the province of Pisa, where the nearest incinerator is. The plant is kept under surveillance night and day, until the last checker and scorpion dissolve in the flames.

Logos started being used in the 1970s, introduced by a major Peruvian trafficker, and spread in the ensuing decade, thanks to the Colombian and Mexican cartels. And then they kept on spreading, multiplying endlessly, along with the demand for white powder. A recent computation, commissioned by the European Union in 2005, counted twenty-two hundred different ones: Some make do with a sober company monogram or pay tribute to a favorite soccer team; others prefer animals or flowers; still others love esoteric or geometric symbols or a luxury car trademark; while others play on a favorite animated cartoon character. It's impossible to list them all. But it's worth collecting a small sample, arranged by type and theme.

**TATTOOS:** a scorpion, a checkerboard, a dolphin, an anchor, a unicorn, a serpent, a horse, a rose, a man on horseback, and other such motifs, similar to the most popular or traditional tattoos, are pressed into the bricks with a metal mold. Along with simple geometric shapes, they are the most common designs and can indicate either the sender or the recipient of the merchandise.

**FLAGS:** the French tricolor, the British Union Jack, even the Nazi swastika. Rather than being pressed into the blocks, these designs are color printed on cards that are slipped under their plastic wrapping. The first two probably indicate the destination, while the last one, found on a load of cocaine paste sent to a Bolivian refinery on the border with Brazil, perhaps conveys the ideological affinity of the parties involved.

**SUPERHEROES (AND RELATED THEMES):** Superman's trademark S, Captain America's portrait, James Bond's special wristwatch, all embossed or printed on cards. Narcos like to appropriate iconic Hollywood fantasies, either as an act of defiance or as a joke.

**CARTOONS:** What do narco-traffickers watch on TV? It's surprising enough to find Homer Simpson wrapped atop every block of coke, or classic Walt Disney characters. But it's really astounding to see Teletubbies or Hello Kitty, the Japanese kitten every little girl in the world adores.

**IDEOGRAMS:** On July 6, 2012, in Hong Kong, more than 600 kilos of cocaine were seized from a container from Ecuador and destined for the emerging market in Southeast Asia or mainland China. All the blocks were adorned with the Chinese ideogram 平, or Ping, which together with another ideogram forms the word "peace," but it may also mean "smooth" or "flat." A good wishes offering to the customer.

**BRANDS:** the Playboy bunny, Nike's wings, Puma's pouncing feline, Lacoste's crocodile, Porsche's lettering, and the Formula 1 and Ducati logos are among the best-known marks, along with the traditional tattoo motifs.

But in the end almost all the symbols drug traffickers choose, from Chinese ideograms to cartoon characters, today are found carved on people's skin. The narcos choose to communicate through the universal language of pop culture, which their merchandise plays as much a part in as do the trademarks they appropriate. Yet they avoid using their most typical symbols, such as the skulls, crossbones, or Santa Muerte with which members of the Mexican cartels and, more often, the Central American maras, get tattooed. Their cult is an internal thing, whereas a brand is something else. These same cartels also use famous logos internally, for marking members' cars, T-shirts, caps, and key rings. Today Los Zetas have adopted the Ferrari pony; the Gulf cartel likes the deer of John Deere, the biggest tractor manufacturer in the world. Stickers and gadgets that are easy to find, and not too flashy. The best-known brands are thus transformed into secret military badges.

The endless forest of symbols the cocaine trade has turned into recalls the ever-changing tangle of routes and handoffs and all the networks that need to be stabilized before a load can depart. The forest's origins can be found in the constant search for boats large and small; crews; the containers that need to be able to be recognized among hundreds of others that all look the same, all stowed in the same mother ship; the legions of people who need to be corrupted in shipping and navigation companies, at customs offices and in ports, in the police

forces and military, in local and national politics. All the coca plantations scattered throughout Colombia, Peru, and Bolivia; all the hundreds of thousands of farmers who harvest the coca in the forests of the
Andes; all the laborers and chemists involved in the chain of production, turning leaves into blocks or liquid cocaine, are only a marginal
part of the whole business. The rest is transportation.

Transportation is what has allowed the Mexican cartels to become
more powerful than the Colombian ones. The availability of the port at
Gioia Tauro has provided the basis of the 'ndrangheta's strength and
transnational prestige, in particular of the Piromalli family and its
allies, which, according to the DIA (Anti-Mafia Investigations Directorate) has become the largest clan in all of western Europe. Since most
narco-trafficking investments and profits are gambled on sea transportation, it has become such a complex problem that it has given rise to a
new and specialized professional figure, who is paid handsomely: the
logistics manager, also known as a systematist or Doctor Travel.
He may be more important and earn more than a broker, especially if
the broker doesn't have the economic and organizational powers of a
Pannunzi or a Locatelli but is one of the many smaller intermediaries
who first contract supplies and then monitor their movement through
the principal phases of embarkation, major stopovers, and arrival at
destination.

The logistical manager—the systematist—has to take care of everything else. Of every leg of the journey, every intermediate transshipment, of every formality, every customs inspection, every kind of cover
shipment. He must also develop strategies for solving or staunching
problems and figure out how to minimize the damage in case something goes wrong. He has to plan every detail, keep every step in his
head, and review in advance all the channels the cocaine takes in the
course of its journey. He has to make transit not a fluid flow but a project that is as differentiated as it is stable: a system.

It requires months of work to develop a transportation system for a
huge shipment of cocaine. And once it has been worked out, tested, and

utilized a few times, it's already time to modify it or think up a new one. Systematists work across the entire surface of the planet, but they're always working against time. They are forever racing against the investigators' skills of intuiting cocaine's movements. Which is why their services are so expensive, affordable only to the major narcotics organizations and the biggest brokers. The richest and most powerful cartels try out new routes by first dispatching "clean loads," with no drugs, as part of a test run for every system.

That's exactly what the Sinaloa cartel did without knowing it was already under scrutiny by the Boston FBI and the Spanish police, who were united in Operation Dark Waters, a key inquest in the history of drug trafficking because it revealed the Mexican cartels' interest in supplying cocaine directly to the European market, which until that point had been dominated by the Colombians. On August 10, 2012, Spanish police arrested four members of the Mexican organization in the center of Madrid, including the cousin of Joaquín Guzmán Loera, at the time the most wanted and powerful boss in the world, the legendary Chapo. Manolo Gutiérrez Guzmán had moved there with a legal adviser and two other of his right-hand men, to lay the foundation for new projects that included regular, easy entry of shipments through the Spanish port.

It all started years earlier, when the FBI came across something more precious than a submarine stuffed with tons of cocaine: a source with access to the upper echelons of the Sinaloa cartel. They decided to investigate the information they received further through a big undercover operation. Starting in early 2010, the infiltrators approached Chapo's cousin and other influential men pretending to be affiliated with an Italian organization already well established in the United States and Europe. They claimed they were looking for new suppliers and had excellent contacts at the Andalusian port of Algeciras. The Mexicans were excited by the idea and began negotiating: They would furnish a ton of cocaine a month, sent by container ship from South America. The "Italian partners" would get 20 percent of each shipment as a reward for getting the cocaine through the port of Algeciras, while the Mexicans would sell off the rest directly, all over Europe, through their new network of operational cells. By August 2011, everything was ready. But before risking such a large quantity of cocaine, the Sinaloa cartel decided to test the safety of the route: Four times in a row they sent containers filled only with fruit through some Ecuadorian companies under their control. Once they'd tested the system the Mexicans let it be known that they were ready to send the first shipment, hidden in a container leaving from the Brazilian port of Santos: 303 kilos, intended for various points of the European market. A rather meager load that was prudently meant to break the ice—a good business practice even for the biggest holding. But not prudent enough this time. On July 28, 2012, the authorities intercepted the shipment in the port of Algeciras, and almost simultaneously, they detained the Mexicans who arrived at the appointment with their fake partners in order to discuss new shipments. The greatest damage to the Sinaloa cartel was that its expansionist aims for Europe had been revealed and temporarily checked. The rest—the seizure of a few shipments, even the arrest of some important men such as the boss's own cousin—are inevitable losses, which such a strong and deeply rooted organization must take into account.

Those who toil in vain, however, even in less dramatic circumstances, are the specialists who plan the whole enterprise. The Doctor Travel systematists get paid just as many other freelancers do. An advance to cover system start-up and development expenses, the rest when the shipment reaches its destination. Payment may also come in the form of a percentage of the merchandise, from 20 percent to 50 percent of the total, after transportation costs. Everything—even transportation costs and the systematist's pay—is calculated on the basis of the end point of the journey. The riskier the final destination, the more perfectly planned the system must be. It's far less expensive to come through the Iberian Peninsula than into Italy, which has become one of the most difficult and thus exorbitant points of entry in all of Europe.

There is an entity that establishes every quotation at stake in the cocaine market, including transportation costs. Much like the diamond exchange, formerly in Antwerp and now in New York, the world cocaine exchange takes place in the major import centers: in the past Amsterdam, and now Madrid. The average costs and prices used to be set in Holland, but ever since the Iberian Peninsula became the privileged delivery point and the place where the principal buyers gather—first among them, the Italian mafias—the bargaining has moved to Spain.

There's no way to explain the systematist's job and the hefty sums the narco-traffickers are willing to pay him unless you look more closely at two crucial problems he has to deal with: ports and cover goods. Big ports—like big airports—most at risk are now equipped with gamma ray or heat-sensitive machines capable of detecting undesirable substances such as drugs or explosives inside containers. A container passes through these immense "metal detectors," where, basically, it is scanned. The various materials inside it show up in the monitor in different colors. Cocaine is yellow. But just as in the Amsterdam airport, a "100 percent security screening" is applied only on planes coming from certain countries, such as the Dutch Antilles, Surinam, and Venezuela; it is impossible for big European ports to fully monitor all incoming shipments. The port of Rotterdam, for example, is not only the largest in Europe but also one of the best equipped in terms of control instruments. Nonetheless, with storage capacity for eleven million containers, the best they can do is to expand as much as possible targeted as well as random screening procedures. And screening takes time, as anyone who has had to endure the endless security lines snaking through the airport on a peak travel day and risked missing his flight knows. No one compensates the unfortunate passenger, but for goods, time is money, money that a company can demand back if a shipment is slowed by customs officials. If a perishable shipment is held up too long, one that, once it's checked, turns out to be just fruit or flowers or frozen fish, the company it is being shipped to—a big supermarket chain, for example—can demand to be reimbursed for the loss. Which means that either they're checked quickly, or they are more likely to pass through customs without undergoing any screening.

So what Doctor Travel does is study security systems and their flaws in order to take advantage of them. State-of-the-art detection system? Just get yourself some carbon paper. Place it in front of your load, and it disappears from the monitor.

A systematist's work includes evaluating a high quantity of complex variables. Let's take, for example, the convenience of concealing cocaine in some kind of perishable merchandise. And let's remember the basic rule that the cover merchandise must be a typical export product of the area where the shipment originates: So, for shipments coming from South America, why not always slip the blocks of cocaine in among cases of bananas? Bananas are, in fact, often used as cover for the very reasons listed above, to which can be added the fact that they have a vast and steady yearlong market. Yet this is exactly why banana shipments may attract more attention. Besides—and this is more complicated—the destination port may be experiencing a drop in deliveries that really has nothing to do with bananas but rather with other kinds of products, which is what seems to be happening with the economic crisis. If customs is less backed up, the chance that the bananas will be waved through diminishes. So you have to modify your plan, betting not on speedy transit through customs but rather on the persnickety perfection and originality of the camouflage. The systematist has to keep constantly abreast of the situation in every port and the success of all the goods being used as cover. A dizzying job, as if he were working simultaneously for every export-import company on an entire continent—two continents, in fact, given that shipments are coming not only from South America but from West Africa as well. The catalog of cover merchandise, like that of the symbols for stamping blocks of cocaine, must be impressive in its variety. It's impossible to list all the cover goods used for transporting cocaine. And even more impossible to know about those where cocaine has never been discovered.

·   ·   ·

Tom Thumb: This tiny hero has to manage without helpers or magic, no resources other than his own vigilant mind. He is the figure who best symbolizes the disparity of forces of those leading the fight against the global cocaine traffic. I've felt like him for years, and I steadfastly follow his example. I try to gather up every bread crumb scattered in the dense forest, to pick up every scrap of knowledge that can help me to get through it. Yet the more I try to look closely at narco-trafficking, bordering on the edge of obsession and exhaustion, the more I sense that something is escaping me, or rather that something keeps getting ahead of my imagination. It's not enough to know, to understand. I need to grasp a more profound dimension, imprint every organ with it, metabolize the mass of notions until they become a mode of natural perception, a second sight. How is it possible otherwise to comprehend that they ship eight tons of cocaine in a single container of bananas, and at the same time have special suitcases made out of fiberglass, resin, and cocaine, which they then treat so as to extract a mere 15 kilos? The first answer is that whoever lost that stratospheric load must have successfully concluded the same operation other times. There's a good chance that they're the same ones who developed new suitcases that look like Samsonites for quick restocking via air, and as a future research investment. Because behind all this there is a logic, just one: sell, sell, sell. Sell any way you can, with whatever system, better to sell a lot than a little. But even if it's less, much less, you can't do without it. It's still business, and it can't be lost. No business in the world is so dynamic, so relentlessly innovative, so loyal to the pure free market spirit as the global cocaine business.

This is the reason cocaine became the merchandise par excellence at a time when markets began being dominated by stocks that were inflated with empty numbers, or securities as intangible as those driven by the new economy, which sold communication and make-believe. But cocaine is tangible. It uses the imaginary, bends it, invades it, fills it with itself. Every seemingly insurmountable limit is about to fall. The new mutation has already arrived, and it's called liquid cocaine. Liquid cocaine can make its way inside any hollow object, can impregnate any saturatable material, can dissolve in any drink, any creamy or liquid product, practically without adding any telltale weight. Half a kilo of cocaine can be dissolved in a liter of water. It's been found in shampoo and body lotion, in shaving cream, glass cleaner, and spray starch, in pesticides, contact lens solution, and cough medicine. It has traveled together with canned pineapple, in containers of coconut milk, in nearly five tons of oil barrels, and in two tons of frozen fruit pulp; it has permeated clothing, upholstery fabric, loads of jeans, canvases, diplomas for deep-sea diving. It's been sent through the mail as bathroom sets and as pacifiers. It has crossed borders in bottles of wine, beer, and other drinks, from Mexican tequila for margaritas to Brazilian cachaça for caipirinha, but mostly in bottles of rum, like the Colombian brand confiscated in the same month in Bologna and Milan: the Medellín brand, aged three years. And as if rum and Coke, which contains much more coke than alcohol, weren't enough, they've also found it in bottles of Coca-Cola. Cocaine can turn into anything at all, yet it always remains the same.

# 15

# AFRICA IS WHITE

The island of Curaçao, part of the former Dutch Antilles, now a constituent country of the Netherlands, is perfect for tourism. Along with the pristine beaches and emerald waters typical of the Caribbean, it can count on many months of good weather annually, because it is outside the path of hurricanes. A paradise, in other words. The Donald Duck Snackbar, in the suburbs of Fuik, in the southern part of the island, is a paradise as well—for narco-traffickers. Between a sandwich and a caipirinha, they talk business. Lately the conversation's mostly about ways to transport cocaine. Controls have grown tighter, so they need new methods.

When you spend years tracking drug traffickers you come to see things not for what they are but for what the traffickers can do with them. I can't look at a world map anymore without seeing transportation routes, distribution strategies. I can't see the beauty of a city piazza anymore without asking myself if it would be a good base for pushers. I can't see the fine, golden sand of a beach anymore without wondering if it would make a good landing spot for an important shipment. I can't fly anymore without looking around the plane and calculating how many mules might be onboard, their stomachs full of cocaine capsules.

It even happens with diapers. What's more innocent than a baby's diapers? They make me think of the woman from the Antilles who was detained at the Amsterdam Airport Schiphol in 2009, after police found a kilo of cocaine hidden in her two-year-old daughter's diaper. There are highly organized gangs that use their own children for trafficking, sticking balls of liquid cocaine inside their diapers. Easy to transport, difficult to pick up on X-rays. But there's a down side: While it's true that coke dissolves easily, it's also true that the crystallization process to render it salable adds not insignificantly to the cost. Even the physically disabled are welcome. Who would ever dream of searching a man with no legs in a wheelchair? No one, as long as the sniffer dog doesn't discover cocaine in the chair's frame, as happened to a young Dominican guy in September 2011. There's no end to it. Cocaine under the cassock of a fake priest. Cocaine in the stomachs of two Labradors. Cocaine in a shipment of two hundred boxes of red roses. Cocaine hidden inside cigars. Candies and cookies filled with cocaine. Loose cocaine inside bags of foodstuffs. Liquid cocaine in condoms tied with elaborate knots.

There's a school in Curaçao. Aspiring mules come from all over the world. Narcos teach them how to package and ingest the capsules without hurting themselves, because they'll use their stomachs as storage during flights. During the first phase of their training the mules swallow big grapes, chunks of bananas or carrots, then condoms filled with confectionary sugar. Two weeks before departure the mule goes on a diet to regularize his digestive cycle. The mule has to eat light: to keep down the capsules, which are the size of those containers inside a Kinder Surprise Egg, you have to stick with fruits and vegetables. It takes a mule two hours to swallow the capsules and settle them in the bottom of his stomach. It hurts; it hurts a lot. So the mule paces, palpitates his stomach to make them go down, helps them along with a little

Vaseline, or at most some yogurt. The stomach is a container that needs
to be optimized, and even half a glass of water takes up space. A begin-
ner manages to ingest thirty to forty capsules, while a well-traveled
professional can get up to 120. The record seems to be held by a man
detained in the Amsterdam Airport Schiphol in 2009 with 218 capsules, amounting to 2.2 kilos of cocaine.

Each capsule contains 5 to 10 grams of cocaine. If even one of them
breaks during the flight, the mule will die an atrocious death from an
overdose. But if it makes it to its destination that cocaine, bought for
about €3,000 a kilo in the Antilles, in Europe will go for €40,000 to
€60,000 a kilo, depending on which country it's sold in. On the street
it can go for as much as €130 a gram. Which is why the couriers have
to follow very strict rules: Before they ingest the capsules they take medicine such as antiemetics, anticholinergics, and antidiarrhetics. The in-
flight menu is rigorous too: milk, juice, rice. From the moment he
swallows the capsules, the mule has thirty-six hours max before expel-
ling them and, finally, as the Colombians say, *coronar*—mission accom-
plished, in other words. The word *coronar* comes from the game of
checkers, when a pawn reaches his opponent's baseline and is "crowned."

Europe needs cocaine, lots of it. There's never enough. The Old
Continent has become the narcos' new frontier: 20 percent to 30 percent
of cocaine production worldwide ends up here. Cocaine has attracted a
new clientele. If until 2000 it was used almost exclusively by the privileged strata of society, now it's more democratic. Adolescents, who
never used to get near this sort of product, are today the most attractive
slice of the market. It was enough for the narcos simply to diversify the
offer and flood the European market with cocaine, lowering the price.
Today a gram of cocaine costs around €60 on the streets of Paris, compared to €100 about fifteen years ago. According to the European
Monitoring Centre for Drugs and Drug Addiction, about 13 million
Europeans have sniffed cocaine at least once in their lives; 7.5 million
of them are between the ages of fifteen and thirty-four. The number of

cocaine users in the UK has quadrupled in ten years. The Central Office for the Suppression of Illicit Drugs Trafficking in France estimates that the number of consumers doubled between 2002 and 2006. By now the market has stabilized; it has its consumers and its habits. The soul of commerce is not publicity but habit. It is the creation of needs, which become so instilled in the user's consciousness that they are no longer considered a need. In Europe, together with the cocaine habit, a silent army has been born, one that marches in close rank, heedless and resigned, with an addiction that has become a custom, practically a tradition. Europe wants cocaine, and so the narcos find ways to get it there.

I'm sitting with Mamadu, a young African man with a sweet but determined face. He tells me he was supposed to be named Hope, but then his parents discovered that in other parts of the world it was a girl's name. He was born at the time that his country, Guinea-Bissau, was experimenting for the first time with multiparty elections. On the horizon loomed an uncertain future but one full of expectation after all the wounds of civil war and repeated coups. His family was originally from the town of Bissorã, but they moved to the capital, Bissau. History repeats itself. People sacrifice their roots for the hope of progress; the city becomes the Eden everyone dreams of. But the hope with which Mamadu's parents wanted to bless the birth of their son is betrayed once again: civil war, coups, and endemic poverty bog the country down in a deadly immobility. Mamadu learns the art of getting by— the profession that, since the beginning of time, employs the most people—and starts to develop the characteristic that many international bureaucrats associate with people from his country: resignation.

But something has changed recently. His continent has become white. It has become an important landing base for narco-traffickers.

"Your country's the center of the world now," I say to him.

Mamadu laughs and shakes his head with symmetrical slowness.

"I'm serious," I insist. "Your country deals in one of the most sought after products there is."

"Why are you making fun of me, my friend?" Mamadu says, serious now. "What resources? Cashews, maybe? Locusts?"

The truth is, Guinea-Bissau, like the countries that border it, is exactly what the narco-traffickers are looking for. Africa is fragile. Africa is the absence of rules. The narcos work their way into these enormous vacuums by taking advantage of tottering institutions and ineffective border controls. It's easy to give birth to a parallel economy, to transform a poor country into an immense warehouse. A warehouse for a Europe increasingly dependent on white powder. If you add the fact that the citizens of Guinea-Bissau, by virtue of their colonial past, are allowed to enter Portuguese territory without a visa, then Mamadu's country really is the center of the world.

Mamadu tells me about the day in 2009 when he happened to pass by the residence of the president of the republic, João Bernardo Vieira. At first he mistook the shots for firecrackers, which he'd always been afraid of, and he turned in the direction of the noise in order to look the little dynamiters in the face. But there was only a throng of people that drew aside in a disorderly fashion as two cars, tires squealing, slalomed their way through the terrified passersby. On the ground the crumpled body of some man he didn't recognize. It wasn't until the next day that Mamadu, glancing at the headlines, learned that it was the president of the republic. Many people saw his execution as a form of revenge at the hands of the military for the killing the day before of the army chief of staff, Batista Tagme Na Waie. Others read the assassination as retaliation on the part of Colombian drug traffickers in Guinea-Bissau for the dismissal of Rear Admiral Bubo Na Tchuto, chief of staff of the navy, on suspicion of conspiring with the drug cartels (a charge to which he would plead guilty in a U.S. court in May 2014). For Mamadu it was simply another wound.

In 2007 *Time* magazine defined Guinea-Bissau as a paradise for traffickers, a state that welcomes drug traffickers and distributes their goods. It helps if you have an archipelago off your coast, eighty-eight islands where small aircraft laden with drugs can land. An open zone for the cartels' personal use. An earthly Eden, practically uninhabited and covered in lush vegetation, bordered by pure white beaches and sliced through by improvised landing strips. It is on one of these strips that the Cessna that changed Mamadu's life landed. Cessnas are perfect for this sort of job: They're nimble and fly at a maximum altitude of sixty-five hundred feet, thus avoiding being picked up by radar. The drugs are crammed inside, in fruit crates stacked one atop another and stashed between the metal panels of the plane. The goods are unloaded and taken to the mainland, and from there they take off for Europe, following three major routes: land, which passes through the Atlantic coast of Mauritania and through Morocco, or over tracks in the Sahara before heading up through Turkey and arriving in the Balkans; sea, the most popular route, where commercial fleets of private container ships carry huge amounts of cocaine; and finally air, where couriers or mules usually ingest capsules filled with cocaine.

"A mule?" Mamadu had asked Johnny.

"A mule, Mamadu. You'll take a little trip to Lisbon and then you'll come back. Aren't you happy?'

The person talking, Mamadu recalls, is a buff Nigerian who has shuttled between Abuja, Nigeria, and Bissau for twenty-five years. He goes by the name of Johnny and is an old friend of Mamadu's father. He says he can give him a hand. Mamadu's parents have gone back to their village: If you have to die of hunger, you might as well do it close to your own family, in the place where you were born. Johnny stands there in his fake Alexander McQueen suit, and as he talks he keeps touching Mamadu on his shoulder, arm, chest. He's a salesman, and he knows that to place his goods, it's not enough to be convincing; he has to establish a contact. Mamadu is hypnotized.

"Lisbon?"

"Lisbon, Mamadu. A few hours' flight, then you take a walk around the old city, pick up a tourist or two, and catch the plane home."

Getting drugs to Europe is easier than you'd think. All you need is a commercial flight, a passenger, and an indefinite amount of cocaine safely stored in special wrapping in the bottom of his stomach. Sure, it's happened that the wrapping breaks during the flight and the mule spends hours in excruciating pain before landing in Lisbon as a cadaver. But most shipments are successful, in part because modern wrapping materials are resistant to gastric acid, to the point that you need to cut them with a knife to open them after they've been expelled,. They used to use condoms, but that's prehistory.

"I have to fly?"

"How else are you going to get to Europe, Mamadu? Swim?"

Solving transportation problems is the narco-trafficker's most pressing business challenge. To get the cocaine to the west coast of Africa they invested several million dollars constructing a veritable highway, the A10, so called because the ocean route travels right along the 10th parallel. Traffic is always heavy on the A10—there's a constant coming and going—but only the tip of the iceberg is visible, thanks to the most spectacular seizures. Like the one on the *South Sea*, a cargo ship intercepted by the Spanish navy with 7.5 tons of cocaine onboard. Or the *Master Endeavour*, the huge merchant ship intercepted by the French navy with 1.8 tons of cocaine: The traffickers had drained the well deck in the stern of the ship normally used for drinking water so as to hide the precious cargo. Sometimes the big cargo or fishing ships moor off the African coast and wait for smaller craft—sailboats, dugouts, or coasting vessels—to shuttle the cocaine ashore. Commercial routes are busy day and night but the increased maritime surveillance and the numerous record confiscations have thrown them into crisis, to the point of forcing the narco-traffickers to aim higher, to opt for those agile airplanes. The most extraordinary example is that of the Boeing 727-200 that landed on a makeshift runway smack in the middle of the

Mali desert and was burned on-site so as not to leave any trace. Investigations following the discovery of the fuselage gave rise to the hypothesis that the traffickers were transporting cocaine and arms and that Islamic radicals had let them use their secret runways to reach Algeria, Morocco, and Egypt, as well as provided them with jeeps and trucks. From there the drugs were supposed to make their way up to Greece and the Balkans, eventually arriving at the heart of Europe. This hypothesis was bolstered by discoveries made a few months later: The Boeing 727-200 was registered in Guinea-Bissau, had taken off from Tocumen International Airport in Panama, and was supposed to stop for refueling in Mali. It did not have authorization to fly, and its crew members were carrying fake documents, possibly from Saudi Arabia. Faced with a burning plane carcass, all the investigators were thinking the same thing: If the narcos can afford to get rid of a vehicle estimated to be worth between $500,000 and $1 million, how much cocaine did they manage to get in? A plane of that size can carry up to 10 tons of cocaine.

It takes preparation and mental strength to become a mule. You have to respect the rules and put your body through harsh training. Mamadu learns the secrets of the profession one suffocating afternoon, inside an abandoned shed on the outskirts of Bissau. Johnny told him to show up with an empty suitcase. "Why empty?" Mamadu had asked, but didn't get an answer. In the middle of the shed is a long, low table on which is a row of capsules only slightly bigger than aspirin. Johnny, like a chef showing off his creations, gestures to Mamadu to come closer. He tells him to sit in the plastic chair in front of him, with the suitcase on his knees.

"Open it. Tell me what's inside."

Mamadu looks at him wide-eyed, he doesn't know what to say.

"Don't be afraid. Open it and tell me what's inside," he insists.

"It's empty, sir."

Johnny shakes his head.

"No," he says. "It's full. You are a tourist, you have some clothes with you, bathing suits. If someone like me wants to know what's inside your suitcase, that's how you have to answer. That's the first lesson, the most important one.

Rules. In order to become a mule, above all you have to be a good actor. A tourist is perfect. But not too overweight. Too many capsules make your belly swell, and the customs officers have a sharp eye: The first ones they stop are fat men traveling alone with just a carry-on. Then there's the payment. On delivery only. Too many mules in the past decided to live the good life in Europe for a few days with the narcos' money and their drugs. And finally there's the physical training.

"I like you, Mamadu. For you, only top of the line products. We care about our employees' health," Johnny says to him.

Mamadu is naïve but he's not stupid. He sighs with relief when he discovers that his mouth is the only orifice of his body he has to open.

"I like you, Mamadu," Johnny repeats. "Let's go just with the main entrance this time."

The training is very simple: You start with one capsule, fighting the instinct to spit it up. The operation is repeated a number of times, until the mule is able to swallow several dozen of them and then walk around like a young African tourist dazzled by Old Europe. Mamadu is ready.

Africa is to Mexico like a giant supermarket is to a food wholesaler. Cocaine is like one of the epidemics that have spread with alarming speed all over the African continent.

Africa is white. The dark continent is buried under a blanket of white snow.

Senegal is white, and so is the Léopold Sédar Senghor airport in Dakar. From a strategic point of view, it's perfect: not far from Europe; not far from the world, thanks to connecting flights to capitals around the globe. Coke has to move quickly, and here, in white Senegal, it finds the energy to do so. Spanish, Portuguese, South African: only three of the nationalities of the most recent mules arrested aboard planes either arriving at or departing from Senghor airport. When the load is much larger, boats are needed. The *Opnor*, for example, which carried in its iron belly almost 4,000 kilos of cocaine destined for European markets before it was intercepted by the authorities in 2007 off the coast of Senegal. Senegal is a turntable, capable of taking in tons of coca to be treated, stockpiled, and then sent on.

Liberia is white. And Fumbah Sirleaf, son of the Liberian president, dirtied his hands white. It is he who works for the DEA, and who contributes to the fall of an organization whose ranks include African bosses and Colombian narcos. In 2010, thanks to a DEA operation, a network of South American, East European, and African drug traffickers was arrested. The associates had been in contact with this Liberian big shot, Sirleaf, for a long time, but they didn't know that in fact he was a DEA informer. Sirleaf discovered that the network could count on high Liberian state officials for their traffic and gave precious information and tape recordings to the DEA.

Cape Verde, a turntable per excellence, is white. The ten islands that make up the archipelago hold out their hands to Latin America while remaining firmly anchored off the coast of Senegal. A drug traffickers' paradise.

Mali is white. And white are the projects of Mohamed Ould Awainatt, a businessman arrested in 2011, the head of an organization that treated the desert as a highway heading north. Jeeps and cocaine.

Guinea is white. White are the affairs of Ousmane Conté, son of the president who governed Guinea for twenty-four years, arrested in 2009 for international drug trafficking. In an interview on national TV, Conté admits between the lines to being implicated in drug trafficking but denies being the head of Guinean narco-trafficking. His brother Moussa is arrested as well, and two years later a huge trial begins, involving dozens of big shots. But nearly all the accused, including Ousmane Conté, will be exonerated. Corruption and precarious institutions: the holes the traffickers slip through.

Sierra Leone is white. Fragile, poor, wounded by civil war right up until the advent of democracy in 2002. And white is the Cessna that in 2008 was supposed to be carrying medical supplies and instead concealed more than half a ton of cocaine.

South Africa is white, and white are her coasts, white her ports, where ships from Latin America arrive. White are the customs of this country. As its wealth has increased, so has its consumption of cocaine.

Mauritania is white. White are the dusty runways where small planes land, jammed full of cocaine. It is the zipper between the Atlantic Ocean and the Maghreb.

Angola is white, because its ties with Brazil are white. Former Portuguese colonies that become brothers through transoceanic coke shipments. Here, as in southern Africa, a good part of the cocaine market is run by Nigerians, who boast of their important criminal history and one of the most organized structures in the world.

Africa is white.


I look at Mamadu and think about how individual stories can reflect the destiny of an entire continent. The hardest part was learning to deal with the stress, he says. To invent another self, as similar as possible to the few tourists he's seen in his short life. Awareness has to be crystallized into habit, routine gestures must supplant instinct's automatic response when faced with danger. Johnny tells him to meet him in front of the Bissau police station. He doesn't tell him to bring a suitcase, because this time Johnny arrives with an elegant overnight bag. When Mamadu is a few steps away he hands it to him and tells him there's five thousand dollars inside.

"You could be anybody. You're a young man with a shiny overnight bag loaded with cash. Go into the police station, chat a bit with the police officers, and then come back out, as if it were nothing."

"I was sure he was joking," Mamadu tells me. "If the police officers caught me with a suitcase full of money, how would I explain?"

But Johnny's not joking in the least. He's deadly serious; even that conciliatory smile he usually wears is hidden between tightly closed lips.

"I plucked up my courage," Mamadu tells me. "I prayed that this was the last test I had to face before starting my new job. Then I went into the police station."

Johnny is the perfect exponent of the most effective and reliable criminal organization on the African continent: the Nigerian underworld.

The Nigerian underworld is an international force that has grown out from its roots to the four corners of the earth. They are small- to medium-size groups with a familial, tribal basis, and the branches of their interests extend to many important open-air drug markets. It's a mix of tradition and modernity, which has allowed the Nigerians to get a foot in all the African capitals north to south, and to spread beyond the continent, thanks in part to the experience they gained selling heroin in the 1980s—international flights loaded with mules, and when those weren't enough, Nigerian traffickers recruited the flight crew. Then cocaine arrives, and the Nigerians throw themselves into the new business. Europe's needs have to be met, and the Africans are ready. So ready that they start obtaining coke directly from the producing countries. Today their presence in Europe is huge, and they're in great demand by the Colombian and Mexican narcos, as well as by the Italian mafias. One of the progenitors is Peter Christopher Onwumere. Before he was arrested in Brazil in 1997, Onwumere proved he was a real international narco. He negotiated, bought, organized transports, and raked in the cash. The Nigerians are phenomenal subcontractors, and they know where to find cannon fodder, like Mamadu.

"I'll never forget my first takeoff," Mamadu tells me. "My stomach sank; it took my breath away. The passenger sitting next to me gives me a paternal smile when he sees me join my hands in prayer; he doesnn't know I'm just begging God not to let one of the sixty capsules inside me explode. It's a Royal Air Maroc flight, with a stopover in Casablanca, then from there to Lisbon. I tell myself that it will all be over in a few hours. I can't help but think how excruciating it will be to expel the capsules, or how I'll survive a whole day in some unknown European capital. I look anxiously at the tourists who've boarded in Casablanca. If I had a sign on my chest that said 'I'm a drug runner' I probably would have been less conspicuous amid all these smiling, carefree men and women in shorts and flip-flops, cameras dangling around their necks. Then, like a lightning bolt, a thought comes to me and suddenly chases away my fear. Are these the people who use the stuff inside of me? Are they my clients? So I start looking at them differently, at the stranger in the center row, this really fat guy who's resting his crossed arms on his belly. The woman next to him, she's big too, is assailing him with words that have got to be important, but he acts like nothing's wrong, or maybe he's fallen asleep. Then I remember what Johnny said about the effects of cocaine, and I think these must be the two principal states: euphoria and oblivion."

I'm struck by Mamadu's wisdom, by his ability to see.

"I've done nineteen trips from Bissau to Lisbon, Madrid, Amsterdam. You could say I have a job with an ongoing contract, at least until I'm caught or a capsule opens inside of me. I've realized by now that I'm a resource that can be sacrificed. Which is why the bosses turn to people like me, even if the amount of merchandise I can carry is small. Because the risk is small too. If I'm arrested, somebody else will be ready to take my place the very next day."

Mamadu didn't start to see any money until after he'd done three trips. Johnny would always drag things out, say he didn't have any cash on him; if Mamadu kept doing such a good job, the small change he had coming to him would soon become a distant memory. But every now and then Johnny would offer him a line, just one, because you have to be familiar with the product you're selling, he'd say. A bit of white powder revs you up to face customs and the cunning gazes of those European women. Not that Mamadu needs the cocaine. He's refined his disguise: Now he's an African until he gets to Casablanca, and then a tourist for the rest of the trip. Tourists have no nationality; being a tourist is an attitude, and at that point the color of your skin, your bloodshot eyes, and your crumpled clothes don't matter. The fear he felt on his first trip has dissolved into routine. Word that controls are being tightened or news of the mounting tide of seizures don't bother him at all. European countries have been flexing their muscles for years now, trying to stop the relentless flood of cocaine. Governments have decided to strike at the heart of illegal trafficking, and the list of detainments and seizures grows longer every day. But those names and facts have nothing to do with Mamadu, nor does the new transportation method some mules thought up: They impregnate their clothes with liquid cocaine. At this point he can toss down capsules as if they were cookies. And besides, he can't stop now. Johnny has told him that there'll be a stewardess on his next flight who is part of the organization, who facilitates the mules' work.

"She's cute," Johnny added, "and it seems she just broke up with her boyfriend. You could ask her out."

"I did the math," Mamadu says to me. "By my thirtieth delivery I should have enough money to treat her to dinner in a fancy restaurant in Lisbon."

# COKE #6

*Andean folk art paintings*

January 21, 2005, Fiumicino airport: A Guatemalan citizen is detained. Five paintings with pre-Columbian motifs are found in his luggage. Behind each painting is an envelope containing a kilo of 92 percent pure cocaine. Total value: €1 million.

*Treated and partially treated calfskins*

September 14, 2005, port of Livorno: The ship *Cala Palma*, which sailed from the Venezuelan port of La Guaira is impounded. Found among the calfskins are 691 kilos of 98 percent pure Colombian cocaine.

*Statues of the Virgin Mary*

March 30, 2006, Brooklyn: The DEA arrests eleven people for cocaine smuggling. They had hidden the precious merchandise—194 kilos of it—

inside statues of the Virgin Mary, destined for various churches and cemeteries.

### Wooden doors

February 24, 2007, Guildford, Surrey, Great Britain: Paul Sneath, an English bloke from a good family, is sentenced to eighteen years for bringing 17 kilos of cocaine into the country. He had purchased handcrafted wooden doors carved with exotic parrots and had them stuffed with sheets of plywood soaked in liquid cocaine. On the market the drugs would have brought about £3 million.

### Statue of Jesus Christ

May 30, 2008, on the Nuevo Laredo border crossing, across from Texas: A Mexican woman is detained at customs. Agents find 3 kilos of cocaine hidden inside the large statue of Jesus Christ in her luggage.

### Fake pineapples

August 22, 2008, Naples: The ROS, which deals with organized crime, seizes 100 kilos of pure cocaine hidden in wax pineapples in a house in Poggiomarino. Value: €40 million.

### Squid

January 2009, port of Naples: During routine controls, the Finance Guard discovers 15 kilos of cocaine hidden among 1,600 cans of squid shipped from Peru.

*Children's books*

April 9, 2009, Christopher Columbus airport in Genoa: An Italian woman, twenty-one years old, is arrested after picking up a package of children's books sent from South America. Inside are 300 grams of cocaine.

**Ceiba speciosa**

April 30, 2009, port of Vado Ligure, Savona: The Naples Finance Guard intercepts a shipment of *Ceiba speciosa*, a tropical tree known in Latin America as Palo Borracho, or drunken tree. Noted for their irregular, bulging trunks, the trees concealed 250 kilos of cocaine.

*Suitcases*

June 2, 2009, Santiago de Chile airport: Sandra Figueroa, a twenty-six-year-old Argentinian woman, catches the customs officers' attention: The bags she is dragging along are too heavy. A chemical analysis reveals that her luggage is made of fiberglass, resin, and 15 kilos of cocaine.

*Frozen sharks*

June 17, 2009, port of Progreso, Yucatan, Mexico: The Mexican navy seizes eight hundred blocks of cocaine, hidden inside twenty or so frozen shark bodies.

*Containers*

June 21, 2009, Padua: The Carabinieri of Padua, with the help of antidrug dogs, discover about 400 kilos of cocaine in containers of bananas and pineapples on a trailer truck.

### Trunks of precious wood

July 22, 2009, Calabria: The Maesano Brothers' network is uncovered. Thanks to their import-export business they were shipping a container a month to Bolivia, with tools for cutting down forests. The container would be sent back full of precious tree trunks stuffed with blocks of cocaine, each weighing at least 100 kilos.

### Transportation trailers

November 12, 2010, port of Gioia Tauro, Calabria: In the context of Operation Meta 2010 an undocumented container from Brazil filled with trailers for agricultural transport is inspected. Sophisticated tests reveal anomalies in the metal tubes that make up the frames. The tubes are opened with gas torches and one thousand blocks are extracted: 1,000 kilos in all.

### Airplane cockpit

February 1, 2011, Fiumicino airport: Two airport technicians, grilled by customs officers made suspicious by their behavior, confess their desire to steal precious objects from the hold of a plane that has just landed from Caracas. But the investigators, alarmed by the antidrug dogs' agitation, discover thirty blocks of cocaine—35 kilos—stuffed behind the instrument panel in the cockpit.

### Frozen fish

March 19, 2011, port of Gioia Tauro: A container that arrived by cargo ship from Ecuador is intercepted. Hidden inside, among the frozen fish, are 140 kilos of pure cocaine.

*Palm hearts*

April 8, 2011, port of Livorno: The Rome Carabinieri seize a container filled with cans of palm hearts on a ship from Chile. In the cans they find 1,200 kilos of cocaine.

*Cookbook*

October 2011, Turin: A package sent from Peru via Frankfurt is seized. Inside is a cookbook, the pages of which are stuffed with cocaine. It weighs 500 grams. The person to whom the package is addressed, an Italian, is arrested in his home. In addition to cocaine, investigators find equipment for preparing individual doses, scales, and a press for packaging blocks. Subsequent investigations uncover a criminal network that was trafficking cocaine from Peru to Italy by way of Germany.

*Coffee*

October 27, 2011, port of Barcelona: The Civil Guard score the biggest drug seizure ever in the port of Barcelona: 625 kilos of cocaine hidden in a container transporting coffee.

*Canned asparagus*

December 10, 2011, Lima, Peru: Five hundred liters of liquid cocaine worth $20 million are seized in a home in a Lima suburb. The drug was in the brine of canned asparagus.

### Artificial breasts and buttocks

December 21, 2011, Fiumicino airport: A Spanish model coming from São Paulo in Brazil is detained. A search reveals 2.5 kilos of pure cocaine crystals inserted in her artificial breasts and buttocks.

### Valentine's Day flowers

February 2012, port of Hull, England: Eighty-four kilos of cocaine hidden in boxes of flowers that an English florist purchased for Valentine's Day are seized. The man had gone to Holland to buy them himself, and sailed from Rotterdam. He was loading his truck when the British police noticed that three boxes weighed five times more than the others.

### Genitals

April 2012, Folcroft, Pennsylvania: Ray Woods, twenty-three years old, from Philadelphia, is detained by the police in an area known for drug dealing. When he is searched they find forty-eight doses of cocaine in a bag strapped to his penis.

### Legumes, aluminum, foodstuffs

June 7, 2012, port of Gioia Tauro: The Finance Guard seizes 300 kilos of pure cocaine onboard the MSC container ship *Poh Lin*, which had set sail from South America. The drugs were found in three containers—in nine large black bags hidden among foodstuffs, legumes, and scrap aluminum— on their way to northern Italian businesses that do not usually import such products.

*Peanuts*

June 8, 2012, port of Gioia Tauro: Discovered in a container from Brazil are 630 kilos of cocaine. It was divided into 580 blocks and stuffed in sixteen bags hidden inside a shipment of peanuts.

*Medical supplies for earthquake-damaged areas*

June 8, 2012, port of Genoa: The Carabinieri find over €1 million worth of cocaine hidden among medical instruments being shipped to a business in Emilia that had suffered serious earthquake damage. The container, which arrived from the Dominican Republic, immediately raised suspicions because such medical equipment usually comes from China.

*Sugar*

June 15, 2012, port of London: Just outside the capital city, in one of the harbor terminals on the Thames, 30 kilos of cocaine hidden in a load of sugar that had arrived on a cargo ship from Brazil are seized.

*Skins*

July 22, 2012, Portugal: The Portuguese police arrest a businessman from Vicenza who works in the tanning industry. The investigators find 120 kilos of cocaine in the container of skins sent from Brazil.

*Cocoa*

August 23, 2012, port of Anversa: Belgian authorities discover just over two tons of cocaine in jute sacks filled with cocoa seeds onboard a container ship from Ecuador. The cocaine, worth €100 million, was on its way to a warehouse in Amsterdam.

### Parquet

August 23, 2012, port of Caacupe-mí, Paraguay: Hidden among irregularly cut pieces of wood for parquet floors are 330 kilos of cocaine; they are seized on a container ship ready to set sail from the private port in Caacupe-mí, on the Paraguay River. A corrupt customs officer is arrested.

### Roast chicken

September 3, 2012, Lagos, Nigeria, airport: A Nigerian engineer returning from São Paulo, Brazil, where he had worked for the past five years, is detained at customs. The police find 2.5 kilos of cocaine hidden among the leftover roast chicken he brought to eat during the flight.

### Hair

September 26, 2012, JFK airport, New York: Kiana Howell and Makeeba Graham, two girls who have just arrived from Guyana, a former British colony between Venezuela and Brazil, arouse the customs officials' suspicion. When they are searched, each is found to have a block of cocaine, weighing about 1 kilo, hidden in her hairdo.

### Chickpeas

October 12, 2012, port of Gioia Tauro: 100 kilos of cocaine sent from Mexico on the ship *Bellavia* are intercepted. The drug was hidden in sacks of chickpeas, officially destined for Turkey.

*Balloons*

October 14, 2012, port of Limón, Costa Rica: During routine checks of a cargo ship anchored in the port of Limón, which leads into the Caribbean, antidrug agents discover 119 kilos of cocaine hidden among multicolored balloons usually used for children's birthday parties.

*Shrimp and bananas*

October 18, 2012, Milan: The Milan DDA arrests about fifty people tied to a huge cocaine network importing into Italy, Belgium, Holland, Austria, and Germany. The loads, hidden among frozen shrimp and cartons of bananas, arrived from Colombia and Ecuador, either in ships that docked at the Hamburg and Anversa ports or in planes that landed at the Vienna airport. The trafficking was managed by the Lombard branches of the most powerful Calabrian families: the Pelles of San Luca, the Morabitos of Africo, the Molès of Gioia Tauro.

*Sweet potatoes*

October 19, 2012, Paramaribo, Suriname, airport: Customs officials, whose suspicion was aroused by the excessive weight of six sacks of sweet potatoes leaving the Johan Adolf Pengel airport, the main airport in this former Dutch colony in South America, discover 60 kilos of cocaine inside the tubers.

*Carpets*

November 27, 2012, Milan: The Carabinieri of the province of Milan arrest fifty-three Italian and Colombian citizens, accusing them of drug trafficking, unlawful possession of weapons, receiving stolen goods, and money laundering. The network, based in Cesano Boscone, was impregnating imported carpets with liquid cocaine. Once the carpets arrived in Milan they were washed with special products to release the drug from the wool fibers, which was then dried.

## 16.

# FORTY-EIGHT

You're dreaming. Another life, more profoundly yours. Money or sex. You dream about your children and your dead, who come back to life. You dream you're falling forever. That you're being strangled. That someone is trying to get in the door, or has already come in. You dream of being trapped, no one comes to free you, you can't get out. You dream that they want to arrest you, but you haven't done anything wrong.

There's nothing uniquely yours about your dreams and nightmares. They're so much like everyone else's that in Naples you use them to play Lotto, the Italian lottery, with the numbers from the Smorfia Napoletana: *'E Gguardie*, the police, 24; *'E ccancelle*, prison, 44; *'O mariuolo*, the thief, 79; *'A fune nganno*, the noose around your neck, 39; *'A caduta*, the fall, 56; *'O muorto*, the dead man, 47; *'O muorto che parla*, the dead man talking, 48; *'A figliolanza*, offspring 9; *'E denare*, money, 46. For sex, you're spoiled for choice. For example: *Chella ca guarda 'nterra*, she who looks at the ground, which means cunt, 6; *'O pate d''e criature*, the father of babies, or penis, 29; *'O totaro dint' 'a chitarra*, a fish inside a guitar, which means intercourse, 67.

I have them too, those dreams. When they start off well, they turn into nightmares. When they're nightmares right from the start, there's little that is dreamlike about them. My days invade my nights, the more or less 3,196 days as of this writing since I've been living under police protection. I've learned to forget my dreams. When they wake me, at most I get up and drink a glass of water. I have trouble falling back to sleep, but at least I've chased away my nightmares with a few sips. All but one nightmare.

I'm screaming, I can't stop screaming, louder and louder. No one seems to hear me. It's a variation on the nightmare in which you want to scream but no sound comes out. Do you know that one? I wouldn't know what number to tell you to play, though. There's 65 for cry, 60 for lament, and 90 for fear. But there's no number for screams in the cabala of the city where everyone screams all the time. Maybe try betting on the mouth, 80. I'm not betting anything.

I write about Naples. But Naples plugs her ears. Who am I to draw attention to things I've not experienced firsthand in some time? I can't possibly understand; I have no right to speak. I'm no longer part of the body of that mother city who welcomes you with her gentle, resplendent warmth. Naples has to be lived, that's all. Either you're in Naples or you're not. And if you're not, you're no longer from Naples. Like some African or South American cities, Naples offers you citizenship right away. A citizenship that you lose, however, when you leave, when you put some distance between your skin and your judgment. At that point, you can't talk about Naples anymore. It's prohibited. You have to stay in Naples, stay inside Naples; if not, you'll always get the same response: "What do you know?"

I know that in Naples the surest number to bet is 62, *'o muort' acciso*, death by murder. I know that Naples treats those murder victims almost as if they were the number 48—the dead man talking—which is what I feel I have become to her. Naples cuts them out, expels them. They're people on the outside, people from Scampia, Secondigliano, or other towns to the north of Naples that have been hit by the feud that exploded after years of steady homicides. Like Andrea Nollino, killed instantly by the burst of gunfire from a motorcycle as he was opening his café in Casoria. June 26, 2012, 7:30 A.M. Or Lino Romano, who on October 15, 2012, goes to the station to pick up his girlfriend, Rosanna, who's on her way back from the wedding of a cousin in Modena, from the same kind of celebration that he hoped to be able to offer her soon. He takes her home and goes in to say hi to Rosanna's parents. Right after he leaves they hear the roar of gunfire, very close, out front in the street. Lino dies while starting up his car, on his way to play soccer with his friends. 9:30 P.M.: It's dark, it's raining, his black Clio looks like all the other black Clios around. Maybe you drive one too, but you didn't get engaged to a girl from Marianella, that clump of apartment complexes in the line of fire between Secondigliano and Scampia.

It seems like a film you've already seen, a story you've already heard. You've read the story of a young man with almost the same name, Attilio Romanò, killed in the cell phone store where he worked. You've seen how they deal coke inside the "Vele" apartment complex in Scampia, how they kill without the least drama, how they betray one another. The scene from *Gomorrah* in which the kids are trained to be shot at really upset you. Those kids are no longer ten, twelve years old, though. Now they're the ones doing the shooting, and the dying.

But you're done with it, you can live with yourself. And I'm done with it too. I wrote a book; they made a film from it. It's my fault if I keep screaming now, if it feels to me as if no one is willing to listen anymore. My fault if the articles I keep writing about the blood spilled in the cocaine markets fall on deaf ears. People can't keep their attention trained on the same scene for so many years; there are other things that are more important, or simply new. My fault if permission is denied to film the fictional TV show based on my first book, *Gomorrah*, on site, with a big protest banner that plays on the name of the town: "SCAMPIAmoci da Saviano," "Let's flee from Saviano." And posters all over the place that shout: "He who takes advantage of Naples is guilty of everything!" I bathed the ears of the world in Naples's blood, but in Scampia nothing has changed. So I'm guilty. Guilty of the new killers whose bodies, brimming with the savagery of youth bolstered by cocaine, go out and murder the umpteenth relative of some affiliate from a rival group. Guilty of the millions in profit for which all those lives continue to be erased. Guilty even of victims like Lino and Andrea.

The entire neighborhood, and even a wider swath of the city, gathered around them. Thousands screamed their innocence; they didn't abandon them—they accompanied them in their final voyage, which followed the final injustice. It's not true that mafia wars only generate fear, cynicism, *omertà*, and indifference. They also generate a special, primitive empathy, because you're forced to see yourself in Lino, in Andrea, in Rosanna, in their parents, siblings, friends, and colleagues. Maybe you too have a cousin who is a cousin of one of the *"scissionisti,"* or secessionists, or to one of Girati, as one of the groups that broke away from the winning cartel in the feud against the Di Lauro clan is called. Your turn could be next. It could have been your son or daughter that December 5, 2012, when Luigi Lucenti, known as *'o Cinese*, the Chinese, tried to escape an ambush by holing up in the courtyard of the Eugenio Montale nursery school in Scampia, while the children were rehearsing a Christmas play. He was supposed to reopen the Cianfa di Cavallo open-air drug market on via Ghisleri, and they killed him. If it had happened just a little later, when the children who don't stay for lunch are picked up by their mothers or grandmothers, a few nursery schoolchildren very likely would have been killed. You could have lost a child, a wife, a mother. It went okay for you that time; now you just have to worry about your child's nightmares, or maybe his wetting the bed just when you'd managed to potty train him. Thank heavens, you keep telling yourself, nothing happened. But it's not enough. So when the occasion arises you find the energy to react, to join forces, to shout along with the others that the blood that flowed was of someone who deserved to live, not to die.

Those screams are about Naples, for Naples. The body of Naples that closes over the wound. Despite everything I'm relieved to know that this happens too, a flow of vital energy that pours from the flood of rage and fear and not just from the spastic contraction with which the intrusive element that went down the wrong way is spit out. Yet the logic by which I am guilty is not all that different from the logic that drives the people in the street to rebel. It's the logic of who's in and who's out. In and out is not determined merely by a certificate of residency. It is determined by the experience of the feud. Only those who live through it can understand; only those who go through it are included, are in.

I tried to find a way to live with the knowledge that, on the one hand, what I have to say about Naples echoes less and less no matter how loudly I scream, and the more painful knowledge that my words are rejected as illegitimate by Naples itself. And so I have spent years studying and chasing the trail that leads out from Scampia and Casal di Principe, to broaden my horizons, to let my investigation take in the whole world. This seems the only escape route available to me, the only way forward.

What are those Scampia area murders compared to those in Ciudad Juárez? How much is the only open-air drug supermarket in Europe worth in comparison with the trafficking managed by the Calabrian families? An 'ndranghetista might not even bother to respond. Wiretappings reveal that the Calabrians despise the Neapolitans. They butcher each other too often and for too little. I hear a laugh coming from Aspromonte. Carried on the wind toward the Tyrrhenian, it reaches Mount Vesuvius and it descends from there.

The Neapolitans despise me more than the Calabrians despise them. But I've never really left Naples. I am always there. To speak about Naples is to betray it a little, but it is in this betrayal that I find my home. The only home, at least for now, that is allowed me.

For me, the pain of the blood that fills the piazzas, the pain of the names that make the lists of the dead grow longer is a sting that doesn't go away, even if I blow on it as hard as I can. A pain that doesn't heal even if I put iodine tincture on it, even if I have it stitched up. This pain has to do with me, for all things that cause us the deepest pain have to do with ourselves, like our flesh, our children, the most untouchable parts of ourselves. All I can do, until someone or something kills me, is to keep betting on my number.

## 17.

# DOGS

A Neapolitan doctor I know finally gave in to his son's pleading and gave the boy a dog. A small dog, relentlessly friendly, with a sweet face. One day he asked his son to go out onto the balcony with him, he had a surprise for him, and in the meantime he went over the little speech he'd prepared in his head. A dog is a delicate creature, you have to respect him, train him, you have to be patient but severe, and above all you have to make him understand that you are the leader of the pack. Liberty, sure, but with hard and fast rules. Necessary preconditions, especially as we're talking about a Jack Russell terrier, a breed that hunters use even today to flush out foxes. Dealing with the dog's daring and explosive temperament would prove to be an important undertaking for his son; it would force him to face one of the basic challenges for a human puppy: to go beyond appearances. Behind those puppy eyes and silly demands to be pet and played with is an unpredictable character that needs to be disciplined.

"Do you understand?"

"Sure, Papà."

Things worked out well. The boy cleaned up after the dog, walked him, played with him, taught him some basic commands: "Stay!" "Sit!" "Heel!" His father swelled with pride, even though his son was sneezing too much and his eyes were always red. He's a doctor, he knows what those symptoms mean: allergy to dog fur. They had no choice. The dog, who had already become a full member of the family, had to go. But for the son the separation would be excruciatingly painful, and it risked undoing everything that they had achieved together: the education of a young boy through the education of a young animal. From now on the child could either fill the emptiness by clinging to his grief and the memory of shattered happiness, or he could overcome the wrenching loss, thus undergoing the most difficult test a human puppy must face: getting used to loss.

Today that dog serves in the canine unit of the Naples police: that is where the family friend to whom he was entrusted works. Pocho, like the soccer player Lavezzi, is the terror of the Scampia and Secondigliano pushers, the "top dog" in the canine unit charged with fighting the Camorra. In contrast to his colleagues, little Pocho can worm his way into the narrowest passageways and slip through the tiniest openings. Innate talent and body type have made him a precious resource, but first he had to go through rigorous training. Play, lots of playing. Because for drug-sniffing dogs, finding a packet of cocaine jammed in a crack in a wall is a game. Great fun. They start with a tennis ball or a rolled-up towel. They play tug-of-war. This is the "attachment stage," in which the dog bonds with objects and its handler. The phase in which an inseparable human-dog couple is formed. During the second phase small quantities of a drug, or a laboratory-created substance that reproduces the odor of a drug, are added to the toy object. This is where an association between toy and drug, between prize and reward, is created. At that point it's time to turn the game into work. Essential work, thus full of gratification. But also full of danger.

Without Mike, that spent eight years with the canine unit of the Volpiano Carabinieri in Turin province, the more than a kilo of cocaine buried under a lamppost would never have been discovered. Without

Labin, the Florence Finance Guard's splendid female German shepherd which while sniffing car seats did not let herself be fooled by a false bottom spread with tar, another 12 kilos would have gone undetected. Ragal—same breed, same profession, Labin's colleague at the port of Civitavecchia—started barking furiously at a car that had just come off a ferry from Barcelona, shattering the Neapolitan driver's presumption that sniffer dogs would not be able to detect his 11 kilos of pure cocaine under the smells of mustard, coffee, and diesel oil. Ciro pointed right at a trailer truck from the Costa del Sol, drawing the curses and clenched teeth of the driver from Castel Volturno. Ufa, who patrols Fiumicino airport, jumped onto a garment bag on the baggage carousel in which were found 2.5 kilos of cocaine. Nearly eight hundred people arrested had failed to reckon with Eola, a veteran awarded for her twelve years of service and more than 100 kilos of cocaine seized.

Agata's existence was much more trying. She was young when she started working at the Leticia cargo airport in the Amazon jungle in Colombia, an important junction for cocaine from Brazil and Peru on its way to the United States. The narcos, tired of seeing cargo planes stopped by that docile-looking Labrador with golden fur, put a price on her head: ten thousand dollars. From that moment until she retired Agata was under twenty-four-hour protection and could no longer accept tasty morsels from strangers. Boss, a chocolate Lab in Rio de Janeiro, has met the same fate. Nine police officers take turns watching over him ever since the order to eliminate him was intercepted, that "little chocolate" who can't be tricked by fake walls or the sewer stench of the *favelas*. When detection dogs dig excitedly, bark, scratch, or paw at an object, it's their way of saying that the drug is right here. It's the signal that they've won the game and are ready to start playing all over again. But for others, there is no game. There's only the humiliation of being flesh and blood. Like Pay de Limón—Lemon Cake—who, along with dozens of other dogs like him, was mutilated and dismembered by Mexican narcos. It's useful to practice on one of them before cutting off the finger of an extortion victim.

Labs, German shepherds, Belgian shepherds, but often even abandoned mutts like Kristal, who risked meeting the unhappy end of a stray but is now one of the most formidable sniffer sleuths in Grosseto. The history of sharp-nosed dogs goes back much further than their specialization in detecting white powder, though. Almost a century of successes in Italy, including that of August 16, 1924, when a stench drew Carabinieri sergeant Ovidio Caratelli's dog into the Macchia della Quartarella woods: There was the body of Giacomo Matteotti, an Italian socialist antifascist politician kidnapped two months earlier by Mussolini's black shirts.

Yet their noses and animal instincts also come in handy for those who, like the Camorra, are on the other side. The Scampia clans kept three German shepherds and a Rottweiler in a condominium courtyard in the Case Celesti neighborhood. Accustomed to the brutality of rusty cages, raised amid broken glass and food scraps, their job was to alert their drug-pusher owners when the cops were coming. Animals in the service of criminal organizations aren't merely faithful watchdogs, though. They are also used as mules, unsuspected couriers, transporting huge amounts of drugs from one continent to the other. Females are ideal: It's hard to say whether that bulge is due to a pregnancy or pellets. Frispa, a black Lab, and Rex, a yellow Lab, were unloaded in Amsterdam from a cargo plane coming from Colombia in 2003. One of the dogs was very agitated and aggressive, the other weak and apathetic. The authorities grew suspicious and had them checked out. They found scars on the dogs' bellies, and X-rays confirmed their suspicions. Eleven packets of cocaine as long as sausages in Rex's stomach, ten in Frispa's. Frispa, the black Lab, had to be put down, because some of the linings had broken, whereas Rex, after another operation and a long convalescence, was saved. One for the many—far too many—sacrifices of man's best friend.

In the summer of 2012 a man went for a walk in a pretty countryside near Livorno. He suddenly noticed a strong stench that led him to make a macabre discovery: a dismembered, disemboweled Labrador lying in the middle of the field. The man, who thought it must have been the work of a sadist or a group of satanists, called the police. But not even a week went by before the stench of fresh death returned: This time the dog, a cross between a Dogue de Bordeaux and a pit bull, had his snout taped shut and a plastic bag sticking out of his cut-open stomach. It's not a coincidence, it's not black magic, merely the tragic end that the white powder commonly deals its involuntary four-legged couriers. It's too hard to make them expel the packets naturally; much easier just to gut them and recover the stuff. Dogs are both victims and soldiers in a global ordeal that for them is still what it has always been: a test of loyalty passed off as a game.

## 18.

# DYING TO TELL

What does one risk by reading? A lot. It's a dangerous thing to open a book and leaf through the pages. Once you've opened a work by Émile Zola or Varlam Šalamov, there's no turning back. I truly believe this. But often the reader is unaware of the risk involved in coming to know these stories; he doesn't realize the impact they'll have. If I could truly quantify the damage that knowing eyes, the damage that people who want to understand, can inflict on the powerful, I'd try to diagram it. For the mafiosi the risk of being arrested, put on trial, and sent to prison is nothing compared to the danger that comes from people knowing the truth, understanding how things actually work—the facts.

If you choose to talk about criminal power, if you choose to stare its secrets in the face, to keep your eyes on the road and on the money, well then, there are two ways to go about it: a right way and a wrong way. Christian Poveda knew them both. He knew the differences—and above all the consequences—of each way. He knew that if you decide to be the extension of your work—a pen, a computer, a lens—then you don't run any risks: You will finish your assignment and come home with the loot. But Christian knew something else as well: If you decide that the extension of your work—a pen, a computer, a lens—is a means rather than the end, then everything changes. Suddenly what you're looking for—and what you find—is no longer a dark dead end but a door that opens onto other rooms, that leads to more doors.

"He went looking for it." "What was he expecting?" "Like he didn't know beforehand?" Callous, cruel questions, yet also legitimate. Cynical maybe, but all things considered, correct. Unfortunately there's no answer. There's only guilt, because you knew the consequences would be terrible, for you and your family. You knew, but you did it anyway. Why? There's no answer to that question either. You see something and behind it you see a hundred other things. You can't simply stop dead in your tracks; you have to keep going, to dig deeper. Maybe you know what awaits you, maybe you know perfectly well, but you're neither reckless nor crazy. You smile at your friends, at your colleagues too, and maybe you share your worries with them, but your outer image doesn't correspond in the least with your inner torment. It's as if two opposing forces were pulling you in different directions. A struggle over where to stand, and the battlefield is your own stomach, because that's where you feel the push and pull, an endless tug-of-war that ties your innards in knots.

Christian Poveda knew this feeling well. He was born to Spanish Republican parents who took refuge in Algiers during the Franco regime, and when he was six he moved with his family to Paris. Curious, questioning, he embraced early on his life profession: journalism. With its extensions—pen, computer, lens—he travels in Algeria, the Caribbean, Argentina, Chile. He covers the war in Iran, Iraq, Lebanon. His reports are different from the sorts of stories you have to file for the TV news. A different quality, you could say, as if he didn't have a job to do. Behind every photo, between the lines of every article there's always a human story that breathes, demanding more oxygen and space.

Christian decides to focus on making documentaries, a new extension of his curiosity, an extension that unites all the existing ones—pen, computer, and lens—and that finally allows him to observe the animal in the wild. He makes his first documentary in 1986, *Shadow Warriors*, about the Chilean rebel group Mapu Lautaro, which opposed Pinochet's fascist regime. But it's when he goes to El Salvador that he seems to find the land he'd been looking for. The place where he was really needed, where everything he'd wanted and all he had trained himself to be converged. El Salvador. A country tormented by a lengthy civil war that Christian himself first documented in 1980, together with the journalist Jean-Michel Caradec'h. He was the first photojournalist to cover El Salvador's guerrilla warfare from the inside. "He went looking for it." "It was his fault." "If you play with fire, you'll get burned." The same remarks, still fair, still pertinent.

Years go by, you accumulate experiences, you build up a protective shell, but the knot in your gut is still there. Christian feels them inside him now, those stories he tells on film. They bite and claw at him from within. And when a story moves inside you it's like your soul is in labor, restless nights, not a moment of peace until you manage to give birth.

His first documentary about El Salvador comes out in 1991. The name Poveda echoes throughout the country. Then the civil war ends; peace treaties are signed. These are years of renewed hope, years in which many El Salvadorans who had taken refuge abroad return home. During the war thousands of children had fled to the United States without their families—either their parents were murdered or their mothers preferred to have them safer far away from a poor land devastated by civil war. Deserters and ex-guerrillas flee as well. That is how the maras are born, the El Salvadoran gangs in Los Angeles that model themselves after all the other gangs there—African American, Asian, and Mexican. The maras are the new families for El Salvadoran kids that form on the streets of California. They start out as a form of self-defense, to protect themselves against the other gangs that target the new immigrants. Many of the people who organize gangs by gathering groups of kids are former guerrillas or paramilitaries: It's not surprising that the structures and modes of operation of these groups resemble military practices. The Mexican gangs are soon defeated, and shortly after, the Salvadoran gangs split into two large families of *mare-ros*, which distinguish themselves by their "street number": Mara 13, better known as Mara Salvatrucha, and Mara 18, a dissident branch. Then the civil war in El Salvador ends. The country's on its knees; poverty is rampant, creating an opportunity for the gangs to go home. For many of them it's a choice; for others their return is decided by the U.S. government, which frees itself of the thugs who'd served time in American jails.

Today the maras have cells in the United States, Mexico, all over Central America, in Europe, and the Philippines; about 15,000 members in El Salvador, 14,000 in Guatemala, 35,000 in Honduras, 5,000 in Mexico. The highest concentration is in the United States, with 70,000 members. Mara 18 is considered to be the biggest criminal gang in Los Angeles. It was the first to accept ethnic diversity and to allow people from other countries to join. For the most part they're kids between thirteen and seventeen years old. This army of children primarily pushes cocaine and marijuana on the streets. They don't handle big orders, they aren't rich, and they don't corrupt institutions. But on the street they guarantee immediate money and power. They're the retail drug cartel and are also involved in activities such as extortion, car theft, and murder. According to the FBI, the maras are the most dangerous street gangs in the world.

Everything is codified within the organization: hand signals, face tattoos, hierarchy. Everything they do is filtered through rules that create and control their identity. The result is a compact organization that knows how to move quickly. In El Salvador mara means group, or crowd. The word implies disorder, but in truth these groups—thanks to their rules, and to the punishments with which infractions are met—have been able to become reliable partners to global criminal organizations. The origin of the name Mara Salvatrucha is disputed. A "salvatrucho" is a young Salvadoran fighter, but the word is composed of "salva"—in homage to El Salvador—and "trucha," which means cunning. You have to pass really challenging tests in order to become a

member: The boys have to endure thirteen seconds of brutal, uninter-
rupted beating—punches, kicks, slaps, and kneeings—which often
leave the new recruits unconscious. The girls are often gang-raped as
well. The recruits are getting younger and younger, and for them there
is just one rule of life: the gang or death.

Christian Poveda wanted to make a feature film about the maras.
He wanted to understand. To live with them. To discover why twelve-
year-old kids become murderers willing to die before they turn twenty.
And they welcomed him. As if they'd finally found the person who
could tell about them, the maras. "Why couldn't he just have stayed
home?" "What did it get him?" "Doesn't he care about the people
close to him?" At a certain point these questions don't bother you anymore; they're as annoying as a mosquito bite. They itch for a while, and
then they fade away, gone for good.

Filming for *La vida loca* takes sixteen months. For nearly a year and
a half Christian follows the criminal bands in search of answers to his
questions. He attends initiation rites, studies their facial tattoos, is at
their side while members—male and female—get high on crack and
cocaine, plan a murder, attend a friend's funeral. Every mara operates
differently, depending on the country it's in. "It's not the same thing
selling drugs in the central market of San Salvador as it is selling drugs
on Sunset Boulevard in Los Angeles," Christian says. Theirs are lives
of shootouts, homicides, reprisals, police checks, funerals, and prison.
Lives that Christian describes without being morbid in the least. He
tells the story of "Little One," a nineteen-year-old mother with an
enormous 18 tattooed on her face, from her eyebrows to her chin. He
tells the story of Moreno, twenty-five, who wanted to change his life
and started working in a bakery set up by a nonprofit called Homies
Unidos. But the bakery closes when its owner is arrested and sentenced
to sixteen years for homicide. He tells of La Maga, another young
mother, she too a gang member who lost an eye in a fight. Christian
follows her to her doctor's appointments, to her surgery to replace the

damaged eye with a glass one. A pointless operation, though, because she's shot dead before he finishes shooting the movie, one of many Mara 18 members killed while he worked on the documentary.

"He's crazy!" "Reckless!" "Out of his mind!" Words thrown to the wind, which Christian Poveda fights with other words. "Most maras members are victims of society, of our society," Poveda says. Because society and the state find it easier to point a finger at their violence, which is so recognizable, rather than to offer opportunities. Maras members look like the dregs of society, like trash; they're revolting. It's easy to consider them public enemy number one. Easy to underestimate them. But Poveda's work dismantles such attitudes.

This is the ultimate meaning of Christian's work. Behind the door of the violence flaunted by the gangs he saw an inaccessible path that leads right to the root of the problem. To get a byline in the newspapers or his name on the opening credits of a documentary it would have been enough simply to affix evil to celluloid, and to speculate a bit. But Christian decides to get to the bottom of things. He wants to truly understand.

On September 2, 2009, Christian Poveda's body is found next to his car, between Soyapango and Tonacatepeque, a rural area north of the capital of El Salvador, with four bullets to the head. His film equipment is lying next to him; it has not been touched. "I told him." "He got what he deserved." "At any rate, he went too far." So say the same old voices over his dead body.

In 2011, eleven people, all Mara 18 members, are arrested and convicted of the murder of Christian Poveda. José Alejandro Melara and Luis Roberto Vásquez Romero are sentenced to thirty years for planning and carrying out the homicide; a third person, a woman, is sentenced to twenty years as an accomplice. Other gang members have to spend four years behind bars for covering up the crime. In August 2013 three more *mareros* are sentenced to ten years for conspiracy to commit murder: They took part in the meeting at which Poveda's death was planned.

Christian was sure he wasn't taking any risks. He had entered into the community of the maras, into their lives. He felt he'd found a sure, safe way in and thought he'd made friends with many of them. But it's a fantasy to think you're ever safe when you're covering a criminal organization.

In Christian's story, bad luck plays a role as well. It seems, in fact, that Juan Napoleón Espinoza Pérez, a former police officer, met a Mara 18 member while under the influence of alcohol and told him that Poveda was an informer, that he had turned his videos over to the Soyapango police. So the gang gathers, and after three long meetings in the El Arbejal farm in Tonacatepeque, decides to condemn Poveda to death.

There are lots of rumors about those meetings, whole orchestras of whispers, symphonies of accusations. Some mara members defend Christian, saying he is honest, that he did a good thing telling about the maras from their point of view. Others are envious: He'll get rich by looking like the good guy against us bad guys. The women defend him. A lot. Or so it seems. The most authoritative members, those who had agreed to be filmed, are frightened by the documentary's success. Too many people are talking about it. It makes its way to the web. So maybe that cop Espinoza wasn't lying, maybe Christian did sell the video to the police. But the sense is that anyone who says too much about the maras, anyone who has in a certain sense taken advantage of them, has to be punished.

On August 30, 2009, the group decides to kill Christian. At the time he's acting as an intermediary for a French journalist who writes for *Elle* magazine and wants to interview some of the girls in the gang. For the first time his contacts ask him for a fee, ten thousand dollars. Even though Christian doesn't like it, he accepts. The magazine has the money and can afford to pay. Christian meets Vásquez Romero in El Rosario. But a little after noon Vásquez Romero gets behind the wheel of a gray Nissan Pathfinder 4 x 4 and drives Christian onto the bridge over the Las Cañas River. That's where they kill him. I can't imagine those final seconds. I've tried. Did Christian realize, even for a moment, that it was a trap? Did he try to defend himself, to explain that killing him was unjust? Or did they shoot him in the back of the head, like cowards? A moment. They must have pretended to be getting out of the car, and in that moment when Christian lifts the handle to open the door they must have fired. I don't know; I'll never know. But I can't keep from asking myself these things.

If the ex–police officer hadn't been drunk that day, if he hadn't told a bunch of lies, would Christian still be alive? Maybe. Maybe not. Maybe they would have eliminated him just the same, because some of the gang members were unhappy with how Christian had portrayed them in his film. Despite his assurances that the documentary would not be released in El Salvador, some pirated versions were making the rounds. Maybe they would have killed him anyway, because the new generation of Mara 18 leadership was even more violent and ferocious than the previous one. According to Carole Solive, Christian's French producer, his mistake was to stay on in El Salvador after he'd finished shooting. Maybe he'd come to know too much about the negotiations between Salvatrucha and 18, two rival bands that were trying to reach an understanding, and that knowledge condemned him to death. No matter how much he trusted those kids Christian never forgot to take certain basic safety precautions. He had a cell phone that he used only to contact maras members. But it wasn't enough.

Christian Poveda believed in the power of images to influence events. That's why he worked as a photojournalist and documentary filmmaker. He devoted all his efforts to chronicling extraordinary political and social situations, making sixteen documentaries that were well received at the world's most prestigious film festivals. I often look for *La vida loca* when I'm in a bookstore, or when I go to someone's home, in the stacks of DVDs next to the TV. I almost never find it. What did you die for, Christian? The question rises up in me like some melodramatic lullaby. What did you die for? Would your life have made more sense if that documentary were in every home? I don't think so. No work of art can make sense of or justify death with a gun to your head. Your last words are more eloquent than any epigraph could be: "Government authorities have no idea of the monster facing them. Now the 18 is full of crazy people. I am very worried . . . and sad."

# 19

# ADDICTED

Writing about cocaine is not so different from using it. You always want more—more news, more information—and the stuff you do find is so potent you can't live without it. It's addicting. These stories, even when they conform to an overarching plot you've already grasped, continue to fascinate in their particulars. And they stick in your head until another one—incredible but true—takes its place. You see that your stimulation threshold is on the rise, and you pray you don't ever go into withdrawal. Which is why I keep collecting stories ad nauseam, more than are needed; I can't bring myself to stop. One evening, long before El Chapo's actual capture, I got a phone call from Guatemala with the news that he was killed in a shootout. I didn't know whether to believe it or not; it wouldn't be the first time that false information about drug lords was circulated. Still, these bits of information roar in my ear. But relatively few others hear the noise. The further I descend into these infernal circles whitewashed with cocaine, the more I realize how much people don't know. There's a river that runs under big cities, a river that starts in South America, flows through Africa, and spreads everywhere. Men and women stroll down Rome's via del Corso, along Parisian boulevards, meet up in Times Square, walk with heads lowered along London streets. Don't they hear anything? How can they stand all this noise?

That old story of Griselda, for example, the most ruthless female narco of all the Colombian drug traffickers. As a child she learned that all men are means, tools to manipulate so as to reach your goals. A reasonable theory if you grow up with a mother who got pregnant by a half-Indian *guajiro* landowner called Señor Blanco, who threw her out on the street as soon as the baby was born. An alcoholic, poor, abused, and desperate, Griselda's mother dragged her daughter through the putrid streets of Medellín, forcing her to beg. A couple of miserable, human beggars who'd part ways only when the mother got herself pregnant by the umpteenth guy she'd picked up who knows where, only to join up later, now with the addition of a half brother or sister. These are the years of La Violencia in Colombia. Brutality is the order of the day, and if you want to survive, you have to be brutal too. Griselda turns thirteen, she starts to prostitute herself. The men she goes with are pieces of meat who vent themselves on her body, and who pay her just enough to get by till the next day. Her amber skin collects bruises and cuts, bites and scars. They don't hurt, though; they're just nicks on her thick armor. Men are a means. Nothing more. Griselda learns the art of pickpocketing to round out her income. She's quick with her hands and doesn't permit herself to steal from her clients, because she doesn't want to risk ruining her beat. For her love is a foul-smelling bed she lies on, waiting while the sweaty creature on top of her does his duty. But one day she meets Carlos. Another man, one of many, and Griselda gives him the usual treatment: indifference. Carlos is a small-time criminal in Medellín, an expert pickpocket and thief who has a thriving partnership with a narco named Alberto Bravo. A long courtship begins between Griselda and Carlos. He brings her a different flower every day, which every day she throws away after accepting it with false courtesy. She never looks him in the eye, but he, unperturbed, makes the rounds of all the florists in Medellín, looking for different varieties.

He teaches her a few tricks to make ends meet; she pretends not to listen but is actually memorizing everything he says. This skirmish lasts a long time, until Carlos's stubborn perseverance breaks through, and Griselda surrenders. For the first time in her life a man has shown her that a relationship does not necessarily have to expire, that there exists a word she has never heard before: trust. They get married, they love each other, they make big plans. He introduces her to Alberto Bravo, who makes her see that the real money is in narco-trafficking. She is young but quick-witted, and doesn't hesitate to set foot in that world. And besides, she has Carlos, who always says yes whenever she asks him if they will be together their whole lives. They move to New York, to Queens, where Colombians are starting to settle and the drug market is really flourishing. A new life. The city that never sleeps welcomes Griselda and Carlos like royalty. Things are going really well, and Carlos keeps saying yes whenever Griselda asks him: "Will we be together our whole lives?" Yes, yes, yes. But then Carlos gets sick— cirrhosis of the liver—and dies in the hospital. Griselda stays at his side till the end, and when her husband dies she doesn't feel a thing, just as she used to feel nothing when she came home after a long night working and counted her new bites and scars in the mirror. Carlos didn't honor their pact to stay together their whole lives; Carlos is just like every other man; men are a means.

She marries Alberto Bravo, but when he goes to Colombia on a work trip and she doesn't hear from him for a while, a furious Griselda catches up with him and kills him in a shootout. By 1971 Griselda has her own narco-trafficking network in the United States. She has understood that the line connecting New York, Miami, and Colombia is the future. She has a lingerie shop in Medellín, where she sells her own designs, which she also has her mules wear. They're the ones who hide 2 kilos of cocaine under their clothes on the Colombia–United States flight. Her name appears in the DEA files for the first time in 1973. She's described as "a new threat for the United States." Business is booming; she's now one of the most important Colombian traffickers.

Despite being a woman—no small handicap in a society where there's no feminine version of the word "narco-trafficker"—Griselda proves to her Colombian colleagues that she can do the job and do it with such violence that she terrorizes people. Her reputation as a wicked woman without scruples precedes her everywhere she goes.

In 1975 she is accused of drug trafficking as part of an investigation in New York, but she manages to take refuge in Colombia. She has already amassed a fortune, $500 million. She returns to the United States a few years later, when things have calmed down, this time to Florida. She founds the Pistoleros, her own army of killers. Among them is Paco Sepúlveda, who slits his victims' throats and then hangs them upside down until the blood has drained out: "The bodies are lighter that way, and it's easier to move them."

The stories about Griselda multiply: hypochondriac, druggie, bisexual, lover of orgies, paranoid, collector of luxury goods. Along with the rumors that feed the myth, Griselda starts collecting nicknames: Godmother, the Queen of Cocaine in Miami, the Black Widow. It's rumored that she slit the throat of some men she'd gone to bed with. She gets married four times, always to narco-traffickers. Marriage is a lever for moving up in the hierarchy of power, and when a husband puts a spoke in her wheels, she has him eliminated. Like Dario Sepúlveda, who contests the custody agreement for their son, whom they named, of all things, Michael Corleone, and so she has him killed.

Griselda's drug empire in Miami takes in $8 million a month. She plays a fundamental role in what will be called the Florida Cocaine War, also known as the Cocaine Cowboys War. Miami is flooded in money, estimated at about $10 billion a year.

In 1979 Griselda orchestrates the Dadeland Mall massacre. Two people are killed in a liquor store in that Dade County mall: Germán Jiménez Panesso, a Colombian drug trafficker who does business with Griselda's organization, and who is the target of the shootout, and his bodyguard. In the 1970s homicides were a private matter. Sure, there were tortures, stranglings, mutilations, decapitations. But they were ways to settle the score. The Dadeland massacre signals instead the beginning of a long series of shootouts in Miami, of battles fought in public places, in the light of day. So-called collateral damage doesn't matter anymore. Now people are shot in the street, in shopping malls, stores, restaurants, crowded locales at the busiest times of day. It is said that Griselda is responsible for the majority of murders committed in southern Florida during that time.

Griselda's ruthlessness reaches epic proportions. Numerous episodes, told as if part of a legend, are passed from one person to the next.

Griselda walks into a bar just for men. Girls are dancing provocatively on their platforms. All heads turn to look at her. A woman who comes into a place like this? Unheard of. What's more, a woman who looks like that: stoned, slovenly, haunted eyes. She sits down, orders a drink, observes the gyrating bodies. She seems about to touch those long legs. Then all of a sudden she gets up and fires a gun. One by one the girls fall to the ground. "Whores!" she screams. "Whores! All you know how to do is wiggle your asses for the men." Griselda is obsessed with those women. For her they don't deserve to live. Another obsession is hunting in bars. She liked to choose her men, and if they didn't go along, they were dead. One time a kid, younger than her, sitting a few tables away, attracts her attention. Griselda wants him and fixes her eyes on him. He avoids her gaze, but Griselda insists. So the kid heads to the bathroom, and she follows, going into the women's room. "Help!" she starts screaming. "Help!" and the kid comes running; maybe that weird woman is sick. Griselda is waiting for him, naked from the waist down. "Lick me," she commands. The kid steps away, his back to the door, but Griselda takes out a pistol and repeats, "lick me." So he does, the barrel of her gun glued to his head.

Griselda holes up in her bedroom, looked after by her German shepherd, Hitler; she's a drug addict by this point. Drugs and the police are only two of her enemies. Rival organizations try to kill her several times. On one occasion she tricks her killers by staging her own death: She ships an empty coffin to Colombia from the United States. In

1984, to escape the continual attacks, she moves her base to Irvine, California, where she lives with her youngest son, the aforementioned Michael Corleone. But she is arrested in February 1985, right in Irvine, accused of drug trafficking by the DEA. She is sentenced to ten years in prison, but even as an inmate she continues to manage her affairs. The Godmother buys herself a luxury prison. From behind bars she comes up with new projects, such as the one—aborted, thanks to wiretappings—to kidnap John F. Kennedy, Jr. In prison she receives jewels, perfume, men.

The Miami-Dade Office of the State Attorney pressures one of her right-hand men, Jorge "Riverito" Ayala, to collaborate, and in 1993 he agrees. They gather sufficient proof to incriminate Griselda for multiple homicide. But it's 1998, and the Miami-Dade Office of the State Attorney is about to be buried in scandal. The man who turned on Griselda is in a witness protection program. He can't take it anymore. The life of luxury and drugs he'd been used to is now just a distant memory, and all the discipline is killing him. He finds a way to put a lot of money into the hands of the DA secretaries. He doesn't want information or cocaine or an escape plan. The money is for sex. Telephone sex, but for him it's still sex. The heavy breathing and moans go on for a while, but in the end an inquiry uncovers the secret hotline, and the DA's authority is undermined. The scandal saves Griselda, who escapes the electric chair as a result. She is freed on June 6, 2004, after almost twenty years in prison, and sent back to Colombia.

September 3, 2012: Griselda, now sixty-nine, is coming out of a butcher shop in Medellín with a friend. Two men on a motorcycle pull up and shoot her twice in the head. The Godmother dies in the hospital a few hours later, killed via the same technique—motorcycle murder—that she herself imported to Miami.

Or take the story of another woman, Mexican this time: Sandra Ávila Beltrán, queen of cocaine. And a sentence I couldn't get out of my head: "The world is disgusting." Sandra couldn't stand hearing that sentence. And if it was uttered by one of her uncle's men, who was none

other than El Padrino Miguel Ángel Félix Gallardo, Sandra felt the
blood rush to her head and pound against her temples. Born into a
narco family, raised in the presence of the greatest of them all, im-
mersed in a macho culture since she was a little girl: How could it be
that those same men who boasted in front of her uncle about their
female conquests and their barbaric slayings of enemies, amongst themselves then would say "The world is disgusting"? Braggarts in front of
the boss, cowards as soon as he turned his back. And if little Sandra
happened to hear them, well, it really didn't matter much; she was just
a girl.

Education is often the drop of water that wears away the stone.
Patient and tenacious, El Padrino's lackeys' words dig into Sandra's
conscience. They make their way deep down, creating an emptiness
that can no longer be resolved with simple rage. She has to look for
other answers. She has to find a lifestyle that contradicts that inescapable sentence. Sandra divides the world into two categories. On one
side are people like her uncle's men. On the other are those who want
to change the world, to win. She can boast of her birthright, the ideal
genetic résumé for a narco-trafficker. But she's a woman; her body bears
the indelible mark of the ineptness of command. Breasts, wide hips, an
ass like a mandolin. These things can't be erased, can't be passed off as
something else. So breasts, wide hips, and mandolin ass become weapons to hone, things she can depend on: fingernails, shoes, hair, perfume,
clothes. For Sandra they are all necessary to make her femininity—her
sensuality and power—explode. Because the more woman she is, the
more the men are going to have to pay attention to her. The very logic
that is used against her, to subjugate her femininity, she will bend to her
advantage, and will teach all women that there is another way to live in
the world.

Men are pawns, to be classified by their usefulness. Sandra gets
sentimentally attached to two federal judicial police commanders, long
a breeding ground for narcos. Then she moves on to seducing important Sinaloa bosses such as El Mayo Zambada and Ignacio "Nacho"

Coronel. And finally the big coup: She gets engaged to Juan Diego Espinoza Ramírez, known as El Tigre, or the Tiger. Diego is a Colombian narco belonging to the Norte del Valle cartel and the nephew of Don Diego, the famous narco Diego Montoya. Sandra is a princess, constantly choosing whom to tie herself to so as to rise in power and social standing. With El Tigre she makes a qualitative leap that allows her to negotiate directly with the Colombian suppliers. So Sandra, El Padrino's niece, becomes la Reina, the Queen. The Queen of the Pacific knows how to exploit clichés. A woman is weak, so there's no point in threatening her: For the Queen this means freedom of movement. A woman doesn't know how to negotiate with men: The Queen takes advantage of the cartel emissaries' embarrassment when faced with a beautiful woman in a low-cut dress.

Now they all have to kneel to her, honor her. She coordinates shipments from Colombia from her luxurious headquarters in Guadalajara and launders the earnings, which get bigger every year. All that money is needed to carry out her most ambitious plan: to give women power. According to the Queen, women need to earn approval and respect, and the fastest, surest way to do that is through beauty. She invests the proceeds from cocaine in beauty clinics, both deluxe and plain, because all women have the right to lovers and husbands, jobs and suitable social standing. It's tangible things she invests in. Bodies and buildings. Breasts and houses. Derrieres and villas. Smooth skin and apartments. Seated on her throne, Sandra rules an army of men who can climb the ranks only to a certain point, because above them, undisputed, is the silent Queen, who never exposes herself, never gets her hands dirty, does not allow her name to appear in the newspaper or, worse, in police reports.

Then one day everything changes. An important shipment has just arrived in the port of Manzanillo, in the state of Colima, on the Pacific: ten tons of cocaine worth more than $80 million. The authorities block it and seize the drugs. For the first time the Queen's name appears in the media. She is now a public figure, and it may not be pure coincidence that a few months later her only son, sixteen-year-old José Luis Fuentes Ávila, who lives in the exclusive Puerta de Hierro neighborhood in Guadalajara, is kidnapped. His captors demand $5 million in ransom. The Queen panics. The only man that really matters to her is in the hands of ruthless killers who threaten to skin him alive. She goes to the authorities. But that turns out to be a serious mistake, because from that moment on the police monitor her phone calls and movements. Which is how they discover that the ransom was paid directly by El Mayo Zambada, because after the shipment was seized in the port of Manzanillo, the Queen is short on cash.

While the Queen embraces her son again after seventeen days in captivity, AFI commander Juan Carlos Ventura Moussong announces that he has proof that the kidnapping was a setup to weaken the Queen's power. Is it really credible that the son of one of the most important bosses can be kidnapped like that? For Moussong, those responsible must be sought among the Queen's own men, who are eager to construct an independent microcartel and, above all, to free themselves of that woman. The AFI director's suspicions are valid, but a short time later he is killed, shot point-blank on the street while coming back from a meeting with the other federal district commanders.

Still, power such as hers cannot easily be defeated, even when it is forced between the walls of the female prison in Santa Martha Acatitla, on the outskirts of Mexico City. It's here that the Queen of the Pacific ends up after being snagged by the police in a fancy Thai restaurant, eating lunch with her companion El Tigre. She'd been going about incognito and using a fake name for years. After her son's kidnapping, things got more difficult for her, but that doesn't mean she is going to give up dining in expensive restaurants or buying the latest Chanel outfit. "I'm a housewife who earns a living selling clothes and houses." In prison she carries on doing what she has always done: fighting for women's emancipation. She teaches her cell mates not to neglect their bodies or their looks even in prison. "If you lose your body, you lose your soul. If you lose your soul, you lose your power. If you lose your power, you lose everything," she keeps telling her new "affiliates," and she tries to set a good example. Apparently she even infects the prison director—a woman. One day some doctors are caught bringing Botox into the prison. The guards immediately think it's for that prisoner who is obsessed with beauty, for the Queen and her new friends. Not true: The Botox is for the prison director. The Queen managed to convince even her that sensuality comes first, before everything else. Sandra parades in the hallways, showing off her big, dark, movie star glasses, and she never complains: never an attack of nerves; never a hysterical crying fit; never a protest other than for the slop the prison guards pass off as food. The Queen smiles at her misfortune and keeps fiery looks for the women who dare to complain to her about the world's injustice: "If it's disgusting to you, then change it!"

August 10, 2012: Sandra Ávila Beltrán is extradited to the United States to face drug-trafficking charges. But at the end of the trial all but one charge is dropped: providing money to her boyfriend, El Tigre, to help him avoid arrest. She is sentenced to seventy months in prison, a term she had already served almost entirely in her previous incarceration in Mexico. In August 2013 she is deported to Mexico, where she is immediately taken into custody in a penitentiary in Nayarit on money-laundering charges. But just after a few months a Mexican federal judge throws out a five-year sentence for money laundering, using the argument that she has already been tried for the same crime in both Mexico and the United States, and orders her immediate release. On February 7, 2015, at 10 P.M., the Queen leaves prison: Three SUVs are waiting for her outside. She climbs into one of them, a white BMW X5, and drives away. She is free. Will she go back to her throne?

Then there's the story of a very special recipe.

"El Teo would bring me the corpses. I'd have everything ready: barrels, water, a hundred pounds or so of caustic soda. Latex gloves, gas mask. I'd fill the barrels with fifty gallons of water and two bags of caustic soda and heat them up. When the mix started to boil, I'd strip the bodies and throw them in. Cooking time's about fourteen, fifteen hours. In the end all that's left is the teeth, but it's easy to get rid of those."

The originator of this recipe is Santiago Meza López, nicknamed, not coincidentally, El Pozolero. *Pozole* is a typical Mexican meat stew. El Pozolero had long been on the FBI's twenty most wanted list, and was arrested in January 2009. He confessed to dissolving three hundred bodies of members of a rival gang. The Tijuana cartel paid him six hundred dollars a week. Teodoro García Simental El Teo, head of a bloodthirsty gang tied to the Tijuana cartel, delivered the corpses and the cash.

"Never a woman, though. Only men," El Pozolero insisted at the end of his interrogation.


Stories, stories, stories. I can't get away from them. Stories of people, of torturers and victims. Stories of reporters who would like to tell about them and sometimes end up dead. Like Bladimir Antuna García, who had become a ghost of his former self. Haggard, prematurely gray around the temples and beard, which only took half a day to grow in. His weight fluctuated; his physique went haywire: two sticks instead of legs, protruding stomach. The prototypical drug addict. A consequence of his work, because Bladimir knew how to tell stories, and knew how to investigate, a difficult occupation in a place like Durango. He had crawled through the grimiest canals, the ones that collect wastewater stories, stories of sewers and of power. But those stories start to gnaw at your insides, you slam into the disgust, and when you can't understand it, you trip, and then look for an explanation elsewhere. Whiskey and cocaine seemed like the solution. But Bladimir decided to leave all that behind; he wanted to go back to being considered one of the best reporters in Durango. He cleaned himself up, found work as a busboy in a tavern in the center of town. He did everything. Humble tasks, but not for Bladimir, who, thanks to his stories, had discovered just how ephemeral the boundaries of human dignity are. Meanwhile he tried to get back into the world of journalism. But the editors didn't want anything to do with him; he was too unreliable, too well known, but for the wrong reasons. Sure, he'd been a talented reporter, but what if they found him crouched over a table again, his nose buried in a line of cocaine? For people who've seen you messed up, even if it was only once, you're always a drunkard and an addict. But a new paper opened in Durango, *El Tiempo*, edited by Víctor Garza Ayala. The paper wasn't doing so well. Maybe some crime stories, which readers really love, could help turn things around. Garza decided to hire Bladimir to cover the crime beat, but just in case, he relegated his section to the back, to the back page, so as not to cut into the politics section on the front page, which is what really matters to him. It's that way all over the world. If a judge is killed or a car bomb explodes, the story conquers the most important pages. Otherwise crime gets relegated to the back. But Bladimir didn't care; what mattered to him was the chance to start writing again, writing about cartels and the Zetas. And avoiding, at least at first, causing too much of a stir. But at a certain point the newspaper vendors started displaying the paper backward, with the last page in full view. Sales went through the roof.

Bladimir was relentless; he wrote dozens of news stories, some of which were exclusives, thanks to his excellent contacts in the army and police. To pay for his oldest son's college education he got a second job with another newspaper, *La Voz de Durango*.

The first threat he gets is on his cell phone, in the middle of the night. A cavernous but clear voice utters two simple words: "Stop it." His wife pretends to be asleep, but she hears everything and bites her pillow in silence. In the months that follow the phone calls become more frequent, always to his cell, always at night, always those two simple words: "Stop it." Sometimes the speaker identifies himself as a Zetas member. Postcards start arriving at the newspaper, tropical beaches and beautiful women, and on the back, in childish lettering, that same command: "Stop it."

"They're just words." That's how Bladimir dismissed the escalating intimidations. He started working even harder, using his articles to attack corrupt policemen in the state of Durango and reporting loudly the threats he was receiving in the media and to the State Attorney's office. Lifting the veil on criminal organizations in Mexico and naming famous narco-trafficking accomplices became a sort of creed for him. In July 2009 he talked about the phone calls in a series of interviews with the Mexico City magazine *Buzos*. He also told of the failed attempt on his life: On April 28, 2009, a man shot at him in broad daylight in the middle of the street, but missed. But when you start talking about threats, the community around you is always ready to say you're paranoid, you're exaggerating. Bladimir reported the threats and the attempt on his life to the authorities, but they didn't do anything. Bladimir was working with Eliseo Barrón Hernández on a story about some policemen in the pay of the cartels. With Eliseo, they did what they always do. They waited till he left his house with his family, humiliated him by kicking and punching him in front of his daughters and wife, then took him away. Then they put a bullet in his head. His mistake had been to stick his nose in a story of corrupt policemen. "We're here, reporters. Just ask Eliseo Barrón. El Chapo and the cartel don't forgive. Be careful, soldiers and reporters." These were Chapo Guzmán's words, which appeared on several narco-banners hung in the streets of Torreón on the day of Eliseo's funeral. A clear claim of responsibility, the way terrorists do it. An unequivocal message. Another one arrives at Bladimir's newspaper office a few hours later: "He's next, that son of a bitch."

Bladimir rarely left his house. Almost never. He would write holed up inside. Some of his colleagues said he'd resigned himself to the idea that he'd be killed: The government offered no assistance; no inquiries were being conducted about the threats; no protection had been assigned to him. His biggest fear wasn't being killed, though. It's the same for everyone. But it's not madness, or a secret suicide wish. You don't go looking for death—you'd be a fool if you did. But you know it's there.

November 2, 2009: It happened very quickly. Kidnapped. Tortured. Killed.

His colleagues' efforts were all in vain. They were scandalized by the apathy of the forces of law and order, who had called Bladimir paranoid. The usual defamation technique: no investigations; no inquiries into what Bladimir had uncovered. There's no investigative journalism in Durango anymore. It died along with Bladimir Antuna García.

# 20

# 000

I looked into the abyss and I became a monster. It couldn't have gone any other way. With one hand you touch the origins of violence, with the other you caress the roots of ferocity. You've got one eye trained on the foundations of buildings, one ear tuned to the beat of financial flows. At first it's all a dark cauldron; you can't see a thing, just something simmering below the surface, teeming as if with worms, trying to break through the top crust. Then the figures start to take shape, but it's still all confused, embryonic, superimposed. Drawing on all your skills and senses you push yourself forward and lean out over the abyss. The chronology of powers begins to make sense, the blood that before ran off in a thousand different directions now flows into one big river; the money stops fluttering around and comes to settle on the ground so you can count it. You lean out a little more. You hook your foot to the rock, practically suspended over the void now. And then . . . darkness. Like at the beginning, but this time there's no simmering; there's only a smooth, shiny surface, a mirror of black pitch. That's when you realize you've gone over to the other side; now it's the abyss that wants to peer inside you. Rummage around. Tear you to pieces. Break you apart. The abyss of narco-trafficking that looks inside you is not the—all things considered—reassuring rite of indignation. It is not the fear that nothing makes any sense. That would be too simple. Too easy. You've identified your target; now it's up to you to strike, up to you to put things right. The abyss of narco-trafficking opens onto a world that works, an efficient world, a world with rules. A world that makes sense. Then you don't trust anyone anymore: the media, your family, your friends. Everyone is talking about a reality that you know is bogus. Slowly everything starts feeling foreign to you, and your world fills with new protagonists. Bosses, massacres, trials. Killings, tortures, cartels. Dividends, stocks, banks. Betrayals, suspicions, accusations. Cocaine. All you know is them, and they know you, but it doesn't mean that the world that was yours before disappears. No. You go on living in the midst of it. You keep on doing what you were doing before, but now the questions you ask yourself rise up out of the abyss. The businessman, the professor, the manager. The student, the dairy farmer, the policeman. Your friend, your relative, your girlfriend. Do they come from the abyss as well? And even if they're honest, how much like the abyss are they? It's not that you suspect they're all corrupt, or mafiosi. It's worse than that. You have looked humanity in the face, have seen how disgusting it is, and now you see similarities to that disgust in everyone you know. You see everyone's shadow.

I have become a monster.

When everything around you starts fitting into this sort of reflection. When you insert everything into the universe of meaning you've constructed by observing the powers of narco-trafficking. When everything seems to make sense only on the other side, in the abyss. When all this happens you've become a monster. You scream, whisper, shout your truths, because you're afraid that otherwise they'll vanish. And everything you'd always considered to be happiness—going for a walk, making love, standing in line for a concert, swimming—becomes superfluous. Secondary. Less important. Negligible. Every hour seems pointless, wasted, if you don't dedicate your energies to discovering, flushing out, telling. You've sacrificed everything not only in order to understand but to show, to point out, to describe the abyss. Was it worth it? No. It's never worth abandoning any path that brings you happiness. Even a small happiness. It's never worth it, even if you believe that your sacrifice will be rewarded by history, by your sense of ethics, by looks of approval. But it's only a moment. The only possible sacrifice is the one that expects no reward. I didn't want sacrifices, and I didn't want rewards. I wanted to understand, to write, to tell. Tell everyone. To go door to door, house to house, day and night to share these stories, to display these wounds. Proud of having chosen the right words, the right tone. That's what I wanted. But the wound of these stories swallowed me up.

For me it's too late. I should have kept a distance I wasn't able to keep. That's what Anglo-Saxon journalists often say to me: Don't get involved; keep a clear gaze between your subject and yourself. But I've never been able to. For me it's the opposite. Exactly the opposite. To have a primary, penetrating, contaminated gaze. To chronicle not the facts but one's own soul. And to imprint on one's soul, like on Play-Doh, the objects and the things one sees, so they leave behind a deep impression, but one that can be eliminated by remolding the Play-Doh. By kneading it. In the end all that remains of one's soul is a frame that could have assumed a thousand different shapes but that hasn't taken on even one.

When you follow the stories of narco-trafficking you learn to read people's faces. Or at least you convince yourself you can. You learn to see if someone was loved as a child—truly loved. If he was looked after, if he was raised with someone at his side, or if he always had to run off with his tail between his legs. You understand right away what sort of life he's had. If he was lonely, bullied, thrown out on the street. Or if, on the other hand, he was spoiled to the point of rotting in comfort. You learn. That's how you learn to sum people up. But you never learn to distinguish the good guy from the bad guy. You don't know who is screwing you or stealing your soul, who is lying to you in order to get an interview, or who is telling you what he thinks you want to hear in order to please you and so to be immortalized in your words. I carry that certainty inside me without too much self-indulgent melancholy: No one comes near you except for a favor. A smile is a way of lowering your defenses; a relationship aims to extort money from you, or a story to tell at dinner, or a photo to give someone, like a scalp. You end up thinking like a mafioso; paranoia becomes your line of conduct, and you thank the people of the abyss for teaching you to be suspicious. Loyalty and trust become foreign, suspect words. You are surrounded by enemies and people eager to take advantage of you. This is my life today. Congratulations to me.

It's too easy to believe what I believed in at the beginning of all this. To believe in what Thoreau said: "Rather than love, than money, than fame, give me truth." I believed that following these routes and rivers, sniffing around continents, sinking my legs into the mire would help me to get at the truth: renounce everything else in order to grasp the truth. But it doesn't work that way, Thoreau. You can't find it. The closer you come to thinking you've understood how markets move, the closer you come to the logic of he who corrupts those close to you, of he who makes restaurants open and banks close, of he who is prepared to die for money; the more you understand the mechanisms, the more you realize you should have taken a completely different route. Which is why I don't have greater respect for myself, that I keep investigating, taking notes, filling agendas, preserving flavors. I don't have greater respect for myself at the end of a journey that is unable to bring me happiness and to share it. And I may not even be aware of it. All I know is that I couldn't have done anything else.

And if I had done things differently? If I had chosen the straight line of art? The life of a writer whom some would define as pure, for example, with his bad moods, his psychoses, his normalcy. One who tells inspiring stories. Who's all engaged in style and narrative technique. I didn't know how to do that. Mine is the life of a fugitive, a story runner, a multiplier of tales. I am a monster, as is anyone who sacrifices himself for something he believed to be superior. But I still have some respect. Respect for those who read. For those who snatch important time from their lives so as to construct a new one. Nothing is more powerful than reading; no one is a greater liar than he who holds that reading a book is a passive gesture. To read, hear, study, understand—these are the only ways to construct life beyond life, life alongside of life. Reading is a dangerous act, because it gives shape and dimension to words, it incarnates and disperses them in all directions. It turns everything upside down and makes change and tickets and lint fall out of the pockets of the world. To get to know narco-trafficking, to get to know the connection between the rationality of evil and money, to rip open the veil that obscures the supposed familiarity with the world. To know is the first step toward change. My respect goes to those people who don't throw these stories away, who don't neglect them, but who make them their own. Those who feel the words on their skin, who carve them in their flesh, who build a new vocabulary—they are altering the direction of the world, because they have understood how to be in it. It's like breaking one's chains. Words are action, connection tissue. Only those who are familiar with these stories can defend themselves from them. Only those who tell them to their child, a friend, their husband, only those who carry them into public places, into living rooms and classrooms are articulating the possibility to resist. Being alone in the abyss is like being in a cage, but if lots of people decide to face the abyss, then the bars of that prison cell will melt. And a cell without bars is no longer a prison.

In the Book of Revelation Saint John writes, "And I took the little scroll from the hand of the angel and ate it; it was sweet as honey in my mouth, but when I had eaten it my stomach was made bitter." I believe that readers need to do this with words. Put them in their mouths, chew them, grind them up, and swallow them, so that the chemistry they are made of can work inside of us, can illuminate the dark night and draw a line between happiness and pain.

You feel empty when your words seem to be enhanced by the threats they provoke, as if people are suddenly listening to every word you utter merely because they risk getting you killed. This is what happens: It happens that silence on these topics doesn't exist. There is a buzz: news flashes, trials, a narco is arrested. Everything becomes physiological. And when everything becomes physiological, no one notices it anymore. And this is how someone writes: He dies writing; he is threatened writing; he stumbles writing. When the threat comes it seems that a part of the world notices what has been written, at least for a while. But then it forgets. The truth is that there's no alternative. Cocaine is a carburant. Cocaine is a devastating, terrible, deadly energy. There never seem to be enough arrests. Policies to fight it always seem to miss the mark. As terrible as it may seem, total legalization may be the only answer. A horrendous response, horrible perhaps, agonizing. But the only one that can stop everything. That can halt the inflated earnings. That can put an end to the war. Or, at least, it's the only response that comes to mind when in the end you ask yourself, now what?

I have let myself be overwhelmed by voices every day for years. Voices that shout at the top of their lungs that alcohol is the substance that claims the most victims. Sharp, hammering voices that every now and then are silenced by other voices that boldly claim that yes, of course, alcohol is bad, but only if you abuse it, if that mug of beer on a Saturday night becomes a habit, and that there's a big difference between alcohol and cocaine. Then the chorus chimes in, those who think that legalization is the lesser evil; all things considered, the voices suggest, legalized cocaine would come under the control of doctors. And so let's legalize murder then! a portentous, baritone voice replies, momentarily silencing everyone. But the silence doesn't last long, because then come those cawing reactions—like knife stabs—one after the other, of those who maintain that drug users really only harm themselves, that if you outlaw cocaine then you have to outlaw tobacco too, and that if you say yes, then the state is a pusher state, a criminal state. And what about weapons then? Aren't they worse? At which point yet another voice— that calm voice with a know-it-all tone that gets stuck on consonants—

affirms that weapons are necessary for self-defense, tobacco can be used in moderation, and . . . But in the end it's an ethical problem, and who are we to curb a individual choice with rules and decrees?

At this point the voices start to overlap and get all muddled. The confusion of voices always ends up this way. In silence. And I have to start all over again. But I'm convinced that legalization really could be the answer. Because it hits where cocaine finds its fertile terrain, at the law of supply and demand. If the requests were to dry up, everything above them would shrivel, like a flower without water. Is it a gamble? A fantasy? The ravings of a monster? Maybe. Or maybe not. Maybe it's another fragment of the abyss that few have the courage to face.

For me the word "narco-capitalism" has become a ball of cud that continues to swell. I can't swallow it; every time I try it goes down the wrong way, and I risk choking to death. All the words I chew on stick to that cud, and the blob expands, like a tumor. I'd like to swallow it down so that it can be attacked by gastric acid. I would like to melt down this word and grab the heart of it. But I can't. Besides, it's pointless, because I already know I would find a grain of white powder. Of cocaine. Regardless of the policies and seizures the demand for cocaine will always be huge: The faster the world moves, the more there's cocaine; the less time there is for stable relationships, for authentic exchanges, the more there's coke.

I calm down; I have to calm down. I lie down and stare at the ceiling. I've collected quite a few ceilings over the years. From those so close to your nose that you can touch them if you stretch out your neck, to those so high up you have to squint to see if they're frescos or humidity stains you're looking at. I stare at the ceiling and imagine the entire globe. The world is a round ball of dough that is rising. It's rising because of petroleum. It's rising because of coltan. It's rising because of gas. It's rising because of the web. If you removed all these ingredients, the dough would risk falling, collapsing. But there's one ingredient that works faster than all the others and that everyone wants. Cocaine. That plant that connects South America and Italy. Like an elastic band across

the Atlantic, an elastic that can stretch infinitely without ever breaking. The roots there, the leaves here. Coke is the ingredient without
which there could be no dough. Just as with flour, which in Italy and in
South America is categorized by zeros, depending on its purity: The
more zeros, the purer it is.

Zeros like wounds through which to see the world. Zeros like abysses
you could sink into.

Zero, like the lens of the telescope through which you can observe
the mirage of white gold, the best cocaine: 000.

# ACKNOWLEDGMENTS

More than anyone else I would like to thank Federica Campana, who has followed this book since its inception, sacrificing her sleep and her free time. She has done it all with true passion. Her research and her analytical approach, her care and her competence have enabled *ZeroZeroZero* to grow with each new edition in every country in which it has been published. I thank her for her dedication and commitment to this work, which were contagious. Collaborators like her are a precious gift; they are what every writer would hope to find in his path: an indispensable ally, a fresh pair of eyes, another heart beating on each story, two more lungs breathing among the same horrifying mechanisms that make you lose your sleep and your faith in the world. I thank her for the work she has done on the language of the book: wherever *ZeroZeroZero* goes, and even though many readers will read it in translation, it has lost none of its original vision, nor seen its spirit diluted.

I would like to thank Penguin Press for believing in this ambitious project. Thanks to Andrew Wylie for our conversations and for the stories only he knows and reveals. Thanks to Ruth Ben-Ghiat, Stefano Albertini, Roberta Garbarini-Philippe, and Annalisa Liuzzo for making me feel at home in New York when I didn't know anything or anyone and when I needed everything, above all advice and tranquillity. Thanks to Rocco Castoro and Professor Gaetana Marrone for appreciating my work. Thanks to Vice and Shane Smith for welcoming my writing and paying heed to my projects. Thanks to Eddy Moretti for loving these stories when I told him about them.

I thank Helena Janeczek, who gave me her advice on literary structure.

I thank Carlo Buga, who dove headlong into this intricate mass of stories and helped me find a guiding light among hundreds of pages. Thanks to Gianluca Foglia, a fierce and determined editor.

To the Carabinieri, the police, the Finance Guard, the ROS, the GICO, the SCO, the DIA, and the DDA of Rome, Naples, Milan, Reggio Calabria, Catanzaro, and all the ones I forgot to mention here, I am extraordinarily grateful for allowing me to read, study, and sometimes experience firsthand their investigations and operations: Alga, Box, Caucedo, Crimine-Infinito, Decollo, Decollo Bis, Decollo Money, Decollo Ter, Dinero, Dionisio, Due Torri Connection, Flowers 2, Galloway-Tiburon, Golden Jail, Green Park, Igres, Magna Charta, Maleta 2006, Meta 2010, Notte bianca, Overloading, Pollicino, Pret à porter, Puma 2007, Revolution, Solare, Tamanaco, Tiro grosso, White 2007, White City.

Thanks to the DEA, the FBI, the Guardia Civil, the Mossos d'Esquadra, Scotland Yard, the French Gendarmerie Nationale, Interpol, the Brazilian Polícia Civil, some members of the Mexican Polícia Federal, some members of the Colombian Polícia Nacional, some members of the Russian Policija, who have accompanied me in their investigations and operations: Cabana, Cornerstone, Dark Waters, Delfín blanco, Leyenda, Limpieza, Millennium, Omni Presence, Padrino, Pier Pressure, Processo 8000, Project Colisée, Project Coronado, Russiagate, Reckoning, Relentless, SharQC 2009, Sword, Xcellerator.

My gratitude goes to all the magistrates I've studied and spoken with for all these years. There are many things I could not have discovered without them.

Thanks to my friends Lydia Cacho, Anabel Hernández, and Diego Osorno, who have made a "Mexican" of me over the years. Thanks to Glenda Martínez, Malcolm Beith, Christophe Champin, Yoani Sánchez for their opinions and their commitment. I am grateful for Robert Friedman's vision, Misha Glenny's intelligence, and Ricardo Ravelo's analytical talent. Thanks to Peppe d'Avanzo; we'd started talking about this book, but as cruel fate would have it, we will never be able to do so again.

Many thanks to the New York police agent AdN. He knows why.

Thanks to Mark Bray, Valeria Castelli, and the Occupy Wall Street guys, who taught me so much.

Thanks to Kim Ziegler and Rachel Love for their guidance with my English.

Thanks to Bono Vox for listening to these stories when I was still wound up in them and for his lifelong open invitation to U2 concerts.

I thank Salman Rushdie, who taught me how to be free even when surrounded by seven armed bodyguards.

I thank Nouriel Roubini, who endured my South American stories one endless night and with whom I talked too much about finance and crime.

Thanks to my followers on Facebook and Twitter: thousands of people who've held my sense of loneliness at bay and made me feel like I was out talking to people even when I wasn't.

Thanks to Sasha Polakow Suransky and *The New York Times*, who allowed me to talk about how the drug trade affected the economic crisis when everyone else was treating it as a marginal issue.

Thanks to David Dannon, who made me another person for six months, free and almost happy.

I thank all the people of the Arma dei Carabinieri who manage my life.

Thanks to Manuela De Caro, always with me, at all times and all costs.

Thanks to my family; I can never forgive myself for the high price they are paying because of me. These lines of thanks will not suffice. This, I know.

And I thank you, American readers, for embracing my stories in your welcoming land. Thank you because, by reading these words, you will make them dangerous. Criminal organizations do not fear writers; they fear readers.

—Roberto Saviano

Angelo De Gennaro, gifted teacher of Italian language and culture, advised and inspired me on nearly every page.

Fellow translator Ann McGarrell buoyed me with her wry wisdom.

Patricia Caprotti, Rita Fabbrizio, Paola Inzillo, Gianni Marizza, Marinetta Piva, and Leonardo Venturini fielded a vast array of questions.

Daniel Jewiss, police officer and soldier, offered his expertise and encouragement.

My editor, Scott Moyers, provided perspective and a sense of humor.

My warmest thanks for their generosity, meticulousness, and patience.

—Virginia Jewiss, translator

# INDEX

# ZeroZeroZero